WESTERN
NATIONAL

Wildlife Refuges

WESTERN
NATIONAL

Wildlife Refuges

THIRTY-SIX

ECOLOGICAL

HAVENS FROM

CALIFORNIA

TO TEXAS

BY

DENNIS WALL

MUSEUM OF
NEW MEXICO PRESS

To Susan, my wife and best friend

Project editor: Mary Wachs
Art director: David Skolkin
Designer: Susan Surprise
Illustrations: Susan Surprise
Mapmaker: Deborah Reade
Manufactured in Korea

10 9 8 7 6 5 4 3 2 1

Library of Congress Cataloging-in-Publication Data

Wall, Dennis M., 1953–
    Western national wildlife refuges : thirty-six ecological havens
from California to Texas / by Dennis M. Wall.
        p.   cm.
    Includes bibliographical references.
    ISBN 0–89013–306–9 (pbk.)
    1. Wildlife refuges--West (U.S.)   2. Natural history--West (U.S.)
3. Wildlife refuges--West (U.S.) --Guidebooks.   4. West (U.S.)-
-Guidebookks.   I. Title.
    QL84.22.W47W37   1996
    333.95'0978--DC20   96–27378
                                                    CIP

MUSEUM OF NEW MEXICO PRESS
Post Office Box 2087
Santa Fe, New Mexico 87504

Contents

Of my childhood years in Albuquerque, New Mexico, when desert scrubland ran unpaved for miles east of town—it's all condos, fast food, and blacktop now—my fondest memories involve long hikes with my friends into the "wilderness." There we spent our summer days among "bluetails" and "horny toads," kangaroo rats and "sand diggers" in a desert scrubland that seemed to run on forever. Red-tailed hawks and ravens rode thermals overhead, cactus wrens constructed their precarious nests in cholla, insects clicked and scuffled in the brush. Whispered tales of bear or cougar in nearby mountains raised shivers of fear—and delight—in our young imaginations. Occasionally, we had the good fortune to share an arroyo bed with a prancing, grinning coyote. All of us loved dogs—but a wild dog! That was something very special.

At our national wildlife refuges, the same sort of wonder and excitement can still be experienced. Many once-prevalent wild species are difficult to locate these days in North America, but at wildlife refuges they continue to roam and wing about freely, sometimes in great numbers. Cranes, bobcats, foxes and pronghorn, waterfowl and perching birds, a menagerie of reptiles, amphibians, native fish, and plants—all find protection and support within refuge boundaries.

To stave off the decimation of wading birds that resulted from a faddish lust for feathered hats, President Theodore Roosevelt created Pelican Island Federal Bird Reservation in Florida in 1903—our first national wildlife refuge. Since then, the system has swelled to over 500 refuges and more than thirty wetland management units. The refuge system is a federal effort overseen by the US Fish and Wildlife Service (USFWS), a division of the US Department of the Interior. The USFWS bureaucratic mission is simple and straightforward: to protect our wondrous wildlife heritage.

Protecting wildlife means protecting habitat. For that reason, our ninety-three-million-acre system of protected natural habitat includes some of the most important landscapes in our nation. A quarter of North America's endangered species resides on national wildlife refuges. Some 400 refuges support endangered creatures at least part-time. More than fifty federal refuges protect "critical habitat" for species in danger of extinction, including the masked bobwhite, the whooping crane, and many other rare animals and plants.

Most refuges were originally founded to bolster migratory waterfowl populations—shootable birds. The system has done quite well in that regard, significantly increasing the numbers of mallards, redheads, gadwalls, canvasbacks, and other species from catastrophic lows suffered in the 1980s and at other times. More recently, the USFWS has begun to emphasize increased biological diversity, because biologists now understand that in diversity lies ecological health.

The term "ecosystem management" is the buzzword for this new philosophy. The concept implies supporting all of an area's resident and migratory species, from pinhead-sized snails to bull elk, from lichens to redwoods. Where an impoundment once simply was flooded each spring to support migratory ducks, its level might now be manipulated to encourage mudflats on its edges for shorebirds, cattails for rails, surrounding cottonwoods for songbirds, and shallows for wading birds and developing native fish.

The thirty-six refuges featured in these pages (and their satellite units) fall within a region of

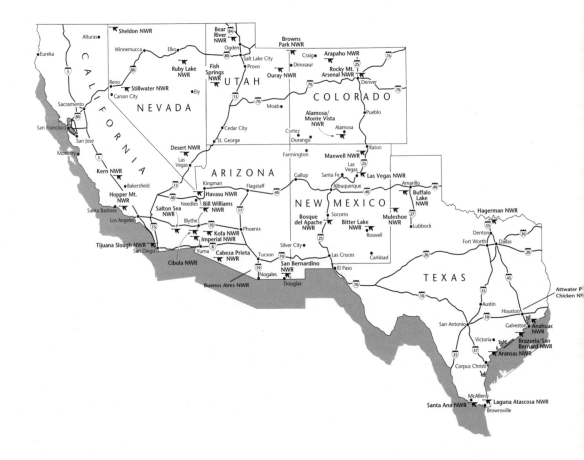

the United States I've labeled "the West." While the West may include any state left of the Mississippi River, I have defined the region somewhat more ecologically as the southernmost states from Texas through California. I have restricted coverage to four southerly California refuges because they fit best with the arid nature of most refuges featured in this book.

New refuges are created regularly, though not as rapidly as the needs of wildife demand. In central Texas, for example, Balcones Canyonlands National Wildlife Refuge (NWR) is one piece of protected land in development to protect endangered golden-cheeked warblers, black-capped vireos, and other creatures. A new unit of Alamosa–Monte Vista Refuge Complex in southern Colorado may soon add needed shorebird habitat to that fine refuge.

Western National Wildlife Refuges range from two thousand-acre preserves to million-acre-plus partial-wilderness areas. They are diverse in character but a factor common to each is water. Most suffer a scarcity of water, struggling constantly to get it or keep it (or to keep it clean), for reasons often as political as they are hydrological. In many cases, the very lack of water—a natural condition—defines a refuge's central character.

Most of the animals featured in Western National Wildlife Refuges reside at more than one refuge. Two north-south migratory bird flyways, the Pacific and Central—along with a slice of the Mississippi Flyway in the case of some Texas refuges—channel hundreds of waterfowl, wader, shorebird, and perching species through all the places featured here.

Most western refuges harbor a core of resident species including coyote, bobcat, mule and/or white-tailed deer, badger, rabbit, porcupine, raccoon, and an assortment of woodland, desert, and prairie bird and rodent species, as well as reptiles such as bullsnake and whiptail lizard. In addition, each one supports at least a few animals and plants found at no other refuge.

How to Use This Book

*W*estern National Wildlife Refuges is designed to offer both ecological insights and practical information for visitors. Generally, the first portion of each chapter presents an overview of the refuge, while latter portions focus on more detailed information regarding the specific offerings of a given refuge. Each chapter begins with traveler and visitor guidelines and ends with partial species listings for the refuge, as well as space for the visitor to note observations and reflections. Each chapter includes ecosystem-indicator drawings to clue the reader into the principal system(s) for each refuge. They are: Desert, Prairie, Upland, Freshwater wetlands, Riparian, Coastal, and Mountain. Many refuges include two or more ecosystems within their borders.

The symbol system that begins each chapter is intended for at-a-glance information. The reader will find fuller details in the main texts.

VC	=	Visitor's Center
R	=	Rest rooms
C	=	Camping
NP	=	No pets
W	=	Water available
B	=	Boating
F	=	Fishing
H	=	Hunting
$	=	Fee

Refuges are grouped in alphabetical order by state, beginning with California and proceeding eastward to Texas. Wildlife photographs are grouped by state and clustered near the refuges they depict. Since even the smallest refuge harbors hundreds or thousands of plant and animal species, only a small portion of

the resident wildlife can be represented in this book.

To gather additional information on refuges prior to your visit, phone or write for brochures and other literature. You can also find information on USFWS World Wide Web page. Additional links and sources of wildlife information are available through the agency's Blue Goose Server.

When You Visit

*V*isitation at our national wildlife refuges will continue to increase as national parks are overrun by visitors seeking to reaffirm their ties to nature. User numbers at our refuges have swelled by around ten percent each year for nearly a decade, straining a system designed first and foremost for wildlife. Still, at certain times of the year you can visit many of the western refuges and encounter few, if any, other people.

National wildlife refuges are not parks, and a subtly different behavioral ethic is required of anyone visiting. At a park, you are a fundamental part of the fauna; at a refuge, you're a welcome visitor whose importance is secondary to that of wildlife.

Even quiet, respectful human visitors may increase the level of stress that resident species faces—to most wild creatures, we appear as predators. Yet without the political support that develops through such personal encounters, our national wildlife refuges may not survive the anti-nature political assaults that have lately grown so forceful.

Fortunately, most refuge managers have developed limited, low-impact visitor routes, while maintaining ample protected acreage where animals may pursue their biological destinies with minimal interference. Within accessible areas, visitors have plenty of opportunity to marvel at the wonders of wildlife, to share space with free-ranging creatures, to connect with the natural world.

When you visit a wildlife refuge, let respect be your guide. Drive, hike, bike, or boat across refuges as unobtrusively as possible, and observe from a distance. If you approach a gathering of ducks or a hillside alive with pronghorns, remain in your vehicle or stay hidden behind cover. After you've absorbed the beauty of the scene, move away slowly and quietly. Keep voices down and radios low. Revealing or exaggerating your presence may frighten wildlife into flight—a visual spectacle, true, but also an unkind act and a possible threat to the creatures you've disturbed. If you've brought a gun in the past, consider replacing it next time with a pair of binoculars or a camera.

Other national wildlife refuge guidelines:

• Utilize refuge visitor centers and displays and take time to read refuge interpretive material such as brochures and signs. All contain useful, interesting information.

• As you explore a refuge, move slowly, settling in periodically to observe all around you. Wildlife magic often unfolds over time, as animals grow used to your quiet, non-threatening presence.

• Binoculars, spotting scopes, and nature guides will dramatically enhance your refuge experience.

• Use your vehicle as a blind. Often, refuge animals are more comfortable with the familiar shape of a vehicle than with a human form.

• Don't approach, touch, or feed animals, even if they appear to be tame or abandoned. Often parents are nearby, waiting for you to leave.

• Obey refuge signs. They're posted for good reasons, including to protect breeding or brooding species. Some areas are closed simply because animals need quiet, secure spaces in order to maintain their health and well-being.

• Respect the needs of other visitors. If you're a photographer, remember that those without cameras have as much right to observe undisturbed wildlife as you do.

Proper refuge etiquette may be summed up by Ernest Hemingway's definition of morality: Doing what makes you feel good after is the right way to behave; doing what makes you feel bad after is probably a mistake.

Acknowledgments

My thanks to all the refuge managers, biologists, ecologists, and others who shared with me their knowledge, insights, and passion for the natural world. Their careful reviews of draft chapters were critical in eliminating errors in content and understanding. Any remaining errors are mine.

I want to specially thank: Phil Norton, Refuge Manager, Bosque del Apache NWR; Brent Guizentanner, Refuge Manager, Aransas NWR; Bob Schumacher, Refuge Manager, Cabeza Prieta NWR; Jim Williams, Refuge Manager, Hagerman NWR; Kevin Desroberts, Refuge Manager, Ruby Lake NWR; Mike Blenden, Refuge Manager, Alamosa/Monte Vista NWR Complex; Thea Ulen, Recreation Specialist, Buenos Aires NWR; Chuck Minckley, Fisheries Biologist, Bill Williams River NWR; Angel Montoya, Biologist, Cibola NWR; Mari von Hoffman, Assistant Manager, Tijuana Slough NWR; Dave Clendenen, Senior Wildlife Biologist, Hopper Mountain NWR; Barney Tomberlin, Hatari Invertebrates, Portal, Arizona; Dr. Nova J. Silvy, Wildlife And Fisheries Science Dept., Texas A&M University; Mary Wachs and the crew at Museum of New Mexico Press for their dedication to quality; Susan, for accepting my gone time with love and support; and Arnie, for being a good boy.

HOPPER MOUNTAIN NWR

ADDRESS, PHONE: PO Box 3817, Ventura, CA 93006, (805) 644-5185.

NEARBY POINTS OF INTEREST: Hopper Mountain NWR also maintains Bitter Creek NWR, a 13,976-acre refuge in southwestern Kern County that is a potential foraging and roosting site for California condors. The grassland and oak/juniper-cloaked refuge is closed to visitors, but Cerro Noroeste Road outside Cuyama, California, cuts through the refuge, offering views of its habitats. A good hawk-watching site, Bitter Creek harbors 117 bird species, numerous reptiles, and endangered creatures that include the San Joaquin kit fox.

I missed seeing free-flying California condors by perhaps a few hours, maybe by a few yards.

On a fall afternoon in 1995 I drove to Pine Mountain, a camping and natural area in the Los Padres National Forest, just off Hwy 33 north of Ventura in southern California. The mountaintop was within range of a condor release site in nearby Lion Canyon and is known as a regular visiting spot for the endangered giant vultures.

After rumbling up the narrow dirt road, which was rutted and precarious in places, I stood at the summit and gazed over a broad vista of grass-carpeted foothills and rugged mountain ranges topped by rock cliffs and ridges. Feeling the heat of thermals rising, I surveyed the high spots that might hold condor nesting caves and perching spots but saw no condors.

mountain

The next day a condor recovery specialist mentioned that several young birds had been spotted roosting on Pine Mountain cedar snags at the time I was there. To have seen the huge, critically endangered birds in the wild, such as it is, would have been a momentous event in my life; I still feel the sting of missing them. But knowing they may be on their way to recovery is good balm for that disappointment.

Since all wild condors have been taken into captivity, the species has, in a sense, been extirpated from its environment. Fortunately, 17 captive-born condors were released into the southern California mountains by March 1996. Those captive-born birds are supplied with stillborn calf carcasses and monitored closely, their biologist overseers ever ready to recapture them if they detect a problem. Time will tell if the latest batch of naive young condors can make its way in the modern world.

The 2,457-acre Hopper Mountain NWR (alongside the 53,000-acre Sespe Condor Sanctuary) is not open to the public. Thus, the refuge may seem an odd subject for a guidebook. Hopper Mountain is included here for two reasons: Activities based at Hopper Mountain are a critical part of what the USFWS is all about; and, though the refuge itself allows no casual visitors, wildlife lovers can reach several areas in southern California (and possibly Arizona) where, with luck, they may glory in the sight of a free-flying condor.

A Study in Magnificence

The endangered California condor is one of the more striking animals in North America, avian or otherwise. Nearly 4 feet in body length, its wingspread may reach 10 feet. Like many highly evolved species, the condor's breeding and incubation periods are long, drawn-out affairs. Pairing can take months to accomplish, with couples usually remaining together as long as both members live.

Courtship among condors is likewise a spectacle of complexity. The male struts about the female, its wingtips pointed to the earth, neck extended, constantly turning back and forth as he makes clicking noises with his tongue. All the while, the prospective bride seems to ignore him.

After making their connubial connection, they proceed to fly from one of several prospective nesting sites to the next until, for reasons known only to themselves, they settle on one particular site. Often they nest on cliffside caves and ledges, though condors also have been known to raise their young in the trunk cavities of giant sequoias.

One egg is generally laid in February on whatever substrate exists at the nest site; condors don't construct cushioned nests. The size of a swan's egg (approximately 4 inches long, 2½ inches thick), the egg hatches a youngster who requires close to 6 months of care before leaving the nest. At some point, the fledgling juvenile is finally booted from the territory when the parents tire of its presence.

Condors are highly intelligent, ever curious and ready to explore new situations and environments. Their intelligence sometimes gets them into trouble, especially when humanity and its development are the targets of that curiosity. Their long-term pair bonding, their intelligence and ability to learn rapidly, their intense curiosity, and their elaborate courtship behaviors make them surprisingly similar to humans.

For example, several "teenage" releasees were recaptured in the early 1990s after wandering into town and "loitering" too close to humans. With carcasses regularly supplied to them, the traditional 150-mile food searches were unnecessary for these kids. They had too much time on their hands; it could have led them into trouble.

Condor Culture

As of March 1996, just over a hundred California condors remained in existence (as many as a dozen eggs were ready to hatch within a month). Most existing condors have been bred in captivity at the Los Angeles Zoo, the San Diego Wild Animal Park, and the World Center for Birds of Prey in Boise, Idaho. Only a few truly wild condors remain alive, and all are presently in captivity.

Each of the zoo-bred newborns is a true condor, genetically speaking. The major problem facing their kind is that, like primitive rain forest dwellers subsumed by rampant development, California condors are losing their culture. Saving the species, which would clearly have gone extinct without human intervention, has meant removing them not only from the wild but from a pattern of life that has sustained them for millennia.

Birds have cultures, especially highly intelligent species such as the condor, which learns much of what it knows from parents and associates. For the condor, culture includes such things as where to find food, how far to range, who and what to avoid, where to nest, and, perhaps most importantly, how to raise their young. As captive-born condors now make up the lion's

share of the remaining population, and most truly wild condors are dead and gone, much of the knowledge once transmitted down through wild generations has been lost.

Condors raised in zoo pens, though fed by condor-shaped puppets and kept strictly removed from human contact, lack the experience that teaches them what it is to be a condor. Some of that extinct knowledge is no doubt so subtle that recovery-minded humans haven't a clue as to what it is or how to teach or restimulate it.

That is one major dilemma facing USFWS experts and others charged with rebuilding the California condor population and returning it to the wild. To help mitigate the problem, recent newborns have been left for several months after birth with their parents, who have been "trained" in childrearing by being induced to raise baby Andean condors. Most of the parents are zoo-bred themselves, but they undoubtedly know more about being a condor than their most knowledgeable human keepers.

Captive breeding is relatively easy in the case of the giant California condor, cousin to the Andean species of Peru and Bolivia. Biologists could go on forever mass-producing the bird in captivity, but a truly wild condor, finely tuned to its environment, is a different animal altogether.

Habitat Recovery, Condor Recovery

Along with the problem of deculturization, another major roadblock on the road to condor recovery is ecological change within their historic habitat. Ten centuries ago, woolly mammoths, giant ground sloths, elk, camels, and saber-toothed cats roamed the hills of present-day Ventura and surrounding counties. Plenty of large carcasses, the condor's preferred food source, lay rotting in the prehistoric sun, offering sustenance during what was likely this carrion-eater's heyday.

Ice Age impacts and human encroachment rapidly reduced the large mammal base from a condor range that once extended across the United States (a pre–Ice Age skeleton was found in Florida). With a sharp reduction in the food base, the condors' range receded, until only a West Coast population remained.

The 1800s and Euro-American expansion into the West marked the beginning of the near end for the huge vulture. Some folks shot them for fun. Others eliminated them for fear they spread cattle diseases such as anthrax. Gold miners slaughtered them for their large quills, which they used for storing gold dust. Predator controls utilizing strychnine- and cyanide-laced carcasses wiped out vast numbers. One varmint killer wrote in the 1880s that after leaving a poisoned carcass on the ground for a few days, he would return to find as many as 25 dead condors lying around it.

Egg collecting, a "gentleman's" hobby, resulted in condor eggs selling for as much as $600 in the 1920s and 1930s. Pesticides, including DDT, may also have taken a toll on eggs, though some biologists dispute that theory. At any rate, by World War II less than 200 birds remained in existence. That number declined over the next few decades. By 1981, no more than 30 condors remained alive in the wild, with only 3 or 4 breeding pairs among them.

A war of genocide had been waged against the California condor, one that very nearly succeeded.

Captive breeding began in the early 1980s. Like its endangered soul mate the whooping crane, the condor's gene pool had declined to such a meager level that few thought the species would survive. After a catastrophic 1984–85 winter, only 9 birds and 1 breeding pair remained in the wild. Many biologists assumed the end had arrived. To save a clearly dying species, government biologists began capturing the remaining condors. They brought the last wild bird into captivity on Easter Sunday, April 19, 1987.

Environmentalists clashed in heated debate over whether or not to capture the last free condors; the debate continued after those last captures were accomplished. Some believed (and still do) that only free condors were worth saving; others insisted that raising captive young at least keeps extinction at bay until better knowledge is gained that might serve to bolster new wild populations. Some were worried that removing the endangered species from its wild habitat would give developers and resource plunderers the excuse they needed to wreak havoc on what would then be "noncritical" habitat.

A few organizations grew weary of talk. In 1986, Earth First! activists threatened to break into a California breeding facility to release captive birds—a sure death sentence for those young condors inside had the plan been carried out. Barbed wire fences were erected to keep misguided condor lovers at bay.

Since 1992, after a long struggle and more than a few mistakes, the multiagency Condor Recovery Team has gradually reintroduced captive-bred condors to southern California mountains. That process continues today with the help of knowledge gained one experiment or error at a time. Recent reintroductions follow on a trail of condor deaths that occurred after earlier releases. Captive-born condors are presently thriving, though the fate of condors in the wild is still very much up in the air.

Recovery Highs and Lows

Since efforts began to save this carrion-eating giant, biologists have learned most of what they know along the way. Maintenance of a captive flock of more abundant Andean condors at the Patuxent Wildlife Research Center in Laurel, Maryland, provided early knowledge later applied to California condor recovery efforts. Still, knowledge wasn't enough—the modern world had developed a host of obstacles to the bird's recovery in the wild.

Power line electrocutions and collisions have killed at least 4 birds. One condor died after drinking antifreeze; many have succumbed to lead poisoning after feasting on the carcasses of legally hunted animals. In fact, ingestion of lead bullets is probably the biggest single threat to the condor's existence in the wild.

Condor intelligence has been responsible for a number of fatalities. They quickly learn that where there are humans, food is likely nearby. Proximity to people often means death. One radio-collared bird simply vanished in 1985; recovery biologists suspect foul play. Two released birds who entered a campground were fed by campers, even after rangers told them not to. One of those birds was recaptured to save it from its new attraction to people.

Immediately after the first 2 birds were released in 1992, two men were caught shooting at one of the releasees with a .22-caliber rifle. One man was tried and convicted. He was fined heavily and sentenced to drawn-out community service.

The condor's flight path to recovery has been a stormy one, indeed.

Focus on Solutions

Numerous concerned individuals and agencies have struggled to save the condor and have refined their management skills to the point that recent releases appear more and more promising. Aversive training with mild electric shock has apparently taught new releasees to avoid power poles. The practice of leaving nestlings with their parents for extended periods seems to result in a wilder bird, less amenable to human approach.

A plan will gradually be enacted to build cliffside nest sites, allowing young to be raised by condor adults amid the panoramas their kind once surveyed when they nested freely. Those setups will be fenced; parent birds will remain captive while children are allowed to fly free. The arrangement will keep precious breeding pairs safe and intact while allowing new condors to reenter the wild.

In the Carrizo Plain Natural Area north of Lion Canyon, the BLM, the state Game and Fish Commission, and the nonprofit Nature Conservancy have teamed up to reintroduce Tule elk and pronghorns to the area. That new stock may eventually provide a source of condor-sized carcasses, reducing or eliminating the need for artificial feeding.

Research into the toxicity of copper bullets, as well as development of a tungsten–bismuth–tin alloy bullet, is in progress. Both materials, though somewhat more expensive than toxic lead, promise better accuracy and higher velocity, which in turn may help reduce or eliminate lead in large-game carcasses. Up to now, every condor found with high levels of ingested lead in its system has died. Steel shot is available for shotgun shells, but condors rarely eat any animal small enough to be legally hunted by shotgun.

By early 1996, 13 birds had been released in Lion Canyon in eastern Santa Barbara County. In February 1996, 4 subadults were released at a new site, Castle Crags, which lies about 40 miles northwest of Lion Canyon in San Luis Obispo County.

A plan to release several condors in Arizona near the Grand Canyon was blocked in early 1996 by a prodevelopment group, CORE, from Kanab, Utah. Resolution of their repeated delaying tactics is pending, with potential lawsuits one dark possibility. Apparently, the extraction-industry group is afraid that allowing an endangered species to return to its historic home may hurt their bottom line—condors be damned.

The condor recovery plan calls for the creation of (at least) two geographically distinct populations, a safety valve to reduce the risk of extirpation due to a single catastrophic event, such as a storm or fire. Arizona once harbored condors; the high cliffs of the Grand Canyon and its surroundings appear to be ideal condor habitat, though large mammal carcasses will have to be supplied to them, at least for a while. USFWS biologists were confident that an Arizona population would be introduced by the summer of 1996, barring lawsuits and other delays.

Condor Watching

Wildlife lovers have several opportunities to observe these majestic birds in the wild, both in California and possibly near the Vermillion Cliffs and Kaibab Plateau north of the Grand Canyon. Though a sighting is far from guaranteed during your visit, patience, good eyes, and strong binoculars will help increase your odds of spotting one.

Pine Mountain in the Los Padres National Forest is a good potential viewing area. Nearer to Castle Crags are two campgrounds, Queen Bee and La Panza, that can serve as base camps for condor viewing. The latter is a much nicer facility, with fire rings, picnic tables, and pit toilets. Queen Bee is rather run-down and primitive, but it can also make a good base for a condor search. A nearby interpretive overlook has been established for viewing. Both campgrounds are marked on California Department of Transportation maps.

A private facility in Big Sur, the Ventana Wilderness Sanctuary is scheduled in early 1996 to take a small number of condors onto their mountain property. The sanctuary's proprietors have already done wonders in aiding the recovery of bald eagles. With that population upgraded from endangered to threatened status, they're tackling the condor problem as their latest gift to the avian world. Sightings may be possible in and around the sanctuary by late 1996.

To identify the huge condor in flight, look for a nearly flat wingspread, extended primary feathers (like long fingers), and triangular white underwing linings. Perching or up close, its odd-shaped, nearly round bald head is one identifying trait. (The juvenile color is black; adult heads are pink.) The condor is more than twice as big as a turkey vulture, so mistaking the two is unlikely. Please don't approach or feed a perching condor. Not only is it illegal but it may also be a death sentence for the bird.

Saving the condor has been a process fraught with tragedy and frustration, but it also offers hope both for a dying species and for a society largely disconnected from the wild world. Every scientific move that condor-recovery biologists make is also a political move, drawing praise and fire from several directions. The eventual success or failure of condor recovery is a reflection of who we are as a people. The California condor's fate may, at least in the spiritual sense, reflect our own.

Impressions and Experiences

Bird sightings:

Other wildlife sightings:

Notes:

				W	H		

ADDRESS, PHONE: PO Box 670, Delano, CA 93216, (805) 725-2767.

DIRECTIONS, HOURS: Drive 19 miles W of Delano to the junction of Garces Highway and Corcoran Road. Open daylight hours. HQ open regular hours Mon thru Fri.

OVERVIEW, ACTIVITIES: Tour road thru marshes, moist-soil units, and desert uplands; wildlife observation, photography, waterfowl, pheasant and dove hunting mid-October thru mid-January.

ELEVATION: From 212 to 222 feet above sea level.

WEATHER: Dry and very hot in summer, mild from fall thru early spring. Fall and winter best seasons to visit.

SPECIAL NEEDS: Drinking water and insect repellent.

LODGING, CAMPING: Motels at Delano (19 miles E), Lost Hills (13 miles SE at Hwy 46 and I-5), and Wasco (25 miles S on Hwy 46); camping at Buena Vista Lake Recreation Area (45 miles S of Kern off I-5) and Allenworth State Park (20 miles E of refuge); RV hookups at KOA campground in Shafter; RV site also at Lost Hills.

NEARBY POINTS OF INTEREST: Tule Elk Reserve, 35 miles S of Kern off I-5, Mono Lake, Yosemite National Park.

Besides Pixley, a third refuge managed from Kern is the 897-acre Blue Ridge NWR. Blue Ridge protects juniper woodland habitat as summer foraging and roosting grounds for endangered California condors. It is closed to the public.

DISABILITY ACCESS: Office is accessible, as is a hunter blind on the refuge.

California's Central Valley offers a good example of the decimation that can befall wildlife in the face of large-scale habitat alteration. It also provides an example of the sorts of steps that can be taken to correct such tragedies. Just a hundred years ago, the valley was the site of a vast wetland of more than half a million acres, along with millions more of grassland, saltbush upland, and riparian forest. For thousands of years, the region drew miles-long flocks of migratory and nesting birds and supported great numbers of deer, elk, and other large mammals.

Then in the late 1800s, the desert farmers came. To supply their fields of rice, cotton, feed grains, and other crops, they dammed and diverted Sierra Nevada runoff water channeled through the San Joaquin and Tule rivers. Over the next few decades, land once rich with wild food and habitat was scraped flat and rendered inhospitable to all but a relatively few wild creatures.

By 1900, just 10% of the historic valley wetland acres survived; now the number is down to less than 8%. The 10,618-acre Kern NWR, along with 6,200-acre Pixley NWR, both located in the San Joaquin Valley (a subregion of the Central Valley), represents much of what's left of the old habitat. Lying on the southern edge of Tulare Lakebed, site of the largest lake west of the Mississippi before levee diversions dried it up, both are critical spots for migratory support and are among the last existing habitat for a variety of native terrestrial creatures.

freshwater
wetlands

Other valley refuges exist farther to the north, joining with Kern to make up a tiny network of remaining water and upland habitat. The San Luis Complex comprises just over 100,000 acres, protecting a variety of biomes, including 40% of the Central Valley's remaining wetlands. Additional wetlands exist at Goose Lake Bottoms, 10 miles south of Kern. There, 4,000 acres of seasonal wet

habitat exist, along with an equal number of upland acres. The Nature Conservancy's Paine Preserve, duck hunting clubs, and other wild acres southeast of the refuge protect uplands and marshes, completing the present-day migratory support system.

Seasons in the Desert

When you first look out over Kern from the visitor kiosk at its entrance, you may find it hard to distinguish the refuge from surrounding farm fields. Its low brush and handful of willows scarcely break the smog-veiled horizon line. Nearly as flat as the surrounding plowed acres, refuge elevation varies by just 10 feet across its entire length. On good days you can make out the low line of the Coastal (aka Temblor) Range far to the south and west.

Kern is not a place of dramatic scenery, though the marsh at sunrise and sunset can be enchanting, warmed by the glow of cattails and bulrushes and reflecting the graceful bend of willows along the banks. The prime fascination of this refuge is realized by entering its depths unobtrusively and watching as wildlife dramas unfold.

Kern's tour road is the primary visitor access. With several pullouts, interpretive displays, and 3 hiking trails into different habitats, the loop offers a good variety of driving, biking, and walking options.

During summer months, especially July and August, Kern can be blisteringly hot (temperatures above 110 degrees F are not uncommon), with water scarce and much of the vegetation withered and drab. Resident species, such as great horned and long-eared owl, mourning dove, and ring-necked pheasant, are often in evidence during those months, along with raptors, such as kestrel and harrier, and the ever-present coots who occupy remnant patches of marsh.

On the uplands, burrowers that include the endangered Tipton's kangaroo rat, blunt-nosed leopard lizard, the secretive San Joaquin kit fox, and a state-listed antelope ground squirrel may show themselves during cooler parts of the day. A variety of waterfowl stays to nest on the refuge, though their numbers are relatively slim. A handful of shorebirds, including curlews and sandpipers, may linger at Kern beyond spring migration. Otherwise, things can be pretty quiet.

From late summer through March, though, Kern is often spectacular. In the fall, between 10,000 and 25,000 feet of water are channeled into 4,000 wetland acres from the California aqueduct and deep wells—wetland acreage that should increase after recent legislation helps increase marsh habitat on the refuge. The goal is an increase to 7,000 acres of marsh by the year 2002.

Close to 1,200 acres are also managed for natural moist-soil plants favored by waterfowl, including wild millet, alkali bulrush, spike rush, barnyard grass, smartweed, and swamp timothy.

Pacific Flyway water birds respond to this bounty in the tens of thousands. First to arrive are August shorebirds. Yellowlegs, willet, marbled godwit, whimbrel, and even red knot at times fly in to occupy the mudflats and shallows. Ruddies and shovelers are among the first ducks to arrive; pintail, green-winged teal, scaup, redhead, Canada goose, and dozens of other species gradually join resident waterfowl, and Kern reverberates in a riot of calls, fluttering, and feeding that continues throughout winter.

With the influx of prey, raptors glide in to take advantage. Golden eagles are common during all the cooler months, along with rough-legged and red-tailed hawks and Cooper's and sharp-shinned hawks in tree-lined reaches. Black-shouldered kite nests here and resides all year round, though the species is not often spotted by refuge personnel. Peregrine falcon and bald eagle come through at times.

The bird list numbers 211 species. Water-loving birds on the list inhabit the refuge in the thousands. Even a few sandhill cranes

show up, though more seem to prefer nearby Pixley NWR, a satellite refuge with 300 to 1,000 acres of seasonal wetland habitat. In 1994, 2,200 cranes jammed into 300 wetland acres on Pixley. That satellite refuge presently has no water delivery system. A new well (pumping is expensive but sometimes necessary) and the year's rain and runoff determine how much water Pixley will have in a given season.

Cranes also visit farm fields around the area and can frequently be seen throughout the valley in September and October. The Sacramento Valley to the north draws more cranes than anyone cares to count.

Springtime at Kern sees vigorous migratory activity, though the wetlands are beginning to dry up by then. Late winter is a better time to come for avian drama. March through May can also be productive, as many of the winter birds, along with a number of migratory species, remain here as the days grow longer and warmer. Species such as white pelican, wood duck, black-necked stilt, American avocet, sandpiper, and dunlin are here in spring.

In the willows, salt cedar, and a smattering of cottonwoods, you may encounter Anna's and rufous hummingbirds, any of a dozen flycatchers, house and marsh wrens, orange-crowned, blackpoll, and black-throated gray warblers, and a variety of sparrows. Hooded and northern orioles both arrive in spring, the northern remaining oftentimes into summer and fall. Cedar waxwing is another of Kern's springtime visitors (they may also be here in fall and winter). A small but productive riparian cluster lies on your left just before the loop's second turn. Six miles of riparian habitat can also be accessed on foot to the south of that spot; a good stand of willow and cottonwood there offers passerine sightings, especially in migration. The slough's riparian structure vanishes into plowed flatlands immediately beyond the refuge border.

desert

Visitor Access

The tour loop that cuts through perhaps a quarter of the refuge carries you close to some of its better wetland and riparian habitats. Among the first marshes you reach on the loop is Unit 1, where water often remains into summer, after most of the refuge has gone dry. That unit is located just beyond your first right turn along the 1-way road.

During wet months, the loop passes marshlands of different depths, allowing good views of waterfowl, shorebirds, and waders, along with various passerines and raptors who perch in the willows and salt cedar that make up Kern's minimal riparian habitat. Cattail and salt cedar between the road and some marshes provide cover; be careful if you approach the marsh on flattened cattails—some of that matting extends over shallow, mucky water.

Upland and wetlands along the loop may yield mammal or reptile sightings just about anywhere, including more than a dozen state and federally protected animals and plants. Grasslands on the refuge are the site of vernal pools, shallow bodies of water that retain winter moisture. Oftentimes they support such interesting plants as coyote thistle (*Eryngium vaseyi*) and dwarf woolly head (*Psilocarphus brevissmus*), along with arrays of wildflowers if moisture conditions are right. During certain years, the refuge may be awash in color, with California poppy, aster, and phacelia painting the landscape.

Mammals on the refuge are furtive, but you may get lucky and spot one, especially in the early morning or dusk hours. They include the endangered San Joaquin kit fox, badger, muskrat, coyote, and raccoon, along with a variety of rodents that are savored by predatory mammals and raptors.

The Beechey (or California) ground squirrel (*Spermophilus beecheyi*) is one active rodent who's hard to miss here. Whitish-flecked fur runs along its body from neck to haunches; a dark V pattern marks its shoulders, pointing forward. The Beechey's bushy, brown-gray tail twitches wildly as it scurries about in search of seeds, plants, and insects, keeping a nervous

eye out for predatory mammals and birds. The squirrels live in mound-entry burrows that may extend for 200 feet. Cute as they are, Beecheys are regarded as a prime host for fleas that carry bubonic plague.

Herp species include the endangered blunt-nosed leopard lizard, which occupies meadowland on the refuge's west side. Grasses on the uplands are clipped short through managed cattle grazing, which with controlled burning comprises much of Kern's vegetation control. Burning will likely be curtailed as air quality regulations grow stricter in this smog-choked region.

Short grass makes good habitat for the leopard lizard, which requires open, low-level views, as it often scans and hunts on its hind legs, searching for tasty insect morsels. The lizard is most active in spring and summer. Other reptiles and amphibians at Kern include the coast horned lizard, pacific gopher snake, western long-nosed snake, pacific tree frog, western spadefoot toad, and bullfrog.

Pixley NWR is home to the largest population of this endangered 9-inch lizard with its narrow range. Due to its sensitive nature, Pixley is not presently open to visitors.

Regional Wildlife Concern

Tricolored blackbirds are monitored and nurtured at Kern and in surrounding areas. In the past they've formed boisterous colonies just south of the first turn on the tour loop, though their choice of yearly nest sites is unpredictable. The state-listed bird nests in cattails, hard-stem bulrush, and farm silage fields and is quite sensitive to storm events and human disruption. In 1994, close to 12,000 blackbird young were born on the refuge. The year before that after a storm hit, production was virtually zero. In 1992, 7,000 tricoloreds were fledged.

Kern biologists, when equipped with adequate funds and the time, survey nearby cropland for blackbird colonies. When a colony is located, they consult with the landowner on ways to encourage successful nesting. Occasionally, they pay farmers to delay harvesting until after fledging to reduce disturbance and nest destruction. Inadequate funding makes this an on again–off again practice.

Water: Blessing and Curse

For all the struggle and expense Kern faces to pump, channel, and otherwise acquire water, there are times when the refuge gets too much of a good thing. Every 8 or 9 years, a massive flood sweeps in. That might be okay for a system prepared to accept it, but Kern staffers are caught in a bind when it comes to floodwater management: They're committed to taking it but have no legal arrangements to release it off the refuge. Sometimes they can work out a short-term deal to release water onto land controlled by the state or other entity, but that isn't always possible.

Smaller floods can be positive events, creating wetlands and facilitating moist-soil plant production, but the big deluges bring an overabundance of water that sits on refuge soil until it evaporates, leaving behind salts and natural contaminants, such as selenium, boron, arsenic, and other biologically harmful chemicals.

Pesticides from nearby farm fields add to the unhealthy mix; water toxicology surveys were planned for 1996. Refuge staffers know the aqueduct water they receive is good, but runoff and subsurface water in this pesticide-heavy, toxin-overloaded region is a different story.

Another problem caused by flooding is the influx of unwanted seeds that it brings, such as those of exotic salt cedar, which arrived during a 1969 flood and have since expanded to crowd Kern's already-scarce riparian vegetation. Removal of tamarisk is an ongoing process, accomplished partly with Civilian Conservation Corps help. Despite improved salt cedar control methods, no one believes the resilient shrub trees will be eradicated any time soon.

While not officially regarded as a "mitigation refuge," Kern does serve the purpose of drawing waterfowl away from some 5,000 acres of selenium-contaminated ponds in the area, including several northeast of the refuge and others along nearby I-5. California's Water Quality Board has been assigned the task of providing 5,600 acres of true mitigation habitats in the valley. By mid-1995 they had managed to create 300 such wetland acres.

Though Kern's water is in fairly good shape, the refuge is hardly immune to contamination problems. Naturally occurring botulism in the moist soil is an ongoing refuge curse, creating the potential for waterfowl disease vectored by invertebrates bearing high levels of the deadly bacteria. Due to heavy consumption of invertebrates by nesting mothers and young waterfowl, whose protein needs are high, development of nesting habitat is a low priority at Kern. Still, dozens of species do produce young here.

The refuge is presently moving toward acquisition of all the California aqueduct water it needs for optimal wetlands production. The hang-up right now involves outdated water structures that make moving the water inefficient. The present infrastructure doesn't aid the flushing process so critical to botulism control. Funding is perennially short, so improvements may take awhile.

Friendly Fire?

Hunters from the Ventura County area have long made Kern a favorite spot for killing ducks and other refuge birds. Their support—including habitat-enhancement funding from the local chapter of Ducks Unlimited—assures that refuge hunting will continue into the foreseeable future.

From mid-October to mid-January, hunting is allowed on a little less than half the refuge. A recent management plan has mandated that 1,000 acres of protected wetlands be flooded before any hunting commences. A closed zone comprising 55% of refuge wetlands will always provide birds with sanctuaries free of flesh-piercing steel pellets, as well as a buffer from disturbances by nonhunters. Generally, the refuge manager sets hunting limits that allow one shooter per 20 acres of huntable area. Some of that area is closed to weapon-less visitors on hunt days.

One positive result of hunters' presence on the refuge is the porta-potties that the state installs during hunting season. Those are the only rest room facilities presently available on the refuge.

Hunters in the region are among Kern's strongest supporters and have much to do with the fact that Kern even exists. It's a sad fact that nonconsumptive wildlife lovers around many refuges seem less passionate about preserving and supporting these places than many hunters. Why the imbalance? Who can say? It's a question only the individual can answer, just as wildlife protection begins on a personal level, with you and me.

Impressions and Experiences

Bird sightings:

Other wildlife sightings:

Notes:

PARTIAL BIRD LIST (OF 211 LISTED SPECIES): Double-crested cormorant, least bittern, white-faced ibis, snow goose, green-winged teal, pintail, gadwall, ruddy duck, black-shouldered kite, golden eagle, Virginia rail, greater yellowlegs, least sandpiper, short-billed dowitcher, Forster's tern, burrowing owl, Nuttall's woodpecker, black phoebe, tree swallow, common raven, water pipit, blue grosbeak, sage sparrow, tricolored blackbird, lesser goldfinch.

PARTIAL MAMMAL LIST: San Joaquin kit fox, coyote, Tipton kangaroo rat, Beechey ground squirrel, muskrat, spotted skunk, raccoon, black-tail jackrabbit.

PARTIAL HERP LIST: Blunt-nose leopard lizard, coast horned lizard, pacific gopher snake, western long-nosed snake, pacific tree frog, western spadefoot toad, bullfrog.

VC	R		NP	W	B	H	F	

ADDRESS, PHONE: 906 W Sinclair Road, Calipatria, CA 92233, (619) 348-5278.

DIRECTIONS, HOURS: From Calipatria, N on Hwy 111, L on Sinclair Road, 6 miles to refuge. Refuge open daylight hours; HQ open 7 a.m. to 4:30 p.m. Mon thru Fri.

OVERVIEW, ACTIVITIES: Some 2,500 acres of wetlands, freshwater impoundments, desert uplands, farm fields, and saltwater habitat. Abundant water-loving and perching migrants. Wildlife observation, photography, hiking, boating, fishing from boats, waterfowl hunting. The Salton Sea International Bird Festival, inaugurated in 1996, is cosponsored by the refuge and the Brawley, CA, C of C. The mid-February event features tours, seminars, workshops, dining, and a collection of "Discovery Nest" wildlife activities for children. For more information, contact the refuge or call the Brawley C of C at (619) 344-3160.

ELEVATION: Sea bottom 260 feet below sea level; refuge averages 230 feet below sea level.

WEATHER: One of the nation's hottest spots in summer (often exceeding 110 degrees F mid-June to mid-September); mild late fall thru early spring; rainfall is rare and generally light. Fall, winter, and spring best seasons to visit.

SPECIAL NEEDS: Water for trail hikes; scope for pelagic birds, flamingos off New River delta; broad-brimmed hat in hot weather; sunscreen.

LODGING, CAMPING: Motels and RV facilities in Brawley (20 miles), Niland (10 miles), Imperial (28 miles), and El Centro (33 miles). Camping at Wister and Finney Ramer units of Imperial Wildlife Area and Salton Sea State Recreation Area.

NEARBY POINTS OF INTEREST: Anza Borrego State Park (excellent desert ecology and exhibits; impressive wildflowers in spring) E of refuge on Hwy. 78; Sand Hills Recreation Area off Hwy 78 E of refuge; Imperial, Cibola, Havasu, and Bill Williams River NWR along Colorado River.

Coachella Valley NWR is a nonaccessible satellite refuge of Salton Sea created to protect the Coachella Valley fringe-toed lizard. The adjoining 20,000-acre Coachella Valley Preserve, managed by the Nature Conservancy and the state of Calif., harbors more than 180 species. The Coachella Valley Preserve is located in Riverside County, approximately 10 miles E of Palm Springs, N of I-10. To reach the Visitor's Center, exit off I-10 eastbound at Ramon Road and proceed approximately 4.5 miles to Thousand Palms Canyon Road. Turn N on Thousand Palms Canyon Road. Entrance to the VC is about 2 miles.

DISABILITY ACCESS: HQ and rest rooms accessible; one hunting blind accessible; observation towers to be upgraded for access (funding will determine when); trails are generally flat but not hard-topped.

It was late spring at Salton Sea NWR, and two endangered Yuma clapper rails were conversing in the marsh. I stood nearby on the dike that holds back the vast inland sea, eavesdropping as the rails traded clicks and rattles. Suddenly, one bolted from the cattails and hop-flew gawkily, brushing the crowns of alkali bulrush as it joined its fellow marsh magician 10 yards away.

In the emergent-tangled shallows, a mother moorhen squawked repeatedly, directing two red-billed fuzzball chicks who bumped about the bulrush maze, learning camouflage. Below the dike ran a second marsh, bordered by a strip of tamarisk and cattails. Half a dozen calls rang from the brush—coots, marsh wrens, a duck or two, others I couldn't place.

Freshwater marshes along the Rock Hill Trail at Salton Sea NWR are just one of a surprising variety of habitats in this small patch of pro-

tected land at the southeastern edge of California's Salton Sea. The 2,500-acre refuge—all that remains after the sea gradually inundated another 44,500 refuge acres—lies below sea level in one of the nation's hottest regions. The area reputedly gets 3 inches of rain per year, but that's often an exaggera-

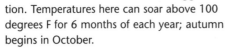

freshwater wetlands

tion. Temperatures here can soar above 100 degrees F for 6 months of each year; autumn begins in October.

Despite the harsh climate (or maybe because of it), Salton Sea attracts one of the largest variety and concentration of bird species in the nation. Some 380 species have been noted here. Many Pacific Flyway birds come in fantastic numbers: tens of thousands of least and western sandpipers, thousands of avocets and stilts, and more than a million eared grebes in late winter. Each year, 15,000 to 20,000 snow and Ross's geese stay for winter, along with no more than a hundred Canada geese, a species that once came in much greater numbers.

Rare and unlikely birds often show up at the three refuge units, including seabirds such as Leach's storm petrel, blue-footed booby, and magnificent frigate bird. Both brown and white pelicans share airspace and loafing islands on refuge impoundments. Two varieties of flamingo wade the shallows here nearly every year, the lesser and Chilean. Some of 10 woodpecker species may be lurching up tree trunks in any season, including the flycatcherlike Lewis's, an occasional resident except in summer.

Dozens of warbler species, along with scores of other neotropical migrants, pass through in spring and fall, drawn to refuge mesquite, willow, and palo verde that jut prominently above the region's endless farm fields. Twenty flycatcher species thicken the mix, many of them lookalike epidomaxes that often provoke fits in ID-conscious birders.

Holes and cracks on and near the refuge, along with artificial box-burrows installed by USFWS staffers, harbor scores of burrowing owls. Some biologists believe upward of 70% of the western race of burrowing owls within California—thousands—live within the borders of Imperial County. The artificial burrows were installed to lessen the owl's damage to nearby irrigation structures, where they may still be found (look along Sinclair Road near the refuge entrance). Indeed, the refuge was originally founded in 1930 to mitigate the impact of wildlife, especially geese, on surrounding agricultural fields. Its mission has changed over the decades, but depradation control is still a primary objective at Salton Sea.

A small assortment of mammals and herptiles resides here, though the demanding environment makes it tough for most to earn a living. Beyond desert cottontail, western spiny lizard, and an occasional western rattler or gopher snake, you won't see many nonavian critters here. At dusk, scan the sky for any of 7 bat species that cruise the refuge on their northerly cycle from Mexico, sweeping the airways for insects. Kit fox, a small dog well adapted to arid landscapes, inhabits burrows in and around the refuge, though its secretive nocturnal habits make it very difficult to see. Monarch butterflies can be thick here some years, passing through on their way to wintering grounds in the Mexican highlands.

Can't Take the Heat

This is one hot refuge, for birding adventures as well as for the human circulatory systems. Late fall through midspring are the best times to come, though such attractors as yellow-footed gull, wood stork, and one of two US nesting colonies of gull-billed terns (the other colony is in San Diego) draw intrepid summer birders, too.

If you go between mid-May and early October, plan a morning visit, with a cool spot penciled into your itinerary by noontime. Except for the trees around the Visitor's Center and the nearby "coverstrip" of screwbean mesquite, lycium, and palo verde that runs along the start of the tour trail, most of the Union Tract must be seen by hiking its 1.25-mile trail. In broiling summer temperatures here, walking the Union Tract's Rock Hill Trail or the half-mile trail on Unit 1 can be extremely demanding. Always bring water on hikes; it can get ridiculously hot by noon, even in nonsummer months.

A viewing platform next to HQ may be a good place for photographers seeking close-up shots of perching birds. Come early and you may avoid the crowds of springtime birders who jam the refuge.

The Rock Hill Trail from HQ can easily yield an all-day birding adventure anytime during fall, winter, or spring without bringing on undue heat stress. The trail begins in a thicket of desert trees that may harbor dozens of passerines, including vermilion and dusky flycatchers, eastern and western kingbirds, Bendire's thrasher, loggerhead shrike (northern shrike come in winter), any of 3 dozen warbler species, colorful lazuli and indigo buntings, Abert's towhee, and white-crowned sparrow.

The tree-lined coverstrip along the first part of the trail may provide food and shelter for numerous perching birds, as well as for desert cottontails, rodents such as cotton rat and pocket mouse, and several lizard species. The strip itself is a good model of habitat mitigation that any farmer can create simply by leaving trees and other cover in place or by planting cover along field edges; food-source plants, of course, add even more support. Here the mesquite beans are eaten by rodents, and the lycium's red berries are savored by many birds. If the practice of leaving coverstrips was widespread, our neotropical migrant populations would be in much better shape—agricultural clearing is one of the chief causes of their decline, along with urban development and destruction of wetlands.

Beyond the farm fields, where some of the refuge's 1,000 acres of winter wheat and alfalfa are grown as wintertime goose feed, the trail leads to a long dike that keeps the sea from swamping the remaining refuge acres. Here the landward side is around 8 feet lower than the looming sea surface. Workers constantly repair and fortify it.

desert

The trail continues over the dike, with good views of the sea and nearby mountains. It leads to several impoundments on the landward side, where abundant bird species may be found. At this point you pass a unique freshwater marsh, bordered by barnacles, which built up over the years to create a dam on the seaward side of the dike. The barnacles originally came from World War II–era seaplanes practicing aquatic landings. Agricultural water feeds the marsh, keeping its salt level fairly low. This is one of the better spots for observing water-loving species, including clapper rail, American and least bitterns, little blue, tricolored, and reddish egrets, and green- and black-crowned night herons.

Settle onto a spot that allows good views into the marsh. Your patience will soon be rewarded. A sparcer strip of marsh lies along a canal on the landward side below the dike, bordering refuge farm fields. Numerous species may be there, too.

Continuing on, you come to a landward-side impoundment that is highly saline due to seawater leakage beneath the dike. The pond supports relatively few birds, though it may harbor avocets, stilts, grebes, and a few others, resting or feeding on the pond's brine shrimp and flies.

Farther inland, freshwater impoundments are more supportive of life. Their tiny islands may harbor dozens of species, including white and brown pelicans, neotropical cormorant, various gulls, including yellow-footed (they often hang out near the seawall), gull-billed tern (a nesting colony resides on a clearly visible bare dirt island), black skimmer, and many more.

Depth gradations in the ponds provide for dabblers that include teal and pintail, as well as divers such as redhead, scaup, and even surf scoter, which breeds in the Arctic, and white-winged scoter, a bird that usually winters on the Pacific seacoast. At least 3 dozen waterfowl species use the ponds and nearby habitat. Most are loafing there and feeding elsewhere.

The trail continues to Rock Hill, an overlook on a small hill draped in brittlebush and silvery desert holly. From there you can scan the entire refuge unit and take in the sea's horizon-filling breadth, which extends between 9 and 15 miles across at various points. From here you may also note eared and western grebes playing along the shoreline. The overlook makes a great vantage point for observing pelicans, gulls, and any of 7 terns who frequent the refuge. Occasionally, seabirds can be spotted from here, including ancient murrelet in spring and summer.

The factories you see across the distant farm acres belching plumes of gaseous discharge aren't nearly as nasty as they look. These are geothermal electric generating plants, and the discharge is steam rather than smoke. They tap volcanic steam escaping from the underlying San Andreas Fault and represent a forward-looking approach to power generation. Earthquakes on the fault line are common because of the underlying geology. A December 1995 quake, one of many that have rocked the refuge, shook objects off refuge HQ walls and desks. The thrill of spotting abundant wildlife isn't the only reason you may feel the earth move at this refuge.

By the Sea

Atop the dike you'll note several large pipes that channel a constant flow of farm irrigation water into the sea. This is "used" water, drawn from the Colorado River, channeled onto fields, then carried to the sea along with concentrations of salt, pesticides, and natural chemicals such as selenium. The outflow keeps both area agriculture and the Salton Sea alive, but it also increases the sea's salt and pollution levels.

Fish were once bountiful in the sea; for decades, a vigorous sport fishing industry thrived on their presence. With salt levels well exceeding sea salt concentrations—and rising—that industry is nearly dead. Various federal, state, local, and nonprofit agencies are debating the future management of this artificial inland sea. Water supply at the refuge, never a problem in the past, may decrease as the city of San Diego vies with other users for limited Colorado River water. With no real water rights, Salton Sea NWR has long relied on the kindness of the Imperial Irrigation District to supply its wetland needs. When push comes to shove, the question will arise: How important is the wildlife? The 6 endangered species living on the refuge may help tilt the balance, but with the anti-nature bias ascendant in Congress, the fate of Salton Sea refuge may be in question.

The sea itself first formed in modern times when a Colorado River dike crumbled in

1905. Within a few months, the breach was a mile wide, and for 2 years there was no stopping its flow into this lowland basin. The flood inundated a region where agriculture had blossomed in this parched desert. This one isn't the first sea that has formed in the area; water has risen and evaporated here numerous times over the centuries. The former body here—Lake Cahuilla, named for a local Indian tribe—was twice the size of today's (fluctuating) 380-square-mile impoundment.

The huge lake serves largely as a depository for salt-and-pesticide–laced agricultural out-flows. As a result, salt levels reached 45 parts per million by the mid-1990s—10% saltier than Pacific Ocean water. Fish transplanted to the Salton Sea in the 1950s, including orangemouth corvina, Gulf croaker, and sargo—and more recently tilapia from South America—once attracted countless anglers. By the 1960s, this was one of California's most productive inland fisheries. Half a million people visited the sea in 1989 (birders as well as anglers), injecting $300 million into the local economy.

By the spring of 1996, the corvina were nearly gone, croakers hadn't been seen in years, and tens of thousands of tilapia were floating on the surface and piled up on beaches. Their deaths come alongside huge eared grebe die-offs that have occurred in some years, including a 1992 mass kill that took 150,000 grebes. Unlike the obvious salt-related problems for fish, the cause of the grebes' demise is undetermined, though biologists are beginning to suspect toxic algal blooms, similar to "red tides" that periodically ravage marine environments.

With the demise of the sport fishing industry here, tourism aimed at Salton Sea NWR becomes ever more important to the local economy. Imperial County seems to recognize the benefits derived from the refuge's 32,000 yearly visitors. Unlike some federal presences, this refuge is regarded as a valued friend and neighbor by most folks in the area.

Unit 1 and the Hazard Unit

Another wildlife-rich portion of the refuge lies a 15-minute drive southwest from HQ at the end of a maze of farm roads. (The refuge brochure will steer you there.) Unit 1 is similar to the Union Tract in that it lies at the sea's edge and contains several freshwater impoundments that support numerous species. Here, cover and perching habitat are somewhat thicker than they are on the Union Tract, and passerines may be more abundant. A loop trail leads past impoundments and marshes. Rattlesnakes are fairly abundant in the brush here, so be alert. More abundant are wintertime snow and Ross's geese; where perhaps 500 geese may reside near HQ, as many as 15,000 often show up on Unit 1.

The New River flows across the farmland from the southeast, emptying into the sea after crossing its mile-long delta. At the tip of the delta, 4 or 5 flamingos have been hanging around for years. They're most easily seen by boat, but a spotting scope may yield faint patches of pink; if the bill is thick and down-curved, you're looking at a flamingo. If it's flat and spatula shaped, you've got a roseate spoonbill in your sights. Spoonbill sightings are uncommon here; refuge staffers heard about one in wetlands along I-8 in 1995; the previous sighting was 4 years earlier.

The landward portion of the New River is accessible by way of a utility road. Don't go there. This may well be the most polluted river in the United States. Pathogens that include polio and tuberculosis thrive in this watercourse that issues from Mexico and is protected by few environmental safeguards. Some people visit its banks, where numerous wildlife species may be found; a few even hunt along the river and eat the carcasses they bring home. Don't be one of these silly people. You'll find numerous reasons to stay within the central part of the unit, and your immune system and loved ones will thank you.

A viewing platform at Unit 1 offers good views of the vegetation, seashore, and marshes. On the wetlands and associated rises, look for black skimmer, Forster's and Caspian terns, white and brown pelicans, pacific and common loons, and any of numerous other wetland species.

In the brush be alert for northern parula, a common winter resident. Other passerines here may include ovenbird, Townsend's solitaire, verdin, Nuttall's woodpecker, and Cassin's kingbird.

On the northeastern end of the refuge lies the Hazard Unit of the refuge. Generally open only to waterfowl hunters on a permit basis in fall and winter, the tract may also be accessible to wildlife lovers during nonhunting, nonnesting seasons. Ask for an entry permit and directions from staffers; if your timing is right you may get lucky and receive one.

The unit flanks the Alamo River, and some good riparian habitat runs through that may harbor any of a number of perching species. Cormorants, egrets, and ibises are commonly found here among freshwater impoundments and marsh habitat. The Hazard Unit is also the only spot on the refuge where wood storks are generally found. They often perch on dead tamarisk snags along Schrimpf Road. If they're present, you can see them easily from your car.

Salton Sea NWR is one of the nation's premier birding spots—a joy to visit, a struggle to leave. In one of the harshest climates in the United States, this patch of protected land and water is truly a national treasure. No birder's tour is complete without a visit to Salton Sea.

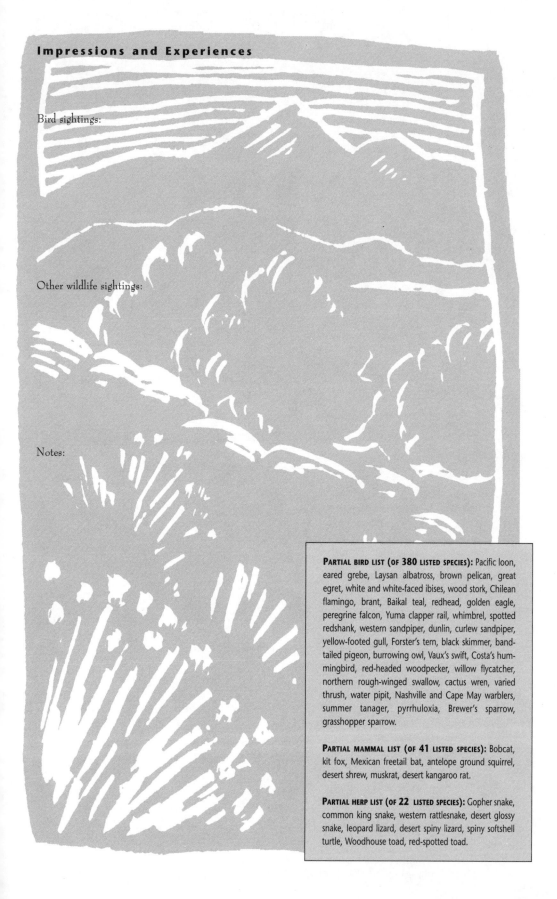

Impressions and Experiences

Bird sightings:

Other wildlife sightings:

Notes:

PARTIAL BIRD LIST (OF 380 LISTED SPECIES): Pacific loon, eared grebe, Laysan albatross, brown pelican, great egret, white and white-faced ibises, wood stork, Chilean flamingo, brant, Baikal teal, redhead, golden eagle, peregrine falcon, Yuma clapper rail, whimbrel, spotted redshank, western sandpiper, dunlin, curlew sandpiper, yellow-footed gull, Forster's tern, black skimmer, band-tailed pigeon, burrowing owl, Vaux's swift, Costa's hummingbird, red-headed woodpecker, willow flycatcher, northern rough-winged swallow, cactus wren, varied thrush, water pipit, Nashville and Cape May warblers, summer tanager, pyrrhuloxia, Brewer's sparrow, grasshopper sparrow.

PARTIAL MAMMAL LIST (OF 41 LISTED SPECIES): Bobcat, kit fox, Mexican freetail bat, antelope ground squirrel, desert shrew, muskrat, desert kangaroo rat.

PARTIAL HERP LIST (OF 22 LISTED SPECIES): Gopher snake, common king snake, western rattlesnake, desert glossy snake, leopard lizard, desert spiny lizard, spiny softshell turtle, Woodhouse toad, red-spotted toad.

VC	R		NP	W				

ADDRESS, PHONE: 301 Caspian Way, Imperial Beach, CA 91933, (619) 930-0168.

DIRECTIONS, HOURS: I-5 exit onto Coronado Avenue, 2.5 miles to Third Street, L .5 miles to signs and Visitor's Center. Open daylight hours; Visitor's Center open 8 a.m. to 5 p.m. weekdays.

OVERVIEW, ACTIVITIES: Some 1,100 acres of estuary, lagoon, and beach shore; trails, landscaped xeroscopic garden, birding, hiking, cycling, leashed dog walking, fishing from beach (see regulation pamphlet available at refuge).

ELEVATION: Sea level to 6 feet.

WEATHER: Mild most of the year. All seasons good for visiting.

SPECIAL NEEDS: Spotting scope for observing shoreline birds.

LODGING, CAMPING: Lodging exists in the surrounding urban area; camping and RV hookups at Silver Strand State Beach, N of Imperial Beach.

NEARBY POINTS OF INTEREST: Chula Vista Nature Center at Sweetwater Marsh NWR; Cabrillo Monument at Point Loma; Hotel del Coronado in city of Coronado N of Imperial Beach, W side of bay; County Regional park, W of refuge—good riparian birding.

Sweetwater Marsh NWR, another Tijuana Slough satellite, is a 315-acre preserve for many of the same species that Tijuana Slough protects, including endangered Belding's savanna sparrow and California brown pelican. Access via East Street exit off I-5, turn W to parking lot, wait for bus to refuge and nature center. Trails to Gunpowder Point (potash from kelp used to make gunpowder prior to World War I); trail from nature center. *Frankinia palmerii*, a marsh plant found nowhere else, can be seen here. Native garden around Visitor's Center, live bird exhibit, reptile exhibit, petting pool for sharks and rays, demos, series of aquaria displaying San Diego Bay marine life. A rare remnant of the natural bayside environment.

Seal Beach NWR features 1,000 acres of Bolsa Chica wetlands, as well as ocean shoreline. It's located within the Seal Beach Naval Weapons Station N of San Diego and harbors many of the same endangered species and other animals found at Sweetwater and Tijuana Slough. Public access may or may not be allowed. Call Tijuana Slough for updated access information.

DISABILITY ACCESS: McCoy Trail is earthen but fairly flat and smooth; Visitor's Center has accessible rest rooms.

One of the smallest refuges in the system, 1,100-acre Tijuana Slough NWR on the coastal edge of San Diego is also one of the least remarkable in appearance. At least at first glance.

Surrounded by city and surf, Tijuana Slough is blanketed in a nearly unwavering coat of cordgrass and pickleweed, interspersed with algal mats and carpet plants such as love grass. Endangered salt marsh bird's beak colonies thrive in the high-tide zone, which grades upward from middle marsh only a foot or two above mean sea level. A variety of exotics, such as crysanthemum, ice plant, and fennel, have also taken root here, creating attractive, though ecologically undesirable, blooms in spring and summer.

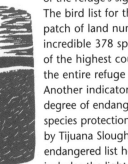

coastal

Despite the monocultural look of the Tijuana estuary, several distinct habitats here support a remarkable variety of species. One indication of the refuge's significance: The bird list for this tiny patch of land numbers an incredible 378 species, one of the highest counts in the entire refuge system. Another indicator is the degree of endangered species protection afforded by Tijuana Slough. The endangered list here includes the light-footed clapper rail, Belding's savanna sparrow, California least tern, least Bell's vireo, and a foot-tall plant, the salt marsh bird's beak. Peregrine falcon and other at-risk creatures pass through in migration, further swelling the protected list. State-protected creatures, such as the coastal race of California king snake and Stellar's sea lion, live here or visit as well.

The refuge is primarily an estuary, meaning its marshes receive both fresh and salt water. One of the Pacific Coast's last remaining estuarine environments—the only one in southern California not bisected by a road or railroad track and the only one with year-round daily tidal flushing—Tijuana Slough provides habitat for many creatures who would likely diminish or disappear if not for this welcoming habitat.

The overlying Tijuana River National Estuarine Research Reserve (NERR), which includes additional state and county land as well as the refuge, totals 2,500 acres. Two refuges managed from Tijuana Slough, Sweetwater Marsh and the more distant Seal Beach in Orange County (both with limited access), supplement the habitat provided at Tijuana Slough, though in somewhat different forms.

The "fresh" portion of Tijuana Slough's estuary arrives by way of the Tijuana River. Two-thirds of the river's watershed is located in Mexico, from which sewage runoff, pesticides, and other toxins present frequent water quality problems. You can look from the refuge into Tijuana, where a massive bullring dominates the scene. When nearby Border Field State Park is open, you can stand at the fence separating the two nations.

The marine environment of the Tijuana estuary is supported by twice-daily tides, channeled through the river mouth into the tidal creeks. A spiderweb of streams and overflow routes known collectively as the "tidal prism" distributes water throughout the marsh. Flushing action through the prism is critical to the system's health.

The refuge environment is imperiled each winter when storms threaten to dam the river mouth with sand buildup, cutting off critical tidal flow. To resist that threat, refuge staffers mechanically build up the massive barrier dunes each November. In 1983 that sand bulwark fell to a huge El Niño–related storm, and the marsh and its inhabitants were devastated by the resulting blockage. A combination of high tide and heavy storm is the event that staffers dread the most. They cross their fingers each year, hoping the sea will show mercy the next time around.

Saving the Slough

Surrounded on the north, east, and part of the west side along Oneonta Slough (the north arm of the marsh) by condos and other residential dwellings, on the south by a military training base, which sends noisy training helicopters over the preserve daily, and to the southwest by an ever-encroaching sea, Tijuana Slough seems an unlikely place to find a national wildlife refuge. A shopping mall would seem consonant here or a dredged boat marina.

Some nearby landowners agree. In the 1960s, when the Tijuana estuary was marked off as the site for a housing development—to be built on a network of dredged high spots, with private docks and other amenities—nearby dwellings were sold as "seafront properties." The fact that the artificial seafront didn't materialize continues to anger some locals, who minimize the importance of the refuge and resent the federal presence here.

But many other locals, led by nearby activist residents, veterinarian Dr. Michael McCoy and his wife, Patricia McCoy, recognized the importance of this remnant estuarine habitat. They were responsible for building community support that eventually wrenched it from commercial hands and into the refuge system. Their tireless political efforts, joined by state and federal agencies, tipped the scales toward preservation in 1980, when Tijuana Slough NWR was formed. Two years later it was designated as part of what is now the NERR. The 21-unit system of protected estuaries includes only four on the entire Pacific Coast managed by the National Oceanographic and Atmospheric Administration (NOAA) and NERR.

Habitats by the Inch

Tijuana Slough's flat reaches appear mundane and relatively lifeless at first—sort of an extended, well-mowed lawn. That image is deceptive, as you'll quickly learn by hiking down the McCoy Trail from the Visitor's Center into the depths of the marsh. Another access point, closer to the lagoon, lies at the corner of Fifth and Iris on the refuge's western edge.

Brackish ponds accessible along the trail are favorites among birders. Numerous winter waders and waterfowl species flock to these less salty impoundments, the remains of old sand mines, to hunt and forage for frogs, fish, and insects. Dabbling ducks, yellowlegs, herons, and many other species can often be seen here with ease, especially during migration times.

Vernal pools—small ephemeral freshwater ponds that harbor numerous specialized coastal animals and plants, including the delicate fairy shrimp—arise and vanish from season to season.

Marsh habitat zones are vertical in structure, lying just inches or feet above or below one another. The keys to the integrity of each are tidal flow, its depth and reach, its flushing and moistening actions, and the minerals it leaves or carries away. The high-saline "low marsh" lies at about mean sea level and supports such plants as cordgrass and pickleweed. Animal species here include the endangered light-footed clapper rail, various crabs and small fish, anemones, and sea urchins.

The "middle marsh" is home to slightly less salt-tolerant species, such as alkali heath, sea lavender, and salt grass. On this level you'll find more plants than in the other zones and a wealth of related animal species. The usually unsubmerged "high marsh" supports alkali weed, the endangered salt marsh bird's beak, spiny rush, and bushy sueada, along with a shrubby form of pickleweed. Both of the latter provide nesting habitat for endangered Belding's savanna sparrows who live here.

Fresh water is the other ingredient that makes a marsh an estuary. The flow from the Tijuana River, which channels runoff mainly from Mexico, constantly alters the salinity level of the various zones, especially the lower and middle. Such chemical changes make this a harsh environment for most plants; only a select few can take the stress.

The delicate chemical balance of the estuary is often altered by influxes of salt or fresh water. Urban environments of more than a million people are not known for their kindness to natural systems, and problems constantly arise due to a variety of human practices upriver.

Despite all the challenges of this overdeveloped environment, Tijuana Slough hangs on in relatively good health—a tribute to careful management.

In addition to the marshes, the refuge contains other habitats. Sandy shore and dunes support California least terns and western snowy plovers, who raise young on the beach in shell-lined sand scrapes. Mudflats and tidal sloughs support numerous waders who feed on small fish, insects, and invertebrates found in the sand and in tide pools, as well as some plant species. Uplands, particularly around the Visitor's Center (operated by the California State Department of Parks and Recreation), support a variety of xeroscopic plants, including sagebrush, lemonadeberry, encilia, sumac, flat-topped buckwheat, and several species of cactus.

A recent volunteer effort resulted in a beautifully landscaped garden of native plants around the Visitor's Center, where cottontails, rodents, whip and king snakes, as well as various birds find good habitat. The landscaping won a prestigious Honor Award in 1994 from the National Society of Landscape Architects.

The refuge also extends a short distance up the Tijuana River, where willows harbor perching birds, including the endangered least Bell's vireo. Cattails, quail brush, desert elderberry, and bulrushes provide habitat for Say's phoebe, marsh wren, sora, and Virginia rail, among many others.

Seasonal Sightings

One of several films shown at the Visitor's Center offers a firsthand (or firstbeak) feeling of what it is to be a bird. In the film, a teacher tells her tiny students they no longer have human mouths and hands; instead, they now have salad tongs, tweezers, and scissors for their "beaks." She tosses a handful of bolts

and other items onto the moist earth and instructs the kids to use their new food-gathering devices to pick up the "morsels."

The teaching technique is instructive, as each type of shore, wading, and seabird does possess a unique feeding tool that determines much of its life-style. Black skimmers, for instance, possess long, hornlike beaks that they drag through the water in full flight, snatching whatever collides with their nerve-rich proboscises. Brown pelicans, which congregate on the sandbars that lie landward of the artificial dike, use suitcase-sized beaks to scoop up mass quantities of fish. Avocets employ their long, up-curved beaks to sweep the freshwater and brackish shallows in a side-to-side motion, stirring up and gulping down dragonfly nymphs, boatmen, shrimp, and various crustaceans.

Just as each bird's facial configuration is unique, so are their mating rituals. The courtship of least terns is fascinating and endearing. The ritual begins when a male tern catches a small fish and approaches a female. He seems to be showing off his catch to her, pursuing her about until she settles on the shoreline. There he prances around her, the fish wriggling in his beak. When she takes his gift, the pair come together to further the species. Female terns, according to refuge staffers, line their nests with shells, probably to aid them in identifying their particular nest from the air.

Least terns were fully protected as far back as 1913, following a slaughter for the millinery trade that was responsible for as many as 100,000 tern deaths each season. Later development along the shoreline, especially on the Pacific Coast, has rendered the least tern once again at risk for extinction. You can distinguish them from other terns by their small size and quick, fluttering wing beats—much different than the slower, more gliding flight behavior of other terns.

The 7-inch western snowy plover relies on its pale color for camouflage against the sand. The snowy uses its thin black bill to forage over the beach, where it snatches up small crustaceans, marine worms, and insects. The female plover also lines her sand nest with shells. Some snowies are quite tolerate of close approaches by thoughtful, gentle humans.

The young of both tern and plover often come under attack from marauding harriers, kestrels, and peregrine falcons. Trapping and relocating raptors is a regular refuge task; nonendangered birds can be shot if other means fail, though trapping is the preferred method of control. Around 75 least terns nest here.

Refuge insects represent another class of fascinating creatures that is fast disappearing along developed shorelines. The globos dune beetle is one, as are several tiger beetles. "Kelp racks" on the shore support rove beetles, as well as flies that have been discouraged by beach managers' attempts to clear kelp and other important microhabitats from recreational beaches all along the coast.

Of Marsh and Humans

The small differences in marsh elevation create fertile ground for damage by invading humans. A hard-soled wanderer can, like some Brobdingnagian rampager, disrupt 3 distinct habitats with just a few careless steps. Unfortunately, waves of undocumented invaders from nearby Tijuana, Mexico, have found Tijuana Slough an ideal spot for crossing into the United States.

They wade the lagoon at night, cut across the refuge and hide near the roadside, waiting for local transit or prearranged rides to the American Dream. Many wear a "traveling" set of clothing that they dump in favor of dry duds after leaving the tidal creek. Huge piles of clothing build up on one popular egress, which staffers have jokingly named "Under-wear Point." Damage from this influx is serious, however, as is further trauma that comes on the heels of pursuing Immigration and Naturalization Service (INS) agents.

Fortunately, Operation Gatekeeper, a federal effort launched in 1994 to bolster enforcement in the area, has resulted in a dramatic decrease in illegal traffic on the refuge. By mid-1995, broad areas of trampled earth were already healing as illegal crossings diminished. White-topped colonies of endangered salt marsh bird's beak were reappearing throughout the refuge, along with salt grass and other native vegetation.

The healing is a secondary result of Operation Gatekeeper, but the benefits are primary to the refuge. Of course, enforcement efforts rely on public funding and political will; there's no telling how vigorously or how long they'll continue.

Staffers here at times attempt to spread the good ecological word to their residents in the area. A case in point: The same cliff swallows that arrive in Capistrano each spring also inhabit the entire San Diego area. Many build their mud nests under the eaves of private homes near the refuge, drawn by a good supply of insects in the marsh, particularly mosquitoes. Some homeowners knock them down, often during nesting time, an act that is both illegal and self-defeating. Like bats that clear the air of numerous bloodsucking mosquitoes, the famed swallows here benefit their human associates in a similar way. They're also a joy to observe.

Management Maze

Management of NERR is divided among a bevy of state and federal agencies. This top-heavy bureaucratic structure—comprising personnel from the USFWS, NOAA, California State Department of Fish and Game, US Navy, California State Department of Parks and Recreation, California Coastal Commission, California Coastal Conservancy, San Diego State University, Southwest Wetlands Interpretive Association, and, at times, the INS—can create unwieldy problems for this delicate ecosystem. (Local agencies and concerned groups also contribute their opinions and influence at Tijuana Slough—I suppose it's good to be loved.) Interagency cooperation isn't always smooth, and problems arise when one generally honorable motive clashes with another.

An example involves periodic controlled burning, which refuge staffers consider helpful to the system's health but which causes a burning sensation in NOAA stomachs due to atmospheric concerns. The state worries about fire for liability reasons in this densely populated urban setting. To the navy, whose young pilots often fly helicopters overhead, smoke clouds are an aviation hazard.

Border control agents pursuing their quarry across refuge land is another example. Agents are simply doing their jobs, but in the process they, along with the border skippers they pursue, have damaged the nests and habitats of numerous birds.

Tijuana Slough struggles constantly from a variety of impacts. Managers wade through the bureaucratic marsh, fighting politics as vigorously as they fight invasive, nonnative predatory species, which have included South American tegu lizards and exotic ferrets. An endangered clapper rail that is now part of the refuge taxidermic display demonstrates the threat by local pets: The dead rail was pulled from the jaws of a marauding house cat.

Feral dogs from Mexico as well as neighborhood dogs and cats constantly threaten nesting and roosting birds here. On contract with the refuge, local animal control authorities run live traps in the area, which they check and empty regularly. Other exotic animal invaders include a colony of voracious African clawed frogs. Until modern techniques were developed, the frogs were used by local hospitals to aid in pregnancy testing, in much

the same way the proverbial rabbit was once used. The prognosticator frogs were released alive in the area and found their way to the estuary, where they've thrived. They're extremely efficient at catching fish and other small prey.

Just as snowy plovers tend to be approach-tolerant, so are many other species here, who negotiate an environment jammed with more than a million people. Their confidence level makes for good birding at Tijuana Slough, even when navy helicopters roar overhead, drowning out conversation and leaving behind clouds of fuel residue. The copters and other training activity are mixed blessings: Without it, there probably wouldn't be a preserve here at all, and military funding sometimes helps with restoration and other refuge projects.

Tijuana Slough NWR is small, but it's hugely important as a link in the chain of natural habitats remaining on this people-heavy coast. The Ramsar group of concerned environmentalists struggling to save the world's wetlands has recently demonstrated that concern by proposing to bring the estuary into its network. Likewise, the Biosphere Reserve Program, also created to preserve the world's important natural habitats, will soon include Tijuana Slough in its system of critically important landscapes. Both organizations, and many others, recognize that the Tijuana estuary is not only important on the local scale but also is a critical piece of the planet's endangered natural environment.

Tijuana Slough's continuing existence is a gift to our world. Its struggle is a valiant one. In that good fight, folks such as Patricia and Michael McCoy are genuine American heroes.

Bird sightings:

Other wildlife sightings:

Notes:

PARTIAL BIRD LIST (OF 378 LISTED SPECIES): California least tern, brown pelican, tricolored and little blue herons, dunlin, black skimmer, shoveler, common merganser, least tern, elegant tern, piping plover, western snowy plover, sora, light-footed clapper rail, black-crowned night heron, peregrine falcon, American kestrel, Belding's savanna sparrow, least Bell's vireo, yellowwarbler, roadrunner.

PARTIAL MAMMAL LIST: Opossum, house cats, feral dogs, coyote, bobcat, California ground squirrel, Audubon's rabbit, jackrabbit, pacific pocket mouse.

PARTIAL HERP LIST: California king snake, whip snake, legless lizard, red-spotted frog, blind snake.

	R	C	W	H		

ADDRESS, PHONE: 1500 N Decatur Blvd, Las Vegas, NV 89108, (702) 646-3401.

DIRECTIONS, HOURS: 25 miles N of Las Vegas on Hwy 95; turn R and drive 4 miles to Field Station. Open 24 hours a day all year. Brochures available from kiosk.

OVERVIEW, ACTIVITIES: 1.5 million acres of Mojave Desert, small wetland, and mountains, with several long, rugged tour roads thru all but high-mountain habitats; wildlife observation, photography, camping, geological study, hunting.

ELEVATION: From 2,500 to 10,000 feet.

WEATHER: Valley floor hot in summer, mild to hot spring and fall, can be cold in winter. Higher elevations are generally warm to cold spring thru fall, cold with some snow in winter. Spring, summer, and fall good seasons to visit.

SPECIAL NEEDS: Self-contained for back road travel; water; good spare tire; register at visitor kiosk.

LODGING, CAMPING: Las Vegas has thousands of hotel rooms and restaurants; primitive camping on refuge and in nearby Toiyabe National Forest.

NEARBY POINTS OF INTEREST: Ash Meadows is a 21,000-acre refuge 90 miles N of Las Vegas, established to protect 4 endangered native fish and 2 dozen other unique species of plants and animals. It has hiking trails but no facilities. Moapa Valley, a nonaccessible, 31-acre site that is 50 miles NE of Las Vegas, was created to provide habitat for the endangered Moapa dace, a native fish. Pahranagat NWR is a 5,380-acre waterfowl area off Rte 93 N of the refuge. Accessible to wildlife observers and hunters. It has a campground, picnic area, and some interpretive displays.

DISABILITY ACCESS: Rest rooms at Corn Creek Springs and Ash Meadows NWR are accessible; hunting blind accessible at Pahranagat NWR.

Soon after you leave the frenzied glitter of Las Vegas and head west toward Desert National Wildlife Range, you enter the Grand Scale. Las Vegas Valley, the refuge gateway, runs endlessly off to the northwest, clouds marching over the far horizon across a sky so vast it hints at eternity. Twenty-five miles up Hwy 95, you reach the refuge turnoff. Heading east now, your view is dominated by the broad, stark Sheep Range and its sprawling *bajada,* the sloping plain formed over countless centuries from mountain erosion. The Sheep Range Mountains extend beyond vision, but that's just 1 of 6 mountain ranges within this 1½-million-acre refuge.

Desert refuge is big—largest in the lower 48. Range after range of mountains tower over the surrounding Mojave Desert, providing habitat for some 800 desert bighorns (1994 figure), the species for which the

desert

Desert National Wildlife Range was established in 1936. Tucked between those mountains, vast desert plains support a unique group of habitats. The refuge offers literally a lifetime of exploration. This is a land of drama and distance, where wild creatures prowl inaccessible reaches; where storms that sweep the desert in winter and late summer are visible for a hundred miles; where primal nature perseveres undiminished.

That Desert refuge is so vast is a wonderful thing; even more of a wonder is that it's nearly untouched by any of the triad of western extractive industries. With few mineral resources, no timber within profitable reach, and scant grazing acreage (mainly due to lack of water), the desert and mountains here remain much as they did a thousand years ago.

If you visit this sprawling refuge, plan to spend at least a couple of days, not only to explore its vastness but to allow yourself the opportunity to experience its beauty and balance. Such a spirit-friendly process requires time, quiet, and contemplation. All three are found here in endless measure.

Timeless Desert

A visit to Desert is a step back into the haze of centuries, when Anasazi and more recent Paiute Indians roamed the canyons and plains, scraping a harsh existence from the land, gathering wild foods, and hunting the deer and bighorn sheep that once roamed these mountains in profusion.

Evidence of that early human presence exists throughout the refuge. You can see some of it along Mormon Well Road, one of three main refuge arteries. Along the road a numbered sign, coordinated with a well-designed visitor brochure, marks the remnants of two agave pits. These limestone circles are the remains of rock ovens in which ancient Native Americans, including the Anasazi, Shoshone, and Paiute, cooked the hearts of the dagger-leaved agave, also called the century plant. (Ecohistorical note: Very few agaves now exist in the vicinity of the pits. In the case of the century plant, at least, those noble ancients may have allowed hunger to rule over sustainability.)

With or without agaves, Desert is one of the most pristine expanses of the Mojave Desert ecosystem still in existence. Though less than half the refuge is open to visitors—the majority doubles as a Nellis Air Force Base bombing range—the open portion is more than most people could cover in a lifetime of visits.

The three vehicle accesses are rough and take you deep into primitive places. Much more of Desert is explorable by foot. Either travel mode requires careful preparation. There's no water to speak of on the refuge; water sources have been constructed or enhanced for the support of bighorn sheep, but those are remote and scattered. Besides, that water is for wildlife, which, despite your fondest fantasies, does not include you.

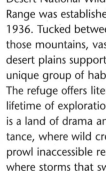

Desert's Oasis

Upon entering the refuge from Hwy 95, you first come to an anomalous wet spot in this parched desert. Corn Creek Springs boasts a perennial water source, a small marsh complete with cattails, and a cool forest of mesquite, willow, cottonwood, fruit, and mulberry trees that support a variety of life. Before Anglo-Americans arrived here in the 1800s, the life-giving spring had long served as an Indian campsite. Later it was the location of a stagecoach stop and railroad storage facility, then a ranch complete with a fruit orchard that still feeds thousands of birds each year. The water source and surrounding acres were purchased by the federal government in 1939 to serve as Desert's field station.

Pathways through the marsh area offer birders the chance to see more species within a confined area than anywhere on the refuge. Scores of birds pause at Corn Creek during migration, and dozens of species live here year-round. As a result, Desert's quirky bird list numbers a phenomenal 240 species. Largely due to the presence of Corn Creek Springs, that list is swollen with an array of regional oddities, including such accidentals as wood stork, double-crested cormorant, Virginia and sora rails, Bonaparte's, ring-billed, and California gulls, and black tern—each a disjunctive presence in this desert environment.

Other creatures, including dozens of lizards and snakes, such as the desert spiny lizard, collared lizard, coachwhip, common king snake, and speckled and sidewinder rattlers, can be found here. Among the 52 mammals inhabiting the area are 3 species of kangaroo rat, western harvest mouse, ringtail cat, and 9 species of bats.

The dragonflies that flit about the cattails are delicate jewels, ranging in color from blue to gold to a metallic rust. Bullfrogs along the trail will keep you hopping with their practice of screaming in alarm at your feet just before they plop out of sight.

Corn Creek Springs is one of the last habitats left for the endangered Pahrump poolfish.

Twenty-nine of the rare pupfish were transplanted here from Manse Spring in nearby Pahrump Valley in 1971, refugees from over-pumping of the aquifer beneath Pahrump Valley and the destruction of their original home.

Several thousand poolfish now live within Corn Creek ponds. You can easily catch a glimpse of these unique, minnow-sized survivors. Two other subspecies of the endangered native fish weren't so lucky; they went extinct before anyone could save them. They're absolutely gone now, and they won't be back.

Refuge Roads

For most visitors, Mormon Well Road is the route of choice. Over its 48-mile length, the road carries you through a variety of eco-zones and offers grand views of the Sheep Range, as well as the possibility of spotting bighorns among the cliffs. It also carries you to hiking access into the wooded eastern slopes of the Sheep Mountains, from the Pinenut and Sawmill trailheads.

mountain

Alamo and Gass Peak roads are the refuge's other driving options. The 16-mile-long Gass Peak Road accesses the flanks of Gass Peak and Fossil Ridge and is the route to Quail Spring, where bighorns may be spotted. Alamo Road remains on the valley floor between the Sheep and Desert mountains throughout its 70-mile reach; 4WD is necessary at times along its northern reaches. Several side routes branch off from Alamo Road, running east to Sheep Mountain canyons that lead to high country. Hidden Forest Trailhead, says one staffer, is his preferred access to high-country adventures.

Vehicle-aided camping is okay anywhere within 100 feet of roadways, but don't pull onto unmarred patches of desert—your tracks and activities will leave scars that take decades or even centuries to heal. Plenty of existing pull-offs, including old road extensions complete with prebuilt campfire rings, can be utilized for overnight stays without damaging the pristine environment.

If you're camper-equipped you can simply pull over on a wide spot in the road and sack out. Those on foot may camp anywhere, but the same light-impact rules apply. If you use local wood for your campfire, keep it small; deadwood litter is critical to desert plant regeneration, and it doesn't develop easily or quickly in this environment.

Seasonal Visits

From late March into June, the desert is often the site of riotous color blooms, when such plants as brittlebush, larkspur, Mojave aster, Indian paintbrush, fleabane, and dozens of others burn brightly in their quest for regeneration. Of course, catching a desert flower show is always a chance encounter. Weather factors and probably the whim of the gods determine when, if, and how intensely the desert will bloom in a given year. But for springtime visitors, gambling on a good floral display at Desert National Wildlife Range, unlike taking chances at the felt tables down the hill, is always a winning proposition.

Summer at the refuge is hot, and relatively few people visit from July through September. Diurnal animal activity in summer is largely confined to early morning and evening forays, when nocturnal species creep from their holes, dens, and perches. Some nocturnal species include great horned owl, night lizard, Mojave rattlesnake, bobcat, cougar, and pocket mouse. Sometimes night creatures reveal themselves at twilight or sunrise. More often they're heard calling or scuffling in the brush after dark. Summer is a good time to see bighorns, when the intense heat concentrates them at water holes, making the usually scattered groups easier to find.

If you visit in summer, the most comfortable place to be is up high. The grass and woodland areas are beautiful, though they don't rival the desert in terms of species variety. Some flowering plants bloom during the broiling season, though, and you'll find abundant beauty in summer if you can appreciate it despite the sometimes numbing heat. Preparation Rule One: Bring enough water to last several days, just in case.

Winter can be a good time to visit, but it may not be the best time to drive the entire Mormon Well Road route, due to occasional winter rains that yield much of the Mojave's yearly moisture. Travelers are sometimes turned back by deep snowdrifts that begin around 6,000 feet; others choose to push on and sometimes lose the road or get stuck— both life-threatening situations. Animal activity and bird presence in winter are minimal, but the landscape, as always, is beautiful.

The bottom line: Spring is the best time to come; fall is second-best. Numerous bird lovers—feeling the pull of nature yet also desiring a little high adrenaline fun—organize gambling/birding trips to the area during those two seasons. They spend half their time absorbing the calm and beauty of the Desert refuge, the other half bumping their blood pressure skyward at the slot machines and poker tables. If your heart can stand the strain, this might be a good way to satisfy both urges.

An Array of Biomes

Changes in the plant and animal communities that correspond with altitudinal differences are obvious as you traverse Mormon Well Road, which takes you from low desert into a "yucca forest" of endless Joshua trees, then to higher woodland country populated by bunchgrasses, sage, juniper, and piñon. Though no roads rise to the highest reaches, you can hike from the roadways to an elevation of nearly 10,000 feet into a forest of Ponderosa pines. The stately bristlecone, earth's longest-living tree, stands upon Desert's highest peaks. Some individuals are more than 3,500 years old.

Far below on the desert floor and sloping plain, Joshua trees first appear as scattered, dwarfish sentinels amid the white bursage, creosote, and soaptree (Mojave) yucca. Continue through the first pass and you're suddenly surrounded by thousands of Joshua trees, which grow larger and taller as you gain in elevation.

On your right as you enter the first pass stands a unique geological formation known as Fossil Ridge. The cleanly defined strata of this tall, sloping mountain, lifted and tilted by ancient earth forces, is a great example of sedimentary layering followed by uplift and tilting. Local science students visit each year to study the formation and hunt for that most beloved of marine fossils, the trilobite, which is abundant on Fossil Ridge.

Once you clear that first pass, you're within bighorn viewing distance. Scan the cliffs to the northwest for the characteristic curved horns and spots of tawny color that appear slightly different than the surrounding rock. Sometimes the sheep pose along the skyline, making identification easier. At any rate, you'll need fairly powerful binoculars or a spotting scope to separate the sheep from their distant habitat. If you fail to find bighorns, you're not alone: Only a small number of visitors ever spot them. If bighorns are a big priority for you, plan to spend a minimum of several hours looking for them. The visitor brochure offers a few other suggested places to find them.

Several miles beyond Fossil Ridge the road enters a blackbrush-creosote association. Peek-a-boo Canyon, named for a tiny stone arch atop a southeast canyon wall, is a good place to study the region's sedimentary geology, which shaped this dramatic landscape with the help of plate tectonics and earthquake action many millions of years ago. The canyon is also a good birding spot. Blue-gray gnatcatcher, Bullock's and Scott's orioles, Wilson's and yellow-rumped warblers, canyon and rock wrens, phainopepla, spotted towhee, brown-crested flycatcher, and many other species inhabit the canyon. A good campsite here, just below and south of a large natural cave, is equipped with a rock-lined fire pit for your ecofriendly convenience.

Drive beyond Peek-a-boo Canyon and you enter rolling desert grassland. The road here is smooth and flat, which may tempt you to increase your speed. Don't do it. A short distance ahead lies at least one deep, hidden crack in the road. Remember that old "Twilight Zone" episode where drivers were cruising along on a highway that suddenly . . . vanished? That's the feeling you'll get if you hit this minichasm at more than 5 miles per hour. It may well break your car and hurt your head, too. Images of the day the truck went airborne remain fresh in my memory.

At its high point, beginning some 16 miles from the main entrance and several miles before you reach the road's egress onto Route 93, Mormon Well Road enters piñon–juniper–sage country, topping off at an altitude of around 6,500 feet. Get out and climb from this point and you'll eventually reach Ponderosa and bristlecone pines, along with a view that is, as they say in Brooklyn, to die for.

The high country along the road, where Joshua trees, junipers, and piñon mingle without prejudice amid sage and bunchgrasses, once was the setting for a limited cattle operation. The land was purchased long ago and taken out of service by the federal government, but the USFWS continues to maintain a water storage facility at the old ranch site, where mule deer often congregate. (Don't stay long; let them drink.) The cattle operation failed not because grass wasn't plentiful but because water was scarce and getting cows to market proved economically self-defeating. Some places are just blessed that way.

After a few miles of high country, the road descends once more into bursage-creosote desert. During favorable springtimes, flower displays here can be even more spectacular than those on the refuge's southeastern side. You can reach this end of the refuge directly from Route 93 by driving 28 miles north of I-15, then going east on the dirt road that lies beneath the intersection of two power lines.

Joshua Tree—Signature Plant of the Mojave

A curious hybrid of yucca and "standard" tree shapes, the Joshua tree is the emblem of the Mojave, smallest of our 4 US deserts. The 19th-century western explorer and revolutionary Gen. John C. Frémont considered it the ugliest plant ever conceived by the Great Tree Farmer, but his attitude was mere ethnocentrobotanism. Once you put aside traditional notions of what a plant should look like, you'll likely agree that the "Dagger tree" is a classic American beauty, both in form and adaptation.

The Joshua tree provides habitat for a surprisingly large number of animal species, from microbes to bobcats. One study estimated that more than a hundred bird species use the Joshua tree habitat at Desert. Numerous birds, including cactus wren, orioles, and gnatcatchers, make their nests in the giant yucca, and the secretive night lizard, which resembles a skink, hides and dines within the leaf litter that builds up beneath the plant as it sheds. The tree has served the animal world since ancient times; the now-extinct giant ground sloth, in fact, found its turgid flesh delectable.

Bighorns and Bureaucracies

The visitor facility is primarily a kiosk sheltering informative displays on the environment and the bighorn sheep that are the main reason for Desert's existence. The self-help nature of the kiosk hints at a curious fact about Desert: The largest refuge in the lower 48 is administered by a grand total of two permanent employees.

Apparently as this isn't a big waterfowl stopoff and visitation is relatively slim, the federal powers-that-be have judged its staffing needs to be minimal. A few volunteers support the understaffed regulars, but don't expect to get much time with them to discuss the refuge or desert ecology.

With the help of a long-term refuge repopulation program, bighorn sheep once threatened with extinction in the early part of this century again roam the high cliffs and hidden draws of Desert's 6 mountain ranges. The mountains here have supported bighorn populations as large as 1,800 since serious management efforts began in the area in the 1930s. Unfortunately, a late 1980s drought reduced that number by more than half—traumatic for an animal that already suffers a perilously low reproduction rate due to the delicate nature of its young.

Disease, lack of water, falls from cliffs, and predation dramatically impact the reproduction of these noble animals. An increase in the area's mountain lion population (whose main course, the mule deer, was also decimated by the drought) has resulted in a predatory shift toward the sheep. By 1995, refuge personnel were considering a fresh importation of bighorns from other areas. Incredibly, despite the need to import sheep, limited bighorn hunting is still allowed on the refuge.

To aid the bighorn's chances for survival, a system of springs and water-gathering devices has long been in place. The structures comprise several types, including rain catchment-and-storage systems, small dams to retain spring and runoff water, and methods to retard evaporation. A current debate among biologists involves whether or not the catchments and dams are even necessary. The species, after all, survived in the area without them for untold centuries.

Some say the structures are little more than predator traps where clever cougars and bobcats lie in wait for sheep and other prey to appear. Others point out that during droughts and population expansions, water holes are critical to a species so limited in number. For now, the water supports will remain. The low number and vulnerability of bighorns are reasons enough to continue maintaining them.

To further protect bighorns and their environment, much of the refuge is in the application

Hopper Mountain NWR in the Los Padres National Forest is a base for USFWS condor-recovery activities.

California condors are once again free and wild in the mountains of southern California. USFWS photo by David Clendenen.

(Left) Andean condors like this one were released for several years in the recovery area, helping biologists learn more about California condor behavior.

Pintail is one of more than two dozen waterfowl species that visit Kern NWR.

Northern oriole.

Kern NWR's cattail-lined marshes reflect the colors of autumn.

Burrowing owl.

Dikes at Salton Sea NWR keep salty seawater from infiltrating most freshwater impoundments. Freshwater ponds in this scorching desert refuge provide habitat for a wide array of avian species.

Cattle egret is one of many waders who use Salton Sea. The ubiquitous egret is an
exotic species. Originally from Africa, it arrived in South America in the late 1800s
and then moved north to the US in the 1940s and 1950s.

Through support by Tijuana Slough NWR and other efforts, the subpopulation of California brown pelicans is recovering after decimation caused by habitat loss and pesticide poisoning. Texas and Louisiana populations are still threatened with extinction.

Tijuana Slough NWR's tide pools along the southern California coast are rich microhabitats. Sea urchins and anemones are two common animals living in these shallow habitats.

Hedgehog cactus stands amid Desert NWR's Mojave Desert lowlands
on the *bajada* spilling from the Sheep Range Mountains.

Mountain lions have preyed heavily on Desert's bighorn population
as deer numbers on the refuge have declined.

Bighorn ewe and kid.

Evening grosbeak.

A trumpeter swan rests in Ruby Lake NWR's marsh shallows.

Ruby Lake NWR's mountain-wrapped marshes support abundant species
in an environment of matchless beauty.

(Top) Pronghorns thrive in the safety of the "Little Sheldon" unit. The fastest land animal in North America, these range dwellers have been clocked at 70 mph for short bursts. They can maintain 40 mph cruising speeds for much longer.

Weathering on Sheldon works its magic on earth and rock.

(Opposite) Downy woodpecker.

American white pelicans roost on marsh islands at Stillwater
and then rise to create aerial spectacles.

Sunset descends over Stillwater NWR's vast marshy acres.

Eared grebes.

stage for wilderness designation. That is, the bureaucratic process is creeping along to designate refuge land as immune from extraction and road-building. Fortunately, the range has few extractable resources, so the usual political pulls against such a designation are minimal. However, with 1990s politics leaning toward a "state's rights" philosophy, no one is hurrying to push the designation through.

A Few Words about the Air Force

The US Air Force has bombing rights to much of the refuge, which hasn't made the job of bighorn preservation easy for biologists and managers. Military actions include claiming wide chunks of refuge airspace as their own after minimal consultation with refuge biologists; overflying the area, dropping bombs, and blasting other high-tech weapons into refuge areas; and demanding time-consuming applications from biologists who wish to enter the restricted areas to do sheep-related work.

Over the years they've blown up water structures and very likely such creatures as bighorns and endangered desert tortoises. Much worse for the ecological big picture was their practice, until recently, of gouging new roads into pristine areas each time they wanted to set up, tear down, or repair targets. Each invasion by military technicians into an unroaded area has meant a new source of long-term erosion, species disruption, and overall environmental degradation.

Military control over these areas (they're technically "tenants" here) often means that yearly surveys are disrupted, maintenance of water sources is badly degraded, and the sheep suffer.

With a "Renewal for Withdrawal" coming up in the year 2001 (determining whether or not they stay), and an environmental impact statement due by 1998, the US Air Force environmental record has improved substantially in recent times. Also, a new generation of air force leaders is gradually taking the reins, many of them well-educated and more

sensitive to environmental problems than earlier leaders. A third positive air force move in recent years has been the advances made in computer and high-tech capability; attack models and simulations allow for fewer actual assaults on the land.

With effort and continued motivation, Nellis AFB could be a model for ecologically sound stewardship of wildlife areas under its watch. Of course, such efforts might possibly cost a little more, though that's debatable. But clearly money is not the issue. Attitude, it seems, is the chief determinant of how the military's wildlife-critical lands are treated.

Defending America from potential enemies is an important goal, and without the military presence here much of the refuge might otherwise be in private hands. Another important military goal should be the use of intelligence and ingenuity to protect our nation's biological heritage.

A Few More Words about Hunting

Permits to hunt a small number of bighorns are parceled out each year at the refuge manager's discretion, based mainly on population figures. The practice does not represent a management tool in the usual sense since there's no need to control the population other than to increase it wherever possible.

Why then is an imperiled species such as the desert bighorn offered up for pleasure killing? The reason, in my estimation, is political. In a strange and somewhat morbid sense, hunters are among the bighorn's best supporters. Hunter groups are quite vocal, making their desires known to those who make the rules. Whatever their motives may be, numerous hunter/volunteers donate hard labor toward bighorn management, installing water equipment and hauling material on their backs. Most never really expect to draw one of the rare permit tags that allows its recipient to climb the peaks and blast a well-horned male sheep into taxidermic eternity. Fewer still can afford to bid the $100,000-plus to win the yearly auctioned tag. Most apparently do it for their "love" of the animal or, more accurately, their love of the hunt.

Much of the money from hunting permit sales and auctions goes toward future transplant and habitat restoration efforts. Restrictions are set on which rams a hunter may kill (leaning toward the oldest members of a group, who theoretically have already passed on their superior genes). Often the new transplants themselves aren't hunted. Still, the system resembles a sort of kill 'em, catch 'em, fly 'em in, kill 'em again, raise more money, catch 'em, fly 'em in, kill 'em again method of "harvesting." Protect and kill. Go figure.

Nevertheless, hunters do contribute much of the effort and funding needed to keep Desert's living bighorns in good health. According to staffers here, that much can't be said for local environmental organizations, whom they say rarely contribute muscle power or money to this important effort.

Environmental organizations unquestionably support the natural world in a number of ways, both in Nevada and elsewhere, but the staff at Desert says they're rarely on hand when the humble but critical heavy lifting begins. Perhaps a meeting of opposing minds at such a basic level would be healthy for both bighorns and the political climate. It's something to consider.

Golden Rules of Survival

At Desert National Wildlife Range, as with most refuges, being prepared for wilderness travel and leaving word for someone on your whereabouts are basic common sense. Upon entering and leaving, visitors are asked to register in a book located at the edge of the visitor kiosk in the parking lot. This is both for management planning information and visitor safety. During summer a stranding here can be life threatening to those unprepared for the searing heat. In winter at higher elevations, people have pushed on into snowy reaches and gotten themselves stuck. In doing so, they have risked tragedy.

Traffic on the major roads running through the refuge, especially off-season, is spotty at best—only around 17,000 people visit this sprawling landscape each year. Self-reliance is critical. Car trouble can force a camping situation for several days before help arrives. Check your vehicle and spare(s) carefully before embarking, drive slowly, and be prepared with adequate food, water, and shelter for the possibility of being stranded. And have a wonderful time.

A visit to Desert is more a contemplative experience than an action-packed wildlife excursion. Here you'll find a fascinating array of life zones, unique plant communities, and the kind of silence and space that most city dwellers have forgotten how to dream about. To experience the beauty and balance here—and to locate your place in it—represents the best reasons for coming. Accomplish those goals to any degree and you'll find that your visit to Desert National Wildlife Range has been a significant life experience.

Bird sightings:

Other wildlife sightings:

Notes:

PARTIAL BIRD LIST (OF 240 LISTED SPECIES PLUS NUMEROUS ACCIDENTALS): Pied-billed and eared grebes, American bittern, black-crowned night heron, ruddy duck, osprey, bald eagle, merlin, peregrine falcon, northern saw-whet owl, Vaux's swift, red-breasted sapsucker, bank swallow, Clark's nutcracker, varied and hermit thrush, Grace's and hermit warbler, rose-breasted grosbeak, lazuli bunting, evening grosbeak.

PARTIAL MAMMAL LIST (OF 52 LISTED SPECIES): Bighorn sheep, pronghorn, coyote, bobcat, 9 bat species (including Yuma myotis, silver-haired bat, and hoary bat), Townsend's ground squirrel, white-tailed antelope squirrel, little pocket mouse, cactus mouse, porcupine, red fox, kit fox, ringtail cat, spotted skunk.

PARTIAL HERP LIST (OF 31 LISTED SPECIES AND 8 HYPOTHETICALS): Pacific tree frog, desert tortoise, collared lizard, leopard lizard, chuckwalla, spotted leaf-nosed snake, western shovel-nosed snake, Sonora lyre snake, speckled rattlesnake.

RUBY LAKE NWR

	R		W	B	H	F	

ADDRESS, PHONE: HC 60, PO Box 860, Ruby Lake, NV 89833, (702) 779-2237.

DIRECTIONS, HOURS: From Elko S on Lamoille Hwy, 7 miles to Hwy 228, S to Jiggs (27 miles); L at fork 4 miles S of Jiggs, 15 miles E on Harrison Pass Road, R to refuge. HQ is 8 miles beyond sign. Refuge open daylight hours; HQ open normal work hours Mon thru Fri.

OVERVIEW, ACTIVITIES: Marsh and sage/grass uplands in a remote valley surrounded by mountains and long views; wildlife viewing, hiking, photography, fishing, hunting.

ELEVATION: 6,000 feet.

WEATHER: Warm days, cold nights late spring thru early fall, with chance for strong rain in summer; winters can be snowed in; spring cool to cold. Spring and summer best seasons to visit.

SPECIAL NEEDS: Warm clothing, self-contained for extended visit.

LODGING, CAMPING: Lodging in Elko; primitive camping at Forest Service campground a mile S of the refuge.

NEARBY POINTS OF INTEREST: Historic Fort Ruby, Bressman's Cabin, Pony Express Trail.

DISABILITY ACCESS: Accessible rest rooms, fishing area at Unit 10.

The moment I descended Harrison Pass and Ruby Valley opened up before me, the world expanded dramatically. Twilight was approaching as I bumped down the winding dirt road and turned toward this high-elevation refuge in northeast Nevada. Just past the entrance sign, I pulled to the roadside to survey the wetlands below.

A filigree of watery strands webbed the grassy valley in a network of marshes that looked like a miniature, treeless version of Minnesota's Boundary Waters. A quarter mile to the east, two oversized dots of white caught my eye. A coyote skulked in tallgrass 50 yards from a pair of trumpeter swans, who were wading in the shallows. The canine was hesitant, clearly daunted by their size.

Throughout the network of hummock-broken waters, brigades of ducks bobbed and fluttered. Occasionally, a diver cranked its wings and trotted across the surface into flight, creating the absurd, shouting ruckus that has earned the duck its cartoon stature.

Another coyote keened in the meadow east of me; then a pack somewhere to the south wailed its strange, beautiful reply. A third howler joined in, completing the mournful harmony.

freshwater wetlands

Several yards beyond the roadside fence, sage grouse muttered in soft, turkeylike voices. Invisible in the big sage, they were near enough that I could hear their scratching and wing flutters. Swallows buzzed about my head, a squadron of trick-flyers delighting in a Red Baron game of tease-tag. A female kestrel whirled through the formation, scattering them. Turkey vultures on rickety wings studied the market.

The scene evolved in evening firelight that warmed the surrounding mountains and threw a pinkish cast against hard-edged clouds. The valley's vegetation—rabbitbrush and big sagebrush rolling down to grass and sedge, then on to hard-stem and alkali bulrush and cattails in the marshes—glowed in the dying light with heightened brilliance.

I was mesmerized. I stood by the roadside for a long time, basking in the glow of this remote place, reveling in its beauty and in my own sense of good fortune.

High-Country Haven

Ruby Lake NWR is an incomparable 40,000-acre piece of northeastern Nevada real estate. The refuge was founded in 1938 as a migratory waterfowl resting and breeding area. That's still its prime purpose; the shallow marshes here, broken by low grassy islands, produce as many as 3,500 canvasback and 2,500 redhead ducklings each year, as well as hundreds of young from other water-loving species.

The term "duck farming" has gained derogatory undertones as the USFWS leans toward the greater diversity that results from ecosystem management. But the term seems appropriate here. There's nothing wrong with a little duck farming as far as I'm concerned. Just knowing they're around, healthy and happy, bolsters my sense of well-being.

North-south–running Ruby Valley is a bolson (undrained valley), once home to a 300,000-acre Pleistocene body of water known as Franklin Lake. You can trace the lines of old lakeshore "benches" on the slopes of nearby mountains that surround the 6,000-foot elevation refuge on three sides. When the environment warmed and the lake began receding around 10,000 years ago, the present expanse of marshes remained, fed by some 200 springs, as well as runoff from the nearby Ruby Mountains on the western boundary.

To appreciate the vastness and complexity of the marshes here, an elevated view is necessary. Several access roads and trails along the western edge of the refuge carry you up the mountain slopes, where you can find such vantage points.

Fount of Life

Native Americans have inhabited Ruby Valley for at least 8,000 years, according to somewhat sketchy archaeological research done here thus far. Numerous sites and artifacts have been unearthed throughout the valley, many at the base of nearby mountains. One site, Bronco Charley Cave, yielded the remains of 26 species, including mountain sheep and bison. Shoshones and a group that Euro-American newcomers called the Rye Grass Eaters occupied the area until historic times, hunting the abundant game that once roamed here. Such game included pronghorns, which continue to inhabit the uplands. Remnants of "drive corrals" that prehistoric residents used for herding and capturing pronghorn herds can be found in several valley locations.

Pronghorns are often spotted on the southern end of the refuge in the meadowland, where badgers and other mammals also prowl. The "antelope" also occupy the northern refuge boundary, just south of Ruby Wash Road.

Sage grouse is another upland species on the refuge. Ruby Valley's grouse population seems to be holding its own more tenaciously than most western populations. At least 2 leks exist on the refuge. Sage grouse are often seen in the upland brush near the southwestern edge of the preserve, as well as on the western boundary of East Marsh and below the road from Harrison Pass. You'll probably hear them before you see them, so try to learn their calls in advance if you're interested in locating them.

Blue grouse reside farther up the slopes of the Ruby Mountains, off the refuge. At the highest elevations, an introduced exotic, the Himalayan snow cock, has gained a solid foothold. For some hunters, this is an imminently killable bird, worth a hard trek over snowcapped ridges. For the rest of us, observing a live one would be thrill enough.

Seasonal Weather

Ruby Lake is definitely a 3-season refuge for visitors. Winters can be brutal here, often dropping to 20 or 30 below zero F, with snow at times blocking roads and sealing off staff members for weeks. Snow can occur any time between early October and May (and on the mountain at any month of the year). Despite frigid winter conditions, a few hardy souls come in winter to fish for trout in valley streams. Call ahead, listen to weather reports, and bring warm clothing no matter which month you come.

In summer, highs here rarely exceed 90 degrees F. Nights are cool enough to require a warm blanket or sleeping bag (there's camping just south of HQ at a primitive Forest Service site). Spring and fall are generally cool and pleasant, but both seasons are unpredictable, always bearing the potential for snow, freezing rain, wind, or thunderstorms.

Habitats from Humanity

The refuge is a third marshland, with wet meadows and sage uplands comprising the rest. Marsh areas can be explored via several roads and dikes, all of them adequate for passenger vehicles. Electric-driven boats and canoes are allowed on the southerly marshes in warmer months, though some restrictions apply during nesting season.

The South Marsh, a broad natural lake on the refuge, is always wet, though water levels vary from one season and year to the next. The northern marshes generally dry up by late summer. Refuge staffers have worked recently to restore the 1,800-acre East Marsh, an emergent-choked impoundment that in the past has offered excellent habitat for colonial nesters and a variety of waterfowl, waders, and shorebirds.

A new levee was built in 1995, burning of peat deposits was in progress, and efforts were ongoing to clear the marsh of a congestion of bulrushes. By 1997, this should be one of the better areas of the refuge for birding. Water habitat here ranges from mud shoreline to around 3 or 4 feet in depth.

The refuge is managed to provide a variety of habitats, which sometimes means diverting water that would otherwise travel on to the South Marsh, the terminus of most Ruby Valley water. A canoe trip into the South Marsh will carry you in silence to an area rich with avian species and natural beauty.

Throughout the marshes, a variety of depths and habitat types creates homes for water-fowl, waders, and shorebirds. Twenty-five species of ducks and geese, including green- and blue-winged teals, cinnamon teal, wigeon, red-breasted merganser, and white-fronted goose, use the marshes. Six pairs of trum-peter swans were nesting here in the spring and summer of 1995. Tundra swans winter at Ruby Lake, with as many as a hundred show-ing up in late fall. You can tell the 2 species apart by the yellow spot on most tundra swans' upper bills, just below the eye—a mark the larger trumpeter lacks.

Not surprisingly, this wet spot in the heart of the Great Basin Desert draws a varied collec-tion of waterbird accidentals. So far they've included rarities such as Eurasian wigeon, Barrow's goldeneye, oldsquaw, white-winged scoter, and Ross's goose.

Virginia and sora rails, along with an occa-sional common moorhen and a healthy popu-lation of American bittern, hide in the cattails and bulrushes along the marsh edges.

Waders and shorebirds commonly found here include yellowlegs, long-billed curlew (scores of nesters inhabit the shortgrass uplands on the southern end), snowy egret, avocets and stilts, great blue heron, willet, greater and lesser yel-lowlegs, white-faced ibis, and several sandpiper species. An occasional marbled godwit drops in, and the refuge has only rarely hosted little blue heron and western sandpiper.

Curlews occupy much of the southern upland area of the refuge in spring and summer, where nesting parents vigorously protect their young. Your presence at brooding time will elicit hazing behavior as well as broken-wing acts to draw you away from nests. Refuge staffers request that you move away from areas where such behavior arises. You can observe these large birds from a distance with scope and binocular; distancing yourself will result

in more natural behavior between parents and young, offering a fascinating glimpse of these Pinocchio-beaked birds.

Sandhill cranes pass through here on the Idaho–southern Colorado River circuit, and a recently declining number of them raise their young "colts" here; 16 pairs nested in 1995. Refuge managers believe Ruby Lake can sup-port up to 60 crane pairs. Part of the man-agement strategy involves development of nesting and foraging habitat to support that number.

An important limiting factor on the crane population is coyote predation, especially in drought years when they leave their traditional upland areas and prowl the marsh. In drought years, the wetlands thus become a natural "predator sink," offering coyotes and other meat-eaters a protein-rich bounty. Currently, managers are not engaged in coyote control, but that could change, especially if sandhill declines continue.

The issue of which species is more important (which should live, which should die) is a thorny one—coyotes nearly always draw the short straw in such matters, when in fact they're only following genetic dictates. Objec-tively, in the face of widespread habitat destruction, cranes do face greater risk than coyotes, who survive in urban areas, farm fields, suburban back lots, and other habitat inhospitable to most species.

Some wildlife biologists would argue that in a natural system, such control of predators is pointless and even immoral, but with most crane habitat gone now, ethical lines begin to fade. Both cranes and coyotes are majestic creatures. It's a tragedy when either has to die.

You can often spot sandhill parents and their young ranging about the meadows on the southwestern portion of the refuge—some-times from the main roadway—and often in the wheat and rye fields across the road from HQ. Cranes nest in the bulrushes, moving out of the marsh to feeding areas by day. Watch-ing the huge birds gliding overhead in twilight, their long necks and legs extended, their calls echoing across the marsh, is a riveting experience that evokes a timeless sense of the wild.

Songbird Sojourns

Riparian strips below springheads, as well as the brush that surrounds wetland areas, draw numerous passerines, especially in migration. Some perching birds who come here include belted kingfisher, red-naped sapsucker, dusky and ash-throated flycatcher, Clark's nutcracker, bushtit, hermit thrush, cedar waxwing, red-eyed vireo, western tanager, yellow-rumped and Virginia's warbler, and several towhee and sparrow species. Most of the 10 warbler species who visit here also nest on the refuge. Rosy finch is one specialty bird that avian lovers may encounter here. Evening grosbeak, whose song is considered by many to be the most beautiful of all North American birdsongs, often performs in Ruby Valley's pine upland and riparian areas.

A spring that feeds the wetlands, creating good songbird habitat in the process, emerges forcefully from a rock outcropping behind headquarters. The dense riparian canyon that lines the waterway is choked with willow, aspen, false cherry, and cottonwood.

Be sure to avoid the nasty thistles that grow near the spring. Their needles burn like fire and the pain is a long time in leaving. Also, step carefully at the springhead; the rocks are slippery.

Relics of a Primeval Lake

Only one native fish survives on this refuge; introduced predatory exotics, including largemouth bass and trout, have lain waste to much of the old aquafauna. The small relict dace isn't endangered (yet) since it inhabits other areas of Nevada as well. Here, though, hybridization with the introduced speckled dace has genetically diluted much of the population.

Seasonal flooding is the cause, overflowing spring-fed ponds and spreading the speckled dace throughout much of the system. This makes management difficult; only a couple of nonflood-prone refuge ponds contain pure relict dace. Recent acquisition of Fort Ruby Ranch on the south end of the refuge offers hope. Two good-sized ponds on the 3,000-acre tract will soon be cleared of all exotics and restocked with the pure strain of dace.

Fortunately, the bullfrog hasn't shown its voracious mug in this insulated valley. Only the northern leopard frog and possibly the spotted frog (a researcher was combing the marshes for this one in 1995) make their home here. Neither poses a survival risk to other aquatic species.

Providing the surrounding streams with trout is the role of the Gallagher Fish Hatchery, a state facility that lies along the highway just south of the refuge. You can tour the ponds here for a view of several trout species.

Anglers with Attitudes

Water diversions from the South Marsh to other wetland areas here are often necessary to fulfill habitat management objectives. This sometimes angers a few of the local fisherpeople, who seem unable to accept the idea that this is a wildlife refuge— meaning it is a refuge for wildlife. They're retired, they want to fish, and that seems to be as far as their vision or ecological concern extends. The nearby retirement community known as Shantytown houses just three permanent residents, but it's the seasonal home of several dozen retirees. Many times they've complained about a lack of water in their fishing hole, the South Marsh. They tend to make their feelings known by calling their congresspeople rather than by discussing their problems with refuge staffers a mile up the road.

This has happened frequently and is always settled in favor of the refuge. Such has been the case since 20 years ago, when disruption of waterfowl habitat here, due mainly to waterskiing, resulted in a federal ban on all powerboats on the marsh during the nesting season. Motors of 10 horsepower or less are allowed between August 1 and December 31.

Fortunately, most Shantytown folk are more reasonable than this handful of irksome anglers, whose disregard for the needs of wildlife is saddening. Also impacting human activity here was a drought in the late 1980s that lowered the water level in the South Marsh. Combined with overfishing, the drought caused a precipitous crash in the bass population. Game fish numbers will likely remain low for several years. With the falling fish count, refuge visitation, which is composed mainly of anglers, has dropped from 70,000 in the late 1980s to around 10,000 in recent years. A new reservoir near the town of Elko also has reduced fishing pressure here. So for now, Ruby Lake is enjoying a rest.

One doesn't need a fishing rod to revel in the charms of Ruby Lake. Canoeing the South Marsh is the best way to pierce its depths—in silence, at eye level with the ducks and other creatures who live there.

A word of caution: People do get lost occasionally in this low maze of channels and islands, sometimes remaining out all night. To lower the odds of this happening to you, choose a reference point on the mountain to guide you and use it like the North Star. In case that method fails you, be prepared with adequate gear, including water and warm clothing. At 6,000 feet, night temperatures here can bring on hypothermia in any season. The refuge brochure lists other ways to avoid such trouble and to get help if you need it.

The storms that hit this part of Nevada in early summer can be particularly hazardous due to lightning strikes and high winds. Storm clouds here should be taken seriously. If you're on the water, head for shore immediately at the sight of gathering dark clouds. That's especially urgent if you note storm clouds creeping down the slopes of the Ruby Mountains. Such movement means hard winds are imminent, and lightning is likely, too.

Management by Mastication

Management concerns here, aside from pole-and-hook politics, largely involve technical aspects of moving water about. That movement is important to the physical condition of habitats in wetland areas, serving to cleanse and freshen the aquatic environment and reduce the opportunity for disease to develop. Antiquated water-control structures make water moving difficult, though work is in progress to improve older structures and build new ones. As usual throughout the refuge system, more money would help.

On the uplands, a small herd of cattle is grazed here as a management tool. If used judiciously, cattle can be effective in reducing unwanted vegetation and may stimulate plant growth by breaking up topsoil, as roving buffalo once did throughout their range. Here, one plant that needs removing (or at least controlling) is the Baltic rush, which offers little nutrition to most species and will take over an area if not cropped.

Cattle also keep the grass low, favoring upland foragers that include long-billed curlew and killdeer—both use meadows on the southern edge of the refuge. Grazing is managed on a "rest rotation" basis that puts cattle in areas only once every 3 years and keeps them there just long enough to perform a single clipping. Traditional grazing often results in grass being pulled out by the roots.

Unfortunately, the trend toward reintroducing extirpated species on refuges rarely includes buffalo, who require heavy fencing, lots of roaming space, and intensive, aggressive management when management is called for. These days, when buffalo impacts are required for a healthy ecosystem, cows usually have to do.

To provide for cattle during winter months, some units are hayed, with the alfalfa raked into bunches and left on the ground. Bunch raking is an old method. In a way, it complements the primeval West feel of this remote, undeveloped region. Ruby Valley and the refuge itself are indeed remnants of a lost era, when deer and antelope played upon broad meadows and human inhabitants gazed out over endless beauty—beauty on all sides, as the Navajo chant intones. Ruby Lake is a truly magnificent place, a part of our wild American legacy that is precious beyond commerce and culture—a place to be protected and cherished.

Bird sightings:

Other wildlife sightings:

Notes:

PARTIAL BIRD LIST: Pied-billed grebe, American white pelican, snowy egret, tundra swan, trumpeter swan, mallard, cinnamon teal, ring-necked duck, bald eagle, sage grouse, sandhill crane, spotted sandpiper, Caspian and black terns, northern saw-whet owl, calliope hummingbird, Hammond's flycatcher, violet-green swallow, bushtit, American dipper, sage thrasher, cedar waxwing, yellow-breasted chat, green-tailed towhee, lark sparrow, bobolink, evening grosbeak.

PARTIAL MAMMAL LIST: Pronghorn, mountain lion, mule deer, coyote, short-tail weasel, piñon mouse, long-tail vole, black-tail jackrabbit, Ord kangaroo rat.

PARTIAL HERP LIST: Great Basin rattlesnake, gopher snake, sagebrush lizard, leopard frog.

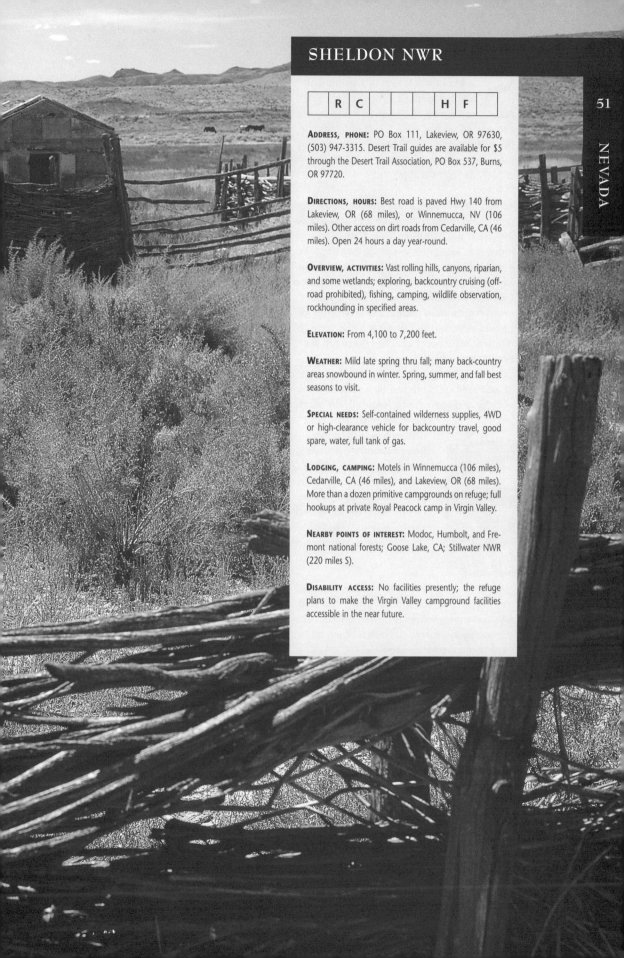

SHELDON NWR

	R	C			H	F	

ADDRESS, PHONE: PO Box 111, Lakeview, OR 97630, (503) 947-3315. Desert Trail guides are available for $5 through the Desert Trail Association, PO Box 537, Burns, OR 97720.

DIRECTIONS, HOURS: Best road is paved Hwy 140 from Lakeview, OR (68 miles), or Winnemucca, NV (106 miles). Other access on dirt roads from Cedarville, CA (46 miles). Open 24 hours a day year-round.

OVERVIEW, ACTIVITIES: Vast rolling hills, canyons, riparian, and some wetlands; exploring, backcountry cruising (off-road prohibited), fishing, camping, wildlife observation, rockhounding in specified areas.

ELEVATION: From 4,100 to 7,200 feet.

WEATHER: Mild late spring thru fall; many back-country areas snowbound in winter. Spring, summer, and fall best seasons to visit.

SPECIAL NEEDS: Self-contained wilderness supplies, 4WD or high-clearance vehicle for backcountry travel, good spare, water, full tank of gas.

LODGING, CAMPING: Motels in Winnemucca (106 miles), Cedarville, CA (46 miles), and Lakeview, OR (68 miles). More than a dozen primitive campgrounds on refuge; full hookups at private Royal Peacock camp in Virgin Valley.

NEARBY POINTS OF INTEREST: Modoc, Humbolt, and Fremont national forests; Goose Lake, CA; Stillwater NWR (220 miles S).

DISABILITY ACCESS: No facilities presently; the refuge plans to make the Virgin Valley campground facilities accessible in the near future.

Sheldon NWR is one of a handful of North American refuges where you can survey all the peaks on every horizon and know that each is within refuge boundaries. At 575,000 acres, this sprawling pronghorn preserve in the northwestern corner of Nevada seems endless.

As you travel north across Nevada to the transition zone dividing the Basin and Range province from the Columbia River Plateau, you move into sagebrush expanses that finger up into Washington, Oregon, and Idaho, gradually leaving behind the desert's stark flats and towering peaks. Here you still find jagged escarpments, long ridges, and an eternity of barren earth, but the landscape also takes in hills that soften until gradually they roll like broad sea swells.

Sheldon refuge is marked by a subtler range of color and form than the land to the south. Here the earth goes gray, pale yellow, and brown. Rough country roads are strewn with volcanic rock (hard on tires) and are lined by occasional rises. Grades can be steep on some back roads, urging turtle-slow driving speeds to avoid free-fall.

prairie

Much of Sheldon appears monotypical. A repetition of tawny rounded hills and grassy valleys is broken only occasionally by a volcanic-tuff outcropping or vertical-sided plateau known in the area as a "table." Look closer, however, and you'll find a rich environment comprising hundreds of plant and animal species in a variety of habitats.

Aside from the long views, Sheldon's magic is in the details—in an aspen grove at the end of a lonely canyon or a pronghorn lit by dusky light. Spring-fed pools are so blue they appear painted in oils. Abrupt chasms plunge 500 feet into stream-carved earth, slicing the plain. Small ponds throughout the refuge may harbor dozens of ducks and other creatures, who take their bathing and drinking where they find it in this largely waterless high desert.

To experience the depth and beauty of Sheldon takes time—a minimum of several days just to scratch the surface. Animals are abundant, though often not easy to find. (One exception is the pronghorn, found in large numbers on westerly "Little Sheldon.") Visit for the solitude and spectacle of long views and tucked-away treasures. When you chance upon a strutting sage grouse, a badger, or a herd of pronghorn, consider yourself doubly blessed.

Hardscrabble History

Millions of years before humans came to the region, volcanic activity covered the refuge land in as much as 100 feet of basalt and created the present-day tables found throughout Sheldon. Mountains rose, faults created low valleys, and the stage was set for the evolution of Sheldon's dramatic character. Over ancient centuries the region played host to numerous large mammals, including 3-toed horses, ground sloths, and saber-toothed cats. Once subject to more than 50 inches of rain each year, the Sheldon area grew dramatically drier over the last several thousand years, until now it is considered upland desert and semidesert, with just 6 to 8 inches of precipitation each year on its eastern side and 14 on its higher western edge. Much of that moisture comes as snow, which melts in spring to fill creeks and impoundments scattered about the refuge.

Long before Euro-Americans entered "the Sheldon" in the 1840s, this region of greasewood, sage, and bunchgrass was inhabited by a succession of Native American cultures. They left evidence of their presence throughout the refuge, particularly near the many springs that erupt throughout the backcountry. Artifacts and petroglyphs, some dating as far back as 12,000 years ago, have been unearthed.

More recent native peoples here included Shoshones and Northern Paiutes, whose ancestors arrived in the area around 1,500 years ago, attracted by the numerous springs and an abundance of wildlife that once roamed the grasslands. Several reservations in the area shelter remnants of those peoples, including nearby Summit Lake Reservation, established in 1913.

Trappers and explorers moved through the area in the early 1800s, followed by a handful of hardy ranchers and later sheepherders who appraised Sheldon's natural wealth of grassland and saw a more fiduciary shade of green. Disputes with local Indians spurred the US Army to erect Fort McGarry nearby in 1866. Once the garrison was in place, intensive ranching began, much of it by corporate livestock kings running thousands of cattle.

Within a few decades, overgrazing had stripped much of the land of its vegetative cover; opportunistic sagebrush and scrub filled the void. Fire suppression further injured the natural succession here, providing brush with a clear field to occupy in all but the low, moist meadowlands.

Bad ecological judgment in such a demanding environment quickly runs its course. Cattle empires that reigned here fell into ruin, replaced by a handful of family-run operations that struggled on into the early part of this century.

Springing Back

Native animals, such as pronghorn, mule deer, and bighorn sheep, hung on for a time, too, but as their environment was gradually rendered more and more inhospitable, they declined to low numbers. Other species, including sage grouse, who now maintain around 50 leks, most on refuge tablelands, were also decimated.

Wild horses living on Sheldon are a legacy of the various settlement efforts here. They create some problems for the refuge, destroying habitat and competing for food and shelter with native wildlife. Some have been trapped and adopted out to horse lovers, but capturing them isn't easy. Refuge overflights for the purpose of rounding up horses or burros are illegal, and landward wrangling on horseback is fast becoming a lost art. So far, refuge managers have resisted the bad option of shooting horses; still, the problem remains.

Fortunately, managers here don't see lethal control of the feral critters as a viable option.

As ranching faded, mining operations were established; however, they've continued to the present as small-scale efforts, never expanding to earth-mover proportions. Basque sheepherders moved in during the early decades of this century, including Thomas Duferrena, for whom the area off Hwy 140 into Virgin Valley is named. His holdings became refuge property in 1937.

In 1918, concerned members of the Boone and Crockett Club and the fledgling National Audubon Society recognized the importance of Sheldon to the survival of the region's pronghorns. Soon they raised the necessary funds to purchase the 34,000-acre Last Chance Ranch, and it was set aside as a game sanctuary.

A portion of the refuge was founded in 1931 by President Herbert Hoover, who took the Last Chance land under federal control to create the Sheldon National Antelope Refuge. This is the western section of the present refuge known as "Little Sheldon," where in an hour's exploration you'll likely spot a hundred or more pronghorns during nonwinter months. The 540,000-acre Charles Sheldon Antelope Range was established in 1936 by President Franklin D. Roosevelt to preserve additional pronghorn habitat.

Both preserves were joined in 1978 to form the Sheldon NWR. Hart Mountain National Antelope Range, 40 miles north near refuge HQ in Lakeview, Oregon, is a 250,000-acre "sister" refuge to Sheldon, also providing good pronghorn habitat and wide-open spaces that support a variety of wildlife species, including the California bighorn sheep. Both Hart Mountain and Sheldon are administered from the Lakeview office.

Nonurban Sprawl

To gain real appreciation for Sheldon you'll need at least 2 days here, preferably 3 or more. Exploring any one of the networks of dirt roads that pierce Sheldon's backcountry is an all-day affair. Fortunately, more than a dozen primitive campgrounds exist through-out the refuge. (If you backpack here, you can camp anywhere, as long as you're 50 feet from water and a half mile from your vehicle.) Some campgrounds have pit toilets and water; others do not. Weather at Sheldon is generally pleasant in warmer months, allow-ing high-clearance access along roads that are often snowed in during winter and early spring.

To get a good feel for the refuge, a few desti-nations are essential. Most visitors spend at least some of their time in the Virgin Valley area, where many refuge habitats exist. The main road is good enough for passenger vehi-cles, and creekside and deep canyon hiking is accessible from here. A rest room–equipped campground lies down the road from the refuge subheadquarters at Duferrena, as do ponds where fishing is allowed.

Several small wetlands in the valley draw waterfowl, especially in spring and fall. Ducks are not the main refuge fauna, but in season you can often find small groups of Canada goose, pintail, green- and blue-winged teal, shoveler, redhead and ring-necked ducks, along with a dozen other species. Shorebirds and waders come, too, including herons, egrets, American bittern, long-billed curlew, greater and lesser yellowlegs, phalaropes, spotted sandpiper, avocet, and stilt. Four tern species also may drop in during all seasons but winter.

Tundra swan visits here from spring through fall. At least 20 raptor species hunt the grass-lands and ponds of Sheldon, including numerous golden eagles, sharp-shinned and Cooper's hawks, northern harriers, and great horned owls. Rarely, bald eagles are found near refuge ponds in winter. Prairie falcons inhabit the refuge year-round.

The Virgin Valley campground is the site of historic McGee Ranch, which operated around the turn of the century on the site of older Native American camps. Semirestored ranch outbuildings still exist on the grounds, includ-ing a mud-and-rock smokehouse. The refuge harbors dozens of historic sites from the Old West settlement era, including homesteads,

livestock management sites, and others. Managers are trying to raise a million dollars in state, federal, and/or private money to maintain them.

A prime draw of the Virgin Valley camp-ground is its rock-lined hot spring pool. (I spent a restful hour soaking in the lukewarm, mud-bottomed pool as small fish, frogs, and a large, gentle garter snake played nearby.) The pool's adjoining bathhouse remained closed in 1995, but volunteer groups were working to raise private donations to restore and reopen it.

From the campground, hikers can trek north to Thousand Creek Gorge, a rugged 500-foot-deep canyon cut by Virgin Creek. Hiking in this high-walled canyon during spring runoff and summer rains may be risky; be prudent regarding weather conditions. If you hike south along the creek or drive south to where Hell Creek crosses the road and hike from there (thereby saving yourself a few hours to get in), you'll find yourself in a luxuriant ripar-ian stretch of Virgin Creek, where in spring you may find numerous passerines, including willow flycatcher, canyon wren, ruby-crowned kinglet, western and mountain bluebirds, and any of 10 warbler species who visit in all sea-sons but winter.

Also in Virgin Valley are two commercial opal-digging operations. For a fee you can root around all day; many visitors return each year to do so. Visit the rock shops for a quick sur-vey of refuge minerals. You can also collect up to 7 pounds of rock per day on most of the refuge. Virgin Valley Mining District is the exception—much of the area encompasses active claims.

Though Sheldon is renowned for the opals beneath its crusty skin, those shiny flecks you'll see on the roadways are not opals. They're obsidian flakes, the remains of ancient vol-canic activity. Razor blades scattered along your path would be no tougher on your tires. Make sure you have decent tread and at least one good spare if you venture onto Sheldon's remote back roads.

A Roam on the Range

Approximately 9 miles west of the Duferrena turnoff, refuge Road 8A takes you south through the heart of the refuge. The road can be quite rough, and traveling its length puts you miles from any aid, should you need it. In the winter of 1992, a couple and their child were stranded on this road in heavy snowfall. The family's exploits made TV movie status when the wife and child found shelter in a cave as the husband walked through heavy snowdrifts to find help, suffering frostbite but making it to rescuers. One such incident is enough for Sheldon, staffers here insist.

An easterly road off 8A takes you to the Hell Creek Sheep Enclosure and good surrounding bighorn sheep habitat. (Road 8A eventually takes you to Cedarville, California, 46 miles away.) The enclosure can also be reached by traveling down the Duferrena road. Refuge maps depict the road system, though traveling them can still be confusing.

Numerous other roads, many of which connect to one another, take you throughout the refuge. Campsites lie along many of them, making good bases for day hikes. Throughout the refuge, creeks and several impoundments create good conditions for various wildlife. Water-fed meadows are often good for sage grouse in spring and summer; canyons offer good birding as well as rest and meditation space.

In general, the refuge rises in elevation as you head west. On the Little Sheldon unit (accessible on refuge Road 34A) you pass through pronghorn-rich country, flanking broad Swan Reservoir and rising into juniper-aspen mountains. That road also heads across desolate open range to Cedarville. A northward turnoff just before Little Sheldon carries you along a rough (4WD) road to the IXL Ranch area, where several impoundments and good rim-country bighorn habitat can be found.

Pronghorns

About 1,500 pronghorns live on Sheldon throughout the year. In winter that number rises to more than 3,500, many of them coming south from Hart Mountain NWR, just over the Oregon border. Big Spring Table is a major wintering area for pronghorn, as is the area west of that large plateau.

Many resident pronghorns live on Little Sheldon, a 34,000-acre patch of rolling grassy habitat on the western edge of the refuge. Little Sheldon was the entire refuge until 1976, when the vast eastern acres were added to it. Little Sheldon remains a sanctuary where hunting is totally banned. The pronghorns' enhanced sense of security here makes them much easier to observe than elsewhere on the refuge. Bands of from 10 to 30 individuals can often be spotted along refuge Road 34A, which bisects the sanctuary, rising toward the west into juniper highlands. Often you'll see them along Swan Reservoir, as well as in the rolling hills to the west. Sometimes they're hard to spot at first, but if you gaze over open areas long enough they generally, increasingly pop into view.

Extractors, Distractors

Game management jurisdiction on Sheldon is a complex issue. Nevada state game authorities have for years conducted wildlife surveys and set hunting limits in the area. They've continued that role after the entire refuge came under USFWS control, despite the new federal boundaries. One advantage of this arrangement is the state's budget, which allows for helicopter flyover surveys. Federal overseers, on the other hand, constantly squeeze every available penny to manage basic refuge functions.

Having one agency manage a piece of land while another manages its game use seems a case of bureaucratic pretzel logic. The state appears to be doing a good job of keeping population numbers at sustainable levels, but one possible hangup in arrangements like this one is the potential that a state may respond to excessive pressure from local, vocal hunting interests—a pressure also shared by the service but rarely to the same degree. It's another "state's rights" issue that poses the question: Does federal control of some aspects of

American society help reduce the impact of local, narrower interests? Or are locals better able to take care of their neighborhoods than federal bureaucrats?

On large portions of the refuge, pronghorns are still hunted, along with deer, a few bighorn sheep (with permits distributed via state lottery), sage grouse, quail, and chukar. Hunter-free zones include the Duferrena area, the Hell Creek bighorn sheep enclosure, and a few other portions of the refuge, including all of Little Sheldon.

Grazing has been removed from the refuge since environmental groups bought up grazing rights from willing sellers and retired Sheldon from that role. Grazing for the purpose of grassland management is still an option for Sheldon's overseers, and such grazing can be useful in some cases. Future grazing activity would likely involve ranchers ferrying small groups of cattle onto specific plots for brief periods. In this sprawling land, such moves probably wouldn't justify the time or cost to cattle owners.

The Hart Mountain refuge in Oregon is another large piece of real estate where grazing no longer takes place. Together they make up two of the largest grassland areas in the West where cows no longer roam. That status offers a great opportunity for land managers to restore the desert grassland to its prehistoric condition—a rare situation anywhere in the country these days.

Controlled burns on Sheldon are part of that restoration effort. Managers here attempt to burn around 4,000 acres of scrub each year. After each burn, native grasses snap back in force, their dormant seeds finally able to pierce through ground once dominated by invading shrubs, such as sage and greasewood.

The grazing issue on Sheldon probably isn't over, however. In the West, it never is. Managers expect at any time to hear renewed calls for "practical use" of this publicly owned grass for the benefit of a few livestock growers. Fortunately, several nearby environmental groups keep eyes and ears alert for signs of such assaults. Any rancher trying to force his way back onto Sheldon faces a protracted legal battle.

Mining has long played a role in Sheldon's history, too, but most of the opal operations here have been mom-and-pop ventures utilizing limited digging equipment. The impact thus far has been minimal, though their presence does cause a small visual jolt to those expecting pristine wild country. Two patented operations on refuge property offer commercial opal-digging opportunities to weekend miners, but they're mere pinpoints on this vast wild range. Their ownership rights superceded federal control, and that could create problems for the refuge in the future if they choose to try to expand. That doesn't seem likely, though, at least in the near term.

The patented companies charge visitors $25 to $50 per day to root in their dirt for fire opals. Ironically, they probably do much better financially than the scores of genuine prospectors who occupy Sheldon for the backbreaking chore of real mining.

Navigational Aids

A refuge map is available by contacting the Lakeview headquarters or possibly from the Duferrena subheadquarters, which isn't always staffed. Managers here are working to improve information access with the addition of new self-serve kiosks. Call or write in advance to be sure of getting the information you need.

A Desert Trail corridor also exists, running north and south on the eastern side of the refuge. As of mid-1995, maps and trail routes were still being developed, though topo maps are already available that are far more detailed than refuge brochures. They're a good tool to have in a land so vast, where the hills and plateaus seem to roll on forever.

Impressions and Experiences

Bird sightings:

Other wildlife sightings:

Notes:

PARTIAL BIRD LIST (OF 192 LISTED SPECIES, WITH 27 ACCIDENTALS): All 5 American grebes, white pelican, black-crowned night heron, mallard, ring-necked duck, Swainson's hawk, bald eagle, common snipe, California gull, screech owl, rufous hummingbird, dusky flycatcher, horned lark, scrub jay, mountain chickadee, northern and loggerhead shrike, warbling vireo, orange-crowned warbler, northern oriole, lazuli bunting, fox sparrow, snow bunting.

PARTIAL MAMMAL LIST: Pronghorn, mule deer, bighorn sheep, short-tail weasel, badger, kit fox, mountain lion, bobcat, long-eared myotis and California myotis bats, raccoon, beaver, pygmy rabbit, Preble's and Trowbridge's shrews, western harvest mouse.

PARTIAL HERP LIST: Rubber boa, night snake, western rattlesnake, collared lizard, western fence lizard, short-horned lizard, southern alligator lizard, pacific tree frog.

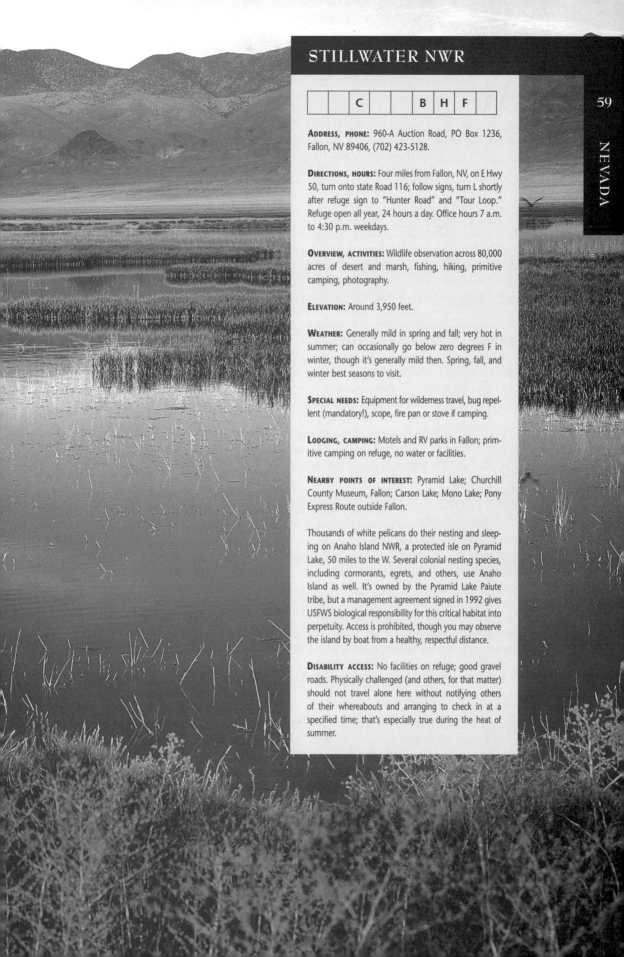

STILLWATER NWR

| | | C | | B | H | F | |

ADDRESS, PHONE: 960-A Auction Road, PO Box 1236, Fallon, NV 89406, (702) 423-5128.

DIRECTIONS, HOURS: Four miles from Fallon, NV, on E Hwy 50, turn onto state Road 116; follow signs, turn L shortly after refuge sign to "Hunter Road" and "Tour Loop." Refuge open all year, 24 hours a day. Office hours 7 a.m. to 4:30 p.m. weekdays.

OVERVIEW, ACTIVITIES: Wildlife observation across 80,000 acres of desert and marsh, fishing, hiking, primitive camping, photography.

ELEVATION: Around 3,950 feet.

WEATHER: Generally mild in spring and fall; very hot in summer; can occasionally go below zero degrees F in winter, though it's generally mild then. Spring, fall, and winter best seasons to visit.

SPECIAL NEEDS: Equipment for wilderness travel, bug repellent (mandatory!), scope, fire pan or stove if camping.

LODGING, CAMPING: Motels and RV parks in Fallon; primitive camping on refuge, no water or facilities.

NEARBY POINTS OF INTEREST: Pyramid Lake; Churchill County Museum, Fallon; Carson Lake; Mono Lake; Pony Express Route outside Fallon.

Thousands of white pelicans do their nesting and sleeping on Anaho Island NWR, a protected isle on Pyramid Lake, 50 miles to the W. Several colonial nesting species, including cormorants, egrets, and others, use Anaho Island as well. It's owned by the Pyramid Lake Paiute tribe, but a management agreement signed in 1992 gives USFWS biological responsibility for this critical habitat into perpetuity. Access is prohibited, though you may observe the island by boat from a healthy, respectful distance.

DISABILITY ACCESS: No facilities on refuge; good gravel roads. Physically challenged (and others, for that matter) should not travel alone here without notifying others of their whereabouts and arranging to check in at a specified time; that's especially true during the heat of summer.

West-central Nevada's Stillwater NWR is a miracle. The fact that a broad, vital wetland exists in some of the driest, most inhospitable terrain in the nation's driest state—despite heavy-handed agriculture-based politics that long ago laid claim to what little water exists here—seems an act of divine benevolence.

Flanked to the east by the rugged Stillwater Mountains, the refuge is almost completely flat, with few trees or rises breaking its broad profile. This is a place of endless views and waterless desert, the sort of environment that reminds you of just how vast the West really is.

In good years, marsh units here run a mile wide and no more than a few feet deep— ideal habitat that attracts some 350,000 ducks, 10,000 geese, 14,000 tundra swans, and many thousands of shorebirds and waders. Up to 15,000 waterfowl young are born here in high-water years, along with numerous wader and shorebird chicks. Half of all Pacific Flyway canvasbacks visit Stillwater. Recently, they've begun breeding on the refuge, as they likely did for centuries before river water was diverted to farm fields and the marshes ebbed.

*freshwater
wetlands*

Several migratory and resident white pelicans, many on fishing forays from their Anaho Island nesting colony 50 miles to the west, often cloud the sky in overflights or cruise at water level, steering and corralling fish in coordinated packs before swarming and consuming them en masse.

Except for desert rodents, mammals here are few. Coyote is the main predator; rodents are the coyote's main feast. A few mule deer wander in from nearby farm fields. Muskrats were rampant in the marshes until a flood in the early 1990s cleaned them out; they're recovering very slowly. More than a dozen bat species cruise the night skies, helping keep down an awesome mosquito population. A few badgers live here, along with black-tail

jackrabbits and a small number of kit foxes. Ground squirrels, kangaroo rats, mice, and voles—burrowers well adapted to this broiling desert land—make up most of the mammal base.

Likewise, reptiles are somewhat scarce due to a sparcity of upland vegetation. Desert survivors, such as fence, zebra-tailed, and side-blotched lizards, have their niches on Stillwater. A few toads make a living on the refuge, estivating for long, dry periods then emerging during wet times.

Snake species include the unusual rubber boa, Sierra garter, California red-sided garter, and Mojave patch-nosed snake. Great Basin rattlesnake is the only venomous species here other than the rear-fanged night snake; its tiny, back-set fangs and mild toxin are no threat to humans.

Remote Travel

Visitors traveling the first stretch of Stillwater's tour road may well ask, "Where's the water?" The start of the road passes little more than a dry, barren reach of greasewood, salt grass, and quailbush, the last sort of habitat you expect to harbor water birds. Patience will reward you. The first of many ponds appears before long, and generally birds will be in residence. In spring and fall there may be tens of thousands of them.

The Carson River enters the refuge from the south and flows north. As a result, salinity increases as the river crosses the refuge. By the time you reach the North Marsh and Nutgrass Lake, you're in the midst of hypersaline pools that may approach 3 times the salt content of seawater. Supporting such delicacies as midges, brine flies, and brine shrimp, they attract several wading species who enjoy such salty treats. This diversity of habitats is partly the reason so many different species live at or visit Stillwater.

Hunter Road is the main entry road into the wetlands. The road takes you past privately owned Canvasback Gun Club and then on to the marsh. Hunting is a major activity on the refuge. Shooters here make up most of Stillwater's 40,000 visitors each year, with most coming during the fall and winter hunting season.

The network of canals along the roads may support abundant life, especially diving birds, such as western, eared and horned grebe, redheads, and scaup, along with waders, including snowy egret, a few great egrets, great blue and green herons, white-faced ibis, and others. Shallow wet depressions throughout the preserve attract avocet, black-necked stilt, yellowlegs, and a variety of small shorebirds, including snowy plover, long-billed dowitcher, and various sandpipers.

White pelicans visit Stillwater year-round from Anaho Island. They often use raised grassy island platforms on the larger impoundments as communal roosting spots. You can't miss these huge masses of white scattered about the wetlands. When they flap their broad wings and take to the air, the result is a true spectacle.

Black-necked stilts inhabit Stillwater in vast numbers in summer and fall; they often pursue each other around feeding grounds, yipping nonstop like poodles gone berserk. Waterfowl dot the larger ponds, bobbing at a distance and bolting from your presence as you enter their safety zones.

Egrets and herons, along with a multitude of white-faced ibises, browse the canal edges. Drive slowly and some species will allow close approaches. This seems especially true of avocets and stilts. Tundra swans, which come in the fall and often stay until the marshes freeze over (this doesn't happen every year), are often found in pondweed-rich areas.

It's hard to predict where you'll find a particular species. Habitat changes from year to year and season to season, depending on water supplies. At least a few tour loop wetlands will be full in any season. Within the tour area are all refuge habitat types except sand dunes, which lie along the northern reaches of the refuge and support just a few plant and rep-

tile species. They're interesting nevertheless and worth the moderate hike. Water bird viewing on the refuge often requires a good scope to pull the birds in close.

Endangered brown pelicans may reside on the refuge during your visit. Unlike white pelicans, who dip food from around them as they bob on the surface, brown pelicans locate their prey from the air and enter the water in spectacular dives, usually emerging with fish in their oversized beaks. A spotting scope will often allow you to observe their angling behavior up close.

Miragelike Marshes

Stillwater's marshes may seem miraculous, but the presence of water here wasn't always so remarkable. For possibly 10,000 years, this glacier-carved Lahontan Valley bolson received the Carson River's flow of Sierra Nevada snowmelt, creating a vast "terminal wetland" that was a source of life for humans and animals alike.

desert

After the explorer Capt. James Simpson traveled the area in 1859, he wrote of the Carson Lake marsh at the valley's southern end and of the Toedokado people (Stillwater Paiutes) who lived along its banks:

The water is beautifully blue . . . margined with rushes; the shores covered with mussel shells, pelicans and other aquatic food . . . and the lake is filled with fish. A number of Paiutes, some two dozen, live near our camp, and I notice they have piles of fish lying about drying, principally chubs and mullet (suckers). They catch them with a seine.

The progenitors of these "cattail eaters," known to moden Paiutes as *Toieikadai*, were an integral part of the life mix, drawing on the marsh's wildlife and vegetal resources. Present-day Shoshone–Paiutes have long since forsaken the mosquito-ridden marshlands and now occupy an upland reservation nearby, but the marshes still mean much to the indigenous people of this land, as they do to late-arriving Anglo settlers and passers-through.

Pony Express riders who pounded across this desolate Great Basin region in the early 1860s described the skies over the marshes as "black with ducks." Indeed, for untold thousands of years, the Stillwater marshes had been a critical wetlands stopover and breeding area for hundreds of thousands of Pacific Flyway water birds.

The archaeological and historical significance of Stillwater accounts for much of its uniqueness. Thousands of Native American graves and ancient habitation sites exist within its borders; artifacts occasionally rise to the surface. Remember to leave such items where you find them. They're federally protected, but even more important, they make up the family legacy of the local indigenous people. Demonstrate your respect by enjoying them where they lay.

Cultivating the Desert

In 1904, Euro-American settlers captured the Carson's flow to irrigate their alfalfa fields. The European tendency to force agricultural production in unsuitable areas had the usual effects on nearby wetlands. Here the natural cycle was disrupted, the river was drawn down, and the marshes were nourished only by agricultural overflow. In many years that excess water was scarce. Sometimes the marsh comprised nothing but dry alkaline soil, broiling under the Nevada sun.

Fallon NWR was formed in 1931 to enhance the waterfowl habitat that regional agriculture had depleted. The idea was good; rewatering refuge wetlands was the hard part.
For decades the refuge went unsupported by either water rights or meaningful legislation. Some years there were no marshes on Fallon at all, just dry, crusty-white alkaline *playa* flats. The same held true for nearby Stillwater Wildlife Management Area, a 224,000-acre on-and-off wetland created in 1946.

The situation began improving in 1976, when 34,000 acres of the Stillwater Wildlife Management Area were given refuge status. That designation was meant to increase wetland habitat that neither Fallon nor the management area had reliably provided.

In 1990, refuge borders were expanded to nearly 77,500 acres, encompassing all of Stillwater Marsh. Water-rights acquisition will eventually sustain 14,000 permanent wetland acres in the area; close to 16,000 acre-feet (providing 3,000 acre-feet of marsh) were purchased by mid-1995. A small series of land acquisitions, many from private inholders, has expanded the refuge to nearly 80,000 acres.

Nearby Fallon NWR remains an erratic wetland that often isn't wet at all. Its fate as a federal preserve is undecided. A third unit of Stillwater refuge complex, Anaho Island NWR on Pyramid Lake (50 miles west of Stillwater), supports a major population of colonial nesters as well as dozens of other species.

Wetland Network

In fall and winter, Stillwater burgeons with life. During nonmigratory seasons, especially early summer, only a small population of waterfowl, waders, and shorebirds lives here amid dense clouds of mosquitoes that might be dangerous were it not for bug repellent and roll-up windows. In any season, the views are epic, and dawn and dusk wrap the sky in rich magenta and gold.

Stillwater's reliable water supply, coupled with agricultural overflow, allows for good wetlands to exist year-round. But Stillwater is only a part of the total wetland habitat in the region. Three major sites—Stillwater, Pyramid Lake, and Fallon in wet years, along with a network of lakes to the south and west of the broad marshes—provide a watery support system for wildlife.

That regional habitat picture applies for most refuges. Few represent the only good habitat within a particular region, though a refuge may be the best-protected and most-carefully managed spot in its area. Inevitably, nearby landowners and government agencies must also do their part to fully provide for the needs of regional and migratory wildlife.

Much more water is needed to help Stillwater meet its optimum potential. That's largely due to the high evaporation rate in this Great Basin desert environment, which runs to 60 inches per year. That means 5 acre-feet of water are required for every actual 1 acre-foot of marsh.

To meet mandated wetland goals, water rights are being purchased in areas around the refuge. Farmland acres have been acquired from local owners, including nearby Fallon Shoshone–Paiute tribe. Water rights are transferred from those fields to the marsh, the land goes back to the tribe, then tribal farmers utilize existing tribal water rights to resupply the same land. It's complicated, but it works.

Fishing and low-power motor boating are still allowed on some refuge marshes as of 1996; several launch sites exist along refuge roads. A long-range management plan may change that. Call ahead if you plan to do either.

Common Sense

A Visitor's Center is planned on a newly acquired piece of land near the hunting club. When erected, possibly by the end of 1996, a resident staffer or volunteer will be there during office hours. However, keep in mind that this is a remote, lightly visited refuge; car trouble may put you 15 or more miles from help. If you leave the main tour road and get stuck, no one may see you for days, and you may have to walk many miles for help. Before you go check your fan belt, spare, and other auto consumables, and come prepared with extra water and food, along with at least basic supplies for an overnight stay.

Camping is okay on Stillwater, at least for now. Contained fires are also allowed. If you make a fire, use a fire pan or otherwise eradicate all traces of its existence before you leave.

The area was used for World War II training maneuvers, and occasionally a piece of unexploded ordinance will surface from the marsh or uplands. Don't ever touch such an object, which may still be active and dangerous. Avoid driving off-road, and stay off alkaline patches, which may appear solid but actually cover a boggy layer that will grab your tires like glue. The main roads here are gravel and generally good; occasionally some are closed due to weather conditions but rarely for more than a day. Call headquarters before you go if the weather seems questionable.

Impressions and Experiences

Bird sightings:

Other wildlife sightings:

Notes:

PARTIAL BIRD LIST (OF 161 LISTED SPECIES, WITH 18 AC-CIDENTALS): Eared grebe, white pelican, white-faced ibis, least bittern, wigeon, redhead, wood duck, canvasback, red-tailed hawk, marsh hawk (harrier), spotted, western, and least sandpipers, dunlin, avocet, black tern, long-eared owl, downy woodpecker, violet-green swallow, bushtit, northern and loggerhead shrikes, yellow warbler, American goldfinch.

PARTIAL MAMMAL LIST: Mountain lion, mule deer, badger, coyote, muskrat, desert kangaroo rat, long-tail pocket mouse.

PARTIAL HERP LIST: Great Basin rattlesnake, Great Basin gopher snake, rosy boa, night snake, zebra-tailed lizard, Great Basin skink, pacific tree frog, boreal toad, bullfrog.

VC	R					H	F	

ADDRESS, PHONE: 866 S Main, Brigham City, UT 84302, (801) 723-5887 (a new Visitor's Center is slated to be built W of I-15; call for directions).

DIRECTIONS, HOURS: W on Forrest Road from Brigham City, 15 miles to refuge. Open dawn to dusk; Brigham City office open 8 a.m. to 4:30 p.m. during the week. Tour road open sunrise to sunset every day; call for hours at new Visitor's Center.

OVERVIEW, ACTIVITIES: Extensive open wetlands habitat; wildlife observation, 12-mile auto loop, photography, fishing, hiking, hunting.

ELEVATION: From 4,802 to 4,808 feet.

WEATHER: Mild spring and fall, moderately hot in summer, cold (sometimes frigid) in winter. Spring, summer, and fall best seasons to visit.

SPECIAL NEEDS: Water, insect repellent, spotting scope.

LODGING, CAMPING: Hotels are available in nearby Brigham City and other surrounding urban areas. No camping on refuge, but campgrounds are available at Cache National Forest, 3 miles E of Brigham City; Willard Bay State Park, S of refuge; commercial campground in Brigham City.

NEARBY POINTS OF INTEREST: Mormon Church in Salt Lake City and its extensive geneological resources; the Great Salt Lake and nearby state wildlife areas on the lake.

DISABILITY ACCESS: Office accessible; new Visitor's Center will be accessible.

For centuries, the freshwater marshes of Bear River NWR (also known as Bear River Migratory Bird Refuge) near Brigham City, Utah, were a setting for one of the great wildlife spectacles in the Western Hemisphere. Until the early 1980s, bird numbers here were nothing short of phenomenal, with more than a million waterfowl, shorebirds, and waders piling into this freshwater delta on their migratory journeys. In the 1940s, more than 400,000 ducks alone came here in migration.

Explorer Gen. John C. Frémont bore witness to Bear River delta's importance as a waterfowl site in an 1843 journal entry:

The whole morass was animated with multitudes of waterfowl, which appeared to be very wild, rising for the space of a mile round about at the sound of a gun, with a noise like distant thunder. Several of the people waded out into the marsh, and we had tonight a delicious supper of ducks, geese and plover.

freshwater wetlands

In 1983, an unlikely natural event devastated this once-productive environment. A massive hundred-year flood sent huge influxes of water down the channel of the Bear River to this terminus on the edge of the Great Salt Lake, inundating tens of thousands of acres that had once been welcoming mudflats and shallow marshes, carrying salt into previous freshwater habitats. The resulting sea of deep, briny, open water supported few of the legions of birds who once relied on the river delta for feeding, resting, and breeding space.

On this flat landscape shaped by ancient Lake Bonneville, a rise in the lake level of just 1 inch can spread water over thousands of dry acres. During those disastrous 3 years, the lake rose 7 feet above its previous level, 13 feet above its lake bottom elevation. Not only was a vast reach of habitat destroyed in the process but dikes and canals, along with modern refuge administration and Visitor's Center buildings, were submerged and ruined.

By 1986, the USFWS learned from hydrologists that it would take 2 decades for the water to recede enough to reexpose marshes and mudflats. Disheartened, federal overseers more or less abandoned the refuge. For 3 years, sporadic caretaking visits comprised the bulk of management efforts.

Strange Luck

The flooding, however, was followed by another hundred-year chance event, this one a multiyear drought. Dry years that meant disaster for much of the West were a stroke of good fortune for Bear River. By 1989, the water had receded dramatically, enough so that habitat restoration could begin. A new refuge manager was assigned; heavy equipment moved in to begin the awesome task of restoring one of the world's premier avian environments. Efforts were also launched (and continue) to purchase upland acres around the refuge, where new facilities will be placed above the floodplain and additional habitat will be developed.

Like the legendary phoenix, Bear River NWR has risen from its sodden ashes. Once again, broad expanses of shallow wetlands, draped in yellow-and-red rafts of sago pondweed, entice waves of waterfowl, waders, and shorebirds during their instinctual yearly travels.

Habitat restoration continues, as it will through the turn of the century (barring more flooding). By mid-1995, 8,000 upland acres had been acquired from nearby willing sellers toward a goal of 17,000 additional acres (most of it along the entry road from Brigham City). When new facilities are built on high ground, the refuge will never again be faced with abandonment when the next long-cycle flood washes over the delta.

Meanwhile, mudflats have reemerged, shallows again provide wading habitat, and spectacular flocks that once darkened the northern Utah skies are returning to the delta. The reshaping of marshes and dikes is now guided by modern understanding of ecological needs and processes. In time, this critical habitat may support (if it's possible) even more species and individuals than ever before.

Desert Estuary

Superficially, Bear River refuge resembles an estuarine environment. As with rivers that run into oceans, the 1.2-million acre-feet of water that flow from the Uintah Range to this Great Salt Lake delta do enter saline water— in fact, the Great Salt Lake is several times saltier than seawater—but unlike an ocean-river interface, there are no tides in the lake to push saltwater back up into the delta. Here a variable salt gradient reaches a short distance into the fresh system, and much of the plant base is salt tolerant. However, most of the freshwater marsh is separate from salty lake water that lies beyond the dikes.

Where freshwater exists in the desert, birds are sure to come. Combine Bear River's freshwater habitat, that of several nearby state-run marshes, and the Great Salt Lake's perennial avian drawing power and you can begin to comprehend the attraction this region has for migrating birds.

More than 60,000 acres of Bear River delta are mudflats and shallows, a vast wetland system that draws huge flocks of waterfowl, such as blue-winged teal, pintail, ruddy, wigeon, mallard, shoveler, and canvasback. By late March, tens of thousands of ducks begin arriving; soon refuge impoundments are a flurry of calling, pairing, and territorial conflicts. In the fall, southward-migrating ducks that stop by the refuge number in the hundreds of thousands.

In a region where water holes lie as much as 75 miles apart, waterfowl concentrate at the marshes, primarily to breed and to feed on endless floating meadows of sago pondweed, a dabbling duck's favorite. Teeming invertebrate populations, particularly midges and brine flies, also supply the dietary needs of numerous species and offer critical protein for egg-producing mothers and their fast-growing young. (The midges here resemble mosquitoes. They can swarm heavily, but they don't bite. Real mosquitoes are rarely a problem at Bear River. Horseflies, though, are a different matter.)

The Great Salt Lake's huge brine shrimp supply also offers meals for a few species, including shovelers and grebes. (Brine shrimp are harvested here by the ton for sale as aquarium fish food.) A modest variety of moist-soil plant species on the delta provides mud foragers, such as curlews and occasional sandhill cranes, with tubers, seeds, and greens.

This rich environment inevitably draws occasional oddball species. Harlequin ducks have shown up at Bear River, as have fulvous whistling ducks and at least 1 pelagic predator, the parasitic jaeger. Wood stork and little blue heron are 2 more of Bear River's surprise visitors.

The refuge bird list runs to 222 species, relatively few passerines in the bunch (up to 96 perchers have been noted here, but numbers are low for most species). Water-oriented birds run the gamut from terns and white pelicans to an assortment of shorebird "peeps." Birds banded here have shown up in at least 31 states and 5 foreign countries, including Siberia, Colombia, and Palmyra Island in the Pacific, a thousand miles southwest of Hawaii. Waterfowl from Bear River have shown up as far eastward as Maryland.

In the marshes in summer, shorebirds that include marbled godwit (Bear River is one of their only known inland stopover points) and masses of sandpipers and gulls create a living shoreline, complemented by a multitude of waders that include thousands of egrets, herons, and long- and short-billed dowitchers. It isn't unusual to see 40 or 50 great blue herons in a single area, fishing in patient statuary poses. Egrets and herons here, as well as cormorants, often nest on the ground due to the absence of trees.

Eighty percent of the nation's white-faced ibises come to Bear River to breed; a summer drive around the 12-mile tour loop will reveal more than you can count. Avocets and stilts number in the tens of thousands in summer. Swarms of Wilson's phalaropes come in spring to breed and perform their erratic swirling feeding dances; they're joined in summer by lesser numbers of red-necked phalaropes.

Four-fifths of North America's tundra swans have stayed at Bear River during October and November—as many as 70,000 before the flood years; back up to nearly 30,000 by

1995—creating a snowy spectacle observable nowhere else except perhaps in the Arctic wilderness. Most of the swans, as with many other species, continue on to southern California, where winter temperatures are mild. In March, thousands of Canada geese move through on their way north, and several thousand snow geese make brief appearances before moving on to California and the Lower Colorado River Valley.

White pelicans come to Bear River to feed in the freshwater marshes. Many fly a 120-mile daily round-trip from Gunnison Island in the Great Salt Lake, where some 17,000 pairs breed (this is one of the nation's few white pelican breeding areas). Since one pelican parent remains with the nest at all times, such commutes are made every other day by alternating parents until fledging time.

Bald eagles come in the hundreds in January, perching on ice and frozen earth as they feed on easily catchable carp, their primary food source here. Refuge staffers have seen dozens of eagles standing in long lines across the flats. Sometimes large numbers of other raptors, including great horned owls and ferruginous hawks, inhabit the refuge. In all seasons except early winter, wildlife activity at Bear River often rises to the level of spectacle.

Passerines have never been numerous on this virtually treeless refuge, but with new upland acquisition and habitat reconfiguration, willows and other trees and shrubs promise to increase their presence substantially.

History and New Beginnings

The Great Salt Lake region was for centuries inhabited by Shoshones, who drew from the rich wildlife resources the lake and delta provided, living in mud and cane houses along the lakeshore, fishing with cane and rush wiers. Other tribes, including the Blackfeet and Flatheads, sometimes raided these local dwellers, especially after horses enhanced their mobility.

The earliest European visit here was recorded in the journal of the Dominguez–Escalante expedition, made in the same year that the United States forged its independence. A succession of explorers, trappers, and others followed. Muskrats drew many early trappers; in a century and a half, millions of the small fur bearers have been taken here. Trapping continued actively into the early 1980s, with more than 100,000 animals killed and skinned each year.

Mormons who arrived in the 1840s brought what would become Utah's defining cultural character. They settled in the grasslands between the great lake and the mountains, farming and raising livestock and proclaiming their God as sovereign over this desert land. Resident hunters such as Frederick Wilson found the delta to be a lucrative resource— in 1905, for instance, he shot around 3,000 waterfowl in the marshes here, selling them for three bucks a dozen.

One of the system's oldest refuges, Bear River was formed in 1928 by presidential proclamation. Unlike many of the Great Depression–era refuges founded over the next decade, Bear River was created primarily as waterfowl habitat rather than doubling as a public employment project.

The refuge was created partially to offset a catastrophic waterfowl die-off that occurred in Utah and California in the early part of this century. That massive death toll was the result of an epidemic of avian botulism, a nerve toxin caused by the bacteria *Clostridium botulinum*.

This virulent mud- and insect-borne disease (known early on as Western Duck Sickness) was long thought to arise from a simple combination of bird crowding and stagnant water. Since then, biotoxicologists have come to suspect that botulism's etiology is more complex. The disease is still not well understood, though it is clearly associated with lowered water levels during summer, along with the presence of numerous flies and animal carcasses. Flies probably represent a significant disease vector, or transfer point, as they ingest the bacteria and are, in turn, ingested by hungry waterfowl.

Research on botulism continues, though it was dealt a blow when a specialized toxicology laboratory on the refuge, built in 1936, was destroyed in the 1983 flood. Presently, there are no plans to rebuild the Bear River lab.

In another sense, however, the flooding that ravaged Bear River brought good fortune, offering managers the chance for a fresh start, unencumbered by long-standing traditions and beliefs regarding waterfowl management. With construction of modern water-control structures and smaller impoundments where water can be better manipulated, managers believe they can exercise improved disease containment. Meanwhile, botulism research may yield new insights and additional techniques to help fight this and other avian diseases.

Smaller marsh subunits also allow for the maintenance of better habitat conditions for various species. For example, deeper water can be drawn down to the mudflat level during summer shorebird migration and then elevated again for the fall influx of diving ducks, such as scaup, ruddy, goldeneye, and canvasback.

Cruising the Tour Loop

As Bear River is redeveloped into the last years of the 20th century, new avenues for visitor exploration will be created, including hiking trails across newly acquired uplands. By 1996, visitor access was confined to a 12-mile tour loop rounding one of the marsh units. Negotiable during all but a few snowbound winter days, the loop carries visitors past most of the refuge habitats, though a scope is necessary for good views of some distant areas.

Before you reach the refuge, the access road from the edge of Brigham City provides numerous opportunities for wildlife encounters. Shallow wetlands—some owned by local hunting clubs—offer good (though at times less than secure) habitat for numerous species. Especially thick in summer along these shallows are white-faced ibis, avocets, stilts, and herons. During a visit in the summer of 1995, I saw more of each of these species—before I ever got to the refuge—than I've seen at all the other refuges in this book combined.

After I entered Bear River NWR, I encountered many times more.

Other common species along the entrance road are long-billed curlews (who often wander upland areas, looking a little lost), willets, killdeer, western meadowlarks, and yellow-headed and red-winged blackbirds, which rise in huge, rounded flocks and fly about in near-perfect unison, as if directed by a single mind.

As you enter refuge wetlands, a kiosk at the old headquarters site orients you to some of the habitat you'll pass through. Here you may also fish—this is the only spot on the refuge where fishing is allowed.

As you cross over the first water-control structures, you'll likely spot pied-billed and western grebes bobbing in the deep canals. The 1-way loop begins to the right and takes you around Bear River's large Unit 2, where much of the delta and lake habitat is represented. Alkali and hard-stem bulrush cluster near the beginning of the loop. Here you may find sora, Virginia rail, or common gallinule, as well as numerous coots, the most easily observed and least skittish member of the rail family.

At the first turn in the loop you're facing open water off to the west, where Canada and sometimes snow geese cluster. Terns, gulls, and other overflying species may be abundant at times. Cruising the long southwestern reach of the loop in winter, you'll likely spot bald eagles on the flats to your right. Scan the broad area that reaches south to Great Salt Bay; just about any out-of-place spot you observe is probably an eagle. Sometimes dozens will be present, perching anomalously on the ground.

On that same stretch to the left, shallows run toward the center of the tour loop unit. There you may see any number of waders and shorebirds, including marbled godwit, golden and black-bellied plovers, ruddy turnstone, pectoral and Baird's sandpipers, and phalaropes. A scope may be necessary for best viewing. Closer to the road the water is deeper, offering good habitat for diving birds that may include western and Clark's grebes. The latter is closely related to the western grebe; the only obvious difference is that in the Clark's, the white on the face extends above the eye.

On the second loop turn, two-thirds of the way along the route, look for eagles on your left. Here you begin to flank a long, shallow canal with plenty of mudflats and shoreline. Shorebirds can be abundant here, as well as herons, egrets, ibis, avocets, and stilts. The broad shallows on the left support a variety of species; often mother ducks and their young cruise the moderately deep water.

Less commonly seen are the mammals that inhabit Bear River. Weasels, muskrats, and skunks are some of the more prevalent species, though you may not see a single individual during your visit. The marmot, generally a high-country dweller, makes its home in rock-strewn areas of the refuge. In fact, locals call the chunky rodent "rock-chuck." Raccoons had just begun reentering the delta by the mid-1990s, a potential problem due to their superior nest-raiding abilities.

More worrisome than raccoons are the red foxes that have rapidly rebuilt their population here after the flood. Foxes are extremely effective nest predators that may become intolerable on this refuge of little cover and long views. No fox control management had been initiated by 1995, but that could change if they noticeably impact the survival rates of young birds.

Herptiles at Bear River are even less prevalent than mammals. That only makes sense; after flooding wiped out the old populations, it will take years for such slow-moving creatures to make their way back. Wandering garter is one of the few herptiles that live here; amphibians are nearly nonexistent due to their sensitivity to salty water.

Postdiluvian Future

Along with improving water-control structures, ambitious plans are being laid to stem the damage from upcoming hundred-year floods. Refuge inundation will occur again at some point—this is a natural cycle that follows its own erratic rhythm. One of the more daunting challenges to future floods is a new pump station, designed to remove floodwater by drawing it onto the flats of old Lake Bonneville. Such a feat would be herculean in nature, and chances are that in any large-scale flood, the pumps will go under before significant water is moved out of the delta. Still, pumping may help during marginal flood events if started quickly enough. All that new wetland acreage would also offer an added bonus, creating additional, if temporary, habitat.

People management at Bear River has never been problematic. Most of the neighbors seem to regard the refuge as an important part of the local economy, drawing as it does a multitude of wildlife lovers and a steady, though smaller, number of hunters. Hunting has long been the tradition here, and it continues with some new restrictions that allow better buffering for birds. For instance, airboat-accessible areas have been somewhat restricted, and rest zones (sanctuaries) have been improved to allow birds the ability to flee from flying buckshot.

Hunters continue to enjoy privileged access to certain areas of the refuge during hunting season, places where nonhunters are not allowed to enter. Some would argue that nonhunters probably don't want to hang around where birds are being shot; others might stress that if people are allowed to enter an area in order to kill animals, it's only fair that others should have access just for a look. The debate continues.

There's no debating the significance of the Bear River refuge as one of our nation's premier breeding and stopover points for many of the Western Hemisphere's majestic avian species. A visit here just about any time of year will delight, surprise, and likely overwhelm you with the sheer numbers of wildlife you'll find. Like mountain man Jim Bridger, who cruised down the Bear River in a leather boat in the mid-1800s, you may leave the Bear River delta feeling that you've just discovered a new frontier.

Mallard.

American avocets visit Bear River in the thousands. When feeding, the avocet sweeps its up-curved bill back and forth to stir up aquatic food. Often Wilson's phalaropes follow along, scooping up leftovers.

Vast reaches of sago pondweed draw waves of waterfowl and other species to Bear River NWR.

(Opposite) Artesian springs on
Fish Springs NWR support a
healthy population of Utah chubs.
They also bring color and life to
a parched, remote desert region.

Common raven.

The declining white-faced ibis visits Fish
Springs marshes during its migratory cycle.
The similar glossy ibis is generally found
from eastern Texas east to Florida and north
to Maine.

Wood duck.

Newborn mule deer fawns in Ouray's Leota Bluffs
rely on camouflage to protect them from predators.

Cliff swallow nests hang suspended from the rocks at
nearby Dinosaur National Monument.

Ouray NWR's unusual upland terrain and rich Green River riparian reaches are home to a wide range of wildlife species.

Bird sightings:

Other wildlife sightings:

Notes:

PARTIAL BIRD LIST (OF 222 LISTED SPECIES): Common loon, eared grebe, snowy egret, black-crowned night heron, tundra swan, mallard, wigeon, Barrow's golden-eye, red-breasted merganser, ferruginous hawk, golden and bald eagle, Virginia rail, lesser yellowlegs, dunlin, American avocet, black-necked stilt, white-faced ibis, Caspian tern, barn owl, calliope hummingbird, northern flicker, cliff swallow, black-billed magpie, water pipit, sage thrasher, common yellowthroat, western meadow-lark, vesper sparrow, snow bunting.

PARTIAL MAMMAL LIST (OF 29 LISTED SPECIES): Long-tailed weasel, striped skunk, marmot, red fox, muskrat.

PARTIAL HERP LIST: Wandering garter.

	R		W	H		

ADDRESS, PHONE: Fish Springs NWR, Dugway, UT 84022, (801) 831-5353.

DIRECTIONS, HOURS: From Salt Lake City, take US 80 W to Hwy 36, then S to Pony Express Route, then W to refuge; or from just N of Delta on Hwy 6, take state Road 174 to refuge; or from Wendover, take US Alt 93 S to Gold Hill turnoff then E to Pony Express Route, which goes to refuge. HQ open regular weekly business hours.

OVERVIEW, ACTIVITIES: Wildife viewing and photography, historical observation, canoeing (with restrictions), hunting.

ELEVATION: Around 4,300 feet.

WEATHER: Very hot in summer; mild spring and fall; can drop below zero in winter but generally mild; 15 inches average yearly snowfall. Spring, fall, and winter best seasons to visit.

SPECIAL NEEDS: Extra spare, sunscreen, insect repellent, self-contained food and water, good map, extra gas.

LODGING, CAMPING: Motels in Tooele, UT, and Wendover, NV; primitive camping just N of refuge on BLM site and 42 miles E along Pony Express Route.

NEARBY POINTS OF INTEREST: Great Basin National Park; Salt Lake City; Crystal Ball Cave (near Gandy); Geode Bed, 14 miles E of refuge.

DISABILITY ACCESS: Wheelchair-accessible rest room at HQ; mobility-impaired facilities at picnic ground, including wheelchair-accessible toilet.

Check a map depicting Utah's Great Salt Lake Desert and you'll find yourself staring at a lot of unmarked space. Besides the military's Dugway Proving Grounds and Deseret Test Center, where weapons of war are developed and tested, greasewood, big sage, and shadscale are the dominant communities in this remote west-central part of the Mormon state. There's little else for mapmakers to mark.

However, take a dusty drive through a hundred or so miles of this outback and you'll reach Fish Springs NWR, where a lush network of marshes rises abruptly from the desert. In this nearly waterless region, the spring-fed wetlands here are a magnet for life and draw tens of thousands of water-oriented birds each year.

Traveling the road to Fish Springs is nearly as much fun as visiting the refuge itself, especially

if getting away—really away—is your aim. In the lower 48, you can't get much more out of touch with urbanity than by visiting Fish Springs. The refuge is a 104 miles southwest of the tiny Utah town of Tooele, 78 miles northwest of Delta, and 102 miles south of Wendover, Nevada. All routes involve long stretches of primitive dirt road, some washboarded and difficult in wet weather.

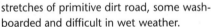

freshwater wetlands

Self-sufficiency is crucial here. Many locals carry two spares, along with extra gas. I learned the purpose of those backups one late September night when I blew a tire and found myself temporarily stranded 50 miles inside the heart of desolation. I babied that spare as if my life depended on it. To top off a truly memorable evening, after taking a wrong turn I drove an extra 2 hours along signless dirt roads before finding my way to Wendover. When I hit town, my gas tank held less than a gallon. It would have been a *very* long walk.

Despite the risks of travel here, the views, the solitude, the sense of history, and the wildness

are magnificent. Endless roads wind through rugged low mountains, crossing sere desert rises, rolling through hills and valleys swathed in tallgrass and desert shrubs. Along the canyon stretch on the approach from Delta, the hills are pocked with mines, both crumbly, sagging artifacts and operational holes that continue to spill pink earth. Antelopes range the flats and leave bedding depressions in the grass. Raptors cruise the airways, scanning for rabbits and rodents. Bobcats and coyotes skulk about the brush, opportunists alert for a meal.

All roads to Fish Springs are demanding, but the paved road from Delta takes you all but 23 miles in asphalt comfort. From any other direction, you're facing a minimum of 60 miles on dirt. Top off your gas tank at the nearest available station before setting out: If you get lost amid the network of unmarked roads, as I did, you can easily drive a hundred extra miles searching for civilization. (When I got lost on that dark and stormless night, I finally had to navigate by the moon's position to find my way out.) Occasionally in winter, the muddy roads require 4WD, as they might during the summer rainy season. Otherwise, slow driving in a solid passenger vehicle will generally get you in and out.

Settlements in the region include a few hardscrabble communities whose inhabitants scratch a rough living from the landscape. A remote Indian reservation, inhabited by the Goshute people whose ancestors have lived here for centuries, lies 25 miles west of the refuge (no services available there). Otherwise, the region is little more than mile upon mile of unroaded, waterless, people-free high desert.

Rough-and-Ready History

The marshes at Fish Springs are nearly all that remain of a vast lake that once resembled an inland sea. Around 50,000 years ago, Lake Bonneville rose to inundate much of the region, reaching 850 feet in depth and covering 20,000 square miles. From 17,000 to 10,000 years ago, the lake began to drop, until only the marshes remained near the present-day refuge. (The Great Salt Lake to the north is the main remnant of Bonneville.)

Benches on the surrounding mountains indicate ancient lake levels. The nearby Bonneville Salt Flats—mirror-flat salt deposits left by several millennia of lake evaporation—are best known for the land speed-record challenges attempted there.

Lake Bonneville's recession wasn't always a gradual process. One geological writer describes a breach of the lake into the Snake River that equaled 5 times the magnitude of any known Amazon River flood event. That deluge, which occurred around 10,000 years ago, equaled an estimated 78% of all the world's present freshwater flow—a flood of biblical proportions.

To add another note of drama to the event, Neolithic humans in the area may well have witnessed the flood. Their presence has thus far been dated back 7,000 years, though they lived in the Southwest for centuries longer and may have been here earlier, too. Numerous obsidian flakes around refuge springs testify to long-standing native presence in the area.

European visitors and settlers came in 1827, including mountain man Jedediah Strong Smith on one of his West Coast forays. Ruins of a way station for the prerail Overland Stage (service began in 1855) lie behind a fence along the road north of the refuge. In 1860–61, Pony Express riders paused at a station here for a sip and a rest; that labor-intensive mail service was soon abandoned when the railroad replaced it. The Lincoln Highway, our nation's first transcontinental thoroughfare, cut through the refuge. Broken stretches of it still remain.

Weathered remnants of the old Pony Express days exist at Fish Springs, though refuge staffers keep their location secret to prevent assaults by souvenir hunters. Even more alluring than any physical artifact is the direct experience one can gain by traveling the old Pony Express route. It runs through hills and valleys and endless flats, offering history buffs a visceral connection to the tribulations of those equine adventurers. Many of the average 5,000 yearly refuge visitors come for just such an experience.

In the late 1880s, a singular Old West character named Thomas settled on what is now the refuge and opened a way station for travelers at the present picnic area site (nicely shaded, with grills and a rest room). According to legend, Thomas was a sort of backcountry Robin Hood. When an obviously wealthy traveler dropped into his establishment for a bed and meal, Thomas fleeced him while hard-luck wayfarers were often treated to bed and board for a minimal fee. Thomas's relatives once owned a portion of the present refuge property and still live in the area.

The refuge was established in 1959, largely from BLM holdings, to support waterfowl nesting and resting along the inland Pacific Flyway. The 17,952-acre refuge has since expanded in concept to support many other species, including large numbers of shorebirds and waders.

Desert Waters

desert

Along with gas, food, water, and a good spare, bring a spotting scope to Fish Springs if you can. The refuge comprises a series of spring-fed wetlands on a tract of land that varies by only 5 feet of elevation across its length. Trees and cover are sparce at the southern edge of the Great Salt Lake Desert. With little cover other than a few trees and stands of common cane lining marsh edges, you're visible to wildlife from a mile away.

The network of ponds and marshes here arises from fossil water flowing from the Deep Creek Range to the west. Rain and snowmelt from thousands of years ago make their way underground from those mountains 1 millimeter at a time, eventually rising again in 5 main refuge springs and numerous smaller ones. Diverted and channeled through more than a hundred water-control devices, the springs supply wetland areas that are managed both for waterfowl and nonhuntable birds, most of whom are migrants. A few species remain for the winter, taking advantage of springwater temperatures that hover around 70 degrees F, even when snow is falling.

Fish Springs water is the only real thirst-quenching option in a 50-mile radius, so Pacific Flyway migratory birds of all types funnel into the refuge during their north-south journeys. Several wader rookeries are supported at Fish Springs, with great blue heron and snowy egret among the resident communal nesters. Black-crowned night heron also use the refuge, as do double-crested cormorant, white pelican, and numerous white-faced ibises. Regional birders often visit to see the only wintering great egrets in the state—2 birds that have been coming here for years. Migrating tundra swans also winter on the refuge.

Shorebird migration—a priority at Fish Springs—begins in July and is nearly over by September. Since many managed wetlands across the nation aren't flooded until after that late summer rush, regional shorebirds find relatively few stopover points on their journey. At Fish Springs, staffers attempt to create shallows and mudflats during the late summer flight period, thus attracting numerous wader and shorebird visitors.

Passerines here are relatively few, and their stays are limited to migratory rest stops. Among them are western kingfisher, Say's phoebe, rock and marsh wren, sage thrasher, Townsend's and yellow-rumped warbler, and a few evening grosbeaks in fall. Raptors are plentiful throughout the refuge; osprey pause here on their migratory travels to feast on the plentiful chub. Bald eagles visit, and a few raptors, such as red-tailed hawk and golden eagle, stay all through the year. Prairie falcons are resident except in the heat of summer.

Waterfowl are hunted on this open refuge in fall and winter; thus, they may be more skittish than usual then. Often when flocks of blue-winged teal, mallard, pintail, shoveler, and redhead rise in fear of approaching autos or booming weapons, they circle the area, evaluate the danger level, then resettle at their original resting spot. Virginia rails and sora also live here, probably in the thousands; spotting these elusive cattail dwellers takes a lot of patience and a practiced eye.

Coyotes at Fish Springs seem more confident than those in many areas—most are used to people and show no great fear of intruders. Some younger individuals go about their hunting and scavenging as if oblivious to you, though they do maintain a prudent distance. During an autumn visit, I watched a young coyote pounce on a large, dark rodent, which it carried about for several minutes before settling in to eat in plain sight. Another stood watching me for a long time from a nearby field of tallgrass before it slumped onto its belly for a rest.

Coyotes are responsible for some predation problems here, but they're tolerated by refuge management, at least for now. The reason: Studies have shown that areas with coyotes generally lack major populations of red foxes, who are highly skilled at finding and raiding marsh bird nests. Since red foxes first showed up at Fish Springs in 1994, managers have relied on coyotes to keep their numbers down.

The most voracious nest-raiding predator on the refuge isn't a mammal at all but the raven, who demonstrates its high intelligence by locating and harvesting large numbers of eggs and nestlings. Study the object you see in the claws of an overflying raven here in spring and summer; you're probably looking at a baby bird. One biologist estimates that 10 ravens have as much predatory impact on Fish Springs nests as 30 or 40 coyotes.

Masses of Utah chub, along with introduced mosquito fish and speckled dace, inhabit many of the ponds. Aided by constant, warm spring temperatures, they're also insulated geographically from exotic game fish such as largemouth bass and sunfish, which tend to wipe out less aggressive locals. The indigenous chub reaches up to 14 inches in length. It's the main food source for a number of refuge birds, including herons, egrets, osprey, and bald eagles.

The native fish, for which the refuge was named, are easy to see; they inhabit most springs and ponds. For now, the Utah chub population is not considered to be in danger. Several desert lakes and springs in the region harbor populations, insulating the species from the effects of local extirpations.

Marsh Management

Managing water at Fish Springs is a tricky business—elevation differences amount to just 5 feet across the preserve. The water-channeling process is further eroded by the actions of thousands of muskrats, who burrow into the dikes and create other problems. The presence of these pesky rodents does have a bright side, however; their incessant traveling to and fro, to and fro (add rodent music here) creates open pathways through the cattails, which aid water circulation.

Some trapping and shooting is allowed in order to control them—there remains a market for muskrat pelts—unfortunately, body-grip traps are often used; they're reputed to kill the little hairballs instantly but don't always work as advertised. When they fail, the muskrats can endure severe pain until the trapper kills and removes them.

To stimulate wetland health, each of the 9 impoundments on the refuge is emptied of water every 6 years. The plug is pulled in February, which dries and exposes bottom sediments to aerobic oxidation, speeding their decomposition. Controlled burns are often used to break down the nutrients locked into marsh vegetation. The result: "Weeds" spring up that are nutritious to waterfowl, and invertebrate populations explode, providing high-protein growth food for mothers and their young.

The technique, instituted in 1991, replaces an older management practice of flooding marshes as deeply as possible in winter and spring, hoping to maintain some depth through the hottest months. That practice was found to damage the natural marsh cycle. Mimicking the natural cycle, though it reduces wetlands acreage in late summer, supports many different species. Managers show some preference for 2,000-acre Avocet Pond during waterless months since its overall structure makes great habitat for the shorebirds and waders that the refuge supports.

Salinity on this Great Salt Lake Desert land is high, and it's aggravated by a dramatic evapo-transpiration rate that concentrates ever-higher levels of salt in areas with low water flow. Where it's highest, salt restricts plant growth to just a few species, such as salt grass and wire rush. (The limited number of salt cedar here also can cope with fairly high salinity.) Though less productive for many wildlife species, high-saline shallows and mudflats support some, including a dozen pairs of snowy plovers who nest on the refuge. (The adjoining Dugway Proving Grounds harbors 2 dozen more pairs.) A high of 175 snowies has been tallied at Fish Springs after summertime births.

Where flow is more vigorous, salts are flushed and a diverse plant community exists that includes several bulrush species, cattails, and, in deeper areas, such submergents as spiny najad and sago pondweed. The spring pools in particular are lush with submergent vegetation. Their vivid colors create jewel-like patches amid this often drab desert environment.

Fish Springs NWR is a marvel, providing life and nursery space for thousands of wildlife residents. A trip here is demanding and requires careful preparation, but the rewards can be abundant for lovers of both wildlife and history.

Impressions and Experiences

Bird sightings:

Other wildlife sightings:

Notes:

PARTIAL BIRD LIST: Eared grebe, white pelican, American bittern, tundra and trumpeter swan, mallard, pintail, shoveler, gadwall, wigeon, ruddy duck, bald and golden eagle, ring-necked pheasant, black-bellied and snowy plover, greater yellowlegs, long-billed dowitcher, ring-billed gull, broad-tailed hummingbird, western wood peewee, horned lark, raven, western and mountain bluebird, yellow warbler, common yellowthroat, rose-breasted grosbeak, green-tailed towhee, savanna sparrow, yellow-headed blackbird.

PARTIAL MAMMAL LIST: Pronghorn, mule deer, bobcat, cougar, kit fox, badger, kangaroo rat, muskrat, desert cottontail.

PARTIAL HERP LIST: Great Basin rattlesnake (never recorded in marsh area), collared and leopard lizards, desert horned lizard, Great Basin whiptail, striped whip snake, wandering garter snake, leopard frog, bullfrog.

OURAY NWR

	R		W		H	F	

ADDRESS, PHONE: 266 W 100 N, Suite 2, Vernal, UT 84078, (801) 789-0351.

DIRECTIONS, HOURS: S from Vernal 30 miles on Hwy 88 to refuge sign. Open 1 hour before sunrise to 1 hour after sunset. Gate locked at night. Field HQ office open from 7:30 a.m. to 4 p.m. weekdays. No Visitor's Center.

OVERVIEW, ACTIVITIES: River, marsh, uplands, interesting geology; wildlife viewing, rafting and canoeing, hiking, geological study (removing material prohibited), hunting in season.

ELEVATION: From 4,660 to 5,072 feet.

WEATHER: Bitterly cold in winter; moderate spring and fall; hot in summer. Spring and fall best seasons to visit.

SPECIAL NEEDS: Self-contained, especially if traveling back road from town of Ouray; insect repellent, water, good spare.

LODGING, CAMPING: Motels in Vernal and Roosevelt; primitive camping at Dinosaur National Monument, Pelican Lake, Ashley National Forest. Dog Lover Alert: Motel proprietors in nearby Vernal comprise the most rigidly antidog crowd I've ever encountered. In 1995, I was refused lodging at nearly a dozen motels before finding the only one in town—the Dinosaur Inn—that would allow my canine buddy, Arnie, to sleep on the floor. Be forewarned, and make your feelings known to locals each time you pull out your wallet.

NEARBY POINTS OF INTEREST: Dinosaur National Monument, nearby forests, Flaming Gorge Recreation Area, miles and miles of wild country surrounding refuge.

DISABILITY ACCESS: Accessible coed rest room.

The term "desert oasis" may be overused, but it's difficult to find a better description of Ouray NWR in northeastern Utah. This 11,827-acre refuge along the Green River provides a marshy wildlife habitat in a region that gets just 7 inches of rain in an average year. It's a visual oasis as well, a green feast for the eyes in a harsh land of barren brown hills and drab, weathered uplands.

Several habitats make up the refuge: multi-hued bluffs of shale and sandstone, rounded by wind and eroded by water and time; riparian corridors thick with cottonwood and willow; marshes and desert grassland; and uplands covered in greasewood, sage, rabbitbrush, and shadscale, where many species find good cover and forage.

Ducks are the main reason the refuge was formed in 1960, though this area could never have been an optimal spot for waterfowl production. The traditional USFWS obsession with ducks result-ed in the development here of habitat that does support around 5,000 waterfowl, including up to 2,000 breeding pairs of gadwall, mallard, teal, redhead, pin-tail, and also Canada goose. In fact, Canada goslings were hand-raised here at one time to help bolster the Great Basin race.

riparian

Despite the long-standing federal philosophy that equated "migratory" with "shootable" birds, Ouray NWR has always supported many nongame migratory species as well. Among them are dozens of water-loving species, including such unlikely incidentals as tundra swan (often less than 10 show up each year) and snowy plover, along with 5 gull and 4 tern species. More common are white-faced ibis, great blue heron, American bittern, avocet, stilt, and double-crested cormorant.

A good assortment of passerines, including more than 2 dozen neotropical migrants, finds habitat here that significantly eases their journey across this parched land. Some are Bell's vireo, black-headed grosbeak, and several flycatchers, including the ash-throated.

Riparian Rarity

A good part of Ouray's uniqueness lies in its riparian system. The 12-mile stretch of Green River floodplain on the refuge has escaped the full fate of most streamside habi-tats along the dammed rivers of the West, where biologists estimate that just 1% to 3% of the environment is riparian. Here water-dependent vegetation regenerates in a fairly natural way, due in part to Ouray's location downstream from the Yampa River conflu-ence. One of very few rivers in the West that has never been dammed, thus the Yampa continues at least remnants of a natural flood cycle to scour and stimulate Ouray's riverside acres. The Yampa hasn't completely "saved" this habitat, but it helps maintain it in a more natural way.

Flooding is a key to healthy riparian systems. Salts are carried away with receding high water, fertile seedbeds are shaped, exotic plant invaders are sometimes discouraged, and saplings of desirable species, such as cotton-wood and willow, are fertilized by nutrients that periodic flooding brings. Flooding also replenishes the water table, benefiting riparian plants during dry seasons. At the same time, floods can visit unruly changes upon areas managed as stable wetlands or upon other seminatural habitats in which succession is disallowed or altered.

The years 1983 and 1984 were both marked by overbank flooding on Ouray, bringing damage as well as seeds of the noxious giant whitetop, a plant that has since taken over large portions of river marsh. That flooding spurred federal overseers to rebuild existing dikes along some managed wetlands. Now, with the emphasis shifting back in favor of natural systems and cycles, they're consider-ing the removal of some of those dikes in the Leota Bottoms section in order to reestablish the natural-flood missing link.

Removing dikes would not only create natural, nutrient-rich wetlands and riparian corridors but would support local endangered native fish, mainly humpback and bonytail chub and Colorado River squawfish. Before damming, these native species found a safe haven in flooded backwaters during their larval stages. There, vulnerable fry grew stout and strong until the next flood overcame the banks and washed them back into the river.

Due to habitat loss and alteration, cold-water dam releases, and an invasion of predatory fish species, all 3 natives are in serious peril. Efforts to restore them to the Colorado River system are ongoing throughout the network of rivers and streams that feeds the mighty river.

Despite the potential benfits of natural flooding, though, removing dikes rasps against the grain of long-standing federal tradition, which tends to change slowly. Attitudes toward natural diversity and natural systems are evolving, however, and knowledge is increasing. A management plan was in the works in 1996, drawing on a variety of ecological and management input.

Natural Riparian Regeneration

Riparian habitat means, among other good things, songbird support. Corridors of streamside cottonwood, peach leaf willow, and understory growth that includes the berry-rich squaw currant, offer a freeway, rest stop, and fast-food market to migrating species, as well as to local inhabitants. With the precipitous decline of neotropical migrants throughout North America, places such as Ouray become ever more critical to their survival.

Additionally, these riparian corridors are crucial to avian reproduction. Here numerous warblers, tanagers, finches, sparrows, and towhees find good nesting habitat. Lewis's woodpecker is one summer resident that nests in the cottonwoods along the river; the migratory yellow-billed cuckoo nests here, too, as do many others, including solitary vireo, mockingbird, yellow warbler, and log-

gerhead shrike. Sharp-shinned and Cooper's hawks nest near the river on the southwest edge of the refuge, and great horned owls raise their young throughout the refuge. Great blue herons maintain two rookeries on Ouray, and cormorants also engage in communal nesting here.

Mammals, including porcupine, badger, deer, and raccoon, also benefit from the cover, shade, and food that riparian systems offer, as do numerous smaller mammals, reptiles, and amphibians.

Native (and some reintroduced) river otters live in the Green, though their furtive, clever ways make them difficult to spot. Sometimes they play in the river just south of Leota Bottom.

In the fall, several dozen elk pass through the refuge. They increase the diversity of wildlife at Ouray, but local farmers resent their crop depradations, giving rise to controversy. The state periodically sends shooters in to thin the steadily increasing elk populations.

freshwater wetlands

When local farmers realize they can make more money from wildlife-oriented tourism than from corn and alfalfa, their regard for the elk may improve. The decision to manage for wildlife as well as for crops, if that day ever comes, will benefit both the ecosystem and the local economy.

Elk can often be spotted in Woods Bottom. Their smaller cousin, the mule deer, also frequents the refuge, with bucks often sporting majestic racks. Deer seem to know the location of refuge safe zones where hunting is forbidden; frequently, they're found in non-hunting areas of the refuge, such as Sheppard Bottom. Oddly, some enjoy ranging about Leota Hills, a barren upland portion of Ouray with little cover or vegetation.

During a summertime visit, I chanced upon a mother and 2 fawns resting in the shade there. When disturbed, the adult dashed to the safety of the nearby marsh, leaving her fawns behind to remain perfectly still and silent, relying on their polka-dot camouflage to protect them.

Pronghorns are another of the large mammals who use the refuge, though they prefer to range on nearby privately owned uplands. Records from the early 1960s mention the presence of black bears on some of the Green's midstream islands and in the Leota unit, but none has been seen recently and those who survived civilization's encroachment have likely ambled on to more remote areas.

Scenery and Solitude

Aside from its varied wildlife, Ouray's landscape and remoteness offer visitors a fascinating foray into geology, solitude, and a true sense of the unfettered Old West. If no animals inhabited Ouray, many visitors would still come just for the scenery.

Leota Bluff along the northwestern reaches of the refuge is a broad canvas of geological art, where the remains of early Cenozoic species, including turtles, mammals, and fish, have been unearthed. Powell Overlook—commemorating Major John Wesley Powell, who came through here in the 1860s in historic trips through the Grand Canyon—offers long views, sullied only by the symmetrical, glaring buildings that lie directly below the bluff. This is the site of a sprawling native fish hatchery, erected a few years back to replace the old one to the north of Sheppard Bottom.

Aesthetically, the hatchery is a disaster, though locating it at the foot of Ouray's most outstanding view is somewhat justified by the presence of a well on the spot (river water would, without careful filtration, bring the eggs of exotic predators into the facility). Some 46 ponds comprise this off-limits facility, where razorback suckers are raised.

Fortunately, the view from here is so vast that with effort it's possible to overlook the glaring visual intruder. Besides, its function is a noble one. Occasionally, visitor groups tour the hatchery, where they get up close and personal

with these virtually unknown fish, who without showing their scaly mugs would have a hard time eliciting any public sympathy at all.

Navigating Ouray

Getting around the refuge isn't difficult, except during and after rain, when the roads turn to greasy mush. Rain at Ouray is as scarce as sage grouse teeth, however, and seldom presents a problem. When rain does come, roads are rarely closed for more than a day; warm winds follow a morning rain and ususally dry the road by afternoon.

Just past the entrance, a tour loop takes you through a variety of habitats in Sheppard Bottom. Numbered signs line the 9-mile route, linked to a brochure available at the loop's kiosk. The flyer offers information on Ouray's hundred-acre farm fields of milo, barley, and winter wheat and describes nearby marshes, salt cedar, riparian, river, and uplands habitats.

In the marshes you may encounter least bittern, white-faced ibis, yellow-headed blackbird, marsh wren, scaup, and possibly hooded merganser, as well as a wide variety of ducks, including ruddies. Red-tail hawk nests are perched on tall cottonwoods just southeast of the observation tower, which provides a good marsh overview.

Beyond the tour loop entrance, the main refuge road takes you nearly the entire length of Ouray's western reaches. The road carries you across uplands, past river marshes, snags, and sandbars where white pelicans and cormorants often rest, along riparian stretches that support numerous perching birds, and over a hilly area that overlooks a broad marsh known as Leota Bottom. Along the way you pass the sandstone and shale hills etched in mesmerizing patterns of erosion and layering. You can hike into the marsh areas anywhere except where signs prohibit entry.

Powell Overlook lies at the road's end, offering grand views of the refuge and far beyond. Leota Bottom is a good place to find virtually every animal species that prefers proximity to water, including many passerines, river-dwelling waterfowl, sora and Virginia rail, and numerous small to large mammals.

Ponds near the refuge entrance are a continuing source of management problems. Contaminated by selenium—probably from agriculture-caused erosion from the Mancos Shelf deposit upstream—they present a serious health risk to the many species who are drawn to them. A propane-powered boomer fires repeated shotgunlike explosions to frighten birds away from the contaminated water, which can provoke birth deformities, as well as sickness and starvation in adult birds.

A refuge plan calls for transforming at least one of the ponds into a moist-soil unit, where migrating sandhill cranes can find safe foraging. Since emergent vegetation has choked many refuge shallows over the years, cranes on the Idaho–New Mexico Flyway have become less frequent visitors. Once in a while a sandhill or whooper will drop by. At least 1 pair of sandhills resided in the wetlands in the summer of 1995.

Rugged Back Road

An access to the east side of the refuge leads to a primitive back road that can yield great wildlife and scenic viewing. It begins from the town of Ouray off Hwy 88. From town, cross the bridge and turn left onto the first paved road. Then turn right onto the dirt road. A tribal "No Trespassing" sign stands here because the entry crosses tribal land. However, visitors may pass along the road if they remain on the refuge. Drive down the road past the sign and you're on a 7-mile route into the most remote part of the refuge.

The road requires at minimum a high-clearance vehicle, preferably 4WD. Good access to several marshes lies along the road. Be prepared before you embark on this journey: stock plentiful water, a full tank of gas, and a good spare; and make sure you have the ability to walk long miles should your vehicle break down. Here you enter the heart of a beautiful, primitive environment. It's definitely worth the bumps and grinds for those in shape for some rough backcountry cruising.

Navigational hint: When in doubt, always keep to the left on your way in.

Halfway down the back road you pass through Wyasket Bottom, where numerous avian species live and play. Sometimes long-billed curlews nest in the uplands along this stretch. Farther down the road you'll approach the river for the second time. Just before you reach the Green you'll come to Wyasket Pond, which in 1995 was jammed with cattails but provided great songbird habitat. At the end of the road a hill offers wild views comparable to those at Powell Overlook. Here you'll very likely have the place all to yourself.

A scope will bring you within good sighting distance of Johnson Bottom across the river. Pelicans and geese frequent the Johnson unit, as do a diversity of ducks and shorebirds, including ruddy and pintail, yellowlegs, stilt and avocet, Wilson's and red-necked phalaropes, dowitchers and snipe.

Raptors, such as peregrine falcon, merlin, Swainson's hawk, and golden eagle, may be spotted here, as well as virtually anywhere on the refuge. In recent winters, as many as 5 dozen golden eagles have made Ouray their temporary home. One recent winter, after Wyasket Lake froze and then dried up, thousands of carp died, and some 70 eagles hung around to feed on the easy pickings.

Nearby Pelican Lake, one of Ouray's main water sources, doesn't always freeze in winter. When it remains open, it can be a good spot for viewing pelicans, eagles, horned grebes (sometimes thousands), and other winter species. Access is limited to the lake. Check with refuge personnel for information.

Seasonal Conditions

Winters get mighty cold here; thirty below isn't unusual. The river often freezes solidly enough to drive a car across (don't, though). The marshes freeze, too.

Summers get miserably hot at times, and mosquitoes can be a problem. Spring and fall, as with most western refuges, are prime times for visitors. Then the weather is mild and numerous migrating species pass through. Flowers can be abundant, particularly on the uplands where larkspur, globe mallow, sego lily, paintbrush, and several cacti spread their colorful blossoms. One endangered species, the Uinta Basin hookless cactus, resides on the refuge. You can distinguish it from other barrel cacti by the presence of a large un-hooked central spine in each barb cluster.

The Water Whammy

Unlike many western refuges, Ouray has sufficient water rights to supply its wildlife needs. The problem here isn't quantity but quality and availability. River water, which at times contains selenium, is pumped and gravity-fed to refuge wetlands during its peak elevation in the spring. That can be good for many species but often is bad for some overwater nesting ducks, whose eggs sometimes float away amid broken bundles of twigs and rushes.

Though overwater nesting may be disrupted, Ouray must take water when it can, as electric pumping always threatens to break the less than ample budget, and the sandy, shifting river creates problems for pump stations. Outdated water-control structures on the refuge contribute to dispersion problems. Conversely, riverside plots that managers try to keep shallow for shorebirds are sometimes inundated by several feet of floodwater.

Pumping water from Pelican Lake is one way to reduce the amount of selenium in refuge marshes, where levels climbed so high in the

1980s that waterfowl hunting was prohibited (to prevent hunters' consumption of toxic ducks). To get that lake water, a pipeline was built from the lake to the refuge. But endangered fish overseers decided the risk of transmitting predatory fish eggs was too high, and the pipeline was shut off. In 1995, the refuge was working to install a fine-mesh screen to filter out such eggs. Managers here also are trying to get the water-rights acquisition moved from late spring to late winter, when the water could provide and entice more waterfowl onto Ouray marshes.

Rafting the Green

The Green River offers rafters a wonderful glimpse at an environment lightly visited by humans. River trips often begin at Dinosaur National Monument to the north, passing through canyons and entering the refuge floodplain near the end of the journey. Rafting takeout is allowed at Ouray Bridge on tribal land, but tribal members require a permit for takeout there, as well as for travel down through the reservation.

One option for boaters is a takeout/launch area located on the refuge, near the silver-roofed buildings that once housed the old hatchery (near the "#9" sign on the main refuge road). The ramp is primitive but adequate, at least as long as use doesn't increase to the point that it disrupts refuge wildlife. Rafting the floodplain is a slow process, but it's one way to discover the meaning of calm and silence and to experience the timeless beauty of wild land.

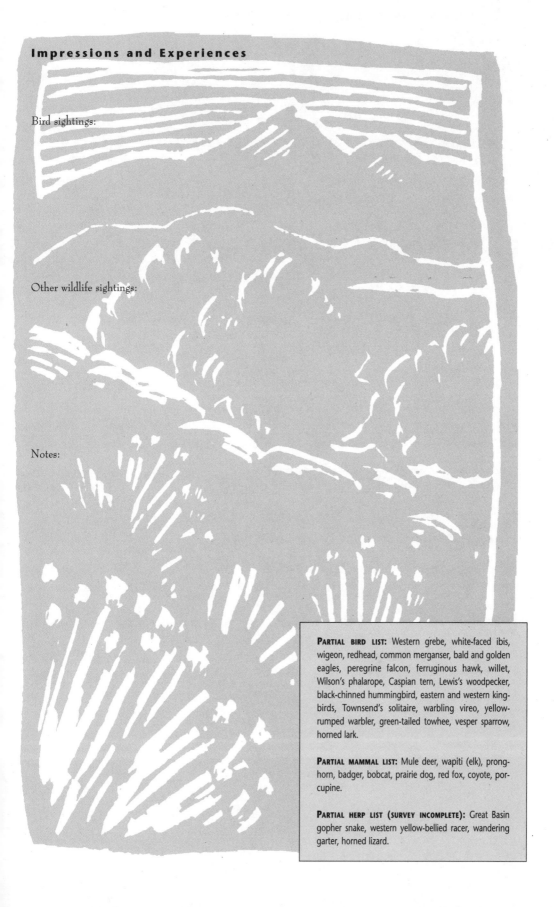

Impressions and Experiences

Bird sightings:

Other wildlife sightings:

Notes:

PARTIAL BIRD LIST: Western grebe, white-faced ibis, wigeon, redhead, common merganser, bald and golden eagles, peregrine falcon, ferruginous hawk, willet, Wilson's phalarope, Caspian tern, Lewis's woodpecker, black-chinned hummingbird, eastern and western kingbirds, Townsend's solitaire, warbling vireo, yellow-rumped warbler, green-tailed towhee, vesper sparrow, horned lark.

PARTIAL MAMMAL LIST: Mule deer, wapiti (elk), pronghorn, badger, bobcat, prairie dog, red fox, coyote, porcupine.

PARTIAL HERP LIST (SURVEY INCOMPLETE): Great Basin gopher snake, western yellow-bellied racer, wandering garter, horned lizard.

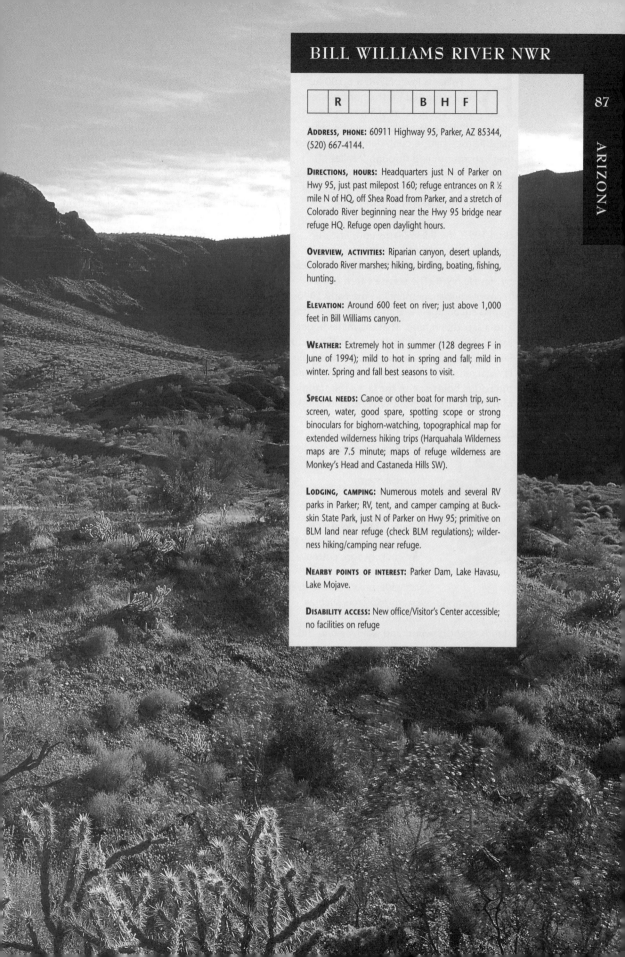

BILL WILLIAMS RIVER NWR

	R			B	H	F	

ADDRESS, PHONE: 60911 Highway 95, Parker, AZ 85344, (520) 667-4144.

DIRECTIONS, HOURS: Headquarters just N of Parker on Hwy 95, just past milepost 160; refuge entrances on R ½ mile N of HQ, off Shea Road from Parker, and a stretch of Colorado River beginning near the Hwy 95 bridge near refuge HQ. Refuge open daylight hours.

OVERVIEW, ACTIVITIES: Riparian canyon, desert uplands, Colorado River marshes; hiking, birding, boating, fishing, hunting.

ELEVATION: Around 600 feet on river; just above 1,000 feet in Bill Williams canyon.

WEATHER: Extremely hot in summer (128 degrees F in June of 1994); mild to hot in spring and fall; mild in winter. Spring and fall best seasons to visit.

SPECIAL NEEDS: Canoe or other boat for marsh trip, sunscreen, water, good spare, spotting scope or strong binoculars for bighorn-watching, topographical map for extended wilderness hiking trips (Harquahala Wilderness maps are 7.5 minute; maps of refuge wilderness are Monkey's Head and Castaneda Hills SW).

LODGING, CAMPING: Numerous motels and several RV parks in Parker; RV, tent, and camper camping at Buckskin State Park, just N of Parker on Hwy 95; primitive on BLM land near refuge (check BLM regulations); wilderness hiking/camping near refuge.

NEARBY POINTS OF INTEREST: Parker Dam, Lake Havasu, Lake Mojave.

DISABILITY ACCESS: New office/Visitor's Center accessible; no facilities on refuge

Bill Williams River NWR, a 6,100-acre refuge located on the northwestern edge of the Arizona Sonoran Desert, has everything a desert lover could want: majestic rock cliffs; a cool, densely vegetated river canyon running through 9 miles of classic Sonoran Desert; and even a marsh harboring rails and waterfowl along a peaceful stretch of cattail-lined Colorado River.

Until 1992, the Bill Williams unit, first purchased by the Nature Conservancy and subsequently by the USFWS, was part of nearby Havasu NWR. The service's turn toward "ecosystem management" in the early 1990s helped encourage the spin-off of Bill Williams into a separate refuge. That move made good sense; the canyon cut by this major Colorado River tributary is located miles from the main Havasu refuge. Perhaps even more significant, the refuge holds one of the last large stands of natural cottonwood-willow riparian forest along the Lower Colorado. Bill Williams is a unique ecosystem, deserving of its own special status in the refuge system.

riparian

Dam Site Worse

A century ago, cotton-wood riparian forest was widespread on the river. In their journals, western explorers such as Gen. John C. Frémont noted miles-thick stands of cottonwood and willow along the banks. They also mentioned the presence of abundant mesquite on the higher reaches. The Colorado's use as a steamboat route for a time placed heavy demands on cottonwoods as engine fuel, depleting the stands severely. The forests resurged in the early decades of this century as boat traffic subsided. For a while, it looked as if the Industrial Age would spare the Lower Colorado River ecosystem.

Then in the 1930s the dams came: 726-foot Hoover Dam on the Arizona–Nevada border in 1935, followed by twenty smaller impoundments over the following decades. As the water backed up into a series of lakes, many of the riparian forests along the river were drowned.

Only a few riparian stretches, primarily on the Gila and Bill Williams tributaries, still harbor the old river forest. Instead, the Colorado corridor these days comprises desert and barren rock, inundating lakes, and cropland in the lower valley. For that reason, resident and migratory wildlife flock to Bill Williams for sustenance.

Unfortunately, the Bureau of Reclamation and the Corps of Engineers weren't satisfied with altering the Colorado River ecosystem. In 1968, Alamo Dam was erected on the Bill Williams, 40 miles above the present refuge site. The old flood cycle was eradicated on the river, and the average flow diminished to a trickle; much of the riparian growth died off here, too. (Few existing cottonwoods on the refuge predate 1968.) Long stretches of opportunistic salt cedar moved in to replace dead native trees along the canyon, choking out natives and substantially increasing the potential for wildfires.

Fortunately, the canyon bottom has resisted full encroachment by tamarisk and still contains a fair number of native trees. Plenty of good habitat exists here for neotropical and resident birds, and larger inhabitants, such as bobcat, mountain lion, ringtail cat, and javelina, and many small mammals and herptiles continue to find the Bill Williams River and canyon a lush living space. Desert bighorn sheep also maintain a foothold on the cliffs surrounding the refuge despite development pressures and rare hunts that take place in the area.

Saving what's left of the old ecosystem and enhancing that system where possible is the twofold purpose of this refuge. That means providing sanctuary for the canyon's desert and riparian species, restoring native vegetation, reintroducing extirpated fishes in both the Colorado and Bill Williams rivers, and otherwise struggling to preserve a tiny fraction of a centuries-old environment from the ravages of a grasping world.

Bill Williams River and Canyon

The refuge follows 9 miles of the Bill Williams River from its delta at the Colorado toward Alamo Dam 40 miles upstream. The canyon is the refuge's center-piece. Flowing gently along except during sporadic dam releases, the river that carved the canyon maintains an average rate of less than 50 cubic feet per second (cfs). Its depth is perfect for wading ankle-deep in the sandy bottom along a canopied passage that cuts a path through dense riparian growth.

Wading the meandering course, either bare-foot or wearing wet-dry sandals, is the best way to explore this section of the refuge. No developed trails exist here, and thick stands of tamarisk impede hiker mobility to just a few yards on either side of the stream-bed. Too, the canopied area can be 10 or more degrees cooler than the surrounding desert.

Birds thrive here, flitting constantly across the riverbed. The bright colors of species, such as yellow warbler, vermilion flycatcher, and summer tanager, flash like sparks in the desert sky.

Wildlife watchers can find sandy stretches along the creek for resting, picnicking, or catching a little sun. Crisscrossing tracks in the sand chronicle the nighttime excursions of cottontails, javelina, and deer, as well as predatory coyotes, bobcats, and less common cougars. The thin, dragged-and-dotted imprints of various invertebrates testify to a parallel microworld along the riverbanks.

In some pools you might spot native fish species, such as longfin dace. Reintroduced with the aid of biologist-led Youth Conservation Corps crews, these and other natives may once more find a finhold in this part of their historic habitat.

A road running off Hwy 95, less than a mile northeast of refuge headquarters, takes you to the lower river, through desert uplands, and past a valley lined with cottonwoods, willows, and salt cedar. Along the way you can stop and explore the desert and cliff-base habitat, where phainopepla and cactus wren are common. Walk out on cactus-flecked rises and look north to scan the cottonwood crowns at eye level. Here you might spot a summer tanager, Bullock's oriole, any of several warbler migrants, or the elusive yellow-billed cuckoo that often perches amid the tree's thick central branches.

The refuge gate, 3 miles up the road, may or may not be locked. (In 1996, an agreement was made to leave it unlocked. That may or may not change.) If it isn't open, no problem. Park and walk the streambed. You'll find yourself in the same cool, canopied environment you would enter farther upriver.

Man-Made Floods

Think twice about proceeding past the gate in a vehicle, especially of the passenger variety. The road is often mushy or obliterated, and it's illegal to leave the right-of-way. Due to the road's condition, you may not know exactly where that right-of-way is, and the result of being caught wandering off-road is a ticket. Hiking up from the gate is the best way to go.

desert

In 1993 the county had recently finished its regular grading of the road; shortly after, a hundred-year flood spurred the Corps of Engineers to release the maximum-allowed 7,000 cfs from Alamo Dam. They regraded the road in the winter of 1994. Another huge outflow was released the following March to save a flood-threatened bald eagle nest on the lake. The 6,800 cfs release inundated the road, the canyon, a 1,500-tree nursery of cottonwoods that refuge staffers were cultivating, and all the work the county had just completed. (Graders finally got the road through to Mineral Wash again in 1995.)

Fortunately, the artificial flood dispersed thousands of cottonwood seeds down the canyon, as floods do in a natural system. Regeneration of cottonwoods has begun due to that inadvertent act of ecological benevolence, and refuge managers actually express delight that the inundation occurred. It probably encouraged the development of many more than the 1,500 trees they were nursing.

Similar artificial flooding can occur any time a heavy rain overfills Alamo Lake. The releases don't come in walls of raging water; rather, the stream rises perceptibly over the course of a few hours. If you've driven beyond the gate and notice the water deepening, it's time to leave. Quickly! Wait too long and you may have to walk out, leaving your vehicle behind for days or even weeks.

Dam operators notify the refuge and nearby landowners of releases, but the refuge staff isn't responsible for clearing people off county roads (even if they had the staff to do so). Recently, various state, county, and federal agencies involved in managing the canyon, lake, and river have begun striving to better cooperate with one another. If you plan to enter the canyon when the lake is likely to rise, call the refuge for information before proceeding.

Hike the full 6-mile length of the refuge's river canyon that lies beyond the gate and you'll eventually reach a stretch bordered by majestic cliffs. There's no camping on Bill Williams; estimate your hiking time judiciously so that you can return to your vehicle before nightfall.

Along with the camping ban, rattlesnakes are another good reason to limit hiking at night. Sidewinders, Mojaves, and diamondbacks are highly mobile at dawn, dusk, and twilight hours, and they may be out roaming during any month. In daytime heat they recede to cooler spots, such as rodent burrows or crevices, so watch where you put your hands and feet. Hike at night and you're tempting fate and fangs, especially when cutting through brush. Be careful, but don't let the fear of snakes deter you from a soul-cleansing hike.

Shea Road

From the nearby town of Parker, you can also reach the refuge via Shea Road, which runs eastward off Hwy 95 on the south end of town. The road runs through BLM desert land and past wilderness-designated stretches. You can camp anywhere on BLM land (learn and obey their regulations), and you can hike and camp in the wilderness areas. Along this stretch you might spot a horned lizard or desert iguana, as well as desert birds including phainopepla, ash-throated flycatcher, loggerhead shrike, roadrunner, horned lark, and many others. Birds are thickest in the washes lined with palo verde, ironwood, and mesquite, though some, including raptors and Gila woodpeckers, often perch on saguaros. Here you may also spot a coyote, badger, or bobcat. If you're truly blessed, a cougar may pad across your path.

Some of the saguaros along this stretch have been shotgunned or otherwise assaulted. Healing of the desert is evident throughout the area. Old roads and tracks disappear (with excruciating slowness) beneath native shrubs; gouged earth smooths out over decades, until it again takes on a less damaged appearance. Wilderness designation and BLM fencing here is just what the land doctor ordered.

Twelve miles up Shea Road, you'll come to an intersection marked "Swansea, 17 miles." The south-running road leads to two interesting sites. Less than a mile from the turnoff on your left, a fenced area protects a huge earthen intaglio of a snake. The raised-earth figure, dozens of yards in length, was constructed centuries ago by resident Native Americans for unknown reasons, though archaeologists conjecture that such earthen forms have ceremonial significance. In spring when desert plants are green you can distinguish its shape most easily; in summer heat and winter repose the brown brush obscures it.

The 17-mile side road continues on to Swansea Ghost Town, an abandoned mining settlement that evokes a long-gone pioneering time in western history.

Return to the main route and you enter a wash-carved area that shelters numerous desert birds. Sixteen miles from the Parker turnoff the pavement ends and you pass over the ill-fated Central Arizona Project canal—a multimillion-dollar project to bring water south from the Colorado River. This mighty effort resulted in the delivery of water so foul that virtually no Tucson resident would drink it. (In 1995, officials were developing a plan to mix CAP water with aquifer water to dilute the salt saturation.)

Three miles beyond the canal, the road brings you down into a sandy wash that enters the river. 4WD is recommended here, though some confident souls regularly make the trip in 2WD. I traveled a short distance through the sandy mush in a 2WD pickup and turned back. If you choose to continue on, you'll find the same type of canyon and river as on the other end of the refuge.

Just before you reach the wash, the road splits off to the right; take this turn and you'll enter the desert uplands on BLM land. Watch for curve-billed thrasher, antelope ground squirrel, turkey vulture, desert iguana, and desert horned lizard, among many other dry-country dwellers.

River Marsh Unit

The refuge encompasses a short stretch of the Colorado River flanked by a shallow, cattail-lined marsh. (Be careful navigating here; boats can get stuck on sandbars.) A small number of birds, such as pied-billed and eared grebes, nest in a few sheltered inlets along this stretch, and Canada geese visit in winter, cruising the river alongside numerous Clark's grebes. About a dozen endangered Yuma clapper rails spend the warmer months in the cattails and may overwinter (no one knows for certain).

Bald eagles winter in the area and may be spotted hunting for fish in the river. Red-breasted merganser is another species that uses the marsh area, along with yellow-breasted chat, common yellowthroat, and red-winged blackbird.

If you visit the marsh by boat, you'll do the birds a big favor by cruising slowly and remaining in the middle of the river. Stay out of backwater areas, especially in spring and early summer—many species hide and nest there. Brooders will leave their nests when frightened, and if they don't return soon, the eggs may broil in the desert sun.

You can launch from a mile below the refuge office on Parker Dam Road, at Take Off Point. Canoes and hand-carried boats may be launched from the refuge headquarters. Be sure to be out by 4 P.M., when the gate is locked, if you wish to take your boat out on refuge grounds.

The "no wake" zone along this river stretch can be a peaceful place, particularly if you go by canoe or kill your motor and paddle once you've reached the marsh. Jagged desert mountains tower above you, wrapped by a searing blue sky; golden cattails wave in the breeze and harbor great blue herons, egrets, and rails. The hiss of traffic on Hwy 95 recedes as you enter body and spirit into this beautiful stretch of river.

If you go by canoe, leave early in the morning when winds tend to be minimal, especially in spring. If the wind kicks up, move your craft to the edge of the cattails, where the surface isn't so rough, and beach it rather than attempt to fight whitecapped waves. If the wind seems brisk, be wise and postpone your canoe trip until a gentler time.

Native Fish Restoration

Just below the refuge headquarters lies a bermed inlet in which thousands of razorback suckers and bonytail chubs are raised. The two species are among 31 native Arizona fish, 28 of which are either endangered, threatened, or candidates for listing. Another is already extinct.

Numerous factors have accounted for the decline of fish native in Arizona and to the western states in general. Damming may be the foremost culprit, disrupting spawning paths and changing river ecosystems. Decreased water turbidity has probably increased the ability of native and nonnative predators to catch and consume vulnerable young. Introduced fish, most from the Mississippi River drainage, bring increased competition for food and space. Voracious species, such as striped bass, channel catfish, carp, and various sunfish, are superefficient predators, consuming millions of helpless natives before they reach survivable size. Pollutants, such as selenium and farm pesticides, have also damaged Colorado River fish reproduction and growth.

All the lower Colorado River refuges are involved in native fish restoration, as is a wide collection of federal, state, and private entities, cooperating in programs such as a coordinated Lake Mojave fish restoration project and other efforts to return native species to the Colorado River, lakes, backwaters, and "free-flowing" stretches.

Recovery of native fish at Bill Williams begins when biologists receive fingerling razorback suckers and bonytail chubs from Dexter National Fish Hatchery, a New Mexico facility that rears endangered fish. The near-microbial fry are placed in aquariums, where they're grown to a few centimeters. From that point, they're introduced into the riverside grow-out facility, where they'll grow to around 10 inches—a size that offers them a chance against predators.

At that point they're released back into the lake and other areas, after being injected with tiny scannable devices known as Passive Integrated Transponders, employed to gather information on recaught fish. Fish biologists use whatever bodies of water they can find for growout purposes. Bonytail chubs have even been introduced into ponds at the Emerald Canyon golf course in the town of Parker.

Native species may live for 30 years or more, so a successful reintroduction may create a stable population for decades. The long-term recovery plan involves first using refuge sanctuaries, then finding off-refuge sites of a hundred or more acres—such as river oxbows—then gradually reintroducing natives into secured stretches of free-flowing river.

Unfortunately, political pressure from water interests has prevented endangered bonytail chubs from being released into the Colorado River below Parker Dam. Those interests fear the restrictions that the presence of protected native fish might cause their commercial operations.

The ecological and political problems that native fish continue to face are enormous. Without sufficient protected river and lake habitat, chances are slim that new recruits will overcome the problems that endangered them in the first place. But we have to try.

Bird sightings:

Other wildlife sightings:

Notes:

PARTIAL BIRD LIST: Yellow-billed cuckoo, yellow-rumped warbler, black-tailed gnatcatcher, ash-throated flycatcher, red-breasted merganser, great egret, bald eagle, peregrine falcon, cactus wren, phainopepla, summer tanager, black-and-white warbler.

PARTIAL MAMMAL LIST: Cougar, bobcat, desert bighorn sheep, mule deer, raccoon, striped skunk, ringtail cat, javelina, antelope ground squirrel, wood rat.

PARTIAL HERP LIST: Mojave and diamondback rattlesnakes, California king snake, gopher snake, desert iguana, desert spiny lizard, desert horned lizard, red-spotted toad, lowland leopard frog (the only population left on the lower Colorado River).

BUENOS AIRES NWR

VC	R	C		W		H		

ADDRESS, PHONE: PO Box 109, Sasabe, AZ 85633, (520) 823-4251.

DIRECTIONS, HOURS: Hwy 86 (Ajo Way) W from Tucson to Robles Junction; 38 miles S to refuge entrance. Sub-station in town of Arivaca. S from Tucson on I-I-19, W at Arivaca Amado exit to refuge. Main section of refuge open 24 hours a day. Visitor's Center open 7:30 a.m. to 4 p.m. Mon thru Fri, except holidays. Brochures available from kiosks at trailheads near Arivaca.

OVERVIEW, ACTIVITIES: Desert grasslands, marsh, riparian canyon; wildlife viewing, birding, backcountry driving, hiking, photography, camping.

ELEVATION: From 3,200 to 4,700 feet.

WEATHER: Moderate fall thru spring (some winter days can get very cold); extremely hot in summer. Spring and fall best seasons to visit.

SPECIAL NEEDS: Self-contained for backcountry travel, water, good spare, sunscreen, sturdy footwear.

LODGING, CAMPING: Dude ranch in Sasabe, small motel near Arivaca; camping and RV hookups just S of Arivaca; also primitive camping on refuge on designated sites.

NEARBY POINTS OF INTEREST: Arizona–Sonora Desert Museum outside Tucson; road up to Mount Lemmon above Tucson (to 10,000 feet; great views) and several mountain and desert areas around city (stop by Visitor's Bureau); Saguaro National Park near Tucson; Biosphere II N of Tucson; Madera Canyon, 50 miles E, and Sycamore Canyon, 35 miles E (birding hotspots, with Mexican species, including elegant trogon and sulphur-bellied fly-catcher).

DISABILITY ACCESS: Rest rooms at HQ; trails in Arivaca are accessible at challenge level.

As you approach the main Visitor's Center of 115,000-acre Buenos Aires NWR in southern Arizona, don't be surprised if you feel transported to the wilds of some misplaced African savanna. The thick carpet of grassland here runs off for miles in all directions, creating a broad, rolling plain reminiscent of east Africa's animal-rich grasslands. The habitat at Buenos Aires seems an anomaly in the heart of the Sonoran Desert, but the elevation here of around a thousand feet above the desert floor is sufficient to create a slightly moister environment, with an accompanying change in biota.

This remote refuge, created from an Altar Valley ranch in 1985 to preserve habitat for the endangered masked bobwhite, is a place of long views, rolling hills wrapped by distant jagged mountains, and burning sunsets over the nearby Baboquivari Mountains. Its habitats are varied, including classic Sonoran

desert

Desert, a lush riparian stretch along the area's only perennial water source, a marshy cienega, and acres of rolling grassland.

More than 100 miles of rough, primitive road-ways wind through the heart and soul of the grass-covered hills. Some 130 ephemeral ponds provide critical seasonal water sources for wild residents and support at least one at-risk species, the Chihuahuan leopard frog. Ninety marked campsites provide visitors with space to settle in and become more intimately involved in the landscape and its residents.

The African analogy is furthered by the presence—generally within a mile or two of the main Visitor's Center—of a herd of some 60 desert pronghorns. These are the originals or progeny of a transplanted herd of the Chihuahuan subspecies. (Transplants are tagged in red; unbanded individuals are refuge-born.) Their familiarity with people has rendered them relatively tame; stay in your vehicle and drive slowly and you'll find you can approach them quite closely.

Pronghorns are often called "antelope," but pronghorns are not actually in the antelope family. They are their own species, one that has evolved in North America for eons. Some of their prehistoric ancestors were huge; at least one species was three-horned, much like a rhinoceros. Pronghorns are swift range dwellers who favor long views on all sides, a safeguard against predators. Though they appear remarkably similar to several African antelope species, they're a truly homegrown, wild American ungulate.

Buenos Aires's African analogy isn't totally fanciful. Rolling hills that cover the lower two-thirds of the refuge to the Mexican border are covered in Lehman's love grass, an African transplant imported by ranchers to repair decades of overgrazing that had left the land severely eroded and nearly barren.

Though it does provide thick cover, love grass is an exotic that aggressively squeezes out various species of native grama and other indigenous plants that otherwise would thrive here. Following their mandate to maintain or redevelop the historic natural environment, refuge personnel are working to induce regeneration of native grass species. The major tool is controlled burning. With the help of fire they're making progress, one fuzzy acre at a time.

Habitat Diversity = Wildlife Diversity

Though located on the Mexican border in the heart of the Sonoran Desert, Buenos Aires contains a variety of habitats that can make animal watching here a surprise-filled treasure hunt. The northern third is Sonoran Desert, characterized by vast acres of creosote, mesquite, desert broom, palo verde, and a few saguaros. Here you may find an assortment of desert dwellers, including javelina, mule deer, antelope, black-tail jackrabbits, Gila monster, western diamondback and Mojave rattlers, and other arid-loving ground species. Birds (the refuge list totals 300 species) may include northern harrier, loggerhead shrike, western kingbird, phainopepla, and many others.

As you cruise down Hwy 286, you climb in elevation. Soon the classic desert biome recedes in favor of grassland—though arid-loving prickly pear, cholla, and other desert plants continue to appear in scattered clumps. Deeper into the grassland you may spot pronghorns, javelina, deer, golden eagle in winter, Swainson's hawk year-round, and along the northern habitat transition line individuals from three nesting pairs of black-shouldered kites in residence since 1995.

In the case of Buenos Aires birds, anything goes. The refuge's proximity to the Gulf of California, for instance, might yield any of a number of seabirds. Aguirre Lake, when it has water, attracts a wide range of species, including waders and shorebirds. Here you might see American avocet, stilt, osprey (who come briefly to fish but generally leave frustrated), blue- and black-headed grosbeaks, and at least one faithful merlin, seen each winter for the past several years. A white-rumped sandpiper was spotted here in 1993. There's no telling what else might show up at this ephemeral pond just southwest of the Visitor's Center.

Antelope Drive, a 10-mile tour road south of the main Visitor's Center, is a good place for spotting pronghorn, Coues white-tail and mule deer, javelina, and possibly a cat or two at dawn or dusk. Desert birds, such as thrasher, cactus wren, phainopepla, and others, can also be found here. Dozens of horned larks and vesper sparrows often inhabit the roadway within the first mile or two of the tour road.

Desert Wetlands

Two of the most interesting areas of the refuge lie on its eastern edge, on the periphery of the town of Arivaca. Here runs Arivaca Creek, the area's only constant water source, which creates two important habitats that draw a wide range of animal species. Since Arivaca Creek and the cienega are located miles from the main Visitor's Center, a substation in town has been established for people whose main interest is birding—although deer, javelina, rattlesnakes, frogs, and many other creatures inhabit these wet areas.

Arivaca Creek lies just southwest of the town of Arivaca. From the parking lot, you can stroll across a mesquite-decked upland area, where you'll find vermilion flycatcher, verdin, Lucy's warbler, and others. A short distance down the trail you reach the creek, a deep-cut arroyo through which the shallow creek meanders beneath a canopy of ancient cottonwoods and overhanging willows.

Here you'll find a wealth of bird life, especially during spring migration. Summer tanagers are abundant, along with a good mix of warblers, including Wilson's, yellow, yellow-rumped (Audubon's), and Lucy's, and more than a dozen other varieties. Gray hawk, thick-billed and tropical kingbird, green kingfisher, buff-collared nightjar, and Costa's hummingbird are just some of the unique species that make their homes in or travel through the area.

A new land acquisition (likely open to visitors by 1997) expands the refuge habitat to include a montane riparian canyon. Brown Canyon, at the base of the Baboquivaris on the northwest corner of the refuge, is a rich environment of sycamore, willow, live oak, and, in its upper reaches, less common hardwoods such as walnut. The creekside habitat attracts numerous species, including ringtail, coatimundi, deer, painted redstart, hooded and Scott's oriole, and 9 species of hummingbirds, including Costa's. This unique hummer species performs a wondrous spring mating ritual, whirring in broad elliptical sweeps through the air, accompanied by a loud, descending buzz that resembles the sound of a bomb falling. The show can go on for hours—a tribute both to the Costa's passion and stamina.

riparian

Link in an Ecosystem Chain

Buenos Aires is important not only for the variety of habitats it holds but because it helps complete a regional linkage of wild land, relatively untouched by progress. To the west run the towering Baboquivaris. That range separates the refuge from the Tohono O'odhams, a desert-dwelling Native American tribe whose ancestors have wrested a living from the area for thousands of years. To the northeast run the Cerro Colorados; to the southeast the San Luis Mountains line the preserve.

The high country of the Baboquivaris, known as a "sky island" due to its discrete rise from an insulating sea of desert, creates fertile ground for a variety of distinct plant and animal subspecies. The montane environment also provides a wild "animal causeway" that allows larger mammals, as well as many bird species, to roam, feed, mate, reproduce, and thrive.

The Pozo Verdes flank the southwest border of Buenos Aires below the Baboquivaris, reaching down into Mexico to create safe passage for numerous creatures, including deer, coatis, mountain lions, and possibly even jaguars, which once roamed the area. Recently, a local cowboy encountered a black cat in the northwest corner of the refuge. Biologists believe he may have spotted an *onca,* which may be a hybrid jaguar–mountain lion or, somewhat less exciting, a cougar wearing its darkest color phase. The spots on the animal, however, are an intriguing anomaly.

Buenos Aires also provides a critical link in a regional ecosystem of connected federal lands. The system includes land managed by the Forest Service, the Bureau of Land Management, the Park Service, and, on its western reaches, Cabeza Prieta NWR, one of the wildest places in North America. As habitat across the West declines, broad, connected wild lands are critical in sustaining numerous populations of wildlife.

Bobwhite Blues

One important native that the USFWS is working to reinstate here is the masked bobwhite, a once-plentiful species that disappeared from the area by the turn of the century. Though a limited population still

ranges freely in Mexico, overgrazing here eradicated the grasslands and encouraged mesquite and other brush to grow in its place, disrupting the bobwhite's lifeways. Later, introduced exotic grasses crowded out the native grass on which the bobwhite depends. With these changes, the US population crashed.

Reintroduction began in the 1970s, 15 years before the refuge was established, but cattle in the valley destroyed much of the habitat and biologists had to start over. Buenos Aires Ranch was purchased by the federal government in 1985 to protect masked bobwhite habitat. Cattle were removed and controlled burns were instituted to enhance the native grassland environment.

The present reintroduction effort involves pairing baby masked bobwhites with their cousin, the Texas bobwhite. Biologists hope that the Texas species can help the masked learn to feed and survive in the wild. By 1995, around 20,000 young masked bobwhites had been released onto the refuge.

The reintroduction process has had mixed results. With the release of around 1,500 birds per year in recent years, the population may be growing. How much is hard to say. The masked bobwhite has an aggravating habit of playing hide-and-seek with surveyors. A biologist can stand 3 feet from a hidden bird or flock and not see a single individual, as one of the bobwhite's main defenses involves hunching down and being very, very quiet. Sometimes researchers remain in a spot for half an hour, seeing nothing; then they get up to leave and several birds bolt from the nearby grass.

Also frustrating biologists is the tendency of adult and juvenile releases to stray from one another. To counter that behavior, biologists are trying such options as releasing young masked bobwhites after the normal breeding and fledging season, when subadults and adults tend to congregate naturally. They're also holding some young back, allowing them to age a few more months in order to increase their survivability. The effort is not pure science; it's learn as you go, and that's what several dedicated biologists here are doing.

For birders, the bobwhite's secretive behavior means that a sighting is unlikely. With luck you might encounter one on a roadway or spot the lone individual who visited the feeder most mornings in the spring of 1995. But chances are you'll never even come close to one—or if you do, you won't know it. Go to Buenos Aires to explore this intriguing environment; don't go to see masked bobwhites.

Reintroduction efforts have hardly been aided by the US Air Force, which maintains a jet training range in the skies overhead. Though they promised refuge personnel they'd keep their jets at least a couple of miles from bobwhite holding facilities, they haven't honored that promise. During my visit in May 1995, I observed loud daily flights directly over the pens. When startled, these highly endangered birds thrash madly about their enclosures. The potential for injury or death is very real, and those errant pilots, and their superiors, could use some attitude adjustment.

Wild, Wonderful Land

Despite those roaring displays, Buenos Aires makes for a rewarding wildlife-oriented visit. Sunsets over the Baboquivaris can be spectacular. Sunrise, raking the grassland, bathes the land in a warm, wavering glow.

Roads that line the refuge are rough in places, requiring at least a high-clearance vehicle, better a 4WD. Getting stuck here, though it might seem a minor problem, still can put you miles from help. In midsummer, or during frequent winter freezes, a stranding can be dangerous. Self-reliance is mandatory for anyone entering refuge backcountry.

If possible, plan at least a 2-day visit to this multifaceted refuge. Spend a day visiting the grasslands and experience the beauty of endless vistas in a prairielike environment, where pronghorns and raptors range about and coyotes howl in the distance. You can easily spend another day in the marsh and creek areas near the town of Arivaca, especially if you're a birder and especially during spring migration—at that time each clump of vegetation, each bend in the trail seems to yield yet another winged surprise.

Birder or not, you'll come away from Buenos Aires refreshed, reinvigorated, and blessed with a new connection to the wild creatures who share our land.

Impressions and Experiences

Bird sightings:

Other wildlife sightings:

Notes:

PARTIAL BIRD LIST (OF 290 LISTED SPECIES): Masked bobwhite, eared grebe, least bittern, snowy egret, black-bellied whistling duck, gadwall, black-necked stilt, Wilson's phalarope, Baird's sandpiper, least tern, Swainson's hawk, black hawk, gray hawk, Montezuma quail, elf owl, Anna's hummingbird, thick-billed kingbird, sulphur-bellied flycatcher, bank swallow, canyon wren, crissal thrasher, Nashville warbler, black-throated green warbler, painted redstart, pyrrhuloxia, Botteri's sparrow.

PARTIAL MAMMAL LIST: Mountain lion, mule and white-tail deer, pronghorn, javelina, coati, ringtail, kit fox, coyote, Mexican opposum, long-tongued bat, red bat, white-footed mouse.

PARTIAL HERP LIST: Sonoran whip snake, long-nosed snake, Mojave rattlesnake, zebra-tailed lizard, Gila monster, Arizona alligator lizard, Great Plains skink, desert tortoise, Sonora mud turtle, southern spadefoot toad, Chiricahuan leopard frog.

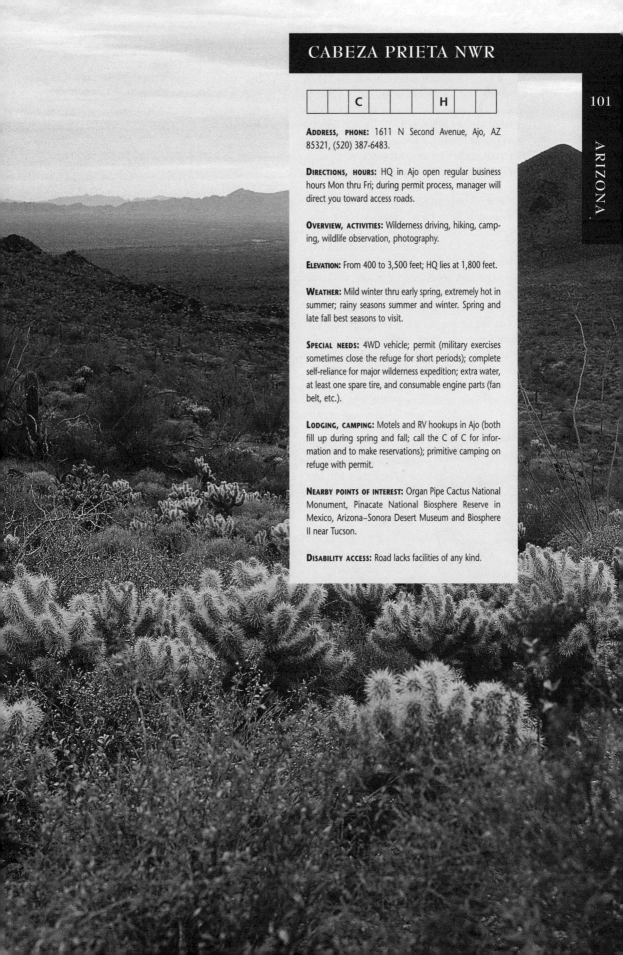

CABEZA PRIETA NWR

		C			H		

ADDRESS, PHONE: 1611 N Second Avenue, Ajo, AZ 85321, (520) 387-6483.

DIRECTIONS, HOURS: HQ in Ajo open regular business hours Mon thru Fri; during permit process, manager will direct you toward access roads.

OVERVIEW, ACTIVITIES: Wilderness driving, hiking, camping, wildlife observation, photography.

ELEVATION: From 400 to 3,500 feet; HQ lies at 1,800 feet.

WEATHER: Mild winter thru early spring, extremely hot in summer; rainy seasons summer and winter. Spring and late fall best seasons to visit.

SPECIAL NEEDS: 4WD vehicle; permit (military exercises sometimes close the refuge for short periods); complete self-reliance for major wilderness expedition; extra water, at least one spare tire, and consumable engine parts (fan belt, etc.).

LODGING, CAMPING: Motels and RV hookups in Ajo (both fill up during spring and fall; call the C of C for information and to make reservations); primitive camping on refuge with permit.

NEARBY POINTS OF INTEREST: Organ Pipe Cactus National Monument, Pinacate National Biosphere Reserve in Mexico, Arizona–Sonora Desert Museum and Biosphere II near Tucson.

DISABILITY ACCESS: Road lacks facilities of any kind.

At 860,000 acres, Cabeza Prieta NWR in south-central Arizona stands nearly alone among a handful of comparably large refuges in the system. Three maps, drawn in progressively greater scale, are required to orient oneself to this vast piece of semi-protected desert along the Mexican border.

Cabeza's rugged Sonoran landscape is not for everyone. Only hardy, desert-loving visitors will find this trip rewarding. A single 4WD trail crosses its 61-mile reach (totaling 125 miles from one highway to another), branching toward two egresses on the west end. Along the way the road passes through endless creosote-bursage flats, with an occasional saguaro jutting from this plain. Shallow washes are somewhat more wildlife-friendly, lined with desert trees that include mesquite, ironwood, and desert willow, along with a variety of shrubs and smaller plants. *Bajadas* sloping down from mountains on the refuge harbor an even greater variety of life.

desert

Broken by a dozen low granite and lava mountains that rise as high as 3,500 feet, the desert flats here create a dry, harsh, silent (at times) ecosystem, largely in balance, as it has been for centuries, and scarcely touched by human ambition.

The somewhat monocultural surface of Cabeza is deceptive: This nearly waterless environment holds some of the most stirring secrets of life on our planet. Survival strategies among the plants and animals of the Sonoran are so ingenious that one might wonder if they don't possess a special intelligence of their own. Otherwise, how could they possibly make it through a single broiling desert summer?

Plants in this harsh land grow waxy coatings; some turn their leaf edges toward the sun during midday to reduce transpiration; others shed their leaves altogether; while still others have adapted hard, sharp needles in lieu of leaves, protecting themselves from browsers and reducing water loss. Such plants generally maintain photosynthesis through their bark or skin. A few flowers bloom only at night or just after sunrise, their cryptic beauty wilting away with the rising of the sun.

Animals such as the kangaroo rat, and possibly the pronghorn and kit fox, can go without drinking water for their entire lives. Wildlife activity is greatest at night. Biologists have reported that during the heat of summer days, they've had normally wary jackrabbits slump down close to share a patch of shade, seemingly oblivious to the human presence a few feet away. When wildlife ignores its survival impulse to rest beside a potential predator, you know things are tough.

Harsh History

The refuge, named for a dark-headed peak on its western side, was founded in 1939 to protect desert bighorn sheep; an estimated 500 now survive on Cabeza. But it also serves as an aerial fighter range for military top guns; thus, permits are required for anyone entering the refuge, and sometimes visits must be postponed. A 4WD vehicle is mandatory here, too, and other strict rules apply to all visitors.

In 1990, much of Cabeza Prieta was added to the National Wilderness Preservation System. The refuge is an anomaly: a "wilderness" with a road running through it. Partly due to Cabeza's status, management directions are presently under review. Options for the future may include reopening the road to 2WD vehicles, staying with the 4WD mandate, or, most dramatic, banning all visitation. (Call before visiting.)

The name of Cabeza's main thoroughfare hints at the sort of trip visitors can expect. *El Camino del Diablo,* the Devil's Highway, is part of a 4-century-old route that began in northern Mexico and continued to Yuma and on to the West Coast. The route was first negotiated by Spanish Capt. Melchior Díaz, who led a detachment of Coronado's expedition through the area in 1540, with the help of local Indians.

The Jesuit priest Father Eusebio Francisco Kino explored the area between 1698 and 1702, preaching to the locals, demonstrating agriculture techniques, and mapping the trail and its water holes. Another route north of Cabeza was easier on the human circulatory system, but raging Apaches along that trail made using it a serious gamble with potentially lethal results.

El Camino del Diablo was used extensively by travelers until the railroad came through in the 1870s. Many early sojourners met eternity along the way, especially during the gold rush days when numerous starry-eyed dreamers traveled the route. With summertime temperatures regularly topping 120 degrees F, hot-weather travelers and their livestock were often desperate and dry-tongued by the time they reached Tinajas Altas, a series of cliffside water holes just off the western end of the refuge. Water wasn't always there when they arrived.

Dozens of human graves on the west portion (some marked by stone crosses) testify to the route's severity. Well into its era of service, the sometimes obscured road could be navigated by following the trail of bleached animal and human bones that adorned it.

Animal Interfaces

Cabeza is still a rough place to visit, suited only for those who love (or wish to learn to love) the desert. It's relatively unvegetated along its extensive flats, except for the creosote and bursage and cacti that go on for mile after mile. Here you can gain a close-up understanding of the desert's "cryptobiotic soil," microcommunities existing within the seemingly barren earth that hold it together and minimize erosion and dust. Balanced deserts generate very little dust—it's generally erosion through road building, grazing, and farming that creates dusty conditions.

Uplands and foothills along the road are more supportive of life, with brittlebush, palo verde, various cacti, and other plants mingling in greater profusion.

This isn't a prime bird-watching place, though migration can bring numerous species (a magnificent frigate bird was spotted over the refuge in the mid-1990s), and brushy washes that support desert willow, palo verde, and other trees attract a variety of desert birds. Nor should you expect to see large mammals, such as desert bighorns or endangered Sonoran pronghorns. Only an estimated 1% to 5% of visitors ever see either species.

Your most likely animal sightings will include lizards and a few desert-tolerant birds, such as phainopepla, turkey vulture, red-tailed hawk, and cactus wren. You'll probably see jackrabbits and cottontails, rodents and invertebrates. If you hike away from your roadside camp at night, your flashlight may turn up a snake or two (possibly a diamondback, sidewinder, or Mojave rattler, so step lightly) or a wandering kangaroo rat or antelope ground squirrel.

Bring along an ultraviolet (UV) lamp to indulge in a lesser-known form of desert entertainment, scorpion-watching. Scorpions are bioluminescent. Under UV at night they glow like poison-tipped windup toys, racing about frenetically, claws outstretched, searching for food that includes any creature smaller than themselves.

mountain

In general, the larger and stubbier a scorpion, the less poisonous is its sting. The tiny, pale yellow, slender-tailed *Centruroides* species are the most dangerous and have been known to cause fatalities. The huge desert hairy scorpion (*Hadrurus hirsutus*) may scare you silly, but its venom won't kill you unless you're highly allergic.

Since it's illegal to use deadfall for firewood on the refuge, you probably won't encounter either in the usual way: by picking up things. At night it's possible, though unlikely, that a scorpion could wander into your sleeping bag. Some desert sleepers prefer zippered tents. I'm one of them. Extended lawn chairs offer a good way to sleep under the open sky, out of reach of wandering critters.

Lizard-watching is another prime amusement at Cabeza—the list here includes whiptails, fringe-toed, zebra tails, desert iguanas, and other species. They're generally most active mornings and late afternoons, especially in hot weather. All can provide fascinating wildlife encounters.

The large, tawny desert iguana is a noble creature whose eyes reflect an intelligence and gentility rarely attributed to reptiles. The fringe-toed lizard is a marvel of desert engineering, with fine hairs on its long toes that aid it in scurrying across the sand. The fringe-toed also has the ability to burrow almost instantly into soft earth when threatened. If you can get close to one, you'll notice that, like the iguana, its eyes also appear oddly intelligent and gentle. Perhaps the sensation is anthropomorphism—these are carnivores, after all, though adult iguanas eat mainly veggies—but a calm eye-to-eye confrontation with virtually any lizard can leave you with the sense that you've shared a unique form of communication.

Western whiptails are fascinating for their slim beauty and erratic, jerky pursuit of insects, but their genetic character is what really sets them apart among lizards: All are parthenogenetic females, capable of reproducing asexually. Basically, each individual within a particular area is the clone of a single ancient Mother Lizard. Their egg hatchings are magical, miracle virgin births.

The chuckwalla, a large desert lizard who lives in rocky, mountainous areas of the refuge, employs a unique survival mechanism: When threatened it wedges between rocks and puffs itself up with air, making it virtually impossible to dislodge. Hungry Native Americans, however, were onto the chuckwalla's scheme. When hunting the oversized reptile, they carried sharp sticks that they used to deflate and hook this tasty morsel.

Vegetal Vigor

Plant species in the Sonoran Desert are equally fascinating. Much of the vegetation at Cabeza resides on the *bajadas*—sloping remnants of sloughed mountainsides—which tend to hold relatively high levels of organic material in their soil. Here you'll find such oddities as the elephant tree (*Bursera microphylla*), whose trunk resembles a pachyderm's leg; wedgeleaf limberbush (*Jatropha cuneata*), a shrub with branches so flexible you can tie them in loose knots (don't, however); and possibly the rare senita cactus, a tall, five-sided "cactus tree" that somewhat resembles its cousin the saguaro. This extremely rare species may or may not remain extant on the refuge. You can see them on nearby Organ Pipe Cactus National Monument.

Horse crippler cactus bears bundled thorns that make the origin of its name painfully obvious. Dune buckwheat, an odd, thin-limbed plant, is a favorite of bighorns and other browsers. The portion of the plant you see atop a dune may be only the tip of a stem that has grown 20 feet or more, reaching ever higher as the dune advances.

Even the ubiquitous creosote has a fascinating character. Long known to poison surrounding earth to stifle competition for water, the creosote has recently been recognized by scientists for its incredible longevity. Creosote "rings," the result of ever-expanding plants propagated via runners, may represent the world's oldest organisms. Some large creosote rings may be more than 10,000 years old.

One of the most beautiful of all the Sonora's plants is often the most difficult to locate. The night-blooming cereus (*Peniocereus greggii*) is a dull gray, sticklike cactus that grows 2 to 5 feet high. Its nondescript appearance is deceptive: In June and July this queen of the night (*Reina-de-la-noche* in Spanish) puts forth a series of two to seven large, stunning white blooms, often one per night, though all buds on a plant may bloom at once. Shortly after sunrise the flowers fold and die.

The cereus's heavy perfume is one way to zero in on a plant, though the easiest way is to locate specimens in daylight and return to them after dark. They're nearly always found growing up through a creosote bush or other protective "nurse plant." In late summer and fall, their bright red, pickle-sized fruits make them obvious.

Spring can be a stunningly beautiful time to visit the Sonoran, especially if winter rain has been abundant. This part of the Sonoran Desert has two rainy seasons, with hard summer rains and long, gentle winter showers. In good years, and sometimes after summer rainfall, entire valley floors and hillsides are awash in floral color, with California poppy, brittlebush, purple ground cherry, Ajo lily, prickly poppy, and desert marigold among the many species painting the landscape.

Desert Balance

The Sonoran is a subtle ecosystem of amazing vitality, a supreme example of the complex balance of undisturbed nature. If you're calmly alert and respectfully patient, and if you maintain the proper internal and external silence, you'll soon come to comprehend some of that balance.

Virtually every creature and every habitat, from micro to macro, is intertwined. Saguaros and bats rely on each other to survive, with bats fertilizing the cacti in exchange for nectar and sometimes shelter. Chain fruit cholla provides sustenance—and may be the key to survival—for the 200 or so endangered Sonoran pronghorn who live here, while pronghorns in turn scatter cholla buds across the desert, where they take root and further the family line.

Cactus wrens build nests in the prickly hearts of cholla cacti, spreading bud plants as they scurry about. Snakes keep rodents in check, while rodents distribute grass seeds and burrow about, mixing nutrients into the soil, aerating the earth, and providing cover and shelter for snakes. Turkey vultures cruise the airways, cleaning up the inevitable and reducing the potential for carcass-borne diseases. Wandering large mammals loosen the soil with their hooves, enhancing new growth they later feed upon. A close relationship also exists between the desert visitor and the washes and soils: You can preserve or degrade them; they can support or engulf you.

Desert interconnections are pervasive, complex, and eternal, but they're difficult to perceive unless you spend time in the environment. A 2- or 3-day trip through Cabeza, with lots of time for hiking and reflection, can reward you with a profound sense of the desert and its ways. The secret is time and patience; the rewards are endless.

Special Rules of Engagement

To enter Cabeza you must obtain a permit from the refuge staff, who prefer that you contact them at least a week before arriving. That way they can help you plan your trip, which will likely turn out to be one of the more beautiful, profound, demanding, back-jolting experiences of your life (unless you happen to be a traveling jackhammer operator or pole vaulter).

A 4WD is a hard-and-fast requirement for visitors for two main reasons: Having total traction makes it less likely you'll get stuck in one of the Camino's broad, sandy washes, which in dry seasons resemble giant flypaper traps; and because in 4WD, coupled with a slow, easy pace, the solid 4WD grip does far less damage to the fragile ecosystem.

Economics is another factor favoring 4WD; you can't expect a refuge staffer to save you when a problem arises, and a wrecker truck dragging you from the refuge will cost a minimum of $500, not to mention the damage that process will create. During heavy rain, especially likely in summer, flash floods can be a problem, and *playas* (shallow lakebeds) may sometimes fill up for days or weeks. When a flooded *playa* blocks your way, even

4WD won't get you through. Be prepared, and willing, to turn back if necessary.

Other rules that apply at Cabeza Prieta are designed mainly to protect the desert eco-system. Don't burn refuge wood. The desert replenishes itself slowly. Ironwood, in particular, grows for hundreds of years, and its deadwood remains intact for hundreds more before returning to the earth. As one staffer put it, "Don't be the dork who takes a 300-year-old piece of ironwood and uses it to cook your weenie." Bring your own charcoal instead, use a fire pan, and pack out your coals and ashes.

You must car camp within 50 feet of the road, though it's better for the refuge if you simply find a wide spot along the Camino and pull over for the night. The desert floor is fragile, and any off-road scars you make will still be there a century later. Leave the car and you are free to hike/camp anywhere—in fact, that's probably the best way to experience the refuge.

Warning: Be aware that Cabeza has been used as a military weapons training range since World War II. Unexploded ordinance remains throughout the refuge. Stay away from any object that might be a bomb or a shell; mark the site with bright cloth tied to a nearby bush and report its location to staffers. Above all, remember that these objects were designed to kill people, and they will. Don't touch.

Substitute Safaris

One option for Sonoran lovers seeking a wild experience but lacking the time, desire, or requisite 4WD for a Cabeza trip is to skip the refuge altogether. Hundreds of thousands of wild acres exist around its perimeter, including land on the Barry Goldwater Air Force Range, the Tohono O'odham Reservation (both require advance permission), extensive BLM land, and Organ Pipe Cactus National Monument. Across the border is the lightly used Pinacate National Biosphere Reserve, part of Mexico's park system and a virtually untouched desert ecosystem. All these places offer back roads and wilderness hiking virtually identical to Cabeza's.

Either way, 4WD is still a good idea—getting stuck anywhere in the Sonoran can be life-threatening, especially in summer. But a high-clearance vehicle and careful common sense will generally get you in and out of less demanding areas, mind and electrolytes intact.

Management Issues

To water or not to water: That is the question at Cabeza and other desert bighorn refuges. Extensive shoring up of natural and artificial water resources, including the use of tank trucks to recharge some water holes, has long been a bighorn support practice here and elsewhere. Bighorns do use the water structures, as do mule deer and many other desert animals, though some experts doubt that pronghorns use them. (I've seen Chihuahuan pronghorns drink, however.) The question is, are they necessary? Do they create imbalances that harm the animals in the long run? Are they little more than predator traps?

For thousands of years, desert bighorns got by on the region's natural water supply, though undoubtedly with heavy die-offs during drought years. Still, they survived until hungry humans came along. With the relatively new philosophy of ecosystem management now ascendant in USFWS policy, some are questioning whether it's prudent to fiddle with natural ways.

Of course, the issue is hardly cut and dry: Humans have drastically altered this ecosystem through overhunting and habitat destruction. In the 1800s and early decades of this century, hunting killed off most of the endangered Sonoran pronghorns (*Antilocapra americana sonorensis*) that once roamed here. Presently, around 200 Sonoran pronghorns exist on the US side, with maybe 300 more living in Mexico. The recovery plan has included removing fences in the area to increase their ability to travel, transplanting some individuals to other supportive habitats, and removing burros and cattle from their range to decrease resource competition. The pronghorns seem to be holding their own for now, but their reproduction rate is agonizingly slow, as it's probably always been in this harsh land.

Sonoran pronghorns were saved just in time, though the subspecies remains at great risk of extinction. Bighorns were likewise slaughtered indiscriminately by settlers and travelers, and their populations were similarly impacted by habitat loss and disturbance.

Since humans bearing killer technologies upset the balance, shouldn't they help put things right again? The debate continues. For now the water structures will remain.

Incredibly, despite all the trouble and debate over protecting Cabeza's tiny population of bighorn sheep, it's still okay for hunters to go there and kill them. (This is true on virtually all bighorn refuges.) Hunting isn't a management tool, it's just for amusement. (Proponents refer to it as "trophy hunting.") Each year the manager sets the number of bighorns that may be blasted off the rocks, based on population surveys—generally it's less than ten. Game tag recipients or auction-winning hunters (the latter sometimes bid more than $250,000 for the privilege) are also allowed to drive onto three nonwilderness service roads off-limits to birders and others.

The Arizona Desert Bighorn Sheep Society invites all bighorn-hunt lottery winners to attend their training course, which, among other things, encourages the hunters to take rams whose deaths will least affect the health of the herd. There's no requirement that they attend, although most do. There's also no requirement that they take the oldest rams, though their horns are often the most attractive. When a healthy young ram is taken, its genes are lost forever. Such genes were vigorous, and their dissemination would have aided the longevity of the species had they not been taken prematurely. In recent years, 7 of the 500 remaining bighorns are killed by hunters each year.

The reason bighorns may be hunted here? Tradition, aided by a politically vocal trophy-hunting community. The status quo will remain intact until enough noise is made by people who think live bighorns are more desirable than dead ones. A wildlife refuge where at-risk animals are killed for sport? The logic of such a policy is difficult to process.

It's No Bird—It's Definitely a Plane

Though a trip across Cabeza can be magical, military exercises overhead make some visits here less enchanting than they might otherwise be. The pro side of a military presence is that it helps ensure the refuge will remain intact and politically viable. (Bighorns and pronghorns don't vote but defense contractors and generals do, with their wallets and influence.) On the negative side of the ledger, sonic booms are regular occurrences here, and bombs explode in the distance, their dust plumes rising thick above the desert floor. Jet roar and vapor trails are constant during regular weekday work hours.

Likewise, travelers along the southern reaches of the Camino will hear a parade of Mexican trucks cruising the interstate just south of the border. If you're going to Cabeza to escape civilization, take note that you won't. But you'll come pretty close.

Visitation to this one-road refuge has doubled each year since the late 1980s. In 1994 the total number of visitors was 640; by mid-1995, 440 people had already applied for permits. The year 1995 was the first in three in which visitation remained flat, probably due to the government furloughs; in the first 4 months of 1996, 375 permits had already been given out. Thus, a trip here during the prime seasons of spring and late fall will probably not result in total solitude, especially if you stay close to the road and your vehicle.

Due to increasing visitation, it's ever more important that you visit Cabeza Prieta with the proper attitude: one of respect, with a nonconsumptive, nondisruptive focus. This is one of the last truly wild places left in the country. By treading lightly, you can help keep it that way.

Impressions and Experiences

Bird sightings:

Other wildlife sightings:

Notes:

PARTIAL BIRD LIST (OF 202 LISTED SPECIES): Pyrrhuloxia, phainopepla, red-tailed hawk, white-winged dove, Gambel's quail, roadrunner, lesser nighthawk, blue-gray gnatcatcher, Say's phoebe, brown towhee, verdin, ruby-crowned kinglet.

PARTIAL MAMMAL LIST: Bighorn sheep, mountain lion, Sonoran pronghorn, bobcat, coati, ringtail, javelina, Merriam's kangaroo rat, Mexican free-tailed bat.

PARTIAL HERP LIST: Mojave rattler, California king snake, bull snake, fringe-toed lizard, red-spotted toad, desert tortoise.

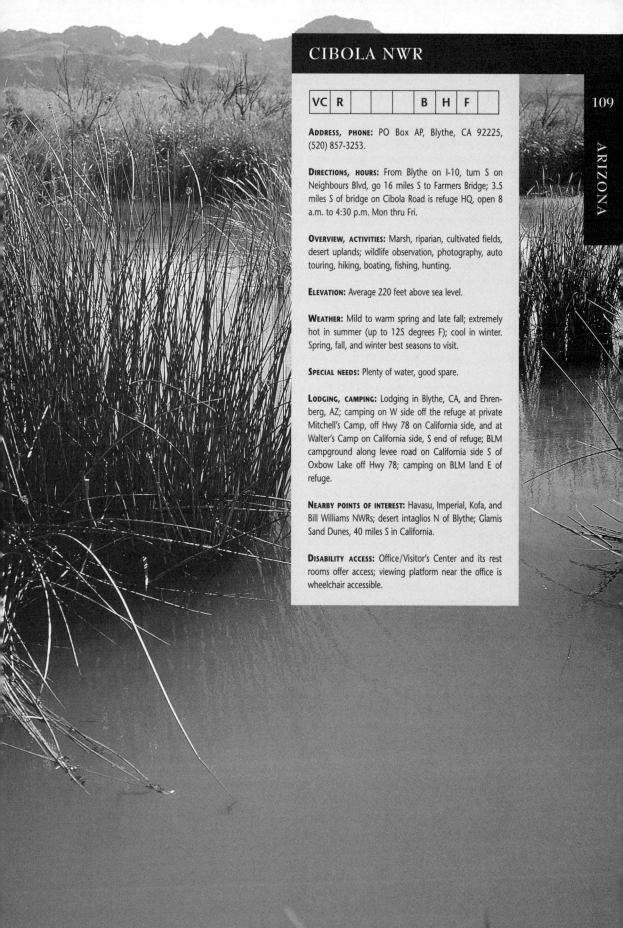

CIBOLA NWR

VC	R				B	H	F	

ADDRESS, PHONE: PO Box AP, Blythe, CA 92225, (520) 857-3253.

DIRECTIONS, HOURS: From Blythe on I-10, turn S on Neighbours Blvd, go 16 miles S to Farmers Bridge; 3.5 miles S of bridge on Cibola Road is refuge HQ, open 8 a.m. to 4:30 p.m. Mon thru Fri.

OVERVIEW, ACTIVITIES: Marsh, riparian, cultivated fields, desert uplands; wildlife observation, photography, auto touring, hiking, boating, fishing, hunting.

ELEVATION: Average 220 feet above sea level.

WEATHER: Mild to warm spring and late fall; extremely hot in summer (up to 125 degrees F); cool in winter. Spring, fall, and winter best seasons to visit.

SPECIAL NEEDS: Plenty of water, good spare.

LODGING, CAMPING: Lodging in Blythe, CA, and Ehrenberg, AZ; camping on W side off the refuge at private Mitchell's Camp, off Hwy 78 on California side, and at Walter's Camp on California side, S end of refuge; BLM campground along levee road on California side S of Oxbow Lake off Hwy 78; camping on BLM land E of refuge.

NEARBY POINTS OF INTEREST: Havasu, Imperial, Kofa, and Bill Williams NWRs; desert intaglios N of Blythe; Glamis Sand Dunes, 40 miles S in California.

DISABILITY ACCESS: Office/Visitor's Center and its rest rooms offer access; viewing platform near the office is wheelchair accessible.

At one time the mighty Colorado River ran wild along its 1,450-mile course from northern Colorado to the Gulf of California. Old-time riverboaters and explorers noted the presence of vast acres of cottonwood-willow forests along its desert banks, sometimes a mile thick or more. Within the river forests, extensive wetlands harbored countless waterfowl. Much of the health of this system depended on floods that periodically swept down the river channel. In this century, damming and channeling began; soon after, the river forest and wetland backwaters were all but eradicated.

The 16,667-acre Cibola NWR on the Arizona–California border is unique in that it was created specifically to mitigate ecological damage caused by the river's taming. Along with Imperial, Havasu, and Bill Williams refuges, Cibola helps restore some of the lost natural balance. However, Cibola, which lies south of Parker Dam, is the only one specifically designated as a "mitigation refuge."

riparian

Habitats here are many— the refuge is a rich mix of lake, marsh, tamarisk forest, creosote-bursage desert uplands, cultivated farm fields, channeled river, and near-barren hills and flats coated in "desert pavement." Numerous waterfowl, including significant populations of Great Basin Canada geese and Platte River sandhill cranes, come each fall to bask in Cibola's moderate climate and feast on a variety of foods, both natural and cultivated. Numerous waterfowl species make Cibola their seasonal home, with a small number of them remaining through summer.

As many as 100 of the estimated 1,100 remaining Yuma clapper rails live in Cibola's marshes. In spring their raucous voices echo over the cattail-lined wetlands, as they call to one another or respond to sharp noises that may include slamming car doors, coughs, or imitative calls.

Arid uplands here support a variety of Sonoran Desert species, including Gambel's quail, white-winged dove, and the sleek, black phainopepla, along with mule deer, rattlesnakes, desert lizards, desert tortoise, and dozens of feral burros—wild equines whose ancestors bore the weight of prospectors' dreams. Forests and riparian habitat here can be crowded with springtime migrants, including numerous warblers, verdin, blue grosbeak, and many others. The refuge bird list numbers 244 species, with heavy representation by passerines, as well as waterfowl and waders. A dozen avian predators, including osprey, bald eagle, and burrowing owl, also find good conditions here; some remain year-round.

Except for the Goose Loop and viewing platform near the Visitor's Center, much of Cibola's best wildlife viewing lies on its southern end. There you'll find an extensive marsh, the 600-acre Cibola Lake, and accompanying shallows and backwaters.

A surrounding lowland tamarisk forest, spotted with mesquite and bare ground, harbors numerous passerines, along with desert reptiles, including western diamondback and Mojave rattlers, and small mammals, such as desert cottontail and several rodent species. Roadrunner and Gambel's quail can often be seen hunting and browsing and, in the case of Gambel's quail, leading a straggly line of chicks through the brush.

Sparcely vegetated Sonoran Desert uplands on the southeast edge of the refuge often harbor mule deer, along with a variety of lizards and several bird species, including black-and-white gray warbler, loggerhead shrike, ash-throated flycatcher, horned lark, and roadrunner. Coyotes move from uplands to marshes, particularly in morning and evening hours, when you'll likely hear them serenading the moon and stars.

Getting Around

The 4-mile Goose Loop tour just north of the Visitor's Center is a good place to begin your Cibola visit in fall and winter. Here you can observe some of the wintering flock of Great Basin Canada geese and sandhill cranes that use the refuge. Cultivated fields of corn, milo, wheat, and alfalfa provide good winter forage for the birds and also help steer them away from nearby private croplands.

Cibola farms around 1,800 acres for waterfowl feeding, supplementing wild foods such as millet and wild grasses. The geese need about a pound of food each per day. Their feeding increases as spring approaches and they ready themselves for the flight back to Idaho, Montana, and other northern-tier states where they spend their spring and summer months.

This is not a refuge best seen by floating the Colorado River. Riprapped along its entire 16-mile length, the riverine stretch of Cibola is a monotonous reach of tamarisk and cane, harboring perhaps a few flycatchers and kingbirds, egrets and herons, an occasional warbler, but little else. Use your time more fruitfully and explore the refuge by vehicle or on foot. Virtually all the visitor-accessible marsh and lake areas can be reached on tire tread or shoe leather.

To navigate the southerly reaches of Cibola, you'll do best to obtain the hunting map from the Visitor's Center display. That map is more detailed than the standard brochure map, though neither contains all the roads on Cibola.

Travel south on Cibola Road from the Visitor's Center and you cross a stretch of nonrefuge BLM and private land. Four miles down, you reenter the refuge and soon come to a road on your right that leads to the Island Unit. That road takes you west into an extensive marsh bordered by tamarisk, cattails, arrowweed, and bulrushes, where rails are likely to be heard but are rarely seen.

In spring, the three distinct calls of the clapper rail seem to fill the morning air all across the marsh. One of the calls is an insistent *kek kek kek*; a second is a sort of *kek kek kek burrrrr;* the third is a clatter, like the rapid shaking of a can with a pebble inside. All are loud and can reverberate a quarter mile or more.

The rail's name derives from the fact that you can get them to call by clapping. One way

biologists elicit responses is by banging a paddle on their canoes. Indeed, just about any sharp noise will elicit calls during the breeding and nesting seasons. An estimated 1,100 of the Colorado River subspecies of this secretive bird existed in 1994. Cibola harbored 80 or 90 of them inside its borders in 1995.

Numerous other species may reside in the marsh areas, including waterfowl such as pintail, mallard, and blue-winged teal. Passerines, coyote, bobcat, an occasional mountain lion, and various desert herptiles also live in the wetlands.

As you enter the marsh you'll pass the ruins of an old settler's cottonwood log cabin. The identity of this long-ago resident has been obscured by time, but the structure itself remains largely intact and may be explored. Watch for rattlers around fallen planks and other cover.

Except for the levee road, Cibola's auto-accessible routes vary in quality, even along a single road. The road marked "Island Unit" is a good one that takes you across a river bridge and into developed wetlands. Less than a mile west of the turnoff from Cibola Road, you can turn south onto a road that takes you into Hart Mine Marsh, a rich wildlife environment. Along the way the road skirts Farm Unit 2, where food crops are raised for wintering geese and waterfowl. (Deer and others enjoy them, too.) Continue west on the Island Unit Road and you'll soon reach the levee road flanking the river. That one carries you past wetlands that harbor a variety of water birds, then on to Cibola Lake and the southern edge of the visitor-accessible part of the refuge.

desert

A north-south county road through desert lowlands south of the marsh is closed to access; it enters a sensitive area where your presence would disturb breeding and resting wildlife.

Along accessible marsh roads, you may encounter any number of avian and other species, including reptiles. If you chance upon a desert iguana and remain in your vehicle, the large, tannish lizard often will hold its ground, offering a good view of its dinosaurish frame. Phainopepla, several flycatcher species, verdin, and any of several warblers, including rust-topped Lucy's, are among the many bird species you may encounter anywhere in the salt cedar, mesquite, and willow forestland.

Cibola Lake's northern reaches begin as shallow wetlands partly obscured from the road by tamarisk. Several access points and overlooks along the way provide views of the lake and its shoreline, where rails, great and snowy egrets, black-crowned night herons, and other waders may be spotted. Various waterfowl, both dabblers and divers, use the lake from fall to spring. An access area brings you close to the water's edge and to a boat ramp there (fishing is allowed in the lake from March 15 through Labor Day). Approach the water quietly, using brush for cover, and you may spot various waterfowl and shore dwellers.

On the south edge of Cibola Lake, a small access trail just off the road takes you through willows and tamarisk to a water-control structure and a brush-enclosed view of the lake. Check the trees for warblers, such as Wilson's and yellow-rumped, and be alert for rails, least bitterns, and rarely seen American bitterns, along with great blue heron and snow egret, who may be settled in the emergents along the lakeshore.

The south-running road from here grows rocky and rough, rising up a steep hill that may be eroded to impassibility. A branch road just before the curve, running up toward a small brick building, generally makes for an easier climb.

Desert Uplands

Once you top the rise, your view of the refuge and river opens up, revealing the dramatic character of this desert region and the California reaches of the refuge, which make up a third of its acres. The uplands are a dramatic departure from the marshes and riparian groves. Sparsely vegetated and largely coated in "desert pavement"—an evenly pebbled surface that results from centuries of silt-washing rains—the dominant biota here includes brittlebush and cactus, creosote, bursage, and other dry-loving Sonoran plants. Note the narrow paths worn into the desert pavement as they descend to the lake edge. These are burro trails, carved by the plodding hooves of an animal who rarely changes its daily watering and feeding routine.

Many of the wild burros at Cibola reside on the flats and in the gently sloped canyon southeast of the lake. As many as 200 of the once-domesticated miners' baggage handlers inhabit the refuge and its environs. Many hang around this area, where views are long and threats are easy to spot. They remain close to the river during warm months, retreating to the mountains east of the refuge from fall through early spring.

Refuge personnel have developed an uneasy truce with the critters. Attractive as they are, the burros can be ecological menaces. They aren't content with merely fouling water holes, competing with deer and other animals for food, or trampling the refuge in general; they also have a nasty habit of taking large bites out of trees. Many of those trees are cottonwoods, which at Cibola are scarce. They're constantly tended and developed here, along with willows, for riparian restoration efforts. Resident deer also destroy trees, but at least they're indigenous, making their depradation somewhat less objectionable.

Cibola's mule deer are natives, with some 250 inhabiting the refuge. Often they can be spotted around the office area or from the observation tower that overlooks farmed acres, as well as on the Island Unit. They're generally near the river in summer, when they seek water and the heavier cover that habitat provides. Other seasons, they retreat into the nearby mountains.

Like those at Bosque del Apache refuge in New Mexico, management efforts here are ongoing to restore cottonwood-willow riparian habitat, which will help to re-create something of the old system the undammed river once maintained through free flow and periodic flooding.

Tamarisk, which has spread extensively throughout Cibola, makes that job difficult at best. Constant budget cuts and manpower reductions don't help either. But each year Cibola's managers attempt to clear a small number of tamarisk-choked acres and replant them with cottonwoods and willows. It's a case of swimming against an overwhelming salt cedar tide, but at Cibola, that's just part of the job.

Cibola at Dusk

Like Imperial refuge to the south, sunset and sunrise at Cibola are times when the world changes. In spring and summer, lesser nighthawks rise from their roosts and sweep over the rolling hills, uttering their melancholy calls. In fall and winter, sometimes spectacular waves of waterfowl and cranes wing overhead, their silhouettes stark against the fading light. The earth turns crimson; the clouds go red and purple. Most of the river powerboaters are at rest. A soothing quiet blankets the land and water.

To the west, the jagged Palo Verde and Chocolate mountains underlie a hazy red sky, defining the dusky horizon, summoning images of fairy tales and far-off lands. If you're vehicle-bound, this is a good time to get out, find a convenient perch, and sit. The overwhelming silence, punctuated by the strange calls of the nighthawks and the soothing rush of the river, will leave you with a cool sense of serenity. Just as Cibola is a gift to wildlife, that peacefulness can be a gift to you.

Impressions and Experiences

Bird sightings:

Other wildlife sightings:

Notes:

PARTIAL BIRD LIST (OF 244 LISTED SPECIES AND 40+ ACCIDENTALS): Eared grebe, snowy egret, least bittern, sandhill crane, tundra swan, snow and Ross's goose, redhead, common merganser, Harris's hawk, prairie falcon, clapper rail, American avocet, long-billed curlew, Forster's tern, burrowing owl, white-winged dove, lesser nighthawk, brown-crested flycatcher, cactus wren, black-tailed gnatcatcher, Lucy's warbler, common yellowthroat, green-tailed towhee, yellow-headed blackbird, lesser goldfinch.

PARTIAL MAMMAL LIST: Mule deer, cougar, bobcat, coyote, feral burro, kit fox, kangaroo rat, black-tail jackrabbit.

PARTIAL HERP LIST: Western diamondback and sidewinder rattlesnakes, desert king snake, desert tortoise, desert iguana, zebra-tailed lizard, bullfrog, Colorado River toad.

					B	H	F		

ADDRESS, PHONE: 311 Mesquite, Needles, CA 92363, (619) 326-3853.

DIRECTIONS, HOURS: HQ is in Needles. Topock Marsh unit is accessible N of I-40 on Mohave County 1. Topock Gorge unit is accessible by boat on the N from launches around I-40 and on the S from Lake Havasu City. Open daylight hours. HQ open regular weekly business hours.

OVERVIEW, ACTIVITIES: Some 37,515 acres of marsh, river, and desert, primarily accessible by boat; boating, wildlife viewing and photography, fishing, hiking, hunting.

ELEVATION: Marsh elevation fluctuates at around 365 feet above sea level.

WEATHER: Hot most of year, extremely hot in summer, generally mild in winter, with occasional freezing temperatures. Spring, fall, and winter best seasons to visit.

SPECIAL NEEDS: Boat and related safety equipment, water, wide-brimmed hat, spotting scope or binoculars, sunscreen.

SPECIAL REGULATIONS: No camping or fires on the refuge; no personal watercraft allowed in marked river backwaters; see brochure for additional regulations.

BOAT RENTALS: Jerkwater Canoe Company, (602) 768-7753 (tours and rentals); Park Moabi, W of I-40 river bridge, rents small boats with *cash* deposits of several hundred dollars; others in Lake Havasu City.

LODGING, CAMPING: Motels in Lake Havasu City; campgrounds at Park Moabi (first exit W of the river off I-40) and at Five Mile Landing off Mojave County 1 on the refuge; wilderness camping on Arizona side of refuge (see refuge map).

NEARBY POINTS OF INTEREST: Desert intaglio 1 mile W of I-40 bridge over the Colorado River; London Bridge at Lake Havasu City; Joshua Tree National Monument.

DISABILITY ACCESS: Some marsh-area trails are fairly flat; HQ in Needles is accessible.

I n Lake Havasu City, Arizona, a local woman was complaining that she couldn't drive her vehicle into most of Havasu NWR. "I always thought wildlife refuges were for people," she told me. This is a true story.

No, this Colorado River refuge, located in northwestern Arizona on the California border, is not (primarily) for people, though people are welcome. Nearby London Bridge, dissembled and rebuilt in tourist-swamped Lake Havasu City, is for people. The malls, highways, condos, and concessions that blanket the town's shoreline are for people. Dams that stifled the Colorado River's annual cleansing floods, monocultural farm fields that crewcut the valley below, concrete-and-glass gambling palaces in nearby Laughlin, Nevada—those places were designed for people.

The 37,515-acre Havasu refuge is for wildlife. People may also visit this wildlife sanctuary of river gorges, backwater, marsh, lake, and sere desert upland, and they do—as many as 700,000 come each year, most for water recreational activities. Unfortunately, many don't even realize they're on a refuge.

riparian

Since wild river habitat has been all but eliminated along the lower Colorado River, Havasu is one of few remaining places where Pacific Flyway migrants and resident birds can still engage in their ageless cycles of meeting, mating, and maternity. The river stretch of the refuge is in high demand as living space for a multitude of creatures whose traditional habitat has been destroyed by damming and rampant development. People place high demands on the river, too. The Colorado River is a navigable body of water, Los Angeles is only a few hours away, and people with a lust for cool water and hot boats visit in the thousands in the hot months. Thus, this stretch of cool water in the parched Mojave Desert serves what seems a paradoxical double duty, both as wildlife haven and watersport mecca.

Three major sections comprise the refuge: The Topock Gorge unit along the river, where most boaters come; the quieter Topock Marsh unit, just north of I-40; and the sparsely visited Needles Wilderness, covering 14,600 acres on the Arizona side, where vehicles are prohibited. Bill Williams River NWR to the south was until recently a fourth unit of Havasu; now it is a separate refuge.

A boat is necessary to see most of Havasu, despite its desert location, but you can approach the edges of Havasu's marsh unit on foot or hike in its extensive wilderness. If you have adequate time, good shoes, and abundant water, you may also walk up to the Topock Gorge unit along the shoreline from Lake Havasu City. However, don't try this in midsummer—this is one of the hottest places in the United States, with temperatures exceeding 115 degrees F not at all uncommon. When the hot wind blows, you'll know what it's like to be trapped in a pizza oven.

One hundred acres of managed cropland provide winter wheat and Bermuda grass for Canada and snow geese; the Bermuda Pasture is observable from a platform near the refuge maintenance yard. A variety of shorebirds, waders, and some passerines come in the spring migration to feed in the marsh shallows and refuge fields.

Mojave Desert upland surrounding both the river and marsh areas provides habitat for a variety of upland dwellers, including desert bighorn sheep, great horned and elf owl, Gila woodpecker, crissal thrasher, a small number of Gila monsters, and canyon and cactus wrens.

Topock Gorge and the River

T he 16-mile stretch of refuge land along the Colorado River is accessible primarily by boat. Much of the upland here is wilderness; on the California side the desert is some of the harshest country in the nation. Hiking across it would take the equivalent of a human mountain goat and requires at least 2 days—if the Chemehuevi Indian tribal police don't turn you back. Wilderness on the Arizona side is more accessible, though also rugged, and offers extensive hiking and abundant solitude.

South of I-40 to the city limits of Lake Havasu City, the river stretch of Havasu NWR runs for 22 miles. Here Topock Gorge, a dramatic stretch of jumbled conglomerates and basalt, rises from the river more than a hundred feet in places, adorned by thick beds of cattails in the river shallows and flanked by desert that begins just a few feet from the water.

The buckled, folded, compressed, and uplifted cliffs along the gorge tell a remarkable story of geological forces that shook the region 17 million years ago. Sandstone here bears footprints of prehistoric camels and other extinct wildlife. The uniqueness of Topock Gorge draws geologists from around the world.

A favorite spot for recreational boaters, the river course is used heavily—and highly inappropriately—in warm months, when a disruptive "freeway culture" dominates, marked by roaring, high-speed aquatic dragsters and personal watercraft, such as jet skis, rumbling along, full bore, between Lake Havasu City and Laughlin.

Accidents happen here, most often later in the day when blood-alcohol levels rise. Traveling the gorge by canoe can be perilous during the raceway season, especially on the three holiday weekends of Easter, the Fourth of July, and Labor Day.

Despite the uproar, cattail-shielded backwaters in and below the gorge provide nesting and living space for a small number of waterbirds. Clark's and western grebes, along with smaller eared and least grebes, nest and play in the shallows. Least bittern is here also, along with soras and clapper rail, common moorhen, and green heron. A few ducks, including redhead, gadwall, mallard, and various teals, also use the backwaters.

Some river backwaters are closed off year-round, for an important reason: If you disturb breeding and nesting sites, birds won't repro-

duce. One study determined that two or three passes from a jet ski at wake speed will tear an overwater grebe nest to pieces. Also, if a frightened bird flees her nest for too long in the desert sun, her eggs will literally cook. During nonbreeding seasons, safe haven is still crucial to the waterfowl who use the backwaters.

The Mojave Desert that lines the river creates a dramatic change in habitat just beyond the waterline. Here you'll find white-winged and mourning doves, raptors (including an occasional peregrine falcon or golden eagle on the high rocks), Gambel's quail, roadrunner, northern flicker, ash-throated flycatcher, gnatcatcher, and western kingbird. During early morning in summer, you may spot some of Havasu's 6 dozen desert bighorn sheep poised on the cliffs or sipping from the river. Other mammals, including bobcat, gray and kit fox, beaver, raccoon, and coyote, are found here and in other areas of the refuge.

During spring migration, songbirds visit the trees, brush, and cattails lining the riverbanks. More common passerines include Wilson's and orange-crowned warblers, common yellowthroat, and yellow-breasted chat. Lucy's warbler, whose reddish crown brings to mind the late comedian of the same name, inhabits the mesquites and other vegetation. Abert's towhee, a local subspecies, can often be spotted ground-foraging around desert trees and brush.

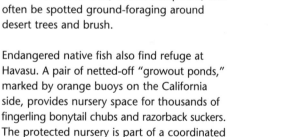

freshwater wetlands

Endangered native fish also find refuge at Havasu. A pair of netted-off "growout ponds," marked by orange buoys on the California side, provides nursery space for thousands of fingerling bonytail chubs and razorback suckers. The protected nursery is part of a coordinated federal and state program to restock indigenous fish to their native habitats. Damming, habitat destruction, and the introduction of aggressive predator fish have driven several native fish to the brink of extinction.

Floating the Gorge

In winter when Topock Gorge boat traffic is minimal, a canoe makes a much safer, and more wildlife-friendly, observation platform. Get an early start and you'll see more critters during your journey, which may be run from Golden Shores Marina to Castle Rock (a 7-hour trip).

Headwinds, especially during warmer months, can slow you down and at times may stop you completely. In winter, tailwinds often rise from the north, quickening your 3-mile-per-hour drift rate and making your paddles superfluous. Competency with a canoe is important here any time of year, and knowledge of how to turn quickly to cut across powerboat wakes when necessary is critical.

If you cruise the river by motorboat in warmer months, move slowly and avoid mucking around too extensively in the cattail-riddled backwaters, where most courtship, breeding, and nesting occur. Try getting to the gorge early and drifting or mooring in a tucked-away cove, and savor the river's beauty and calm. Some backwaters are closed completely during breeding months, and disruptive personal watercraft are never allowed into backwaters between I-40 and Castle Rock. Signs are posted to that effect.

In many places you can pull your vessel onto shore and hike into the desert beyond the riverbank. This is the Mojave, though it lacks the trademark Joshua tree, a species found just 20 miles to the west in California. The aspect here is creosote, bursage, and saltbush. A fascinating collection of plant species also thrives under the towering cliffs. They include pencil cholla and barrel cacti, cheeseweed, and a variety of spring and summer blooms, including false heliobore, phaecilia, lupine, brittlebush, desert marigold, and, on river-carved dunes, the elegant sand verbena.

The Devil's Elbow area of the gorge, where cliff walls come within 30 yards of each other, is one of the most picturesque stretches anywhere on the Lower Colorado. The Grand Canyon it ain't, but in this desert flatland, these cliffs are a dramatic departure from the surrounding terrain.

Topock Marsh

Nesters on the snaggy, 4,000-acre Topock Marsh unit are mainly herons, egrets, and cormorants. But in winter, close to 10,000 ducks spend their days here, along with 1,500 Canada geese and 4,000 snow geese, which fly out mornings to browse in local farm fields, returning near dusk to the sheltering marsh.

Topock Marsh is accessible in a few spots by foot or bike. In spring and summer you can drive to the northeasten edge, off the Bullhead-Topock Road (Mojave County 1). From there launch your boat or walk or bike across the dikes and levees. Here you'll find good views of the water and surrounding brush, which supports perching birds that may include verdin, blue grosbeak, and vermilion flycatcher.

The New South Dike, accessible a mile north of Golden Shores Marina off Mojave County 1, is a good walk-or-bike route with broad views of the marsh. On the western portion of the marsh, signed areas are closed from October 1 to the end of January.

A west-running dirt road just north of Five Mile Landing across Fort Mojave tribal land takes you across a mile of desert to the refuge fence, a few hundred yards from the water. From here you can survey the eastern marsh with a scope or binoculars. You're likely to find a number of creatures along the way, too, including cactus wren, phainopepla, loggerhead shrike, various lizards, and (rarely) a desert tortoise or Gila monster. Several varieties of rattlesnake are also here, so watch your step.

The marsh is landlocked from the river, so boaters must launch from one of several areas around the marsh, including Five Mile Landing, a federally licensed commercial operation on the refuge, or from refuge launch areas on the south and north ends of the marsh. (Please don't tie your boat off to nest-covered snags. Wakeless speed and general unobtrusiveness are desired etiquette on the marsh; cruising at wakeless speed may also save your prop from treacherous underwater projections.) The marsh and river offer good bass, crappie, and catfish fishing, and there is waterfowl hunting here in winter, when sections are closed off for hunters.

The Trouble with Tamarisk

An impenetrable tamarisk thicket covers the landscape north of the marsh, supplanting native riparian habitat and creating a constant fire hazard. A recent fire burned several hundred acres of the refuge and 3,300 more on the adjoining Fort Mojave Indian Reservation. Managers feel the tamarisk, along with thick stands of abundant, oil-rich arrowweed, represents a powder keg. Sadly, managers expect a fire, either lightning or human caused, to extensively damage the refuge at some point in the future.

As with most western refuges, fighting the exotic tamarisk requires constant effort, one ruled by budget and manpower limitations and frustrated by the salt cedar's resiliency. Managers here work to restore cottonwood, mesquite, and willow to patches cleared of tamarisk. Progress is slow, but the results are beneficial to a wide variety of bird species that once had miles-thick groves of native trees along the river in which to nest, feed, and hide. That was many decades ago, however, before tamarisk infiltration and damming crowded them out.

On the highway east of Topock Marsh, as well as in nearby towns, a giant form of tamarisk thrives in limited groves. Athel tamarisk hasn't spread like its prolific smaller cousin, probably due to the massive tree's enormous water needs. The species grows to 40 or 50 feet in height and provides limited habitat for songbirds while harboring fewer insects than native cottonwoods and willows and providing less adequate nesting support.

The athel is quite beautiful, though, with heavily grooved bark, evergreenlike foliage, and showy spring blooms. Tamarisk is a species that land managers never take for granted, and biologists are keeping an eye on the giants to assure that they don't proliferate and further threaten native species. So far that hasn't happened, and many local residents enjoy the groves. So for now they'll stay.

Wild Things

Havasu serves as a migratory rest stop for birds traveling along the eastern reaches of the Pacific Flyway, but a fair number of year-round residents are also found at Havasu. (More than 80 birds nest here.) Endangered and threatened creatures, such as peregrine falcon, snowy plover, golden and bald eagle, and Yuma clapper rail, are just some of the locals and migrants at Havasu. A total of 292 species is listed in the refuge brochure, though other reports put the number above 300.

Yuma clapper rail surveys conducted periodically along the river by refuge biologists yield rough population estimates, but such surveys can be tricky. The count is taken by pulling a boat up to a backwater area, playing a taped rail call, and counting the number of responses. During a May survey I attended in Topock Gorge, taped rail calls produced markedly fewer answers than the same area had generated just days earlier. The birds were still there, they simply didn't have anything to say this time.

Because of the rails' secretiveness and the technique's resulting error margin, surveys are used to compare estimated numbers of rails from year to year rather than as hard population counts. In this way, population trends can be roughly tracked and management methods shaped. The estimated 50 endangered clapper rails here seem to be maintaining themselves for now, despite intense human pressures.

Snakes Alive

While hiking down the dirt road just north of Five Mile Landing on a May afternoon (wearing shorts and sandals), I nearly stepped on a mating pair of sidewinder rattlesnakes. Even from close up, their pale coloration made them difficult to see against the tawny-colored earth. Until that moment I hadn't realized how well I could jump while loaded down with photographic gear.

Their pairing behavior was fascinating, almost thoughtful—not the sort of behavior one expects from cold-blooded creatures. First the male approached the female and touched her gently with his snout. She rattled and flailed at him and he thrashed out of fang's reach. A moment later he nudged her again, and once more she rattled and jumped. On his third attempt she twitched, but this time she didn't rattle—she was softening. He moved closer in this perilous dance and slowly, carefully slid his head and neck across her back. He then proceeded to massage her jerkily with his upper belly. Once she seemed comfortable with his familiarity, he moved over her and penetrated her with one of two hemipenes, which all male snakes possess. They remained joined for a long time.

If all went well, the female rattler would soon give birth to between 5 and 18 young. As with garter snakes and some fish, pit viper births are ovoviviparous: The female gestates the eggs inside her body; the eggs hatch while still inside; and the young exit her body free and functional, their little poison glands and fangs primed and ready for business.

Sidewinders get their name from their loco-motive style when crossing loose sand. The motion consists of sideway-looping move-ments that leave a series of parallel, J-shaped tracks. Sidewinders eat mainly mice, rats, and lizards, using their keen sense of "smell" via a sensitive organ on their tongue to pick up prey trails. Like all pit vipers, they can locate and strike prey in total darkness with the help of heat-sensing pits on either side of the face. The "horns" on their foreheads are hinged scales that fold down to protect the eyes, probably to protect them during rodent bur-row hunts from rocks, roots, and the brief, desperate struggles of their victims.

Neighborhood Cooperation

An interesting archaeological remnant across I-40 near the bridge has recently been acknowledged with a prayer ceremony and the installation of a plaque by Native American tribes, USFWS representatives, and other interested parties. What locals have long called the Mystic Maze—a 30-acre network of furrowed lines across the hilly desert terrain— is now accepted by many archae-ologists, as well as local tribes, as a "purification maze," believed by some to have been used by ancient natives to cleanse themselves after battle.

Some believe the maze has more recent roots than that, but the tantalizing patterns across the landscape suggest more than just some Industrial Age tinkering by a bored farmer.

Other Native American sites, including a signed area a few yards off the river, also commemorate the region's early inhabitants. Havasu maintains good relations with the tribes, as it does with numerous other federal and state interests.

Such cooperation is critical in an area where wildlife, water, and recreational needs are overseen by half a dozen agencies. Havasu's managers hope to access additional Colorado River water flow-through rights in order to cleanse the overrich marsh. In doing so, they may add even more to the richness of this desert wildlife haven.

Impressions and Experiences

Bird sightings:

Other wildlife sightings:

Notes:

PARTIAL BIRD LIST (OF 292+ LISTED SPECIES): Pied-billed and Clark's grebe, great egret, great blue heron, blue-winged teal, ring-necked duck, red-breasted merganser, northern harrier, Cooper's hawk, golden eagle, Gambel's quail, Yuma clapper rail, snowy plover, least sandpiper, common snipe, Forester's tern, white-throated swift, belted kingfisher, black phoebe, cliff swallow, cactus wren, warbling vireo, common yellowthroat, black-headed grosbeak, Abert's towhee, swamp sparrow.

PARTIAL MAMMAL LIST: Bobcat, cougar, gray fox, antelope ground squirrel, feral burro, wood rat, western pipistrel bat.

PARTIAL HERP LIST: Western diamondback rattler, California king snake, shovel-nosed snake, collared lizard, desert banded gecko, desert spiny lizard, Gila monster, western whiptail lizard, red-spotted toad, bullfrog, desert tortoise.

VC	R			W	B	H	F	

ADDRESS, PHONE: PO Box 72217, Martinez Lake, AZ 85365, (520) 783-3371.

DIRECTIONS, HOURS: From Yuma, 30 miles on Hwy 95 to Martinez Lake Road, 15 miles W to refuge. Open daylight hours. HQ open regular hours Mon thru Fri.

OVERVIEW, ACTIVITIES: Sonoran Desert, lakes, wetlands, and riparian habitats along the southern Colorado River in Arizona and California. Hiking, car touring, birding, fishing, exploring in upland Sonoran Desert, wetlands, and mesquite/tamarisk thickets. River cruising (best by canoe or raft). Hunting in fall and winter for birds, rabbits, deer, and bighorn sheep.

ELEVATION: River approximately 600 feet.

WEATHER: Extremely hot in summer, moderate fall thru early spring. Spring, fall, and winter best seasons to visit.

SPECIAL NEEDS: Water, hiking boots, bug spray, Imperial's hunting map (more informative than the general pamphlet map).

LODGING, CAMPING: Motels in Yuma and at Martinez Lake; camping at Martinez Lake, Walter's Camp, and Picacho State Recreation Area (California side).

NEARBY POINTS OF INTEREST: Kofa, Cibola, Bill Williams River, and Cabeza Prieta refuges, Organ Pipe Cactus National Park, Yuma Territorial Prison (a historical museum).

DISABILITY ACCESS: HQ accessible; rest rooms there accessible.

Sitting quietly near dusk within Imperial NWR's "Painted Desert" can be an oddly stirring experience. A moonscape of rounded desert hills rolls off in every direction, nearly devoid of vegetation except for a coat of fine grasses, a few scattered beavertail cacti, and a handful of scrubby mesquite, palo verde, and ironwood trees. The soft pastel hills, crumbly remains of volcanic flows and ancient seabeds, evoke images of some distant lifeless planet.

Imperial's least-vegetated region is hardly without life, though. At dusk, lesser nighthawks dart about in low flight, nearly clipping the hilltops as they call to one another in ghostly trills. Kestrels, too, join the fray, as do common poorwills, who often perch on the roadway, rising to snatch insects and then returning to the same spot. Shrikes and western tanagers pose on scattered limbs. Bees swarm the palo verde blossoms, and crickets drone incessantly while lizards creep about the rocks, regarding trespassers one-eyed, heads tilted. From beyond a nearby hill you may hear the mournful braying of a feral burro, the rhythmic crackle of its hooves on gravel lending cadence to this symphony of desert sounds.

riparian

As the sun falls beyond the Colorado River, the hills turn to embers. This moonscape, the peculiar calls, the deepening glow of sunset—all conspire to create an experience that is unique and unforgettable.

Imperial is the southernmost of four refuges along the riverine border that separates Arizona from California (the refuge spans both sides) and is unique for a number of reasons. Perhaps its most singular trait is that it encompasses the last unchanneled stretch of the lower Colorado River, the sole remainder of vigorous Corps of Engineers flood-control efforts. The river's taming has created a new and artificial cycle—it may rise or fall by a foot within a week, depending on regional agricultural demands. Generally, it's lowest on weekends.

A rich collection of backwater lakes and marshes offers productive habitat for waterfowl and other birds. The terrain is also unique because its topography includes a meeting of dramatically diverse biomes: parched upland Sonora (3 inches average rain per year) grading into lush backwaters melding into river, with all the varied life-forms that such a meeting attracts.

Established in 1941 by executive order to provide habitat for migratory birds and other wildlife after the creation of Imperial Dam in 1937, this 30-mile-long, 25,625-acre refuge retains a small piece of once expansive habitat lost to wildlife as a result of river alterations. The system here is artificial, in a sense, brought about by large-scale tinkering. But it does support many of its previous wild residents along a stretch of the Colorado River where little natural riverine wetland survives. That makes it critical to wildlife that once reigned here and that remain, though in smaller numbers.

Fooling with Mother Nature, as usual, has resulted in unfortunate consequences. Before Hoover Dam tamed the river in 1935, followed by further damming above and below, the Colorado was a roaring, seasonally changing force that regularly overflowed its banks. That periodic flooding flushed the extensive wetlands along its borders, carrying countless tons of silt to the Gulf of Mexico and keeping the vegetation that lined its banks in a balanced state.

After the damming, the river's entire ecological balance changed. No more are its wetlands scoured each spring of debris and silt. Natural plant succession consequently has been altered. Open-water flood catchments now transform in short order to silted, cattail-choked shallows, then to congested phragmites (common reed) communities, and finally, when silt has piled up above the high-water level, to impenetrable reaches of salt cedar, an exotic species of relatively scant value to wildlife.

Paradoxically, farmland on the refuge that once generated row crops for migrating waterfowl has been flooded, and some is now managed as moist-soil units that produce natural food sources. Close to 500 acres are farmed in grain and forage crops; a hundred acres will soon produce moist-soil plants, including edible hard-stem bulrush, spike rush, smartgrass, and wild millet. Close to 1,500 Canada geese and 50,000 ducks benefit from those vegetal food sources.

Hundreds of Imperial's bottomland acres are choked with salt cedar, reducing usable habitat and creating a nearly overwhelming management challenge. Refuge staffers fight the tamarisk jungle 15 or 30 acres at a time, clearing away patches and planting native cottonwood, willow, and mesquite as dwindling finances allow. The David-and-Goliath battle is a noble one, though with a bigger slingshot (read "budget"), progress would likely increase significantly. For the cost of one wing strut off a B-1 bomber—a plane that in 1995 the Pentagon didn't even want—the refuge could be improved in a major way for the wildlife it was meant to support. So it goes. In *The Territorial Imperative* (1966), author Robert Ardrey argues that if we were as creative in peacetime pursuits as in our wartime efforts, the cultural landscape would be unrecognizably changed. That goes for our physical landscape as well.

Critical Life Support

Despite its broad tamarisk coat, Imperial remains a critical migratory stop, wintering ground, and wildlife home base for hundreds of bird species and many other life-forms. Four species of geese use the refuge yearly, with Canadas the most prevalent. Nearly 20 varieties of duck come from northerly summer grounds, including, on rare occasions, old-squaw and surf scoter. Numerous waders and shorebirds flock to refuge backwaters and river sandbars.

An estimated 125 endangered Yuma clapper rails live here. (Experts aren't sure of their numbers nor certain whether clappers migrate south in winter or remain. When clappers aren't calling, it's almost impossible to survey

them. See Cibola NWR, AZ.) In spring, you can sometimes get them to call by imitating their *kek kek kek* call (one of three calls they make), by clapping your hands sharply a few times, or by banging on something that resonates loudly. If you decide to converse with the clappers, please do so sparingly.

Black rail (smaller than a robin) and Virginia rail, as well as sora, moorhen, and coot, also occupy the cattail-crowded backwaters of Imperial. American and least bitterns live in the emergent vegetation with their rail cousins; when threatened, these secretive marsh dwellers stand in the reeds with beaks skyward, blending in with surrounding plants.

More than a dozen raptors come here. Year-rounders include Harris's hawk and northern harrier, kestrel, prairie falcon, black-shouldered kite, and red-tailed hawk. In the spring you may find osprey, sharp-shinned and Cooper's hawk, and sometimes a peregrine falcon. Fall and winter bring around 2 dozen bald eagles, as well as rough-legged hawk and an occasional ferruginous hawk. Owl species here include western screech, burrowing, great horned, and long-eared. Less common are short-eared and northern saw-whet, which appear in winter.

desert

Perching birds make up a large portion of Imperial's 271 listed bird species, especially during nonsummer months. Flycatchers are particularly abundant; vermilion, olive-sided, and Hammond's, as well as Cassin's kingbird, are among the more notable. Phainopepla inhabit the desert uplands and mesquite/tamarisk reaches. Three goldfinches—lesser all year, American in spring and summer, and the rarer Lawrence's in fall and winter—bring color to the trees and brush.

A small army of sparrows enjoys Imperial during cooler seasons; savanna, song, Lincoln's, Brewer's, and white-crowned are the most abundant, but you may spot a fox, sage, vesper, or even grasshopper, too. Abert's towhees are 1 of 3 subspecies found here. The abundant Abert's can be distinguished from the brown towhee by its black mask and lighter beak. It appears in desert brush and riparian growth of southern and western Arizona. Its westward range ends abruptly along the Colorado River.

You can distinguish Imperial's legions of lesser nighthawks from their cousin, the common nighthawk, in numerous ways: The lesser is smaller, it tends to fly much lower to the earth, its white wing bars are closer to the wingtip than the common's centered wing-bar, and, perhaps easiest of all, the common nighthawk doesn't live here.

Except for summer-dwelling Lucy's, yellows, common yellowthroats, and yellow-breasted chats, warblers inhabit the refuge largely in migration, though a few remain in winter, including yellow-rumped, Wilson's, orange-crowned, and black-throated gray. In every season except winter you might find summer, western, or possibly hepatic tanagers (present here in the fall); blue grosbeaks and black-headed grosbeaks dart about riparian vegetation in spring and autumn, and lazuli buntings come in winter and spring.

Varied thrush has been seen on the refuge in winter, though you shouldn't expect to encounter this rarity. For that matter, magnificent frigate birds soar over on occasion, perhaps blown in on gulf storms; but don't bet your binocs you'll spot one. More frequently seen but unusual birds found here include Lapland and chestnut-collared longspur, both of which come in fall. Red-eyed vireo, Clark's nutcracker, northern parula, and palm warbler are among dozens of accidentals that stray to Imperial.

The Long and Winding Road

A 6-mile road from the headquarters to Yuma Wash, the refuge boundary on the north, is Imperial's main land artery. It leads through the refuge past several wetland overlooks, the Painted Desert self-guided trail, and the upper desert reaches north of the refuge.

The road is narrow and winds sharply through hills and washes, demanding caution and alertness for other vehicles. Yuma Proving Ground and BLM property borders the refuge from Yuma Wash northward; military police patrol this stretch of the road.

The wash itself can be treacherous in dry weather, with deep sand that grabs tires and refuses to let go. Walk it before attempting to drive across. Beyond the wash lies a desert of white bursage, mesquite, cottonwood, smoke tree, and desert willow, as well as tamarisk; much of the growth is along periodic arroyos that cut their way down to the river. Get out and walk the arroyos and you'll likely spot a good variety of birds, small mammals, and reptiles, especially in cool morning and evening hours.

The road eventually reaches Red Cloud Mine, where a form of crystal is privately mined. The mine is closed to the public, but you can bird your way up to its border, 16 miles north of HQ. Camping is allowed along BLM land north of the refuge.

Wet and Dry Birding

One of the best auto-accessible spots for viewing waterfowl here is Mesquite Point, just before the Painted Desert on the main north-south road. Park well away from the road's end and walk, using brush as cover; otherwise you'll almost certainly frighten the birds down below.

Northwest of the point is river-fed McAllister Lake, which often harbors large numbers of ducks, including blue-billed ruddies in mating season, as well as shoveler, goldeneye, three teal species, and gadwall. Six grebes (least, pied-billed, horned, eared, western, and Clark's) also use the refuge and may be found here. Dozens of egrets and herons congregate on lake snags in the evenings while even more use nearby river habitat.

Conversely, nearby Palo Verde Point overlooks a sea of salt cedar and reed; the dense vegetation makes wildlife spotting difficult. Ironwood and Smoke Tree Point take you above Butler Lake, where you'll likely find numerous water-loving birds.

Greater waterfowl concentrations are often found in less accessible marshes and ponds, including the Island and Adobe Lake areas. If you hike off the road in warm weather (during any season), watch for rattlers and be sure to bring sufficient drinking water—people have gotten turned around here and wandered for hours before reorienting themselves.

Another way to view Imperial is by boat—either your own launched from Picacho State Recreation Area, from the privately operated Walter's Camp on the California side, from the town of Martinez Lake (rentals are available there), from two launch ramps on the refuge at Meers Point near Martinez Lake, or from two ramps near Clear Lake, also on the refuge. From Picacho, you can walk to Taylor Lake, where large concentrations of waterfowl reside in winter (along with duck hunters). Small boat and canoe launches from Picacho also can be a good idea, considerably mini-mizing the paddling distance to Adobe Lake, another good birding and wildlife spot.

Unless you're interested in floating more than birding, though, the river isn't the best way to see the refuge, as most of the shoreline is lined with a solid green barrier of tamarisk. You'll spot a few egrets and herons, maybe a flycatcher or two, but most of the time you'll be staring at that unbroken wall of salt cedar.

During cold months, a cruise of the 26-mile stretch of river on the refuge may offer better birding, but it also presents problems. Water depth is extremely low in winter, with numer-ous sandbars and shallows to avoid, and your presence may frighten birds resting on exposed sandbars. The landward side of the refuge offers several river overlooks; with binoculars or scope you can probably get your fill of river-perching birds without upsetting them.

If you decide to travel the river, a motorless raft or canoe launched from above is the best way to pass through this narrow, exposed stretch. Be prepared to get out and haul your craft over emergent sandbars; water depth averages 4 to 8 feet, with much deeper holes here and there, but in winter siltation creates sandy dams throughout the watercourse. Also, strong winds may arise, making a long-distance paddle exhausting. Rafts may fare even worse in winds; strong southerly blows can severely impede your progress. A good rule with motorless vessels is to explore only a few miles from your launch site.

When the water level is high, narrow cuts will get you into several of the riverside lakes and backwaters, but during breeding season you may be intruding, and you'll likely frighten many creatures off. Better to beach (and secure) your craft somewhere nearby and hike in, using cover to remain unobtrusive. All back-waters on the refuge are "no wake" zones.

In spring and summer, river birds are few, and the scores of powerboats that roar and roil the water chase off all but a few resilient egrets and herons. Water skiing is prohibited on the refuge, except near Martinez Lake and Picacho State Recreation Area; but that doesn't stop boaters here from constantly challenging aquatic speed records. Their insensitivity to the wildlife is a major problem, but river jurisdiction is shared by numerous state and federal agencies; thus, enforcement policies and responsibilities remain at this writing unsettled.

A half-acre growout impoundment for native Colorado River fish is located in an area north of Martinez Lake, but that facility is closed to visitors. The pond maintains 10,000 razor-back suckers. Imperial is one of four refuges along the river trying to restock native species, such as the razorback, humpback chub, and squawfish (see Bill Williams River NWR, AZ) after damming wrought havoc on their lives and futures.

Equina Non Grata

Burros represent a toothsome challenge for Imperial's management. Descendants of miners' pack animals, a hundred or so of the equines live on the refuge in a wild state, ranging into nearby mountains in winter and descending to the river in warmer months. Their penchant for destroying trees, shrubs, and water holes makes them undesirable residents, as does their trampling of ground plants and their food competition with indigenous mule deer and bighorn sheep.

Controlling feral burros is difficult. Periodic adoption roundups on nearby BLM land help, but the hardy equines reproduce efficiently, so their numbers rebound quickly after thinning. The critters are protected by the federal Wild Horse and Burro Act (a few wild horses live here, too), so refuge staffers grudgingly tolerate their presence.

Along with the burros, many other mammals are well represented on Imperial. Mule deer frequent the refuge, as do badger, bobcat, cougar, skunk, coyote, jackrabbit, fox, and ringtail. A few bighorns range from nearby mountains to riverside cliffs, where they're occasionally spotted by boaters. They also appear in the Painted Desert area but are more often seen around the mountains north of Clear Lake.

Reptilian life also is abundant here, including chuckwalla, desert iguana, collared lizard, gopher snake, and several rattler species. Scorpion, tarantula, and black widow reside at Imperial. Leave them alone and they'll do the same for you.

Maneuvers and Merriment

Neighbors around the refuge, many of them military retirees, seem to have mixed feelings about the federal presence in their backyard. Some support the refuge, including several who make a big slice of their living from birders and other refuge-goers. (Be sure to mention to locals why you're here; it helps.) Others resent having any restrictions placed on their fishing, boating, and camping.

At one time, camping was allowed on the refuge, but garbage buildup, wildlife disturbance, and fires—99% of which are human-caused and difficult to fight in remote refuge areas—resulted in a camping ban. Nearby Picacho State Park was once part of the refuge but was withdrawn to help satisfy the demands of recreational users.

Picacho State Park is heavily used, but in a sense that activity has been counterbalanced by the wilderness designation of land on the north and south sides of the park. The California Desert Protection Act of 1994 set aside 9,200 acres on the Arizona side and 5,880 acres on the California side as land that will never be roaded or developed. Hiking and camping are allowed there but no motorized travel.

Nearby Yuma Proving Ground generates both support and challenges for the refuge, as well as for those who visit. Wildlife surveys by military personnel are shared with the refuge, providing useful management information, and military patrols help in law enforcement and visitor aid. Unfortunately, unexploded ordinance remains alive and well in test and training areas along the refuge periphery. A sudden loud blast, dust plume, or ground tremor may remind you that training continues just a few miles past the fence.

Imperial represents a good compromise for time-pressed nature lovers who wish to visit desert, riparian, and marsh habitats in a single trip. This compact refuge can be covered in a day or two, with plenty of time in each habitat for easygoing exploration.

Bird sightings:

Other wildlife sightings:

Notes:

PARTIAL BIRD LIST (OF 271 LISTED SPECIES): Canada goose, American white pelican, Yuma clapper rail, cattle and snowy egret, white-faced ibis, northern pintail, green-winged teal, common merganser, ruddy duck, osprey, ferruginous hawk, greater yellowlegs, Wilson's phalarope, Caspian tern, lesser nighthawk, ladder-backed woodpecker, ash-throated flycatcher, Swainson's thrush, phainopepla, orange-crowned and Audubon's warblers, vester sparrow, lesser goldfinch.

PARTIAL MAMMAL LIST: Cougar, bighorn sheep, badger, coyote, feral burro, California leaf-nosed bat.

PARTIAL HERP LIST: Sidewinder and western diamond-back rattlers, gopher snake, desert king snake, desert iguana, chuckwalla, red-spotted toad.

KOFA NWR

		C			H		

ADDRESS, PHONE: 356 W First Street, PO Box 6290, Yuma, AZ 85366-6290, (520) 783-7861.

DIRECTIONS, HOURS: S from Quartzsite, AZ, on Hwy 95 to several refuge entrances. Palm Canyon entrance is 18 miles S of town. Refuge open 24 hours every day. Info brochures from kiosks at some entry roads.

OVERVIEW, ACTIVITIES: Vast reaches of rugged Sonoran Desert and mountain habitat; wildlife observation (bighorn sheep and others), hiking, camping, hunting.

ELEVATION: From 680 to 4,877 feet.

WEATHER: Very hot from late spring thru early fall; mild spring and fall; winters generally mild but can drop below freezing. Spring, fall, and winter best seasons to visit.

SPECIAL NEEDS: Good spare, water, complete self-containment for wilderness travel and camping, spotting scope (to observe distant bighorns and other creatures).

LODGING, CAMPING: Motels and RV parks in Quartzsite and Yuma; primitive camping on refuge; vehicles must remain within 100 feet of designated roads.

NEARBY POINTS OF INTEREST: Imperial, Cibola, Havasu NWRs.

DISABILITY ACCESS: No developed facilities.

I reached Kofa Queen Canyon a few hours before sunset on a warm May afternoon. During a pause in the bumpy drive across the creosote-bursage flats, through boulder-strewn uplands and along a rocky arroyo, I'd spotted a dozen desert bighorn sheep lounging on a high cliff a mile or so to the east. The sighting had been mainly luck—I'd glassed the ridge for several minutes before the symmetrical curve of a horn popped into view against the darker basalt.

As soon as I caught sight of that first ram, several more sheep seemed to appear from the cliffside. Soon, an entire community was visible, lounging on rocks, grazing on the high slopes, lambs hovering close to mothers. One lamb stood proudly on its own boulder, a soft silhouette atop the crimson ridge.

Half an hour later, I settled into camp near the canyon's narrowest gorge. A clatter of displaced rocks above camp signaled that visitors were nearby. On a hunch, I began making odd noises—grunts, hoots, chattering sounds.

desert

A large ram leaned over the bluff to study me. Another bighorn appeared, and then another, the third a female with shorter, less-curved horns that resembled those of a domesticated goat. Over the next few minutes, the rams and ewe watched me in dusky light.

I spoke softly to them and they seemed to listen, apparently noting my peaceful intent. I was profoundly moved by their visit. This was a gift, a rare encounter with majestic wild mammals who not only trusted me but seemed to welcome me to their home.

Kofa's greatest gift to any visitor may be the feeling of freedom it affords. The thousand or so bighorns on the refuge are a big reason for that feeling. Knowing the indigenous sheep inhabit Kofa's highest reaches, living wild and free, evokes a sense of spaciousness, of wild grandeur.

Refuge for the Spirit

Fifty miles north of Yuma in southwestern Arizona, this rugged 665,400-acre desert preserve is bordered on the west by a major highway that a century ago bore 20-mule-team freight wagons. But once you leave Hwy 95 and delve into Kofa's backcountry, the world of asphalt and ego recedes far behind you.

Two rugged mountain ranges rise from the refuge floor, the Kofas and Castle Domes, along with a few smaller ones. The broad King Valley, where Gen. George S. Patton trained his desert-rat troops during World War II, bisects Kofa at its center. This scenic desert/mountain refuge is extremely rough in places, full of jagged, vertical canyons cut by "roads" that can pound a vehicle silly and eat tires without effort.

Long flats reach to the horizons, adorned with desert plant communities. Broad stretches are coated with the curious natural phenomenon of "desert pavement," where fine silt has been washed from the surface by centuries of rain, leaving "paved" areas of even-sized pebbles, sometimes for miles. (Don't drive on desert pavement; your tracks will leave scars for centuries.) Gently sloping *bajadas* spill from the crusty mountains, supporting denser plant communities; winding arroyos cast shadows, channel water, and support life.

Most of the refuge has been designated wilderness, meaning no roads or vehicles are allowed on much of it and no development will occur within its borders—at least as long as the political will remains sufficiently strong. Some 327 miles of existing roads form a network of access into the refuge's wild places, but at some point, to delve most deeply into Kofa's secrets, you must leave your vehicle behind.

Getting Around

Except for a handful of well-graded access roads, most of the dirt tracks that web Kofa's backcountry require 4WD or at least a high-clearance vehicle; ubiquitous oil stains on the rocks attest to that fact. A map is available from kiosks on refuge roads east of Hwy 95 or from the headquarters in Yuma during regular office hours.

Thick lines on the map indicate Kofa's few graded roads, upon which passenger vehicles can generally do fine, though high-clearance is better. If you traverse double-lined routes, you'd better have a vehicle that can scramble, along with at least one good spare. Some double-liners aren't roads at all, in the strictest sense, but washes, twin tracks across jagged rocks, or partially obstructed strips of rocky ground.

Beyond these narrow ribbons you'll find a desert world of incomparable balance and beauty. The northern section of the refuge is the place to be. Nearly untouched by human activities, this is the Sonoran as it has existed for thousands of years.

The southern fifth of Kofa, conversely, is a wasteland of discolored mine tailings and discarded equipment, the remains of a once-vigorous silver and gold extraction industry. Discouraged miners did virtually nothing to clean up their mess, a tragic (and hazardous) legacy that has destroyed the beauty and integrity of thousands of Kofa's acres.

Refuge managers work to repair the damage, but inadequate funding and laws protecting "historical" artifacts (anything more than 50 years old, including garbage) slow their progress. Also, many of the shafts provide homes for such creatures as bats and ringtails, making them important habitats. Placement of wildlife-friendly grating over those shafts is a process that creeps along as funding allows.

Warning: Many of the mines in the Castle Dome flatlands are unmarked and unobvious. Some vertical shafts plunge straight down 700 feet and more. **Don't walk around out here.** Better to stay away from the area completely. By all means, never stroll these acres at night.

The northern and central reaches of Kofa are everything the Sonoran Desert should be.

Relatively low visitor use enhances the primitive feel, and the sheer size of the refuge cushions you from other people, even during the "busy" winter season. You can get lost here, more easily in the figurative than in the literal sense.

Spring may find portions of the refuge drenched in wildflower hues; summer is searingly hot, a time when highly adaptive desert plants shed or curl up leaves, recede into tangled masses of dead twigs, or fold skin plates inward, tapped dry.

Fall can be hot, too, but it's generally mild. Winter is the time most visitors come. Many are "snowbirds" from northern states, residing in RVs at Yuma and Quartzsite, cruising Kofa's better roads on day trips. Winter may be the least picturesque season for the refuge, but except for occasional temperature plunges and chilly nights, the weather is generally comfortable.

mountain

Desert Life

A walk into Kofa's brush any time of year reveals an incredible variety of plant species. USFWS biologists have collected and listed 289 plants on Kofa; many more have yet to be added to the list, as the Sonoran Desert is believed to support close to 2,700 species.

The most obvious here are creosote, ironwood, mesquite, palo verde (an often leafless green tree, frequently bearing sprigs of desert mistletoe), ocotillo, brittlebush, and the giant saguaro. In addition, Kofa harbors a multitude of plant wonders, including parasitic ratany with its royal purple spring blooms, desert marigold, tackstem, globe mallow, Mariposa lily, and the paperflower shrub, whose yellow petals glow in spring before drying to a faded flesh tone and remaining attached for months. Prickly pear, hedgehog, barrel, teddy bear cholla, and long-spined pencil (or Christmas) cacti put forth spectacular floral shows in spring and summer.

Jojoba sprout beans that yield a waxy substitute for the oil once derived from slaughtered sperm whales. Commercial jojoba farms have taken root in other parts of the Sonoran, one of few cash crops appropriate and sensible to cultivate in this arid land.

Where water sporadically flows, Kofa's desert willows grow. In spring the delicate pink blooms of this pseudowillow attract a multitude of Costa's and black-chinned hummingbirds, who often hover, apparently without fear, to meet your eye.

In a few canyons, hollylike Kofa Mountain barberry grows in low bunches. Palm Canyon (accessible via passenger car and a half-mile uphill hike) harbors some of the only known native stands of remnant California fan palms (*Washingtonia filifera*). One tiny grove survives in a narrow crack high on the north face. Sunlight touches the giant fronds no more than an hour or two each day, around noon. Apparently, the canyon's microenvironment is sufficient to keep these biological fossils healthy. A brochure from the kiosk at the base of Palm Canyon offers good information on the palm and other species.

Dry-Country Miracles

Most of Kofa's resident wildlife species are secretive and difficult to observe without a serious expenditure of time and patience. Founded in 1939 to protect threatened desert bighorn sheep, Kofa has been quite successful in its primary mission. But "ecosystem management" has been a guiding rule at Kofa for decades. With the refuge and all its biota under federal protection, scores of creatures and plants find secure homes in this vast, undeveloped range.

As water defines the desert, so does it define the lifeways of desert dwellers. Mammals here are among the most fascinating of all creatures. Often their survival modes defy accepted notions of what animals need to exist. Merriam's and desert kangaroo rats, for example, never drink. The long-tailed rats derive all necessary moisture through a metabolic process that

transforms chemical constituents of dry seeds into water—a remarkable desert alchemy.

Big-eared kit foxes also may never drink, though biologists have yet to confirm that suspicion. Most desert predators, including badgers, gray foxes, coyotes, and cougars, have minimal water needs, drawing nourishment largely from blood and moisture in their prey. They are "opportunistic" drinkers, taking water when it's available but doing without it during dry times. Other desert dwellers have the ability to store several degrees of heat in their bodies, releasing it during cooler evening hours. Such nighttime heat release requires less perspiration, thus conserving precious body fluids.

One heat saver and water storer is the desert bighorn, which utilizes water at least as efficiently as the camels that briefly roamed these parts after the Civil War, in a failed military experiment. Often when bighorns come to drink from water holes in summer, they arrive looking gaunt and shrunken. As they guzzle perhaps 2 gallons in several brief bouts, they begin to swell up. Gradually, they fill out, and when they leave, they look like different animals. A satiated bighorn may not drink again for 5 days. Bighorns also have the ability to store heat by day and release it at night or in cooler environments. Rather than perspire, as equines do, they dissipate heat mainly by panting. Bighorns also release heat by direct contact with cool structures, such as shaded rocks and earth.

Desert predators, and most of their prey, prowl at night, when temperatures can be 40 degrees cooler than in the day. The large eyes of many species, including ringtail, bobcat, and various rodents, reflect their night-roving ways. Predators tend to have binocular vision while prey species are constructed with side views to help them spot and evade pursuers.

Ringtails, raccoonlike creatures also known as "miner's cats," live in caves, canyons, and mines throughout the refuge. They show little fear of humans. Campers at Kofa have sometimes awakened to find the fuzzy critters perched on their sleeping bags. Wood rats,

Humpback chub is one of several native Colorado River fish being captive-raised and then reintroduced into the river system.

Desert cottontail.

The Bill Williams River winds through the heart of the refuge, providing life support and good habitat for numerous creatures.

With the help of wildlife biologists, the endangered masked bobwhite is likely regaining a foothold in its old grassland habitat on Buenos Aires NWR.

Arivaca Creek on Buenos Aires NWR provides lush habitat in the heart of the arid Sonoran Desert.

Vermilion flycatcher.

Coati.

Gila monster.

The red-spotted toad is one of the relatively scarce desert amphibians. This nocturnal species can be found near some of Cabeza Prieta's scarce water sources or moving about arroyos and *playas* during wet weather.

The elephant tree is one of several rare plant species found on Cabeza Prieta NWR.
It generally grows on *bajada* slopes. The species is found only in southern
Arizona and northern Mexico.

(Opposite) Roadrunners are found throughout the Sonoran and Chihuahuan deserts.

A Cibola NWR burro trail etches desert pavement on its way down to Cibola Lake.

Clark's grebes inhabit river, lake, and marsh habitats at Cibola NWR.

Topock Gorge on Havasu NWR is a dramatic region of high cliffs
and cattail-lined backwaters.

Desert iguana.

Mating sidewinder rattlesnakes entwine. The venomous species moves over desert
sand in a unique motion that leaves discrete J-shaped tracks along its path.

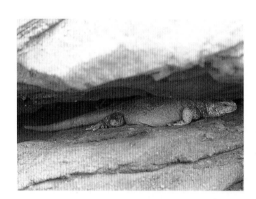

Chuckwalla.

Mourning dove.

Feral burros.

Imperial NWR protects rich habitat and scores of wildlife species along the lower Colorado River.

Desert spiny lizard.

Desert willow is an indicator of subsurface water. It's often found along arroyo edges.

Evening light warms a western face of the Kofa Mountains. Here Palm Canyon harbors
native California fan palms and the unique Kofa Mountain barberry. Kofa Queen Canyon
to the north supports a band of bighorn sheep.

Ringtails find good habitat in Kofa's abandoned mines and in mountain caves.
The nocturnal creature employs oversized eyes and ears to hunt for its omnivorous
diet of insects, birds, and various fruits.

Bighorn ram.

The javelina (or collared peccary) is a piglike native found from southern Arizona east to south Texas. It feeds on various vegetal morsels, including prickly pear pads, which it devours spines and all. When danger threatens, peccaries clack their tusks and emit musk from a gland on their backs. Usually they flee, but sometimes they will attack.

Bullfrog, scourge of western wetlands.

Black Draw's creekbed at San Bernardino NWR harbors numerous
riparian birds, as well as desert mammals and tiny native fish.

commonly known as packrats, create rock-crevice nests formed from twigs and other plant matter. Mixed with their droppings (which some archaeologists call "rachit"), the nests expand over time until huge middens of hardened material build up. The crusty remains last for centuries and sometimes contain artifacts of early human presence—a time capsule useful to archaeologists in their quest to decipher ancient human lifeways.

The nocturnal habits of most desert mammals make them tough to see. Early mornings and late afternoons are best for mammal observation, with water holes being prime activity centers. If you locate a water hole that's observable from 50 yards or so away, you probably won't disturb visiting species too much—if you stay quiet and well hidden. Still, limit your stay to a brief period, especially in hot months. Never forget that water is a life-or-death resource for many desert dwellers. Any campsite must lie at least a quarter mile from the nearest water hole.

Scaly Survivors

Lizards are a major exception to the night-roaming rule that guides most desert creatures. The desert spiny lizard can often be found in daylight, glued to the side of a palo verde or smoke tree trunk or darting across an open stretch, heading for cover. Collared lizards favor rocky outcroppings, where they sun themselves for hours and wait for prey, which they swallow whole with the help of backward-slanting teeth. They'll sometimes remain in place as you approach quite closely, secure until you enter their invisible safety zone.

Whimsical zebra-tailed lizard, with striped tail curved over its back as it runs, resembles a scaly, four-legged scorpion. You'll spot it dashing along roadways and clearings, wearing what seems to be a constant grin.

The regal desert iguana lives among the vegetation, pursuing insect prey and munching on flowers and other vegetable goodies. Iguanas often sit in calm repose, a state that to some

human eyes (mine, at least) resembles meditation. They seem particularly still and thoughtful in the presence of nonthreatening observers.

The venomous, slow-moving Gila monster is another of Kofa's residents, though it's rare and not often encountered. The tail of this thick, orange-and-black, bead-scaled lizard swells to store food and moisture, which it draws upon for sustenance during lean times. This "monster" is actually a docile creature if left unmolested. A sighting of one is a gift bestowed by kindly gods.

Study any lizard and you'll probably notice that it's studying you back. Intelligence is a tricky trait to measure. Their thoughtful eyes and steady gazes, not to mention their wondrous desert survival strategies and clever evasive moves, seem to belie our assumptions about the microintelligence of saurians. At any rate, a few minutes spent observing a lizard in its natural habitat can be a journey back through the eons—a 3-D diorama of dinosaur lifeways played out in real time.

Snake species here number more than a dozen. Five rattlesnakes inhabit the refuge, including western diamondback, Mojave, western, speckled, and sidewinder. The rosy boa, one of North America's most unique and beautiful snakes, also roams Kofa's rugged countryside. Collectors and poachers take a few illegally; fortunately, the refuge is so large their numbers are likely secure from wildlife thieves. The lyre snake is harmless to humans but can envenomate small prey with fangs set deep inside its mouth.

A victim of habitat loss and overcollection, the protected Sonoran Desert tortoise can sometimes be found in late winter and early spring creeping across Kofa's flats or boulder-strewn slopes, feeding on annuals and other flowering plants and shrubs. Recent radio tagging of tortoises on the refuge reveals that most spend their lives within a territorial radius of just a few hundred yards. Perhaps more amazing than those little turtle transmitters are fiber-optic camera cables used to probe the creature's burrow, which may run 15 to 30 feet deep. One biologist used such a probe to photograph a tortoise 7 yards beneath the earth, tucked away in its subterranean living room.

Bird Life

Though 185 bird species have been listed at Kofa, you'll rarely find more than a dozen or two species during your visit. They're most often found in cooler, shadowed canyons and thickets or on upland slopes where vegetation is dense. Ash-throated and western flycatchers and Say's phoebes are numerous at Kofa, along with both blue-gray and black-tailed gnatcatchers, who play in the low brush and respond well to a birder's "pishing" enticements. Slate-black phainopeplas can often be spotted on treetops; their deep, questioning *Whirp?* often causes human heads to turn.

Raptors, including the Krider's phase of red-tailed hawk, nest in the saguaros. The Krider's upper body and tail are paler than those of the common redtail; light patches often adorn their upper primaries. Kestrels are another common predatory bird here, along with little sharp-shinned and slightly larger Cooper's hawks.

Cactus, canyon, and rock wrens are common at Kofa; loggerhead shrikes impale their prey on cactus spines or barbed wire for later consumption. Gila woodpeckers flit about the saguaros, landing vertically and utilizing holes they or others hack into the saguaro's soft flesh.

White-winged and mourning doves call from the brush, and Gambel's quail (possibly an opportunistic drinker) hustles from shrub to shrub. In cold months, as many as 40 adult and juvenile Gambel's may assemble in ragtag groups. In late spring, a dozen or more new-borns form unruly lines behind their mothers, often with a male or two in attendance helping to herd the youngsters along.

Bighorns, Water Management

The 800 to 1,000 bighorn sheep at Kofa constitute the most stable population of the *mexicana* race of desert bighorns anywhere. Only around 2,000 members of this dry-country subspecies exist in the United States. Living in small family groups, they range about the refuge's highest cliffs and ridges, descending periodically to visit a water hole or forage for food.

Their dinner plants represent a wide variety of species, including jojoba, mesquite beans and leaves, brittlebush, and many others. Witnesses have observed the sheep straddling and "walking down" tall agave stalks in order to feast on the blooms. They often eat spring flowers, creating a comical image as buds and blooms protrude messily from their mouths.

Kofa's bighorns are most easily seen in Burro Canyon, Kofa Queen Canyon's high ledges, and the Castle Dome Mountains, where you'll have to do lots of difficult rock scrambling to get within view. Occasionally, you'll encounter one dashing across a flat or lying alongside a King Valley roadway, though the latter doesn't happen often. Along higher-elevation road-sides, chance sightings are more frequent.

Management of Kofa bighorns largely involves water. About a hundred water holes have been enhanced here through the addition of concrete lips, by blasting water-bearing depressions into cliff walls, and lately by shading ponds to reduce evaporation.

Traditional bighorn theory mandates placing water holes no more than 3 miles apart to correspond with the sheep's maximum wandering distance from water. More recently, holes have been maintained a little farther apart in order to separate bands, reducing the possibility of disease transmission. Bighorns are highly susceptible to lung diseases, especially those of domestic sheep and goats. Losing a band of 40 sheep to blue tongue or brucellosis would be tragic; spreading a killer disease to hundreds more would be a catastrophe. It's happened before, notably in Wyoming and

Montana, where domestic-borne diseases have killed thousands of mountain bighorns.

The debate continues regarding how much "artificial" water is too much in a desert environment. Negative arguments include expansion of food-competing deer populations, encouragement of predators (including bighorn-eating cougars), and overtaxing of plant resources due to expanded herds. Right now, Kofa's population appears to be in balance. In fact, approximately 30 individuals are transplanted from Kofa each year to mountains in Arizona and other southwestern states.

Some end up at the business end of high-powered hunting rifles. The "privilege" of killing a bighorn at Kofa is extended to around 16 or so permittees each year, a "safe" number derived from research on the effects of hunting on wild populations. The hunt is strictly for the amusement of hunters rather than serving as a management tool. However, outdoorspeople with cameras may shoot all the bighorns they want, and the sheep can still go home to their families.

Taming the Human Herd

With some 60,000 visitors each year traveling its near-endless reaches, Kofa is able to absorb human impact without much disturbance to wild residents. That could change with increasing visitation, an impact seen throughout the refuge system.

More troubling is the potential that owners of patented mining claims will develop their land for tourism or sell parcels to entrepreneurs. In one recent case, a helicopter flight-seeing business over bighorn areas was proposed (and discouraged). In 1993, a religious commune brought in nearly 100 trailers to house 250 of their faithful for several months until they moved on to greener pastures.

Such activities could seriously degrade Kofa, one of the last protected large tracts of wild country remaining in the West. To counter the possibility of future ecological myopia, refuge managers attempt to buy up private refuge-enclosed land as it becomes available. Additional funding would make that job easier.

For now, most of Kofa NWR remains a gem-like reach of undisturbed Sonoran ecosystem. Those who appreciate this natural treasure can only hope future visitors will come to appreciate Kofa, not to possess it, to immerse themselves in this wide open world rather than diminish it. The harsh desert is fragile, too. Lands such as Kofa remain precious only so long as we walk softly upon them, leaving nothing but tracks, taking nothing but inspiration.

Impressions and Experiences

Bird sightings:

Other wildlife sightings:

Notes:

PARTIAL BIRD LIST (OF 185 LISTED SPECIES): Krider's red-tailed hawk, golden eagle, greater yellowlegs, white-winged dove, common poorwill, western flycatcher, phainopepla, black-tailed gnatcatcher, cactus wren, loggerhead shrike, black-throated gray warbler, MacGillivray's warbler, house finch, lesser goldfinch.

PARTIAL MAMMAL LIST: Desert bighorn, mountain lion, gray fox, ringtail, coyote, desert cottontail, Arizona pocket mouse, Harris's antelope squirrel, western pipistrel bat, California leaf-nosed bat.

PARTIAL HERP LIST: Western diamondback rattlesnake, Mojave rattlesnake, desert king snake, rosy boa, lyre snake, western banded gecko, Gila monster, desert iguana, zebra-tailed lizard, desert tortoise.

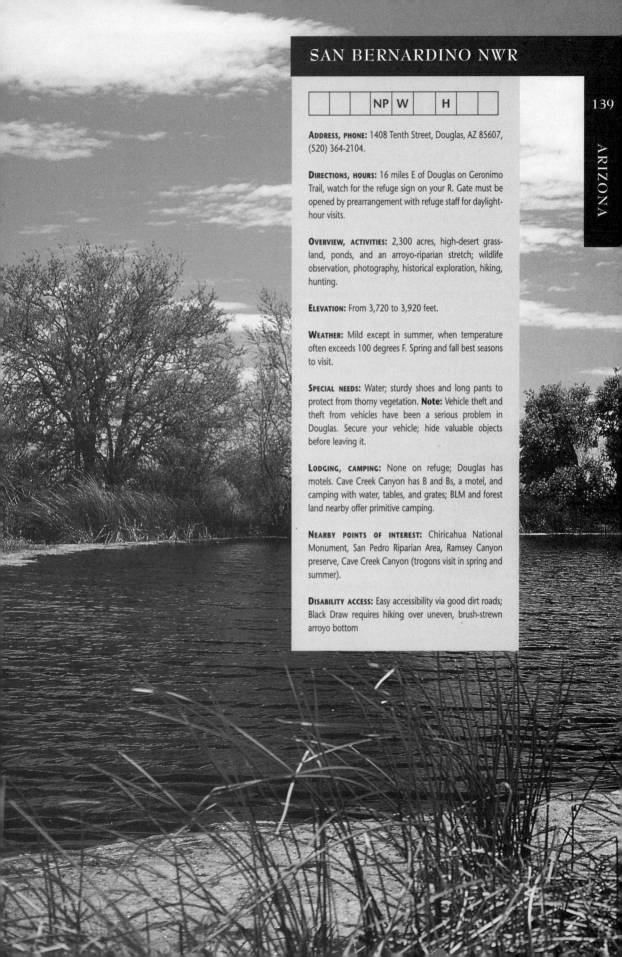

SAN BERNARDINO NWR

				NP	W		H		

ADDRESS, PHONE: 1408 Tenth Street, Douglas, AZ 85607, (520) 364-2104.

DIRECTIONS, HOURS: 16 miles E of Douglas on Geronimo Trail, watch for the refuge sign on your R. Gate must be opened by prearrangement with refuge staff for daylight-hour visits.

OVERVIEW, ACTIVITIES: 2,300 acres, high-desert grassland, ponds, and an arroyo-riparian stretch; wildlife observation, photography, historical exploration, hiking, hunting.

ELEVATION: From 3,720 to 3,920 feet.

WEATHER: Mild except in summer, when temperature often exceeds 100 degrees F. Spring and fall best seasons to visit.

SPECIAL NEEDS: Water; sturdy shoes and long pants to protect from thorny vegetation. **Note:** Vehicle theft and theft from vehicles have been a serious problem in Douglas. Secure your vehicle; hide valuable objects before leaving it.

LODGING, CAMPING: None on refuge; Douglas has motels. Cave Creek Canyon has B and Bs, a motel, and camping with water, tables, and grates; BLM and forest land nearby offer primitive camping.

NEARBY POINTS OF INTEREST: Chiricahua National Monument, San Pedro Riparian Area, Ramsey Canyon preserve, Cave Creek Canyon (trogons visit in spring and summer).

DISABILITY ACCESS: Easy accessibility via good dirt roads; Black Draw requires hiking over uneven, brush-strewn arroyo bottom

When you're a bird, it's often the little things that matter most. So it is with tiny San Bernardino NWR and its sister refuge, Leslie Canyon, located in the extreme southeastern corner of Arizona on the Mexican border, amid a valley strewn with cattle and carpeted in a sea of grass.

On their yearly migratory journeys, birds find welcome respite on these two small patches of protected high-desert land, which lie within a habitat-poor region of agriculture and nearly treeless ranch country. An array of desert-dwelling reptiles and mammals who live here or visit from the surrounding countryside also benefits from this crucial patch of habitat.

If you're a desert fish, a refuge such as San Bernardino matters even more. Fish are the major reason the former Slaughter Ranch was purchased by the Nature Conservancy in 1980 and transferred to the USFWS 2 years later. Tough little critters, the endangered Yaqui chub and Yaqui topminnow, and two federally threatened species, the Yaqui catfish and beautiful shiner, are extraordinary piscine survivors. Some are able, when nature turns particularly belligerent, to make homes in little more than oxygen-depleted, overheated mud puddles. Nearby Leslie Canyon provides them with additional habitat.

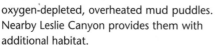

desert

The term "desert fish" may seem an oxymoron. Fact is, more than 30 indigenous fish exist throughout Arizona's desert country, all but one of them at imminent or probable risk of extinction. Tough as the various species are, modern-day water demands have imperiled these hardy desert dwellers as severely as at any time along their entire evolutionary journey. Overgrazing (which destroys habitat), agriculture (which removes water), and introduced predatory game fish are the main culprits, with help from a scattering of retirement communities and small towns that draw precious water from an area where water is always at a premium.

The water table has dropped dramatically in recent years due to overpumping. Bathhouse Spring, an artesian water source on the refuge that once gushed 6 feet into the air and provided a natural shower for early inhabitants, is now erratic and undependable. Now solar-powered pumps and haphazard artesian wells keep the moisture topside in a network of tiny scattered pools. These ponds are some of the last habitats for local indigenous fish. Each day is a coin toss for them: Heads means survival for a while longer; tails will mark their oblivion.

San Bernardino is accessible to visitors, while Leslie Canyon is not. The latter, a 2,700-acre satellite preserve, is closed off to casual visitors because its critical fish habitat is highly vulnerable to human disruption. To enter San Bernardino, you need a special-use permit, which is simple to get—just call or write for your permit and arrange for someone to unlock the gate. Exploring the tiny refuge is a 1-day affair. You can see a good deal of it by vehicle, but the most productive stretch is along an arroyo bottom that requires hiking and a little fancy footwork.

Slaughtered Landscape

San Bernardino refuge is one of the smallest in the system, barely 2,300 acres. The terrain is covered mainly by great and alkali sacaton grass, bunchgrasses that grow prolifically and remain straw colored most of the year. Scattered among them are creosote, mesquite, desert willow, and catclaw acacia, as well as various cacti and such dry-country plants as brittlebush, sandpaper bush, and allthorn. The head-high allthorn (or "all thorn"), whose name says it all, is nature's way of causing pain to the careless. Masses of hard thorns make up the body of this dark green, leafless plant, which sometimes responds to overgrazing by expanding into the mother of all briar patches. The plant grows from southern California to southwestern Arizona.

At least one plant proposed for protective status, the Huachucan water umbel (also called the Cienega false rush), was recently discovered along the moist edges of some cattail-lined ponds here. The tiny follicles of this low-lying plant make it nearly unnoticeable. But someone noticed, and there's no other plant like it. Now it has a place where it may possibly survive, as the Great Gardener intended.

History Rolls By

The land that makes up San Bernardino has been occupied sporadically for at least 10,000 years. Evidence of a Paleolithic Clovis culture has been excavated on refuge grounds. Spanish history dates to 1694, when Arizona's premier Catholic proselytizer, Father Eusebio Francisco Kino, passed through. In 1822, a Spanish land grant was deeded to a man named Ignacio Pérez.

The grassland that seems to roll off forever here is the reason cattle have so impacted the area's recent history. Texas John Slaughter was a colorful character who bought the present-day refuge land from the Pérez family in 1887 and whose own family lived here for decades after. Slaughter's personality made a good fit with the harshness around him. He was a sworn (some say brutal) Indian fighter and one in a series of sheriffs who employed strong measures to keep the streets of nearby Tombstone safe for decent folk.

Slaughter amassed his fortune through the mysterious acquisition of thousands of head of cattle in Texas. When his ownership was questioned (no receipt), he exited stage west to Arizona. Soon he was running as many as 100,000 hoofburgers over the grassy hills. His homesite, complete with a large, cottonwood-lined pond that now harbors endangered desert fish, has been meticulously restored and is open to visitors. A pamphlet leads guests, for a small fee, on a self-guided tour of Slaughter's life and times.

Several droughts in the late 1800s killed off most of the Slaughter cattle. Soon after, a series of destructive monsoons hit the live-stock-decimated terrain, tearing topsoil away like a blade through skin. Most arroyos in the desert are a recent phenomenon; before cattle and other forces disrupted the land, relatively few of these gullies were torn away to form seasonal watercourses—and even less were cut into grassy high desert. On San Bernardino, the erosive side of Slaughter's legacy is evident in the form of Black Draw, a 15-foot-deep gash that bisects the refuge.

A Draw for Wildlife

For both animals and human visitors to San Bernardino, Black Draw is the place to be. Walk through this quiet arroyo over the shallow, sometimes pooled, creekbed and a variety of life reveals itself. Birds such as hooded and Scott's orioles, summer tanager, verdin, ladder-backed woodpecker, and, in season, large numbers of migrating warblers fill the willows and cottonwoods with color and song. Gray hawks live and nest in the canopy (check the three tall cottonwoods midway along the draw). Bullfrogs scream in alarm as you approach; dragonflies hover while blue-throated, black-chinned, and rufous hummingbirds buzz in for a closer look. Green kingfishers, more common at nearby San Pedro Riparian Conservation Area near the town of Sierra Vista, stop in on occasion. The northern beardless tyrannulet, a favorite of birders, can sometimes be found here during warmer months.

riparian

Abundant vermilion flycatchers—the male a brilliant red with black wings and a dark mask, the female mostly brown—make their homes throughout the refuge, perching on low limbs and shrub tops. They're relatively unafraid of people and will perch fairly close if you remain calm and quiet. The little winged spot of fire calls with a whistled, 2-note *pee*. During breeding, the male courts its brownish, streak-breasted counterpart by singing a thin, 3-note song while hovering and fluttering, a sort of air-dance that must be both arousing and entertaining for prospective females.

Lizards and small mammals rustle in the brush, including the kangaroo rat, desert king snake, 3 species of rattlesnakes, and the gentle, foot-long Arizona alligator lizard. If you get here early enough or stay into late afternoon, good fortune may grace you with a glimpse of a javelina, a deer, or even a bobcat or mountain lion. Ocelots have been seen in the past at nearby Coronado Monument, but so far, none of these furtive cats have been spotted at the refuge (though they are spotted— wherever they live).

Scattered small water holes and a few larger ponds (some accessible, most off-limits) provide homes for desert fish. The trees and brush that surround them are often populated by various songbirds. Cooper's hawks perch on limbs over the smaller ponds, waiting for a chance at thirsty prey or maybe just to enjoy the view.

The water holes also make good living quarters for bullfrogs, the single most problematic species on the refuge—other than an occasional drug smuggling "mule" from Mexico, a long-term problem that had decreased significantly by 1995. The voracious frogs eat anything they can stuff in their gaping mouths, including birds, snakes, bats, rats, turtles, and their own family and friends.

Bullfrogs have devastated several populations here, including the endangered Mexican garter snake and the nearly extirpated Sonoran mud turtle. A single mud turtle was discovered on the refuge in 1984, the first to appear in 6 years.

Refuge personnel built a fence exclosure against the bullfrogs (accessible to visitors) to protect the dwindling number of Chiricahuan leopard frogs on the grounds. When depre-

dations continued, they set up an experimental miniexclosure at headquarters, introduced bullfrogs, and found that the little assassins were actually scaling the fence to reach their victims! An improved barrier design seems to have slowed the attack considerably, though bird predation still takes a toll on the endangered leopard frogs.

Swimming the Desert

The 4 endangered or threatened fish that the refuge protects are marvels of evolutionary engineering. Endangered, threatened, or candidate species include the Yaqui chub, Yaqui catfish, Yaqui topminnow, and beautiful shiner. They're delicate in the sense that few are left, and extinction is a real possibility; but given their survival characteristics, these fish are also as tough as the most grizzled desert prospector. They survive in pools and streams on the two refuges, as well as in cienegas (marshes) in the area. Some of the pools are fed by solar pumps; others remain full through spring action alone. The latter are rare, as the water table is far lower now than it was before Mexican and American residents began pumping it out. A few of the ponds are located in visitor areas; others are in a section of the refuge that is closed to all entry.

Experts believe these desert fish have always been few in number, eking out their obscure lives in the meager runoff and spring-fed watercourses of the Yaqui River drainage basin, which lies mainly in Mexico but also encompasses the refuge. Four other indigenous fish, the longfin dace, endangered Mexican stoneroller, roundtail chub, and Yaqui sucker, also live within the drainage and environs. All are slated for reintroduction on the refuge at some point.

These and other indigenous fish are now being bred and studied at the Dexter National Fish Hatchery in southeastern New Mexico, a last hope for numerous southwestern fish— most of them unknown to all but a few biologists. Why save them? Because they exist. Because they are beautiful and fascinating creatures. And because we diminish our collective spirit when we let another being slip into extinction.

Table Talk

Neighbors around the refuge are mostly ranchers, a life-style that often suggests conflict with the feds. Poorly managed cattle inflict environmental damage, and the presence of USFWS operations often translates into off-limits land.

In the case of San Bernardino and its water needs, you might assume ranchers would accuse the USFWS of caring "more about some mud-sucking fish than they do about people." Here, however, such conflict is minimal. The reason is coincidental interests. Water, or lack of, is the make-or-break factor both for ranchers and the refuge. The two sides are equally concerned about surrounding development and agricultural forces that threaten to take precious water away.

As a result, a regional interest group has sprung up, partly comprising ranching interests who often welcome refuge personnel to their meetings and even let them speak. The Malpai Borderlands Group meets regularly to discuss water and wildlife and to maintain political influence within the region.

Their agenda goes beyond water needs and uses. Convinced that prescribed burns are a good way to enhance habitat both for cattle and wild creatures, group members are pushing federal agencies, such as the BLM and Forest Service, to make fire a regular management tool in the area. That includes allowing lightning-caused fires to burn freely where appropriate. They're also maintaining grass banks and arranging conservation easements on private and leased lands, which will benefit both their cattle and regional wildlife.

The group represents the best kind of cooperation between commercial and wildlife interests, and it offers a model for regional problem-solving.

For now, tiny San Bernardino remains a secure living space for a surprising number of species. This is a refuge you can see in a single morning, though you may choose to spend an entire day here if the weather is mild. Bring plenty of water; if you need more, a wellhead on the refuge can be tapped for a cool drink.

The refuge is small but can often pack a powerful wildlife punch. Its scant acreage allows visitors to observe a good variety of species in a brief time. Spring and fall are the best seasons to visit. If you go in summer, plan to be gone by noon or visit in late afternoon, the other magical wildlife time.

Impressions and Experiences

Bird sightings:

Other wildlife sightings:

Notes:

PARTIAL BIRD LIST (OF 231 LISTED SPECIES): Vermilion flycatcher, loggerhead shrike, phainopepla, yellow warbler, black-bellied whistling duck, ruddy duck, American kestrel, common ground dove, Gila woodpecker, northern beardless tyrannulet, Cassin's kingbird.

PARTIAL MAMMAL LIST: Javelina, bobcat, mule deer, kangaroo rat, raccoon.

PARTIAL HERP LIST: Chiricahuan leopard frog, Mexican garter snake, diamondback and Mojave rattlesnakes, Gila monster, Sonoran mud turtle.

VC	R			W		H		

ADDRESS, PHONE: 9383 El Rancho Lane, Alamosa, CO 81101, (719) 589-4021.

DIRECTIONS, HOURS: To reach Alamosa refuge, go 4 miles E of Alamosa on Hwy 160, turn R on El Rancho Lane; 3 miles to Visitor's Center. Monte Vista NWR is located 6 miles S of the town of Monte Vista along Hwy 15. Visitor's Center open 7:30 a.m. to 4 p.m. weekdays; refuge roads open daylight hours year-round.

OVERVIEW, ACTIVITIES: Tour loop roads thru rabbitbrush and greasewood uplands and marsh habitats; Visitor's Center at Alamosa has information and exhibits; hiking trails on both units. Wildlife observation, photography, biking in some areas; hunting on both units.

ELEVATION: From 7,500 to 7,600 feet.

WEATHER: Mild from late spring thru early fall; can get very cold in winter, though many winter days are relatively mild; spring typically very windy. Spring and fall best seasons to visit.

SPECIAL NEEDS: Scope, window pod for in-vehicle photography (good in Monte Vista marshes).

LODGING, CAMPING: Motels and RV facilities in Monte Vista and Alamosa; camping at commercial campgrounds in both towns, at Great Sand Dunes National Monument (15 miles), and in San Juan National Forest.

NEARBY POINTS OF INTEREST: Great Sand Dunes National Monument; Zapata Ranch (resident bison herd and often elk herds on ranch); Mishak Lakes, a Nature Conservancy preserve, is difficult to access but is said to be a rewarding journey for hardy wildlife lovers.

DISABILITY ACCESS: Walking trail at Alamosa accessible; rest room facilities at both refuges are accessible; much of the visitor area on both units is accessible by vehicle only. Dike-top accessible trails were in the planning stage in early 1996.

When spring rolls around and it's time for western waterfowl to head north, many leave their wintering grounds for the northern-tier, glacier-carved "pothole" states or the cool reaches of Canada. However, others avoid those long journeys, opting for the convenient southern Colorado wetlands of the Alamosa and Monte Vista refuges.

The resemblance of Alamosa/Monte Vista NWR Complex to more northerly waterfowl habitat is what sets these high-country refuges apart. Nowhere else in the United States do such large concentrations of ducks and geese nest at so low a latitude. Thousands of mallards, cinnamon and green-winged teal, Canada geese, and other species raise their young on these 26,000 acres. Some years, the Monte Vista refuge has supported more than 1,200 nests per square mile.

freshwater wetlands

Up to 20,000 members of the Rocky Mountain population of greater sandhill cranes pass through Monte Vista on their way to and from nesting grounds in the northern-tier states. At Monte Vista they fill the sky with their trumpeting calls and enliven refuge grain fields with their leaping presence. In mid to late March, thousands of human visitors come to celebrate the grace and beauty of these magnificent birds.

Marshes along the Rio Grande River in Colorado's San Luis Valley have for centuries harbored significant bird populations. After the mid-1800s, when farming and ranching invaded an area long inhabited by Ute Indians and the wildlife that sustained them, bird and mammal numbers seriously declined. The Migratory Bird Conservation Commission responded to the losses in 1953 by creating Monte Vista NWR. Its sister refuge, Alamosa, was established in 1962. Separated by 20 miles and two small towns, the two units were combined in 1979 to form the present national wildlife refuge complex.

The San Luis Valley is part of a hydrologic system that funnels water from the bordering San Juan and Sangre de Cristo mountains. Snowmelt each spring swells the Rio Grande and recharges the groundwater system. Canals built more than a century ago, as well as artesian and pumped wells, are the lifeblood of the two refuge units, which lie on the valley's southern edge. Uplands blanketed in greasewood and four-wing saltbush comprise most of the hilly, riparian Alamosa refuge; Baltic rush is the major ground cover on table-flat Monte Vista. Each refuge unit is distinct in character, but both offer abundant life support for birds and other creatures.

Alamosa's Riparian Reaches

Alamosa is a 12,000-acre refuge of greasewood and rabbitbrush uplands, cut by the Rio Grande to form a series of channels and marshes. The refuge unit lies in the shadow of Colorado's Sangre de Cristo Mountains, a rugged high range topped by snowcap for most of the year. As it meanders through the refuge, the river's many oxbows create wetland ponds and shallows; short stretches of deeper channel attract some diving ducks and security-oriented geese.

A Visitor's Center on the western edge of Alamosa is the site of seasonal wetland shallows that often support small numbers of lingering migratory waterfowl through the warmer months. The wetlands here vibrate in early spring with the rasping of countless cricket frogs. A slow approach along the road may yield sightings of species such as pintail, cinnamon teal, northern shoveler, and others. The Visitor's Center itself is a good place to orient yourself to the wildlife, history, and ecology of the refuge complex.

A trail from the Visitor's Center parking lot takes you on a 2-mile round-trip along the river, where with proper stealth you might encounter pied-billed grebe, great blue heron, cattle and snowy egrets, and any of nearly 2 dozen waterfowl, including green-winged teal, gadwall, mallard, ruddy duck, and common merganser. Mudflats and shallows along the shore may yield common snipe, solitary and pectoral sandpipers, long-billed dowitcher, Wilson's phalarope, avocets and stilts, and other waders and shorebirds.

Brush, trees, and grass along the way may harbor willow flycatcher, Say's phoebe, western kingbird, mountain bluebird, yellow-rumped warbler, American and lesser goldfinch, vesper sparrow, ring-necked pheasant, meadowlark, and yellow-headed and red-winged blackbirds. A few mule deer, as well as badger, coyote, gray fox, long-tailed weasel, and kangaroo rat, may show themselves in the uplands, especially during early morning and dusk hours. Reptiles that range about the refuge include western garter snake, Plains spadefoot toad, Great Plains toad, leopard frog, and eastern fence lizard.

On your way to the tour loop east of the Visitor's Center, power poles along the road may support golden eagles in late winter and early spring; bald eagles are more common on the refuge in winter months, mainly along the river. Raptors cruise the entire area, preying on waterfowl and upland rodents and reptiles. Prairie falcons and kestrels and Swainson's and red-tailed hawks can often be spotted here. Along the eastward-running county road you'll pass broad, shallow wetlands that often teem with ducks, along with waders such as white-faced ibis, snowy egrets, and great blue herons.

A short distance after you cross the railroad track, a right turn takes you on a road passing in and out of refuge borders several times before you reach the bluff's loop road. Along the way you'll pass several *playa* wetlands that may or may not hold water and associated wildlife. A broad reach of scrubland here may be home to black-and-white warbler, sage thrasher, meadowlark, horned lark, jackrabbit, lizards and snakes, and an array of summer wildflowers.

The river channel that lies below the bluff often holds pied-billed grebe, redhead, scaup, ruddy, and other divers; broader shallows are home to mallard, pintail, shoveler, and numerous other dabblers. For best viewing,

take advantage of the rabbitbrush along the loop road to partially hide your vehicle. Refuge rules mandate that you remain in or near your vehicle while on the loop, which is exposed to broad reaches of the marsh. Your on-foot wanderings might otherwise frighten hundreds of birds into flight, disrupting their peace and chasing them out of sight of other visitors.

In early spring when frozen wetlands begin to thaw and cold-killed carp are everywhere, 4 dozen or more bald eagles may be perched on overhanging tree limbs or poised on ice, hunched over frozen fish dinners. Though they clearly savor the carp, bald eagle numbers often correlate with waterfowl densities, suggesting that bald eagles take more ducks than many people realize. Carrion always makes for an easy meal, but baldies can be efficient predators when they need to be.

During midwinter few eagles are in residence. Several other raptors inhabit the refuge in the coldest months, however. Great horned owls can be thick in winter, many of them staying year-round and nesting on both refuge units. Prairie falcon are numerous, too. Peregrine falcon may pass through during any season, but most often that recently down-listed species appears in spring and fall.

riparian

Monte Vista Unit

Monte Vista offers a more intimate connection with the creatures living amid its flat marshes and grassy uplands. Shadowed by the San Juan range, with its "fourteener" mountain peaks and year-round snowcap, the refuge is wrapped in farm fields marked by livestock, old log buildings, and picturesque weathered haystacks.

A 4-mile tour loop road (for vehicles only—no foot or bike travel is allowed) provides access into Monte Vista's 14,000 flat acres of marsh and grassland. The small wetland on your right as you enter the loop is an elegant example of a well-balanced marsh, both in ecological and aesthetic terms. From your vehicle you may spot any of dozens of water birds, including waders such as great blue heron and white-faced ibis, assorted waterfowl, yellow-headed blackbird, muskrat, and leopard frog.

The road rolls on past several shallow ponds that hold numerous waterfowl from spring through fall. Though water birds come by the thousands, Monte Vista is thickly vegetated and offers few mudflat margins for waders and shorebirds; thus, their visitation is light here. During one of three visits to the refuge, I spotted only 3 American avocets, hunched against the late April wind (which can be brisk), and a few killdeer in flight or scurrying across the roads.

In winter, waterfowl numbers decrease as icing steals habitat. An exception was the large mallard population that until recently hunkered down around warm water from several artesian springs. There they stayed through the cold months, surviving in weak physical condition, their population ravaged by avian cholera—a deadly disease that thrives on crowding and stress.

In 1992, refuge staffers began encouraging those birds to adopt a healthier life-style. Through a complex arrangement with other nearby water users, they developed more than 20 temporary warm-water wetlands. The birds dispersed onto these new habitats, cholera dropped to nearly zero, and most of the mallards have since begun to migrate normally.

Autumn at Monte Vista brings numerous birds in transit, including around 20,000 sandhill cranes heading for the southern reaches of New Mexico, where they winter at the Bosque del Apache refuge and nearby state-managed habitats. The 3 remaining whooping cranes in the Idaho–New Mexico flock, along with a hybrid "whoophill," often show up at Monte Vista for brief rest stops in spring and fall. During the last 2 weeks of March (dates change according to conditions), the refuge and city of Monte Vista sponsor a 4-day bird festival that attracts close to 2,000 crane-watchers each year. The festival features workshops, birding tours, conferences, and other events. (For information call [719] 852–2731.)

Passerines make use of both refuge units but not in great numbers. Small groves of cottonwood and willow scattered about the refuge may harbor perching birds, especially in migration. Trees, brush, and grasslands here support a relatively small number of species, including resident vesper and song sparrows, horned lark, black-billed magpie, short-eared owl, and American kestrel. Many more passerines are here in all but the winter months, including small numbers of shorebirds, numerous raptor species (a recent Christmas bird count turned up 70 harriers in just a few hours), red-shafted flicker, several swallow species, and yellow warbler. Trees along Hwy 15 near the refuge office are a good place to spot perching birds. Look for ring-necked pheasants and mule deer in the nearby fields.

A large pullout off the highway provides views of cranes and geese who feed in the refuge's 400 acres of organically grown crop fields, where barley, wheat, oats, and alfalfa are rotated yearly to provide browse for the birds. In the surrounding fields you may also spot mule deer or in winter some of the 600 elk who have been showing up regularly since the late 1980s.

The elk may become a source of problems for refuge overseers. They don't do much harm to Monte Vista refuge in normal years, but staffers expect them to move off the refuge and attack nearby haystacks and farm fences when a hard autumn snow hits, preventing them from reaching the natural browse. That may cause political problems for the refuge, and managers are studying ways to reduce the herd's presence. A special hunt is one option, though the cranes who visit in autumn are incompatible with high-powered rifles—

particularly in the eyes of the avid birders, who keep an eye on the refuge and might also feel threatened.

Nearby housing and highways are another reason to avoid the shooting option. As it is, some hunters line up along refuge boundaries, staring wistfully at their untouchable prey, who seem to understand that the refuge means sanctuary. When an elk bolts off the refuge, its flight may draw a flurry of hunters who blast away and then drag the carcass from nearby private land. Not a healthy situation for elk, neighbors, or hunters. As of 1996, the problem remained unresolved.

Monte Vista (along with 8 other refuges) has recently been challenged with a potentially far-reaching lawsuit over the impact of cattle grazing on refuge wildlife. For years, grazing had been allowed on Monte Vista. Recent studies indicated that the cattle were eradicating grassy "residual cover" needed by nesting waterfowl in spring. Though newer, more sophisticated grazing techniques had been adopted in recent years, the inverse relationship between grazing and nesting success remained significant. Several environmental organizations joined forces to stop grazing on this and other refuges.

In 1995, the parties settled out of court, agreeing that the USFWS would launch extensive research on the wildlife impacts of various grassland management techniques: prescribed burns, mowing, herbicides, and grazing. That study began in 1996. The results may be applied to management practices throughout the refuge system.

Shorebird Support

Though the deal wasn't finalized by early 1996, the refuge was in the process of acquiring a third unit. The 3,200-acre White Ranch—which will likely be renamed the Sangre de Cristo NWR when acquired—is a marshy area located in the flatlands just west of Great Sand Dunes National Monument. Its *playa* mudflats would add a needed third dimension to the refuge complex: good shorebird habitat. Refuge staffers expect to have the new unit under their wing by early 1997, if all goes well.

Impressions and Experiences

Bird sightings:

Other wildlife sightings:

Notes:

PARTIAL BIRD LIST: Great blue heron, cattle egret, white-faced ibis, sandhill crane, whooping crane, Canada goose, mallard, gadwall, cinnamon teal, ruddy duck, Swainson's hawk, golden and bald eagles, prairie falcon, Virginia rail, spotted sandpiper.

PARTIAL MAMMAL LIST: Mule deer, elk, coyote, badger, gray fox, muskrat, long-tailed weasel, striped skunk, kangaroo rat.

PARTIAL HERP LIST: Gopher snake, western garter snake, Plains spadefoot toad, Great Plains toad, leopard frog, eastern fence lizard.

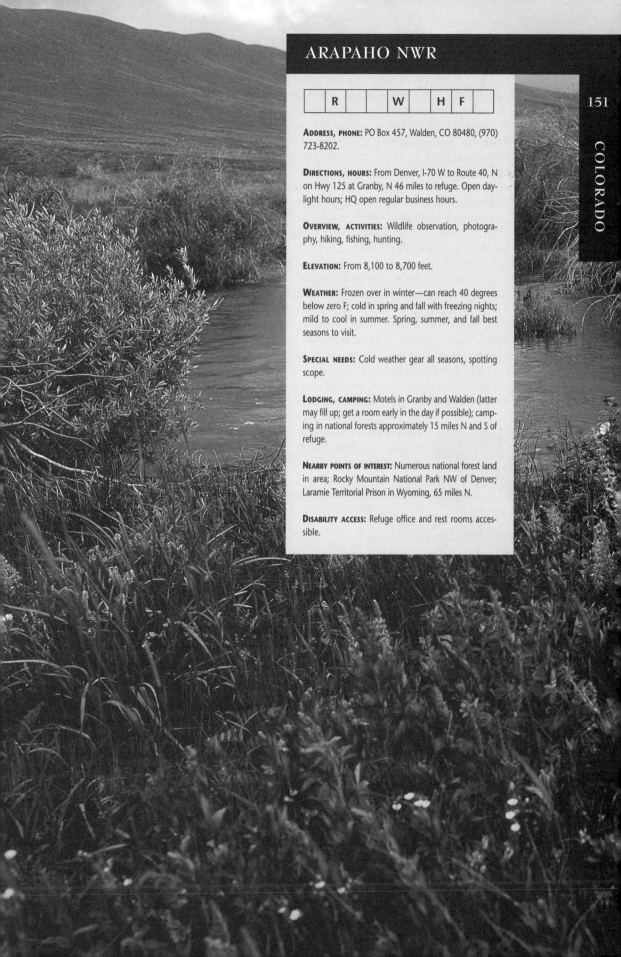

ARAPAHO NWR

	R		W		H	F	

ADDRESS, PHONE: PO Box 457, Walden, CO 80480, (970) 723-8202.

DIRECTIONS, HOURS: From Denver, I-70 W to Route 40, N on Hwy 125 at Granby, N 46 miles to refuge. Open daylight hours; HQ open regular business hours.

OVERVIEW, ACTIVITIES: Wildlife observation, photography, hiking, fishing, hunting.

ELEVATION: From 8,100 to 8,700 feet.

WEATHER: Frozen over in winter—can reach 40 degrees below zero F; cold in spring and fall with freezing nights; mild to cool in summer. Spring, summer, and fall best seasons to visit.

SPECIAL NEEDS: Cold weather gear all seasons, spotting scope.

LODGING, CAMPING: Motels in Granby and Walden (latter may fill up; get a room early in the day if possible); camping in national forests approximately 15 miles N and S of refuge.

NEARBY POINTS OF INTEREST: Numerous national forest land in area; Rocky Mountain National Park NW of Denver; Laramie Territorial Prison in Wyoming, 65 miles N.

DISABILITY ACCESS: Refuge office and rest rooms accessible.

Arapaho NWR stands literally at the top of the refuge system. This high intermountain 24,000-acre refuge lies more than 8,000 feet above sea level. It is located in the heart of what Coloradans call North Park, a 30- by 45-mile reach of glacier-carved basin that is one of four such grassy reaches in the state's northern section. Irrigated primarily by the Illinois River through a complex network of irrigation canals, the refuge offers waterfowl and other wildlife ideal breeding, feeding, and nesting habitat.

Surrounding the park is an enfolding horseshoe of mountains: on the west runs the Park Range, on the south the Rabbit Ears Mountains, on the southeast the Never-Summer Range, and to the east and northeast the Medicine Bows. Opening north into Wyoming, the basin delivers the Illinois, Michigan, Canadian, and Grizzley rivers into the North Platte. Several endangered species, including the whooping crane, piping plover, and a high-country orchid, find critical habitat along the Platte, and thousands of sandhill cranes arrive at the riverbank each spring to feed and breed there.

upland

Arapaho is a place of great diversity in a setting of long views and lush surroundings. Inhabited by 187 bird species, nearly 3 dozen mammals, and a dozen fish and herptiles, its irrigated meadows, sage uplands, wetlands, and willow riparian acreage offer critical support for creatures large and small. Wildlife viewing opportunities here are many, often within easy view of car travelers.

Longtime Land Use

For centuries, the grassy reaches of North Park provided grazing and calving grounds for vast herds of bison, whose weather-sculpted horns have been unearthed on the refuge. Ute Indians followed the herds here in spring and summer, moving to lower environs in fall as each year's 60-inch average annual snowfall and below-freezing temperatures set in.

By 1820, trappers such as Frenchman Jacques Bijeau entered the basin in search of beaver. The year 1844 brought famed western explore Gen. John C. Frémont to North Park, where he recorded this entry:

The valley narrowed as we ascended and presently divided into a gorge, through which the river passed as through a gate—a beautiful circular valley of thirty miles in diameter, walled in all around with snowy mountains, rich with water and grass, fringed with pine on the mountain sides below the snow, and a paradise to all grazing animals.

By 1878 (as bison were being driven to near-extinction throughout the West), Euro-Americans arrived to plumb the park's riches. Extremely harsh winter weather chased most ranchers and miners away in time, but a few hardy families held out. Some of those families remain in what is now Jackson County. Half of the 1,800 residents here are active ranchers.

A few graze their cattle on the refuge, an arrangement designed to manage the grasses, which would otherwise grow too matted in time even for duck nesting. The cattle are grazed in a short-duration, high-intensity manner, a practice developed by Holistic Resource Center founder Alan Savory. The innovative technique mimics the grazing style of now-extirpated bison. Such grazing clips grasses once, where cows left untended often browse grass over and over for long periods, stressing plants and often leaving erosion in their wake. Short-term grazing in selected areas also helps break up the earth, allowing oxygen and nutrients to move downward, enriching the soil.

Such grazing benefits more than the ecosystem—it also helps keep federal/private relations in the area cordial. Remarkably, ranchers using the refuge pay premium fees for running their cattle on this rich meadowland, and they seem glad to do so. The federal government actually profits from such payments, as opposed to the situation that now exists on BLM land, where grazers pay far below market value and exercise much less control over their animals.

Restoring the Big Picture

Arapaho refuge was formed in 1967 to help mitigate the loss of prairie glacier-created pothole habitat in states to the north. Where countless glacier-carved water holes in the Dakotas and other northern-tier states once provided breeding grounds for millions of US waterfowl, modern development, agriculture, and other human-made alterations erased thousands of those north country wetlands.

Arapaho's numerous natural and artificial ponds mirror some of that lost pothole country. Most are fed by a system of ditches put in place by ranchers over the past hundred years.

Waterfowl support remains a primary role here, though the newer "ecosystem management" philosophy (supporting a region's full diversity of plants and animals) has broadened Arapaho's mission. Until the decade of the 1990s, wetland development within the refuge system was designed almost solely to bolster the number of shootable birds. Newer impoundments are designed in varying levels of depth and within varying habitats. The practice supports a much wider variety of water-oriented species, including waders, mudflat browsers, and upland nesters.

On the political side, ecosystem-oriented programs are ongoing at Arapaho and sometimes beyond its borders. They bring together a multitude of federal, state, and private entities that attempt to solve land and water problems while accommodating the interests of each party.

The local Owl Mountain project is a prime example. Formed initially to solve problems related to elk overabundance, the project has brought together many divergent interests. All seem to acknowledge the importance of maintaining a healthy, balanced ecosystem in the face of their varied commercial and environmental efforts. Though problems may arise due to opposing needs, the members maintain an ongoing dialogue. Talking is always good business when "competing" interests seek their share of an area's natural bounty.

Refuge staffers here also involve themselves in a variety of voluntary restoration and habitat improvement projects off the refuge, backed by government programs and money, some involving private landowners. They see their role as going beyond refuge management activities, since wildlife respects few lines on the map.

Diverse Habitats

Arapaho is a diverse refuge, but it's also a seasonal one. With an average of only 30 consecutive days of frost-free weather each year, the refuge is often snowed in, blocked up, or frozen over. Your chances of exploring its back roads between October and March are virtually nil—only the short headquarters road from Hwy 125 is snowplowed during those months.

A few brave souls do make the arduous trip in winter, and there are good reasons for such a visit. Elk often winter on the refuge in the hundreds, pawing through snow to get at grass and other forage. Golden eagles and rough-legged hawks also winter at Arapaho, feeding on such delicacies as long-tailed

riparian

weasel, ermine, marmot, hardy Nuttall's cottontail, and other prey who dare to leave their dens and holes in the subfreezing weather.

The refuge is sometimes accessible in March and April, but snowmelt often leaves behind muddy, sloggy conditions that can bog tires and make road hiking a messy chore. Refuge staffers run water into numerous refuge impoundments in the late winter months while ponds are still frozen. The practice creates habitat that draws in early bird migrators, helping build their numbers at the earliest opportunity.

May through early October are the best months to visit, with May–June and September–October the best of the best. I visited in July and found conditions windy and cool, with daytime temperatures in the low 50s (often they'll reach the 70s this time of year) and nights dropping just below freezing. Birds were relatively few in number then, possibly due to stiff winds that blasted the refuge. I encountered a few Wilson's phalaropes swirling about in the flooded fields, killdeer teaming on the roadways, Brewer's sparrow, American goldfinches, and marsh wrens hopping about in the low brush. Snipe perched on low posts along the refuge back road to Hwy 14—an odd place to find long-billed mudflat dwellers—and Swainson's hawks and kestrels hovered over the meadows in search of prey.

A Forster's tern made a brief appearance, 1 of 2 tern species (with the black) who visit here, most likely from the Great Salt Lake area. A birder's favorite, the rosy finch inhabits the refuge all year. Oftentimes this semicolonial finch can be found at HQ feeders. The life of the male rosy finch isn't really that "rosy." Outnumbering females by 6 to 1, the male finch spends much of its life fighting other males. Along with the finch many songbirds at Arapaho migrate vertically rather than horizontally, cruising up and down nearby mountainsides as the seasons dictate rather than hundreds of miles to warmer climes.

Several of the dozen moose who browse Arapaho's willow riparian reaches were easy enough to spot. A dirt road leaving the HQ parking lot, running north for 6 miles to Hwy 14, is a good place for encountering these Colorado Division of Wildlife transplants. Generally, they're visible a hundred or more yards from the road along the willow-lined river course. (If you approach the refuge on Hwy 125 from Granby, scan the riverbed along the way for browsing moose.)

Beaver also live along the back road to Hwy 14; their amazing architectural creations line the river all along its course. In this area you might also find raccoon, badger, red fox, muskrat, and porcupine, especially early in the day.

This road, which can get mushy in wet weather, is also your best bet for spotting

sage grouse, who live in the uplands east of the roadway but visit the water near dusk and dawn. The short stretch of road running between two cattle guards is where this largest of US grouse species most often shows up.

Sage grouse are declining in Colorado; in 1995 the state was considering them for its threatened species list, though that effort has been halted for now. No one is sure why their numbers are shrinking, but grazing and development are two likely suspects. Curiously, the state and refuge still allow sage grouse hunting. Erring on the side of caution would seem a more prudent way to go, as everyone agrees the grouse population has plunged dramatically.

An off-refuge sage grouse lek (mating ground) is occupied in late spring on nearby BLM land. Ask refuge personnel where it is if you're interested in observing the antics of these ostentatious breeders. Please respect the birds' reproductive needs, however, and keep your distance.

Once you've driven the 6-mile back road and reach Hwy 14, turn left toward the town of Walden. On the way you'll pass the Brocker Overlook, a good spot from which to survey the valley and visually trace the river meander for miles. Few moose are found here since there are almost no willows, and a moose without willows is a sad moose, indeed. You might spot deer in the area, though, as well as coyotes and any of several raptor species.

Another dirt road, running up the hill southeast of HQ, takes you to a second overlook, this one tracing a ridge top for several miles. Below runs a dense, willow-lined stretch of the river, where there is also a walking trail. To the east is endless sage upland. Moose often turn up along the river here, and the heights make a good platform for spotting raptors, as well as sage dwellers, such as meadowlark, Brewer's sparrow, and lark bunting, the Colorado state bird. Occasionally, a Harris's sparrow appears on the refuge, throwing local birders into a generally dignified frenzy.

Wildflowers, including lupine, narrow-leaf

paintbrush, larkspur, and wild iris, grace the meadows and riversides. One of the most prolific wildflower sites lies in the meadow along the self-guided riparian trail. That trail begins at the end of a road running south from HQ (turn left just after the bridge from HQ). From the parking lot (and a handicapped-accessible rest room) you'll find a winding path through willows and along the crisp, gurgling Illinois River.

The trail takes you through a beautiful stretch of riverside habitat, good habitat for birds as well as small mammals, such as porcupine, muskrat, and possibly weasels that live here. I spent hours on the trail strolling about, taking in the beauty of wildflowers, rushing water, and swaying willows. Benches are in place here, allowing you to settle in.

Moose Moods

One of the charms you may encounter on this path is the same moose you may have spotted from the ridge above. Part of a group of animals transported to the region from Utah's Uinta Mountains and the Yellowstone area, these largest members of the deer family have spread throughout middle Colorado to the New Mexico border. Since their arrival in the 1970s, the few dozen original transplantees have expanded to an estimated population of 500.

Unfortunately, as the herd has expanded, so has moose hunting. Close to a hundred permits are now assigned to moose hunters, up from less than half a dozen a decade ago. The "sport" involves finding a barn-door-sized moose (who is generally browsing contentedly on willow leaves), lining up the sights, and blasting away. Some who have seen the hunt say it resembles assassination more than sport, but state game officials have chosen to keep the population at its current level due to riparian damage these willow-munchers cause; sadly, hunting is probably the most cost-effective way to maintain that balance.

A little caution is in order anytime you're in moose country. The riparian trail south of HQ,

for instance, carries you along a winding path flanked by thick willow stands. Within this network, moose enjoy browsing, mating, and chaperoning their young. The willows obscure parts of the river and meadows from view.

Moose are gentle, somewhat timid creatures, sedate most of the time and ready to flee at the sight of humans. But there are notable exceptions to this rule. During mating and calving seasons a protective, aggressive nature ascends, a fact that visitors should always keep in mind. Never approach a moose calf. If you find yourself between Mom and her little stumbler or between a male and female who seem in an amorous mood, move away quickly.

In 1994, a local woman attempting to pull her dogs off a moose calf was savagely attacked by its mother—akin to being repeatedly rammed by a car. She barely escaped with her life and spent weeks in the hospital and much more in rehab. Keep your distance. If you see a nearby moose's neck hair stiffen, you're facing imminent attack. In that case, back away calmly but rapidly, be ready to run, and try to move in the direction of such cover as large trees.

Despite the relatively small risk they pose, moose are wondrous creatures to behold. In company with common sense, a sighting will likely be one of your most treasured memories of an Arapaho visit.

Tour Loop Road

The most frequented part of the refuge (and the only area permanently closed to the waterfowl, rail, antelope, and sage grouse hunting) begins 4 miles north of the headquarters road off Hwy 125. Here, a 6-mile, self-guided tour loop carries you past several larger refuge ponds, where much of the waterfowl activity takes place, including the rearing of young.

By the end of each September, the refuge supports up to 8,000 waterfowl, and more than 7,000 ducklings and up to 300 Canada goslings are born here each year. With planned habitat expansion, those numbers should increase to around 12,000 ducklings and 500 Canada geese.

A brochure available from the loop's kiosk provides information on various habitats along the roadway. The tour road runs past sage flats, ponds and mudflats, nesting upland and emergents, and an urban center for white-tailed prairie dogs. White-tails create smaller towns than their black-tailed cousins, who live at lower elevations. The town is also inhabited by Wyoming ground squirrels, a much smaller species of burrowing rodent. Burrowing owls live here, too, and are occasionally seen perched beside holes, standing guard.

Two other roads running east off the refuge portion of the highway offer interesting wild-life encounters. One brings you to a river overlook northeast of the roadway. The other, which begins near the Adopt-a-Highway sign, takes you along a narrow meander to a high spot above two ponds. Here waterfowl such as teal, gadwall, eared and pied-billed grebes, and others may be found, often with their young, in midsummer.

The second of the two ponds—the one con-taining both cattails and bulrushes—has for several years been a communal nesting site for black-crowned night herons. More than 30 nests exist within surrounding vegetation. Stay near the gate and use a scope for heron-watching; approach more closely and you'll likely spook the birds, disrupting their breed-ing and nesting. The herons hatch their young at different times throughout the summer; a scan of the pond's edges in midsummer will reward you with views of the full range of hatchlings, juveniles, and adults.

Multitude of Management Voices

Water is a big issue here, as it is through-out the West. Because the North Platte and its critical habitat receive water passing through the refuge, Arapaho must "reim-burse" the river when water is drawn out. That entails closing a headgate for a specified period or enacting some other method to replace captured water. Water parceling is complex, a bureaucratic hassle requiring much paperwork and effort. But as we've learned through so many past mistakes, once a species is gone, you'll only find it in picture books and on TV nature programs. So God bless bureaucracy. Sometimes.

Grazing on this and other refuges, however sensible a management tool, may not be an option if a recent compatibility-related law-suit by environmentalists goes in favor of the plaintiffs. That would leave fire as the primary grassland management tool at Arapaho. Con-trolled burns here are troublesome and not always practical due to winds, short burn seasons, and other factors.

Innovative grazing techniques, such as those developed by Holistic Resources Center founder Alan Savory, create new options for refuge managers. Here, grazing may be the best option for grass management, one that also takes into account the needs and desires of neighboring ranchers. If overseen carefully and used strictly for management needs, grazing on Arapaho may be a good way to solve both biological and political problems in a single effort. To keep the refuge system healthy in the face of powerful, divergent interests, such practical choices may be the best way to go.

Impressions and Experiences

Bird sightings:

Other wildlife sightings:

Notes:

PARTIAL BIRD LIST (OF 187 LISTED SPECIES): Eared grebe, mallard, gadwall, pintail, lesser scaup, golden and bald eagles, killdeer, spotted sandpiper, American avocet, black tern, great horned owl, belted kingfisher, Lewis's woodpecker, willow flycatcher, American dipper, house wren, sage thrasher, mountain bluebird, Wilson's warbler, yellow-headed blackbird, western tanager, lark bunting.

PARTIAL MAMMAL LIST (OF 32 LISTED SPECIES): Pronghorn, moose, mule deer, elk, red fox, ermine, bobcat, muskrat, golden-mantled ground squirrel, least chipmunk, Nuttall's cottontail.

PARTIAL HERP LIST (OF 5 LISTED SPECIES): Barred tiger salamander, western toad, striped chorus frog, wood frog, wandering garter snake.

BROWNS PARK NWR

	R	C		W				

ADDRESS, PHONE: 1318 Highway 318, Maybell, CO 81640, (970) 365-3613.

DIRECTIONS, HOURS: Hwy 318 E from Dutch John (40 miles); I-40 to Hwy 318 W to Maybell, CO (50 miles from Maybell to refuge); Hwy 500 N from Vernal (50 miles dirt); Hwy 430 from Rock Springs, WY (95 miles). Refuge always open. HQ open regular business hours Mon thru Fri.

OVERVIEW, ACTIVITIES: River, marshes, riparian canyons, uplands; wildlife viewing, hiking, biking, canoeing/rafting, camping, fishing.

ELEVATION: From 5,355 to 6,200 feet.

WEATHER: Cool days spring thru fall, very cold winters with mild snowfall; temperatures generally close to or below freezing at night year-round. Spring and fall best seasons to visit.

SPECIAL NEEDS: Self-contained for remote, service-free area; warm clothing, full tank of gas from source nearest the refuge, high-clearance vehicle for cruising S river road, 4WD best for back road trips, bug repellent.

LODGING, CAMPING: Motels in Craig, CO; Vernal, UT; Rock Springs, WY; primitive camping on refuge.

NEARBY POINTS OF INTEREST: Flaming Gorge Reservoir and Dam; three historic sites on refuge: Lodore Hall, Two Bar Ranch, Fort Davy Crockett site; also several historic homesites.

DISABILITY ACCESS: HQ and Visitor's Center wheelchair accessible, with accessible rest rooms. Both campgrounds have wheelchair-accessible rest rooms. Physically challenged—accessible fishing pier. A waterfowl hunting blind and fishing pier are also accessible to those with impaired mobility.

Despite its accessibility by paved highway, Browns Park NWR in the northwest corner of Colorado is among the most remote federal refuges in the lower 48 states. From its sage uplands, cottonwood-lined creeks, rocky river cliffs, marshes, and backwaters, the nearest community of any size is nearly 50 miles away—and there you'll find little support in case of medical or mechanical problems. A trip to Browns Park is a major expedition that requires total self-sufficiency.

Except for the sad absense of wolves and grizzlies, the ecosystem at Browns Park closely resembles its primeval aspect. In colder winters the high-desert region draws hundreds of elk from the surrounding mountains, along with lesser numbers of mule deer and a few of the bighorn sheep reintroduced to the area by the state around 1980. Moose and deer wander the draws and trace the river course. Sage grouse strut and pronghorns browse

the greasewood and sage uplands. A colorful variety of passerines inhabits the trees and shrubs along the river and its brushy feeder canyons. The long views here are awe-inspiring.

riparian

In the Green River's cold depths, hardy representatives of 4 endangered native fish species are occasionally observed despite dam-chilled water temperatures that challenge their viability and limit their procreation. (Flaming Gorge dam lies just 25 miles upriver.) The Green and inflowing creeks also support, along with nonnative game fish, indigenous species, including Utah chub, mottled sculpin, bluehead and flannelmouth suckers, and fathead minnow.

A small but vigorous collection of waterfowl comes in spring and stays into fall, brooding their young in this tiny patch of remaining wetland along their migratory path. Bird life is scarce here in winter, mainly because the marshes freeze over in November and remain locked in ice until March. (Canada geese and a few ducks do, however, hang around on the icy river.) In winter, management emphasis turns toward support of large mammals, who

find sustenance on the upland reaches of this 13,455-acre refuge.

History: Characters and Conflicts

Located in its namesake region known as Browns Park—one of four extensive grassy meadows in the northern reaches of the state—the refuge sits at the confluence of colorful historic forces. "History" here more accurately begins in Mesozoic prehistory, more than 60 million years ago, when dinosaurs inhabited the region. Remnants of those scaled giants can be seen at nearby Dinosaur National Park, which borders the refuge to the southeast. Dinosaur artifacts occasionally surface on the refuge, too.

Thousands of years ago, native peoples known to us as the Fremont Culture lived in this mountain-flanked valley. Over more recent centuries, a succession of aboriginal groups, mainly Snake and Shoshoni peoples, hunted buffalo here and maintained themselves amid the park's abundance.

After Euro-Americans arrived—a flamboyant parade that included the Dominguez–Escalante expedition in 1776; soldiers and trappers, including Kit Carson and Jim Bridger, in the 1830s and 1840s; and gold chasers, cattlemen, and outlaws by the 1860s—the character of the park began to change. Criminals, such as Butch Cassidy, "rustler queen" Ann Bassett, and other assorted robbers, horse thieves, and generic scalawags, used the park and its proximity to the Utah state line to evade the law and graze their ill-gotten herds. Historians say criminal behavior other than unprovoked murder was accepted as the norm by most park residents.

The Indians and buffalo were largely gone by 1873, when white settlement began. Three national historic sites on the refuge serve as reminders of that past. They include the still-active Lodore Hall, a local community center; Two Bar Ranch; and the site of Fort Davy Crockett, a settler/Indian contact and trading point.

From the late 1800s until recently, excessive grazing overtaxed much of the grassland, allowing sage and other shrubs to increase their presence and creating erosive conditions. Exotic plants such as giant whitetop and salt cedar later invaded, altering the biotic balance even further. Construction of Flaming Gorge Dam in 1962 brought dramatic changes in the river system and accompanying marshes—impacts that further aggravated the loss of prairie pothole waterfowl habitat to the north, degrading the ancient migratory system of stopover and breeding habitats.

Restoring Balance

The refuge was approved in 1963 and opened in 1965, mainly through a Duck Stamp–funded purchase of private land. While not officially acknowledged as a Bureau of Reclamation mitigation refuge (the designation has political/economic ramifications, and this refuge, like most, is a political beast), Browns Park was formed to support migratory waterfowl after Flaming Gorge eradicated riverine wetlands in the area. With river flood and flow now tamed and the Green subject to wide fluctuations, electric water pumps are required to support the life-giving marshes.

Here ducks, grebes, herons, bitterns, rails, and other bird species breed and raise their young in spring and summer. Around 2,500 ducklings are hatched in the marshes each year, along with close to 300 goslings of the Great Basin Canada variety (recently rechristened the "western" race). Westerns are large birds, just a few pounds smaller than robust midwestern giants.

Redhead, gadwall, mallard, and a small number of canvasbacks represent the major duck species who use Browns Park. Passerines are well represented during warm months—a total of 195 bird species have been identified here. With its rich mix of desert upland, riparian, river, and marsh habitats, the bird list is eclectic. It includes tundra swan, bald and golden eagle, merlin, sora and Virginia rail, sandhill crane, mountain plover, marbled godwit, red-necked and Wilson's phalaropes, white-winged dove, pygmy owl, 4 humming-

bird species, 6 swallows, red-breasted nuthatch, Clark's nutcracker, sage thrasher, blue-gray gnatcatcher, 8 warblers, and assorted buntings, grosbeaks, sparrows, towhees, and finches.

In winter, scores of mountain bluebirds congregate here, along with perhaps 300 Canada geese and 600 ducks, who reside on the unfrozen river and its sandbars.

Along with elk, deer, moose, black bear, and bighorns, numerous smaller mammals find welcoming habitat at Browns Park. Among them are black- and white-tail jackrabbits, several species of mice, rats, voles, and shrews, and the evocatively named star-nosed mole. This tiny, secretive burrowing creature, listed here though its territory is theoretically restricted to the northeast United States, is a fascinating critter. In warm weather, it uses 22 (count 'em) sensitive probes on its nose to root about for earthworms, its favorite food. In winter, when the ground is frozen, the near-sightless creature takes to the frigid waters, swimming rapidly about and preying on fish and aquatic morsels. Truly a mole of many talents.

upland

Other mammals here include 3 species of fox (gray, kit, and red), beaver, raccoon, mink, long-tailed weasel, mountain lion, and river otter. Herptile species include a small number of western rattlers—the only poisonous species extant at Browns Park— Great Basin gopher snake, the rare rubber boa, 6 types of lizards, 5 toad and frog species, and the seldom-seen tiger salamander.

Though the area's climate was less arid in past centuries, Browns Park is a desert now, receiving an average of around 9 to 10 inches of rainfall each year. Mountains surrounding the valley are responsible for this lack of precipitation, capturing most incoming moisture in the form of snow. Whitecapped higher reaches around the park add yet another element to Browns Park's incomparable beauty.

The highest reaches of Browns Park support juniper and pine. Upland benches are cloaked in sage, greasewood, shadscale and hopsage, rubber and other rabbitbrushes, and various grasses, including western wheatgrass, Indian ricegrass, Great Basin wild rye, and needle and thread. Desert conditions support a variety of cactus species, including the dwarfish plains cactus, barrel, claret cup, and pincushion, along with sego lily and wild buckwheat. Typically, desert-dwelling species such as kit fox and spadefoot toad are found here, too.

Winters can dip below zero degrees F, but the park's erratic snowfall is light and rarely stays on the ground for long. Thus, one can visit at any time of year and find conditions that may be demanding but that are tolerable to those who prepare adequately.

One of three access roads to the refuge, the dirt back road from Vernal, Utah, is the most interesting. It's also the chanciest in terms of weather and road conditions (call ahead for road conditions). Hwy 500N runs from Vernal through sparsely vegetated hills and grass-decked ranchland, then over a beautiful mountain pass a few miles south of the refuge.

Along the way you may camp on BLM land, but choose your campsite carefully, as much of the area is privately owned. Near the refuge you'll pass the edge of the Diamond Breaks Wilderness, which borders the refuge along most of its southern reach and offers good hiking and exploring. In 1995, this land was actually a "wilderness study area," slated for designation in the state's system of wild, roadless areas. With antinature politicians on the rise, its designation may be on hold for a while.

Beaver Creek

Just west of HQ, Beaver Creek runs northward across Hwy 318 and southward down to the river. The creek is aptly named—beaver dams line its entire length, with more than a dozen dams and associated ponds per mile. You can hike the winding creek or more easily hike the benches above it. Here you'll have a

good chance of spotting moose browsing in the creekbed. Thick growth along the creek also provides good habitat for songbirds, including cedar waxwing, a variety of warblers, marsh wren, and many others. Small mammals, such as mink, raccoon, and others, also occupy the creek habitat.

Riverside Sights

Several habitats comprise the refuge, all of them rich with life. Sage upland benches cover nearly 7,000 refuge acres, where you can find many of the large mammals, especially in winter. Here the at-risk sage grouse cavorts, pursued—along with other prey, such as rats, reptiles, and rabbits—by coyotes, foxes, and other carnivores. A long access road takes you across the uplands, allowing good overviews of the 9 marshes along the river. Signs along the way explain the significance of various refuge habitats.

The same road leads you down the benches to close proximity with the north marshes. Find a perch along the edge of marsh vegetation in spring or summer, close to a stand of cottonwoods or willows, and you'll likely spot a variety of passerines. Some of them may be yellow-breasted chat, lazuli bunting, and yellow and Wilson's warbler, but many more pass through on their way north and south. Here you may also spot a moose or two browsing in the willows. The road offers high points for viewing raptor flybys, and in the evening it allows for spectacular sunset views to the northwest.

A couple of miles from the turn onto the northside road is a blind and accessible fishing pier. The blind can be good for bird photography. From the Crook Campground you can see the refuge housing area to the east. In the tall cottonwoods above the houses is a small great blue heron rookery. Please stay out of the housing area (unless you get permission). From the river you can get good binocular views of the nests and possibly of young herons trying out their new wings on the high limbs.

Return to the eastern side of the refuge and cross the swinging bridge (an accessible rest room and a primitive campground are located here), and you'll reach a 2-way road running along the southwest side of the Green. The bridge itself dates back to the first decade of this century. For decades, would-be crossers had to leave their conveyance, rearrange the scattered wood slats on the bridge, then proceed across the rickety structure, hearts thumping along with their tires. It's been improved, though it still sways as you cross, providing a touch of adventure.

Take a right on the other side and you enter the back road to Vernal. A left turn carries you along a marsh-side route where some of the best water-bird viewing on the refuge can be found. The marsh areas are closed to entry from March 1 until July 31 to give breeders some peace; they often nest right on the dikes. Visitors may hike the area at other times, so it's important to honor this regulation.

The road itself is fairly smooth along its first few miles, but it gets rougher as you continue on. In wet weather it can be a vehicle-bogger, so use your best judgment about proceeding. High clearance is a must here, and 4WD is a good idea if you wish to travel the entire 8-mile length.

The best marshes for wildlife contain a 50–50 mix of emergent vegetation and open water. Succession constantly moves that mix in favor of emergents. Management efforts such as controlled burns and clearing help keep the balance intact, allowing migratory waterfowl good habitat year after year. Wildlife refuges, if allowed to go unmanaged, would be far less valuable to wildlife in some years. Management may sometimes seem like meddling, but it is a crucial element in wildlife support in these modern times.

Flynn Bottom, the first marsh area you'll reach, is one of the better places at Browns Park for spotting moose. White pelicans also prefer this marsh and the sandbars that line its riverside edge. Warren Bottom is a favored waterfowl spot that often produces up to 7 broods of geese and many ducks each season.

Horseshoe Marsh across the river was the site of a recent attempt by refuge staff to transplant cottonwood poles. Around 75 trees were planted. Beavers destroyed every last one of them.

Many of the culprits are known as "bank beavers," so named because rather than dams and ponds, they construct their lodges by digging into riverbanks. Other than their choice of homes, though, they have the same big-toothed habits as their pond-dwelling brothers and sisters.

Nelson Bottom, the site of a Ducks Unlimited/state habitat rehabilitation effort, is the site of a bank-widening effort that began in 1995 and is scheduled for completion by 1997. At that time, it should provide good wildlife viewing.

Shorebirds can be abundant in season in Hoy Bottom, which also lies on the north side of the Green. Here you'll likely find the greatest concentration of black-necked stilts, red-necked and Wilson's phalaropes, long-billed dowitcher, avocet, spotted and western sandpipers, and an occasional solitary sandpiper. Herons and egrets will usually be here, too.

The last few marshes along the road are generally less productive for wildlife viewing than those you've already passed, but the trip is rough and primitive—and experiencing its raw nature can be rewarding in and of itself.

Management

At one time, the land and water here were seen through the limiting lens of migratory game bird preservation; thus, grazing wasn't regarded as a big problem—that despite the cow's competition for grass with elk and deer who also use the refuge.

Times change. In the late 1980s, the refuge manager recognized that cattle grazed here were not compatible with native species, and there was no clear management justification for their presence (a more legitimate reading than most refuges' interpretations of "compatibility"). They disrupted the environment, damaging upland nesting areas for meadowlarks and other brush nesters, and they competed with native wildlife for both habitat and food. So the refuge manager phased them out over several years, banning their presence in 1994. His actions drew ire from local ranchers, including the main permitee, who also happened to preside over the Colorado Cattlemen's Association.

The move was accomplished despite congressional meddling, along with a few bouts of foot-stomping by local ranchers who believe that all grass is simply cow cud waiting to be ingested. In the end, wildlife needs won out, area ranchers reached a level of peace with refuge staffers, and the ecosystem will continue to provide for the critical needs of habitat-starved wildlife in the region. The move was a courageous one, and former manager Jerre Gamble deserves credit for placing wildlife needs at the top of the priority list.

Managers here still reserve the right to bring in cows in the future, should they require a grass-thinning alternative to controlled burning. Limited grazing can indeed be a good way to control thatched-up grasses without the dangers and damage fire can cause.

Controlled burning is now the major grassland management technique at Browns Park. Generally, 2,000 acres or less are burned each year, most lying along the river. Tamarisk is present in still-manageable numbers. Staffers attack the noxious invader through a combination of mechanical clearing and plant-specific applications of the EPA-approved herbicide Arsenal. Giant whitetop (*Lepidium latifolium L.*), which covers 1,200 acres of marshland, is less amenable to control. Though

some clearing and burning reduces its presence, the exotic is here to stay. Russian olive, leafy spurge, and Russian napweed are some other exotic residents on the refuge.

To provide for the growing influx of moose on Browns Park, grassy areas near willow stands are no longer burned, even when they turn decrepit. Willow is a moose's favorite food, and burning can damage the delicate tree.

Browns Park bugs can bring on severe aggravation in summers following mild winters. The summer of 1995 was a case in point: Mosquitoes and flies that swarmed about my head and that of my dog, Arnie, were maddening. (They made us really mad!) But we did discover a good way to discourage them: Keep moving. If you leave your vehicle during such attacks, simply walk 10 yards down the road, pause to draw the bugs to you, then hurry back to your vehicle, hop in, and start driving. You'll leave most of the little demons behind.

Two nice campgrounds make visiting Browns Park a convenient and comfortable affair. Both are primitive, offering spaces laid out beneath giant cottonwoods, equipped with iron grills and pit toilets. It's nice to be able to camp on a refuge without adversely impacting wildlife. So far, Browns Park's remoteness makes low-impact camping feasible and nondisruptive. However, visitation numbers are rising here and elsewhere; at some point, visitation may need to be restricted.

For now, this high-country refuge offers responsible wildlife lovers a wildly rewarding experience with relatively few restrictions. You'll find the beauty of Browns Park nearly unlimited, too.

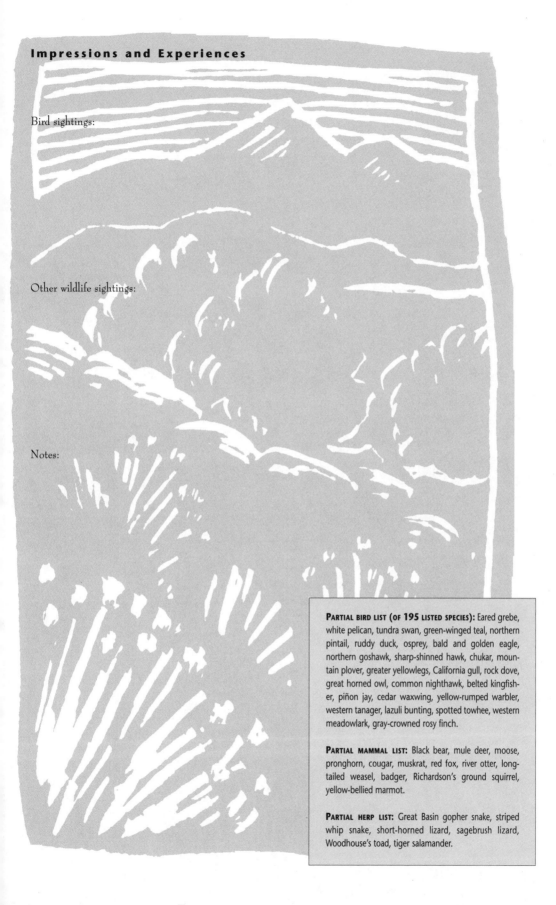

Impressions and Experiences

Bird sightings:

Other wildlife sightings:

Notes:

PARTIAL BIRD LIST (OF 195 LISTED SPECIES): Eared grebe, white pelican, tundra swan, green-winged teal, northern pintail, ruddy duck, osprey, bald and golden eagle, northern goshawk, sharp-shinned hawk, chukar, mountain plover, greater yellowlegs, California gull, rock dove, great horned owl, common nighthawk, belted kingfisher, piñon jay, cedar waxwing, yellow-rumped warbler, western tanager, lazuli bunting, spotted towhee, western meadowlark, gray-crowned rosy finch.

PARTIAL MAMMAL LIST: Black bear, mule deer, moose, pronghorn, cougar, muskrat, red fox, river otter, long-tailed weasel, badger, Richardson's ground squirrel, yellow-bellied marmot.

PARTIAL HERP LIST: Great Basin gopher snake, striped whip snake, short-horned lizard, sagebrush lizard, Woodhouse's toad, tiger salamander.

ROCKY MOUNTAIN ARSENAL NWR

VC	R			W		F	

ADDRESS, PHONE: Building 613, Commerce City, CO 80022, (303) 289-0232.

DIRECTIONS, HOURS: Take I-15 E from downtown Denver, N at the Quebec Street exit several miles to entrance. Eagle Watch viewing area just N of intersection at 56th Avenue and Buckley Road. Call first. Parts of refuge, including hiking trail and Visitors Center, open in fall on Sat, 8 a.m. to 3:30 p.m. Eagle Watch open 3 p.m. until dusk and 6:30 to 8 p.m. on Sat, Dec thru mid-March. Wildlife tours every Sat and Sun—tour buses depart from West Gate at 72nd and Quebec (call for times). Seasonal events thruout the year (call or write for schedules, brochures).

OVERVIEW, ACTIVITIES: Controlled visitor access into prairie and wetlands; bus tours; views of eagle communal nesting in winter; extensive environmental education programs.

ELEVATION: Average 5,300 feet.

WEATHER: Mild late spring thru fall; cold in winter with common freezing days; snow tends to melt soon after falling; accessibility in winter is generally good. All seasons good to visit.

SPECIAL NEEDS: Advance reservations except Saturday A.M. drop-in program (bus from main gate).

LODGING, CAMPING: Extensive lodging and several RV parks in the Denver area; camping in commercial campgrounds, nearby national forests, BLM land.

NEARBY POINTS OF INTEREST: Denver Museum of Natural History (good display on prairie history and ecology); Denver Museum of Art; Rocky Mountain National Park.

Two Ponds NWR is a satellite unit of the Rocky Mountain Arsenal NWR. The 47-acre refuge is upland with three human-made impoundments and associated marshes. The refuge harbors some 85 species of birds, as well as fox, beaver, vole, field mouse, and an occasional deer. Two Ponds NWR is located at 80th Street and Kipling in Arvada, 15 miles NW of RMA. A section of the refuge, the Prairie Management Zone, is open to public daylight hiking on a drop-in basis, with parking on 77th Street or in the nearby Lutheran Medical Center parking lot. Access to the Environmental Education Study Area requires advance permission. Call the park ranger at RMA's main number, extension 127, for information and access.

DISABILITY ACCESS: Visitors Center and its rest room, trails and walkways, present and upcoming interpretive sites (including Bald Eagle blind), outlying rest room facilities all accessible.

Scores of mule deer lounge in the ash and cottonwood thickets of Rocky Mountain Arsenal (RMA) NWR. White-tailed deer dash across open stretches of shortgrass prairie, their snowy rumps flagging distress as they leap in graceful arcs. Pintail, ruddy duck, canvasback, and other waterfowl species bob on ponds lined with matted, overaged bulrushes and cattails. Dozens of eagles hunt the wetlands of this Denver met-ropolitan-area refuge in winter, perching atop leafless cottonwoods that in other seasons shelter numerous avian woodland and grass-land species. Meadowlarks and mountain bluebirds sing and chatter from mullein stalks, rejoicing in spring's arrival. Badgers root for prairie dogs amid extensive townsites that also harbor burrowing owls. Reptiles dash and slither through stands of prairie grass.

An uninformed observer dropping in on this 17,000-acre site, 10 miles northeast of down-town Denver, might con-clude that RMA refuge is just another link in the fed-erally managed habitat chain that supports Central Flyway migratory birds and resident terrestrial creatures.

RMA is a part of that chain, offering good habitat for a wide range of species. But beneath its exterior of

prairie

prairie, woods, and wetland lies a toxic legacy, a chilling example of the harm we can do to our natural environment.

Together with the US Army and Shell Oil Company, the USFWS is working to change that legacy. If funding and political will remain intact, RMA will in time come full circle from its former role as death-dealer back to a semblance of the healthy northern short-grass prairie it once was. Restoration efforts here represent a model of how our society can right a terrible wrong—if only we accept responsibility for our actions and expend the resources necessary to correct our errors.

Hazards and Habitat

In 1992, RMA was designated by Congress as a national wildlife refuge. Six years earlier, it had been named a Superfund federal clean-up site, adding it to a list of our nation's most lethal landscapes. At that same time, the USFWS began activities on RMA after discovering a large eagle roosting site on the grounds. The arrival of biologists began a process that would eventually lead to the Arsenal's refuge designation.

Bringing RMA to full-scale refuge status won't be quick or easy. This close neighbor of Denver's old Stapleton International Airport and "suburb" of Commerce City had for 40 years been one of the country's primary man-ufacturing sites for toxins—first for chemical weapons, such as white phosphorus and nerve gas, and later as a Shell Oil Company com-mercial manufacturing site for a wide range of pesticides, under contract with producer Julius Hyman and Company.

Rachel Carson's groundbreaking book, *Silent Spring* (1962), chronicled the ecological dam-age that unregulated pesticides can do. No ambiguity ever existed on the effects of army-produced toxins: They were created specifically to kill human beings. Chemical manufacturing processes during the Arsenal's productive years were careless by today's standards. We know that now, though chemical makers in past decades were merely following estab-lished development and disposal methods of their time. Their toxin-handling practices disregarded obvious future consequences, and scientists even then should have known bet-ter. But that's organochlorine over the dam.

From the mid-1940s until 1982, an array of lethal compounds flowed from "core-area" factories into open earthen pits lined with asphalt that inevitably buckled and fissured. Wind carried toxins far and wide on clouds of dust. Chemicals leached downward into the water table, poisoning groundwater beneath at least a third of the Arsenal, sending a plume of toxins down through an equal area north of the site's border. The walls and frames of buildings used to house manufacturing processes absorbed deadly doses of a variety of agents. At least a third of RMA was, and is, a deadly place for humans and animals alike.

Healthy Habitat Amid the Ruins

Despite its poisoned past, much of the Arsenal, particularly on the south side, has long been a rich wildlife environment, supporting more than 330 species. The 14,000-acre buffer zone around the most dangerous areas received lesser (and in some cases nonmeasurable) concentrations of toxins. Wildlife who lived and bred in the buffer seem relatively healthy, producing normal young at rates similar to those in noncontaminated areas along Colorado's Front Range.

Researchers have found that a fairly sharp dividing line exists between deadly and supportive habitats and that some animals fare better than others as they hunt and forage around polluted areas. Mammals, for instance, seem to tolerate Arsenal contamination better than birds, whose livers are less able to cleanse toxins from their bodies. Birds whose feeding behavior encompasses broad areas are less at risk than those living and feeding in restricted ranges near contamination. Burrowing mammals, such as prairie dog and badger, have been minimally affected, except those living inside highly toxic earth.

The large herds of mule and white-tailed deer on the refuge—even those who often cross the most dangerous areas of the Arsenal—appear to reproduce and survive as well as deer in other areas. Mule deer, in fact, are overproducing and must be culled to match the land's carrying capacity. (Hunting them is prohibited by Superfund regulations.)

Raptors who hunt around toxic buildings, conversely, often died (and still were dying as of April 1996) within days or weeks of eating rodents amid contamination. Many show classic symptoms of dieldrin poisoning: clenched claws, wings posed in a stiffly downcast man-

ner, heads twisted in contorted death poses. Other terrestrial birds also face short and painful lives if core areas comprise their main foraging grounds.

Despite the horrors of core-area pollution, biologists who arrived in the mid-1980s recognized that good habitat does exist on RMA. They also knew that extensive site mitigation would be required if the Arsenal were to support a healthy wildlife population into the future. The Arsenal's designation as a Superfund site had already resulted in preliminary efforts to contain the mess. To minimize wildlife mortality, a speedy resolution of cleanup policies was needed.

Political forces, however, soon began to clash, a situation that would continue for a decade. The state and EPA wanted all contaminated solids and liquids to be incinerated, an expensive process that would take decades to complete. Others favored a "cap and containment" strategy that would result in a faster and cheaper—though less permanent—eradication of toxic material.

Finally in 1995, after local congressional representatives had forced the issue by warning that their cleanup funding had limits, an agreement was reached among the concerned parties. The most contaminated solids would be taken to a central landfill, where they would be capped and contained and then covered with 4 feet of native-vegetated earth; liquids were incinerated. Lesser contaminated solids were to be consolidated in Basin A; even lesser contaminated solids were to be capped and contained in place. By the time that agreement was reached, nearly $800 million had already been spent on interim mitigation and liquid incineration.

Burning of RMA's toxic liquids was completed by late 1995. The final cleanup agreement was to be signed the following summer. If the process remained on schedule, cleanup crews were to begin dissembling toxic structures by 1997, bulldozing contaminated soils, and disposing of all these toxic solids in sealed landfills, designed to meet "thousand-year" standards of unbreachable containment.

Toxin monitoring will continue indefinitely. Shallow groundwater (30 to 50 feet down) will be cleansed by giant filters for as long as a century and then returned to the aquifer clean enough, they say, for drinking, fishing, and swimming.

A realistic cleanup procedure is now in effect. In the 1996 federal budget, however, Congress cut funding for RMA cleanup by 15%. If that funding level continues, the cleanup process will require at least 5 years longer than initially planned. Environmental shortsightedness has not yet been vanquished; policies and priorities based on willful ignorance continue to influence the process.

Limited Access

Until toxin containment is complete sometime in the first decade of the 21st century, RMA refuge will maintain careful control over public visitation. But refuge overseers have big plans for RMA. Though the design has not yet been finalized, they envision a full-scale, posttoxic refuge that is a model of visitor access and education. It would include a network of trails, several wildlife viewing areas, an environmental education center, and more.

Presently, the refuge is accessible on a restricted basis. Prearranged bus tours ferry schoolkids and other visitors along a roadway through prairie, along wetlands, and past structures once used for chemical manufacturing. Biologists here seem to view the lethal character of the core sites with clear, honest eyes. None seem motivated to cast rosy colors over this tragic situation. They acknowledge the mistakes; correcting them is their main effort now.

A Saturday "drop-in" program from 8 A.M. until 3:30 P.M. allows visitors to explore the refuge along walkways and hiking trails. Bus tours that leave from the west gate provide guided tours into otherwise restricted areas. In winter months, a bald eagle communal

roosting site over First Creek, the only natural watercourse on the refuge, harbors as many as 40 eagles. That roost is viewable on the eastern edge of the refuge off Buckley Road. It's open from midafternoon until sunset. A few spotting scopes are available, though you may wish to bring your own.

An ever-changing variety of programs are presented at the refuge Visitor's Center and on tour roads throughout the year, helping educate thousands of visitors, many of them students from the Denver metro area. Despite the long work ahead, wildlife tours and workshops, night fishing on refuge ponds, birding, and many other activities already combine to make RMA one of the most visitor-oriented refuges in the federal system.

Prairie Ways

Shortgrass prairie comprises most of the refuge's 27-square-mile reach. For centuries, Northern Pawnee, Cheyenne, and other tribes ranged over the rippling grasses, hunting bison, pronghorn, deer, and other species. Euro-American farmers arrived in the late 1800s, remaining until the advent of World War II. Their efforts included construction of canals and impoundments on the present refuge grounds; most existing ponds were built in that era. Plowing and cultivation altered the prairie ecosystem, an impact that lingers in some areas.

Regeneration of healthy prairie habitat is a long-term goal of refuge managers. Some areas remain blanketed in healthy stands of western wheatgrass and other native species; other acres have fallen to the dominance of invaders, such as low-crested wheatgrass. Prescribed burning began in early 1996 and will continue as a means of reinvigorating native species.

To some, the monocultural prairie may appear incapable of supporting a wide variety of life. Actually, hundreds of species live amid the largely treeless plains. Burrowers are prevalent here, including the ubiquitous black-tailed prairie dog—a joy to watch as they bob and hustle about their den entrances, shaking their heads vigorously and whistling when danger approaches. In early May young gophers jut their tiny heads from the burrows.

Plains pocket gopher, a smaller cousin of the prairie dog, lives here, too. The pocket gopher uses mouth pouches to store dirt as it digs. The silky pocket mouse, another resident, uses its mouth pouches for food storage, extracting all its water from those seeds.

Among the prairie's predators and omnivores are the coyote, who takes a large share of white-tailed fawns in spring, favoring mule deer reproduction (they're born slightly later, when coyotes are somewhat satiated); red fox, whose numbers are controlled by more aggressive coyotes; badger, a weasel who thrives on prairie dog dinners; and raccoon, skunk, long-tailed weasel, and mink.

Badger, prairie dog, and white-footed mouse are 3 "sentinel species" monitored by refuge biologists for signs of toxin intake. Birds studied in the same way include starling and kestrel; nest boxes scattered throughout the refuge serve as collection points for study animals.

Burrowing owls arrive in April to share the prairie dogs' earthen dwellings. Swainson's hawks come in large numbers in spring, remaining through summer to feast on the many small mammals here. Red-tailed hawk, prairie falcon, golden eagle, and other raptors also feed on mammals and birds who live in the grasslands and wetlands. In fall, Swainson's numbers decline and lesser numbers of ferruginous hawks take their place, a long-declining species that seems to do well at RMA.

Some of the woodlands here were planted either by earlier residents or by refuge staff. Ash lines the main entrance road, and clusters of ash and locust around the Visitor's Center harbor passerines in migration, along with residents, such as sharp-shinned hawk, blue jay, western wood-peewee, downy woodpecker, yellow warbler, and others. A total of 227 species have been recorded on the refuge, about half of them seen once a year or less.

Migratory water birds may pass through here in large numbers. More than a dozen duck species, along with Canada goose and hooded and common mergansers, share wetland areas with shore-dwelling sandpipers, long-billed dowitcher, Wilson's phalarope, greater yellowlegs, and others. Three species of gull come through, the ring-billed being a year-round resident. Waterside birds, such as common yellowthroat, belted kingfisher, Virginia rail, and marsh wren, are sometimes seen here, too.

Snapping turtle, spiny softshell, and western painted turtles are among the shelled creatures found in refuge marshes and impoundments. Striped chorus frog and northern leopard frog are 2 of the half-dozen marsh amphibians identified here.

Upland species, including horned lark, several owls, common poorwill, sage thrasher, and others, inhabit the grassland, trees, shrubs, and prairie edges. They share upland reaches with a variety of reptiles, including prairie rattler, western bullsnake, western hognose, and eastern yellow-bellied racer.

The Future of a New Refuge

Rocky Mountain Arsenal NWR has a long road ahead. The cleanup itself isn't a particularly complex operation. More challenging will be the political and funding aspects involved in turning a chemical production site into a wildlife refuge. Army funding for USFWS cleanup support is scheduled to begin declining in 1997 by 17% each year.

With the refuge management plan completed, plans have been drawn up for a Visitor's Center on the southwest corner of the refuge, at a gateway from Commerce City. The site will include a Visitor's Learning Center and a trail-and-tram system from that point. Those facilities should be completed within 2 years after the cleanup is wrapped up.

As army support money is phased out, US Interior Department appropriations will take its place. Presently, there is some question as to the support that the underfunded USFWS is willing to earmark toward this new refuge. Wildlife concerns will most likely be supported; visitor programs, a secondary interest of budget-conscious refuge system overseers, are the part of RMA that may be in peril.

If you consider that the service's refuge appropriations amount to $1.81 per acre— as opposed to Park Service per-acre funding of $13.23 and Forest Service funding of $6.83 per acre—such priority-setting can be better understood. But considering RMA's position as a major urban refuge, the notion of reducing or ending visitor education programs here seems a wasted opportunity to inform and build partnerships between the public and the refuge system. At a time when Congress seems bent on abdicating its environmental responsibilities, the refuge system needs all the friends it can get.

Impressions and Experiences

Bird sightings:

Other wildlife sightings:

Notes:

PARTIAL BIRD LIST (OF 227 LISTED SPECIES): American white pelican, Canada goose, northern shoveler, ring-necked duck, belted kingfisher, horned lark, house wren, mountain bluebird, yellow warbler, grasshopper sparrow, yellow-headed blackbird, American goldfinch.

PARTIAL MAMMAL LIST: Mule and white-tailed deer, coyote, red fox, black-tailed prairie dog, striped skunk, long-tailed weasel, badger, least shrew.

PARTIAL HERP LIST: Prairie rattlesnake, western bullsnake, western hognose snake, lesser earless lizard, many-lined skink, common snapping turtle, Plains spadefoot toad, Woodhouse's toad, tiger salamander.

BITTER LAKE NWR

	R		W	H		

ADDRESS, PHONE: PO Box 7, Roswell, NM 88202, (505) 622-6755.

DIRECTIONS, HOURS: From N end of Roswell off US 380, the refuge lies 8 miles E at the end of East Pine Lodge Road. Open daylight hours every day.

OVERVIEW, ACTIVITIES: An 8.5-mile auto tour loop around marshes, impoundments, upland grassland. Wildlife observation, hiking, photography, picnicking. Hunting on southern edge of middle section and in Salt Creek Wilderness. Hiking and camping in Salt Creek Wilderness.

ELEVATION: From 3,450 to 3,550 feet above sea level.

WEATHER: Mild spring and fall, hot in summer, mild to cold in winter. Heavy rains may fall in late summer. Mild winter showers, rarely snow. Spring, fall, and winter best seasons to visit.

SPECIAL NEEDS: Sign in at tour road entrance; permits for group camping from October thru March.

LODGING, CAMPING: Lodging and RV parks in Roswell; prearranged group camping on refuge; camping at Bottomless Lake State Park 10 miles E.

NEARBY POINTS OF INTEREST: White Sands National Monument, Carlsbad Caverns, Roswell Museum, Sacramento Mountains (sky island with unique species), Bosque del Apache NWR.

DISABILITY ACCESS: HQ and adjacent public rest rooms are accessible; observation platform on tour loop accessible.

L ocated on the ecotone where Chihuahuan desert melds into Great Plains grassland, the 24,536-acre Bitter Lake NWR in southeast New Mexico provides the best of four worlds. Both desert and grassland inhabitants find comfort and sustenance in Bitter Lake's rolling grasslands and Pecos River marshes and impoundments. This semi-desert refuge also straddles a larger dividing line that separates eastern and western US species. Creatures residing or visiting here represent both sides of the nation's biota, especially bird species but also mammals, herptiles, and plants.

Eastern and western forms of meadowlark and bluebird (a third species, mountain bluebird, also passes through), yellow-rumped warbler (Myrtle's and Audubon's), and red-headed and ladder-backed woodpeckers—and even Lewis's on occasion—are a few of the avian species who share ecotone habitat with one another.

desert

The tiny, predatory grasshopper mouse—ounce for ounce one of the more vicious hunting mammals on the planet—lives in Bitter Lake grasslands, at the eastern edge of its range, along with kangaroo rat, a desert species. Javelina, a decidedly western desert critter, shares space with the eastern white-tailed deer, who ranges along with its western cousin the mule deer. Thirteen-lined ground squirrel, a Great Plains dweller, wanders brushy habitat on the refuge alongside the western spotted ground squirrel.

Bitter Lake is also unique as one of the few reliable water sources in this dry region, which reputedly gets 12 average inches of rainfall per year but lately has been lucky to get 7. Even the quality of the wetlands is unique: Fed by the Pecos River, which gathers high levels of salt as it crosses Permian Basin soils, the impoundments and natural *playas* of Bitter Lake are fed a constant load of salts and minerals. High evaporation in the region's warm, dry winds builds saline levels ever higher. In spring, *playa* flats appear coated in

snow as salts that have risen with water levels remain as water recedes. Into summer, that coating begins to ease back into the mud and the snowy appearance fades.

Water chemistry on Bitter Lake encourages and sustains a variety of wildlife species found almost nowhere else. Exotic snails the size of pinheads, a form of marine algae found elsewhere only in the Gulf of Mexico, salt-tolerant indigenous fish, localized dragonflies, and other specialized creatures find safe haven among the sinkholes, *playas,* and streams of the refuge. The special nature of the water at Bitter Lake NWR is one reason that 23 federal or state listed species, along with one hypothetical resident (the swift fox), live or visit here.

Bird Magnet

W hen most of Bitter Lake's 40,000 yearly visitors cruise the 8½-mile tour road, it isn't snails and algae they seek but more dazzling wildlife displays. Rarely are they disappointed. Thousands of migratory cranes, geese, and ducks find good habitat on the refuge among 6 artificial impoundments, a natural *playa,* and expansive acres of salt-crusted mudflats. Upland acres attract even more species.

Several grand avian events occur here each year, exploding against a backdrop of red rock, long views, and cloudless blue sky. In late August and September, harbingers of the coming migration appear with the arrival of ruddies and wigeon, who often lead the waterfowl pack. Then come cinnamon and green-winged teal, along with pintails, mallards, lesser scaup, ring-necked, and 2 dozen other species. Soon the ponds are alive with wild shouts and flailing wings.

Snow goose, Canada goose, and a few white-fronted geese also arrive to join the winter fray. By midwinter, ducks often number as high as 20,000, with twice that number of geese inhabiting refuge waters and farm fields. Cranes can number 70,000, though most often between 5,000 and 15,000 settle at Bitter Lake.

Oddballs may accompany the normal visitors. Over the past several years, refuge accidentals have included white-winged scoter, oldsquaw, greater scaup, and even garganey. An unusual species may also visit after being blown off course or following an urge for adventure. Magnificent frigate bird was once spotted here. Roseate spoonbill has also browsed in refuge shallows.

A new farmland acquisition on the southern end of the refuge helps maintain the migratory hordes with corn and wheat. Managed by a local cooperative farmer who cultivates in return for a share of the bounty, 600 farmed acres help reduce depredation on neighboring farmland. Taking the consumptive heat off area farmers is one good way for any federal refuge to demonstrate its value on the local level—important in these antifederalist days.

Fall migration and its aftermath is Bitter Lake's most impressive time, but various seasons offer avian treasures as well. Spring migration brings thousands of shorebirds flocking onto the muddy *playas;* some remain into the heat of summer. Their southerly migration over Bitter Lake, which begins as early as July and intensifies in August, offers another showy spectacle of shore and shallows birds, including endangered interior least terns, who nest on refuge mudflats.

As many as 300 pairs of snowy plovers arrive in early March to inhabit the salty mud around the Bitter Lake wetlands; they breed and brood rapidly, leaving again in early fall. Until recently considered for listing, the snowy's population is still in question among biologists. Many here nest along the Bitter Lake *playa,* which isn't directly accessible to visitors but may be viewed from an overlook on Bitter Lake Road. (A self-guided tour pamphlet will lead you there.) White pelicans also arrive in late winter months to bob among deeper portions of Bitter Lake's 6 managed impoundments, all of which lie along the tour loop.

Except after particularly harsh rains, the tour road will accommodate passenger vehicles. It offers good viewing of refuge waterfowl and shorebirds, as well as upland and riparian

species. Elevated viewing areas and picnic tables along the way enhance the amenities. Even when wildlife is scarce, the panoramic landscape here can be reason enough for a trip, especially in late spring, when wildflowers bloom and many plants take on their finest colors.

Early summer is probably the least impressive time at Bitter Lake. It's hot then, and most migratory species are busy elsewhere, raising broods or fattening themselves for their return to wintering grounds. A good number of shorebirds and waders do hang around, however, including avocet, black-necked stilt, yellowlegs, sandpipers, killdeer, and Wilson's phalarope.

Midwinter here hosts ducks, geese, and Platte River sandhill cranes, along with a lesser number of passerines and ground dwellers, such as savanna and song sparrows, desert-dwelling pyrrhuloxia, white-winged dove, and roadrunner. Chestnut-collared longspur may appear at Bitter Lake some winters.

Water birds who use the refuge quickly learn where freshwater springs emerge from the floors of saline impoundments. They visit those favored spots daily to drink their fill, then wander back onto saltier waters to rest, find partners, and socialize.

freshwater wetlands

Raptors come to Bitter Lake in large numbers. Bald eagles may stay through winter, leaving by late February. Harriers cruise the low skyways throughout the year. Kestrels, ferruginous hawks, red-tails, prairie and peregrine falcons, and several other predators take advantage of the rich prey base in Bitter Lake's grass- and marshlands. Mississippi kite feeds here, though nesters haven't yet been documented nesting on the refuge. You may find the kites at all the golf courses in nearby Roswell, especially at Spring River Golf Course and the Roswell Country Club.

Wingless Wonders

Mammals on the refuge include a small number of pronghorns (easier to see along Hwy 70 south of the Salt Creek Wilderness). Mule and white-tail deer, mountain lion (a hypothetical that likely visits here), a surprisingly large and visible population of bobcats, coyote, at least 3 fox species, badger, and a host of rodents are also here.

Snakes on Bitter Lake include three rattlers, the prairie, massasauga, and western diamondback. A rattlesnake predator, the desert king snake, is also in residence. The king is able to constrict and consume rattlers with an ease known to few other snakes—or to any other snake-eating species, for that matter. Rattlers seem to know the danger of kings; when confronted by one of these elegant, black-and-white creatures, they rarely strike. Rather, they present a curved portion of their body to the king, apparently in hope of discouraging it. If the king is hungry, the rattler's posturing rarely succeeds.

Hognose and a disjunct population of ribbon snake are also in residence. Collared lizards dash about the bluffs and Salt Creek Wilderness dunes. Several whiptails live here, including the noble checkered whiptail. At least 9 amphibians inhabit the wetlands, among them spadefoot toad, tiger salamander, green toad, leopard frog, and cricket frog. Fortunately, no predatory bullfrogs have made their way into Bitter Lake marshes and creeks.

Other herps include barking frog, an eastern species, and 6 types of turtles, the common box turtle, yellow mud turtle, painted, snapper, softshell, and the rarely seen river cooter, which is much more common in the Mississippi River system.

Grassland Forever

Rolling grassland makes up most of the refuge, a rich food source that once supported massive herds of cattle run by legendary Texas cow baron John Chisum. In the late 1800s, Chisum ran the show from the Texas border to Fort Sumner, New Mexico, 150 miles north of the refuge, leaving extensive grassland damage and alteration in his wake.

Alkali sacaton dominates but shares the highly saline soil with around 50 other grass species. One dominant grass here is gyp grama, a gypsum-obligate species. That low bunchgrass also grows around this region's premier gypsum sandpile, White Sands National Monument in the nearby Tularosa Basin. Tarbush and creosote make up much of Bitter Lake's upland shrub base.

Small clusters of salt cedar line waterways and ponds; some is burned to keep it from spreading and sucking up excessive water. The area never provided major passerine support, so managers here maintain just a small amount of perching habitat, some in the form of tamarisk. Cottonwood and elm trees around refuge headquarters are probably the first perching structure that migratory passerines notice on their cross-country approaches. That area is a good place to find northern oriole, redheaded woodpecker, northern flicker, yellow-billed cuckoo, blue and scrub jays, red-breasted nuthatch, and any of 2 dozen warblers who may pass through in spring and fall.

Iodinebush is a significant wildlife food plant around Bitter Lake's *playa* edges. The salty succulent, also known as seepweed or *quelite-salado,* is unique but hardly showy; the flowers are small, greenish, and lack petals, and the plant itself runs from dull green in moist times to a flat brown the rest of the year. Raised in Arizona by Pima Indians and other desert tribes, its seeds are roasted to make a food known as *pinole*. A black dye has also been extracted from this member of the goosefoot family. At Bitter Lake, wandering tribes who visited the refuge in centuries past may have used iodinebush as a food source, though the high-saline water here apparently never supported significant or long-term human settlement.

In streambeds and along some spring-fed creeks and wetland marshes, phragmite communities have emerged, displaying their wheatish-looking crests in waves of amber that ripple and shimmer with the slightest breeze. Mormon tea is another common upland resident at Bitter Lake, along with several cacti species, including prickly pear and cholla.

Geological Oddities

A weak earthern crust here is the reason Bitter Lake contains such a large number of sinkholes. Water draining from the Sacramento Mountains comes this way along the Hondo River, which meets the Pecos on the refuge. Some water goes underground into the Roswell artesian basin, whose pressure forces it upward on the refuge. Dissolving sedimentary soil beneath Bitter Lake leaves gaps in the earth. When their roofs collapse, they become sinkholes.

As many as 60 of the near-concentric sinkholes have formed on the refuge, most on the northern part of the middle unit, where visitation is prohibited. More lie just beneath the surface, waiting for some small weight to crack their thin earthen skins and open a new pond to the New Mexico sky. In years past, cattle have broken through and drowned in the underlying pools. Salt levels vary widely from one pool to another; rainfall and other factors create varying levels within individual ponds. Some sinkholes that have appeared in recent years already supported fish populations. The fish, including the endangered Pecos gambusia and salt/fresh-water-tolerant Pecos pupfish (a candidate for federal endangered status), either lived without sunlight or traveled an underground aquatic labyrinth from dark to light.

Fortunately, several game fish transplant attempts here have failed, with the exception of carp. Give a carp a puddle and a few minnows to feed on and it'll probably survive to roil the mud and keep sunlight from reaching aquatic plants. Periodic drainages help keep

their numbers down, as do the hungry bald eagles, egrets, and herons who feed on them.

Bitter Lake itself (the only natural lake on the refuge) lies within the nonaccessible north-central area, as does a 60-foot-deep sinkhole at the Lake St. Francis Research Natural Area. Refuge staffers maintain a monitoring station at Lake St. Francis. A computerized sensor device on its shoreline measures more than a dozen environmental variables, from wind speed to temperature changes to saline levels. Part of a global warming research network, the sensor also helps feed big-picture climate information to global scientists studying this troubling phenomenon.

Human Demands, Wildlife Impacts

As usual, water creates conflict here, as it does throughout the West. Pecos River water has been the source of contentious, ongoing legal challenges between New Mexico and Texas, the latter believing it's entitled to a larger share. Eventual settlement of that sticky issue will affect local New Mexico farmers and refuge water managers in equal measure.

Oil and gas operations that dot the upland terrain have a mixed impact on area wildlife. From ground level, visitors may see an occasional rise here and there, topped by a drilling device. From the air it's a different story—roadway grids completely checker the land like some massive subdivision.

Many lizards and rodents probably find these barren roadways a deathtrap, as great horned owls and kestrels scoop up road-crossing prey with ease. Conversely, roadrunners enjoy skipping along wellhead roads, nailing insects and lizards as they go. Habitat alteration here has clearly upset an ageless biological balance; how that balance is rearranging itself is anyone's guess.

If proof of the value of biological diversity is really necessary, Bitter Lake offers good evidence in the form of the state-listed Pecos sunflower, which grows only in the area. The survival of this plant amid some of Bitter Lake's saltier uplands got food scientists curious. They hybridized the species with other sunflowers and created a new variety that thrives in saline soils—a boon crop for areas heavily infiltrated by salt. The species has been a commercial success, opening what were alkaline dead zones to productive agricultural use.

Several unique species of snail that make Bitter Lake their home pose a more philosophical challenge to those arguing the value of

diversity. Just a little larger than sand grains, the Roswell spring snail, Koster's spring snail, Pecos assiminea snail, and shrimplike Noel's amphipod are unique creatures whose ranges are limited to the refuge and similar nearby habitat.

You can't eat 'em, can't fish with 'em, they would never sell on the open market, so why save them? It's a fair question. The answer is: They're part of our world and deserve to live. To argue against such a basic ethical principle is to deny our role as caretakers of the planet. That role is ours, even when there's no money in it.

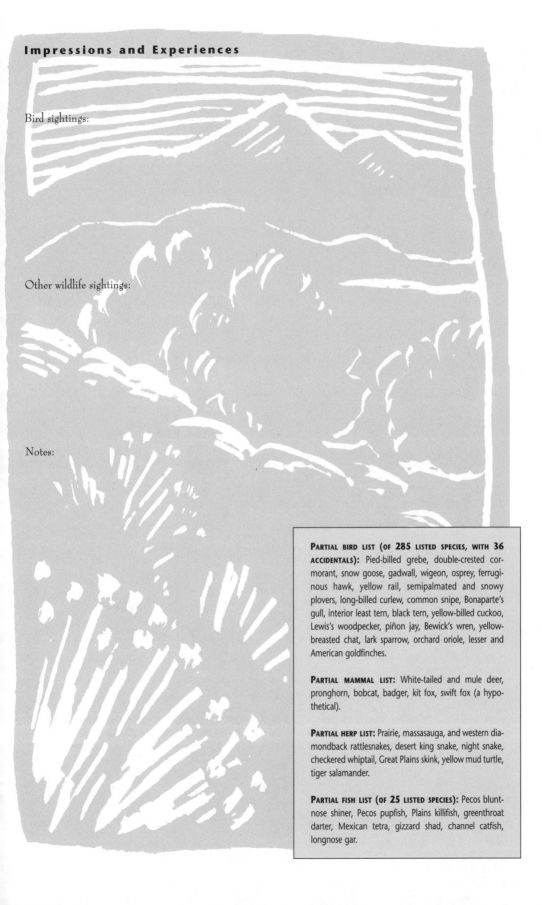

Bird sightings:

Other wildlife sightings:

Notes:

PARTIAL BIRD LIST (OF 285 LISTED SPECIES, WITH 36 ACCIDENTALS): Pied-billed grebe, double-crested cormorant, snow goose, gadwall, wigeon, osprey, ferruginous hawk, yellow rail, semipalmated and snowy plovers, long-billed curlew, common snipe, Bonaparte's gull, interior least tern, black tern, yellow-billed cuckoo, Lewis's woodpecker, piñon jay, Bewick's wren, yellow-breasted chat, lark sparrow, orchard oriole, lesser and American goldfinches.

PARTIAL MAMMAL LIST: White-tailed and mule deer, pronghorn, bobcat, badger, kit fox, swift fox (a hypothetical).

PARTIAL HERP LIST: Prairie, massasauga, and western diamondback rattlesnakes, desert king snake, night snake, checkered whiptail, Great Plains skink, yellow mud turtle, tiger salamander.

PARTIAL FISH LIST (OF 25 LISTED SPECIES): Pecos bluntnose shiner, Pecos pupfish, Plains killifish, greenthroat darter, Mexican tetra, gizzard shad, channel catfish, longnose gar.

BOSQUE DEL APACHE NWR

VC	R			W		H	F	$

ADDRESS, PHONE: PO Box 1246, Socorro, NM 87801, (505) 835-1828.

DIRECTIONS, HOURS: 15 miles S of Socorro off I-25; turn at San Antonio exit; go .5 miles then R on Hwy 1; refuge is 8 miles S on Hwy 1; open 1 hr before sunrise and 1 hr after sunset; small entry fee. Visitor's Center open Mon thru Fri from 7:30 a.m. to 4 p.m., and on weekends from 8 a.m. to 4:30 p.m. year-round.

OVERVIEW, ACTIVITIES: Auto tour loop and hiking trails thru 7,000 acres of upland desert, wetland marshes and ponds, riparian areas; Visitor's Center with extensive displays and windowed bird observation area. Wildlife observation, hiking (including into 3 refuge wilderness areas), photography, November crane festival with workshops, tours, and other events. Prearranged group camping, tours, and programs for educational and volunteer groups.

ELEVATION: From 4,500 to 6,272 feet.

WEATHER: Generally mild fall thru winter, though it can drop below freezing in winter. Summer very hot from late morning until dusk. Spring, fall, and winter best seasons to visit.

LODGING, CAMPING: Socorro has numerous hotels; campground on Hwy 1 N of refuge; camping in Cibola National Forest 25 miles W. RV park in Socorro, another in San Antonio, NM. Other lodging, including B and Bs, in Socorro and San Antonio.

NEARBY POINTS OF INTEREST: Very Large Array radio telescope 70 miles W on Plains of Saint Agustin; Elephant Butte Reservoir 60 miles S; Old San Miguel Mission in Socorro; Water Canyon 30 miles W.

Sevilleta NWR is a 220,000-acre research area in Socorro County harboring desert grassland (some in pristine condition) and protecting a portion of the Rio Grande River valley. In 1989, the refuge was designated a Long-Term Ecological Research Station (LTER) by the National Science Foundation, one of twenty in the nation. The designation brings Sevilleta into a network of ecosystems where research on global warming trends and other major ecological concerns is carried out. It is closed to the public.

DISABILITY ACCESS: Visitor's Center, rest rooms, and observation stands on the refuge are accessible.

Sixteenth-century Spaniards called the arid reach of the Chihuahuan Desert that now encompasses Bosque del Apache NWR the *Jornado del Muerto,* or Journey of Death. During their travels north along *El Camino Real,* or the King's Highway, from Chihuahua, Mexico, to Santa Fe, those early New Mexican settlers dreaded this part of their journey—water was scarce, summer heat unyielding, and attacks by Apaches and Commanches relentless.

However, these days for tens of thousands of migrating waterfowl, cranes, and songbirds, the Bosque del Apache refuge means life.

This desert and wetland refuge sits amid a broad stretch of scrubland flanking the Rio Grande just south of Socorro. Wrapped by the Chupadera Mountains to the west—a range that resembles rough-edged heaps of lavender pudding—and the San Pascual Mountains to the east, the 57,191-acre site is one of the most intensively managed refuges in the nation. The refuge offers its myriad wild (and human) visitors a variety of ecological zones, including wetland marshes, ponds and mudflats, riparian woods, grassland, desert, and backwater sloughs. The diversity of Bosque's habitat provides for a large number of species throughout the year.

*freshwater
wetlands*

Most of Bosque's acreage is restricted (scopes and binoculars allow access to some of that area). The accessible parts, including 7,000 central acres whose wetlands and desert support most of Bosque's wildlife, can be viewed along two broad auto loops, bisected by a 2-way road running east and west.

November through February are Bosque's most dramatic months. That's when as many as 20,000 sandhill cranes, 45,000 snow and Ross's geese, and some 60,000 ducks make the refuge their cold weather home. Raptors seem as common as sparrows here in winter,

including numerous eagles. Arrive near dawn or linger at dusk and you're treated to one of nature's most riveting spectacles, as tens of thousands of cranes, ducks, and geese flap and glide their way over the refuge to and from feeding areas and roosting sites. They come in deafening, uncountable numbers, darkening the sky as their heavy wings beat in primal, whispering rhythm. The sight and sound of all those birds against the backdrop of a Bosque sunrise or sunset is magnificent.

The Socorro Chamber of Commerce, conservation groups, and government agencies join forces each November to celebrate Bosque's most notable species. The Festival of the Cranes is held the third weekend in November. The several-day event features tours, bird and wildlife classes, photo workshops, and the chance to commune with thousands of wide-eyed bird lovers.

Getting Around Bosque

The northern part of the 12-mile tour loop is where you'll find most cranes and snow geese during fall and winter; both loops offer you the chance to observe more than a dozen species of ducks, as well as numerous shorebirds in spring and fall and passerines and waders throughout the year. Hybrid white-winged/Bianchi's pheasants and wild turkey are among the ground species you'll probably see.

More than a dozen raptor species, including bald and golden eagles, and numerous other aerial hunters make Bosque their temporary or permanent home. In fall and winter, chances are you'll see at least 4 or 5 eagles, both bald and golden, on an average winter day. Harriers are abundant during the cooler months. Redtailed hawk, including members of the dark Harlan's race, are here in abundance.

Hiking trails into riparian woods, marshes, and deserts total around 9 miles and include a recently built boardwalk to the Rio Grande River. Several viewing stands around the tour loop offer good vantage points of the marshes.

Frequently seen mammals include coyote, porcupine (look in the branches of cotton-wood trees), mule deer, beaver, and muskrat. Herps may include diamondback rattler, gopher snake, Texas night snake, twin-spotted spiny lizard, whiptail lizard, desert box turtle, and bullfrog.

A 145-acre wetland area, located half a mile north of the Visitor's Center off Hwy 1, is often a gathering spot for several waterfowl species. The new wetland was built in 1994 with financial assistance from Ducks Unlimited, a hunter-oriented organization that has provided matching funds for additional wetlands development on the refuge.

A Congregation of Cranes

The thousands of sandhill cranes who come here in the fall are 1 of 15 crane species worldwide and 1 of 2 species residing in North America; 3 subspecies make Bosque their temporary home.

Resident from Florida to California during the cold months, sandhills summer in Alaska, Siberia, Canada, and the northern prairies of the United States. During their migrations they pause to feed and drink in prairie pot-holes, mountain meadows, lakes, and tundra, usually in groups of two to four. Huge num-bers of these subgroups travel together, form-ing raucous winged mobs whose loud calls can be heard for miles.

Though the sandhills' main coloration is gray (with a red head patch), its plumage is often stained a rust color; that's due to the bird's habit of rooting in iron-rich earth and staining its coat during preening. Young sandhills are often heavily rust-hued; occasionally, an individual appears nearly white (especially in glaring light), like the much less common whooping crane. But when you see a snow-white whooper, you'll know it isn't a sandhill.

If in doubt, you can distinguish the sandhill by the absence of black wingtips and by the whooper's noticeably taller (up to 56 inches)

stature. Whoopers also have a pointed patch of black extending from beneath the bill to the sides of their cheeks, and their call is high-pitched rather than gravelly like the sandhill's call.

Sandhills (and whoopers) feed on grain, tubers, berries, and a variety of small mam-mals, birds, insects, and amphibians. As the temperature drops they prefer high-energy grain, such as corn grown on the refuge in a cooperative arrangement with local farmers.

The sandhill pairing and/or territorial display is a dramatic dance, during which partners leap up to 8 feet in the air with wings spread, shouting their distinctive, brassy *garr-okk* call.

Whooping Cranes: A Second Chance?

The few endangered whooping cranes who frequented Bosque in 1995 represented the last of an experimental flock that has wintered at Bosque since the 1970s, when an experi-ment was launched to bolster the critically small number of whoopers in the wild. The experimental flock was developed to help cushion the main Aransas–Saskatchewan flock from the threat of extinction due to disease or accident.

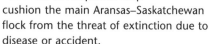
desert

To create the new flock, biologists took eggs from the nests of existing wild whoopers. (They usually lay 2 eggs but raise only 1 chick successfully, so the practice doesn't harm propagation.) The eggs were planted in the nests of sandhill "parents" at Gray's Lake Refuge in Wyoming. From the late 1970s through the mid-1980s, as many as 34 adoptee whoopers were making the trip from Wyoming to New Mexico.

The experiment, recently abandoned by the USFWS, hasn't failed completely but it's certainly been discouraging—though much has been learned in the process. Male adoptive whoopers seemed to behave normally, surviving well, setting up nesting sites, and waiting for females. Apparently, however, female adoptees have reacted differently to the experimental situation. Some have gone haywire in a sense, flying off to parts unknown and otherwise refusing to cooperate. No known wild births of pure whoopers have occurred among the experimental flock.

Avian cholera and tuberculosis, at times endemic to wild flocks such as those that populate Bosque, have taken their toll. Other whoopers probably fell to goose hunters' shotguns, as well as to collisions with fences and power lines.

Only 3 pure whoopers have shown up at Bosque each fall for the past few years, along with 1 sandhill/whooper hybrid, known to biologists as a "whoophill." The fate of the other transplants is unknown, though most almost certainly perished. Aransas NWR in south Texas continues to draw around 150 of the snowy white cranes each fall, up from a low of 16 in 1941.

Aransas is the whooping cranes' only other known southern migratory grounds, making the Rocky Mountain flock that visits Bosque a crucial component in the species' chance for survival. An experimental Florida resident flock was established on the Kissimmee Prairie in central Florida, using chicks from captive birds. Unfortunately, by the fall of 1994, the 33 captive-bred whooping cranes transferred there from the International Crane Foundation in Wisconsin and the Patuxent Wildlife Research Center in Maryland were lost due to bobcat predation. The transplant process continues, though its future remains sketchy.

By 1996, the Bosque crane program was undergoing a major reevaluation. Several proposals were being weighed, including one to teach new whoopers to migrate by using an ultralight aircraft as guide. Matching surrogate whooper parents with captive-bred newborns is another possibility being studied.

The endangered species debate these days has taken a turn for the worse, as far as whoopers are concerned. Some ask whether species so close to extinction should be targeted for restoration at all, given the limited resources citizens are willing to expend. Is it better to focus financial resources on species that still have a reasonable chance for survival? That's one side of the argument. The other side is more easily understood if you're lucky enough to observe one of these beautiful cranes in the wild. Once you've seen a whooping crane, you'll likely want to see the species saved.

Other Winter Residents

Bald and golden eagles are common at Bosque during the cold months, along with northern harrier, red-tailed hawk, kestrel, prairie falcon, and its less common cousin the merlin. Occasionally, a fourth species of falcon, the peregrine, sweeps overhead, scattering waves of terrorized ducks. Golden and bald eagles both take their share of ducks, as do other raptor species. Curiously, waterfowl bobbing beneath the flight paths of harriers seem to tolerate their presence without undue alarm, though harriers also enjoy a good duck dinner now and then.

Long-billed dowitcher, greater yellowlegs, and Wilson's phalarope reside here during winter; depending on where water is channeled, they may be spotted on both loops.

In late winter, scores of colorful green-winged teal sweep in and begin their mating rituals. Bufflehead, mallard, and northern shoveler are abundant during fall and winter, as are pintail and gadwall. Snipe are common here, too, at this time of year. Finding these masters of camouflage on Bosque mudflats is an exercise in eyestrain. Chickenish pied-billed grebes often bob in drainage canals lining the roadways.

Occasionally, a black-crowned night heron fishes the shallows of the southern ponds, though the species may appear anywhere there's water. Many roost in the submerged tamarisk to your right as you approach the east end of the 2-way road. Great blue herons are abundant at Bosque in winter, and many remain all year round.

Coyotes are ever-present on Bosque and take their ration of snow geese; most appear well fed. Observant visitors may luck upon the drama of several coyotes working in unison to trap weak or unwary geese. Coyotes generally don't go after cranes, whose big beaks and strong, clawed feet make them formidable prey. Mountain lions and bobcats in the area generally don't pay much attention to the cranes or snow geese.

Some of Bosque's coyotes have grown accustomed to humans and will approach quite closely. A few are captive-raised releases. Don't be fooled; these are not puppy dogs and they can hurt you. Feeding them is illegal and unethical: Such familiarity puts the animals at risk by making them too people-friendly for their own good.

Warm Weather Wonders

Fall and winter are the seasons when Bosque shows its best face, but spring and summer here offer their own special charms, including the stately white-faced ibis (scan the mudflats), American avocet, and black-necked stilt. A dozen duck species are also found here during the hot months. Loggerhead shrike is one of several species who perches in refuge cottonwoods and tamarisk snags.

Hummingbirds come in large numbers in spring, hovering and fighting at the feeders around the Visitor's Center. Hummer species include the black-chinned, broad-tailed, rufous, and an occasional calliope. The federally en-dangered southwestern willow flycatcher is an occasional resident in spring and summer.

Upland "game" residents include wild turkey and pheasant, most of the latter being hybrids of Bianchi's white-winged and ring-necked subspecies.

A flock of several hundred introduced Canada geese lives on the refuge. At one time thou-sands of Canada geese arrived each fall, along with a few dozen snow geese and their small-er cousin the Ross's goose. But damming and leveeing of the Rio Grande and its tributaries in Colorado and New Mexico dramatically altered their migratory habits, and the Canadas quit coming. Snow geese, for some reason, found the changes appealing and are now the main goose species at Bosque. On occasion, white-fronted geese can be spotted mingling with the more common Canadas.

Spring is a productive birding time at Bosque. Many neotropical migrants return in March and April, and the refuge comes alive with their songs. Migrating shorebirds can also be abundant here. A number of spring arrivals remain through summer to nest and fledge their young, though others continue north to cooler climes. In spring Bosque plays host to a variety of raptors, shorebirds, and perching birds, such as solitary and warbling vireos, Bewick's wren, canyon towhee, blue gros-beak, northern oriole, and lesser goldfinch. Bell's vireo can be spotted here, too.

Summer at Bosque can be hot—for many people unbearably so, with the temperature often climbing above 100 degrees F. Bugs arrive in late spring and can be quite annoy-ing well into fall, especially mosquitoes, which thrive in the abundant wetlands.

Still, if your bug lotion is effective and your tolerance for hovering bloodsuckers high, summer offers the chance to encounter abun-dant wildlife at Bosque, including many species who depart in the fall for Mexico and points farther south. Such species include vari-ous warblers and vireos, Forster's tern, belted kingfisher, yellow-breasted chat, and summer tanager. Chipping and lark sparrows are com-mon then, and you may see dozens of blue grosbeaks during the warmer months, partic-ularly along the east-side tour road flanking the south ponds.

Apache Woods

Prehistoric Native Americans, known to archaeologists as Piros, inhabited the Bosque area for hundreds of years, finally escaping to the El Paso area with Spaniards during the Pueblo Revolt of 1680. Ruins of their dwellings still exist within the refuge. Spaniards first crossed the region in the 1600s on their way north to settle and trade in what was then Spanish territory. Apaches lived and hunted in the area, often attacking Spanish and Mexican interlopers. They continued to skirmish with American settlers until the late 1800s, when treaties and military campaigns forced those longtime residents onto reservations.

Bosque del Apache NWR was founded in 1939 as a migratory area for waterfowl, with an emphasis on bolstering the number of greater sandhill cranes. Once endangered, it is one of our nation's great conservation success stories. The refuge name means "Apache woods" in Spanish, deriving from the presence of Apaches who often camped in the cottonwoods along the river.

Built with WPA and CCC labor, the makeshift nature of Bosque's irrigation system created a challenge that the present staff has only recently overcome. Under the direction of refuge manager Phil Norton, the old irrigation system has been revitalized. Most floodgates have been ripped out and replaced with efficient designs via labor by eager volunteers working alongside refuge staff. (Bosque's volunteer program is one of the most dynamic in the refuge system.) Heavy equipment for the job has been borrowed or scrounged, repaired, and put to work in an effort that demonstrates the ingenuity and dedication of those involved.

Some of Bosque's heavy equipment has come from drug enforcement confiscations, army surplus auctions, and other on-the-cheap methods. Funding for Bosque and the rest of the federal refuge system—at a time when even the school lunch program is under assault—is perennially inadequate, forcing managers to develop creative means of get-

ting hold of the equipment they need to do their jobs.

For instance, at Bosque a superb building-material operation has been instituted on the refuge's southern boundary, employing little cash but lots of ingenuity and volunteer labor. Dirt and rocks from the operation, which staffers affectionately call "Bosque Sand and Gravel," are used throughout the refuge.

The old flood-or-famine method of irrigation created poor habitat and aggravated soil problems. Evaporation of standing water concentrated salt, a natural process in dry climates where irrigation and/or a high water table exists. Before the Rio Grande was dammed and leveed, natural flooding served to periodically flush out salt buildups.

Land grading, aided by high-tech, laser-directed equipment, allows for more efficient shallow-water management of wetland habitat areas and croplands.

The relatively new science of "moist-soil management" allows for balanced wetland maintenance and native plant germination, which in turn provide food and habitat for many more wildlife species than the refuge could otherwise support. Essentially, the system mimics the Rio Grande floodplain's natural state before the river was tamed, a system of periodic flooding and good drainage. About a quarter of Bosque's river-bottom land is presently under moist-soil management.

Wild foods arising from Bosque's moist-soil acres include a crane's favorite, chufa, a small sedge that grows nutty tubers on its roots. Watch the cranes probing what looks to be bare earth; it's likely they're snacking on chufa. Other moist-soil foods eaten by cranes, geese, and other waterfowl include bulrush tubers, wild millet, and smartweed.

Cattail shoots and roots, as well as seed-bearing grasses, are also encouraged by this process. Numerous invertebrates that provide birds with needed protein are also supported. Bosque is presently experimenting with moist-soil techniques that may encourage cottonwood germination, once a natural process on nutrient-rich, flood-borne riverside soils. That's particularly important after a 1996 fire decimated as many as half of Bosque's cottonwoods.

Feeding the Flocks

Innovative row crop management helps to stretch Bosque's food supplies for cranes and waterfowl while allowing managers to control the number of cranes and geese residing on Bosque at a particular time. The system, used in some fashion at numerous other refuges, works like this: Some 1,200 acres of Bosque land have been turned over to local farmers. Three-quarters of that cropland is used to grow alfalfa, which the farmers keep; the other quarter is corn, which feeds refuge cranes and geese.

Generally speaking, cranes are food-managed to keep them inside the refuge. That's accomplished by knocking over controlled amounts of the tall, sturdy corn plants, which the cranes consume. Keeping cranes within Bosque's borders is a good way to keep nearby farmers happy since the birds might otherwise plunder their fields.

Geese, which can outnumber Bosque cranes by 3 to 1, are generally food controlled to keep them *out* of the refuge. Otherwise, their swarming presence would overtax the environment and contribute to the spread of disease. Controlling their numbers is accomplished by knocking down just enough corn near the outer edges of the field to provide for, say, 15,000 geese at any particular time. This and similar techniques succeed because geese won't enter tall corn for fear they'll be waylaid by predators. They only eat what's available on field edges, which refuge staffers can control.

Keeping neighboring farmers happy, especially in these politically fractious times, is a critical part of refuge management. The ability to control the movement of geese also helps bolster hunting opportunities on nearby state-managed refuges. That's important to area

hunters since hunting is banned on the river-bottom acres of the refuge. It's important to Bosque, too, helping maintain the refuge as a true sanctuary for wildlife—one of few such federal refuges in the West.

Salt Cedar—Pioneering Control Methods

Another plant-related challenge at Bosque involves the African invader tamarisk, or "salt cedar." The shrub tree has caused untold environmental degradation throughout the desert Southwest by supplanting riparian vegetation, drawing excessive water, and providing little useful habitat for native species. At one time managers and private landowners tried burning the rapacious shrub, which was brought here as an ornamental and erosion-control plant. They soon discovered that fire actually stimulates the growth of tamarisk, a root-sprouting species.

Bosque's staff has declared war on salt cedar— you'll see one battlefield shortly after entering the refuge. Note the barren earth to your right as you begin your cruise around the southern loop. That area, as well as hundreds of acres on the south and east perimeters of the wetlands area, has been mechanically stripped of salt cedar and planted with cottonwood "poles." Salt cedar is tenacious, though, and requires a full-frontal, no-mercy assault. It must be cut off at ground level, plowed under, then plowed again and ground into smaller pieces—all just to *slow* its return long enough for native riparian species, such as cottonwood, willow, and wolf berry, to take hold.

Where thick tangles of tamarisk once existed, cottonwood is again growing. Bosque ecologists hope the plantings result in a renewed native forestland. Other areas are left bare so that nature may replace on its own the predamming environment that characterized the river's edges.

Tamarisk eradication techniques developed at Bosque del Apache are already used far and wide throughout the salt cedar–infested

Southwest. Such capability is critical to numerous western refuges; most also suffer some degree of tamarisk infestation.

Bosque del Apache is important not only as habitat for hundreds of wild species but it's also a showcase of sorts, a model of the kind of environment that once existed all along the Rio Grande system before damming, grazing, and agriculture altered its natural character. Management techniques here may serve in future years as models for ecosystem rejuvenation all along the river—a healing process that will benefit both animals and humans for generations to come.

A visit to Bosque is always an adventure; you never know quite what you'll find here. In November of 1994 I was one of a lucky handful of visitors to encounter a groove-billed ani,

a Mexican bird seen at Bosque just a few times in more than 5 decades. In February of 1995, 4 tundra swans dropped in to mingle with the geese and cranes. In the spring of 1995, Eurasian wigeon and surf scoter both showed up, along with ovenbird. Other rarities here have included common loon, snowy plover, Montezuma quail, and gray catbird. (One catbird returns to a particular spot on the refuge each fall; as you approach the final pond on the east end of the 2-way road, look in the cottonwoods to your left.)

Visit Bosque in the fall or winter, if you can, and watch as one of nature's most spectacular events unfolds before your eyes and ears. Still, a visit to this rich desert habitat in any season is worthwhile. Bosque del Apache is a magical place with an unending store of surprises.

Bird sightings:

Other wildlife sightings:

Notes:

PARTIAL BIRD LIST (OF 325 LISTED SPECIES PLUS ACCIDENTALS): Sandhill and whooping cranes, snow and Ross's geese, great blue heron, sora, American avocet, greater yellowlegs, killdeer, bald eagle, roadrunner, northern flicker, barn swallow, vermilion flycatcher, southwestern willow flycatcher, Gambel's quail, horned lark, yellow-rumped warbler, indigo bunting, blue grosbeak.

PARTIAL MAMMAL LIST (OF 75 LISTED SPECIES): Mountain lion, bobcat, mule deer, porcupine, coyote, beaver, weasel, badger, valley pocket gopher, rock squirrel, black-tail jackrabbit, striped skunk, muskrat, meadow jumping mouse.

PARTIAL HERP LIST (OF 67 LISTED SPECIES): Sonoran gopher snake, desert king snake, western diamondback rattler, prairie rattler, Texas night snake, twin-spotted spiny lizard, southern prairie lizard, whiptail lizard, western painted turtle, desert box turtle, bullfrog, tiger salamander, New Mexico spadefoot toad.

PARTIAL FISH LIST (OF 35 LISTED SPECIES): Largemouth bass, channel catfish, flathead catfish, black bullhead, gambusia (mosquito fish), carp.

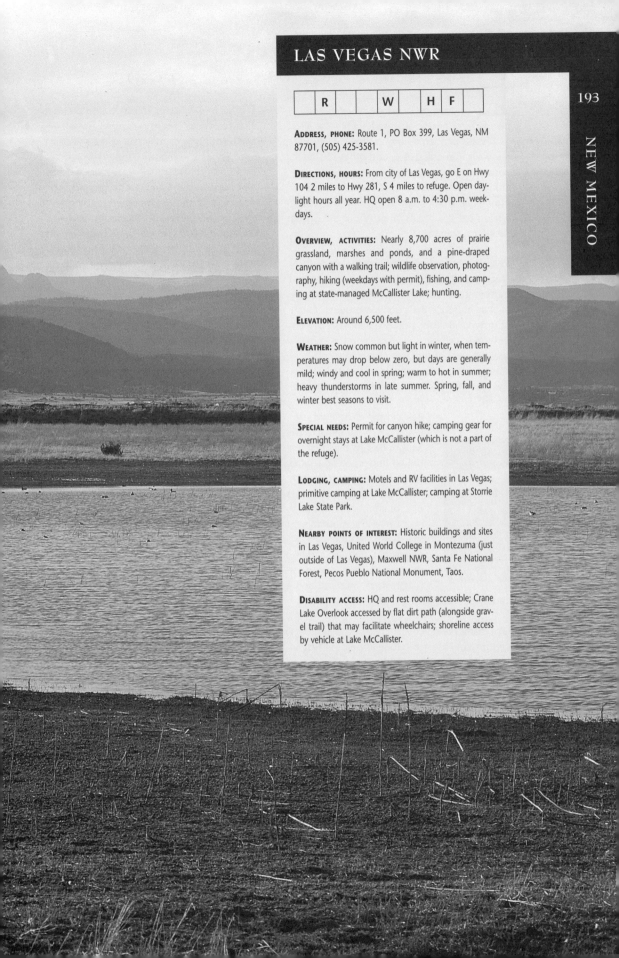

	R		W		H	F	

ADDRESS, PHONE: Route 1, PO Box 399, Las Vegas, NM 87701, (505) 425-3581.

DIRECTIONS, HOURS: From city of Las Vegas, go E on Hwy 104 2 miles to Hwy 281, S 4 miles to refuge. Open daylight hours all year. HQ open 8 a.m. to 4:30 p.m. weekdays.

OVERVIEW, ACTIVITIES: Nearly 8,700 acres of prairie grassland, marshes and ponds, and a pine-draped canyon with a walking trail; wildlife observation, photography, hiking (weekdays with permit), fishing, and camping at state-managed McCallister Lake; hunting.

ELEVATION: Around 6,500 feet.

WEATHER: Snow common but light in winter, when temperatures may drop below zero, but days are generally mild; windy and cool in spring; warm to hot in summer; heavy thunderstorms in late summer. Spring, fall, and winter best seasons to visit.

SPECIAL NEEDS: Permit for canyon hike; camping gear for overnight stays at Lake McCallister (which is not a part of the refuge).

LODGING, CAMPING: Motels and RV facilities in Las Vegas; primitive camping at Lake McCallister; camping at Storrie Lake State Park.

NEARBY POINTS OF INTEREST: Historic buildings and sites in Las Vegas, United World College in Montezuma (just outside of Las Vegas), Maxwell NWR, Santa Fe National Forest, Pecos Pueblo National Monument, Taos.

DISABILITY ACCESS: HQ and rest rooms accessible; Crane Lake Overlook accessed by flat dirt path (alongside gravel trail) that may facilitate wheelchairs; shoreline access by vehicle at Lake McCallister.

Evening at New Mexico's Las Vegas NWR can be a wild experience. In fall and winter in refuge marshes and ponds, a multitude of waterfowl fills the air with vocal pandemonium as shovelers, ruddies, gadwalls, Canada geese, and other species announce their presence. During those same colder months, bald eagles prowl the rolling prairie hills that comprise much of the refuge while small mammals range about the grasses seeking sustenance.

In spring, red-winged and yellow-headed blackbirds stand poised on tree branches and mullein stalks, flaring their wings, necks jutting as they annouce their dominion over a patch of ground. Brilliant yellow meadowlarks seem to be everywhere; they, too, favor the crimson mullein perches for their crooning displays, along with the fence posts and cattails that line the refuge's network of irrigation canals.

prairie

Beyond the rising lights of Las Vegas, New Mexico, the Sangre de Cristo Mountains roll off in deepening shades of blue. Clouds top Hermit Peak, gathering the last rays of sunlight. As the sun drops over the mountains, marshes turn a metallic silver-gold, framing cattails that may harbor sora and marsh wren, muskrat, and a variety of water-loving birds.

Like many prairie environments, this north-central New Mexico refuge appears at first to support minimal wildlife. Your view from the state highway, which doubles as the main refuge tour road, takes in long reaches of blue grama, western wheatgrass, and other native grasses, along with a few scattered patches of cottonwoods and willows. Farm and ranch houses on the refuge periphery contribute to the illusion that refuge acreage differs little from surrounding private fields. Patience and careful observation are sometimes required to unlock the refuge's more dramatic wildlife secrets.

Seasons and Secrets

In fall and winter, it's easy to find the magic at Las Vegas. Then, waterfowl and other marsh-loving birds may crowd the skies and pond edges and raptors fill the skyways. In fall, hundreds of sandhill cranes pile in from their northwestern summering grounds, some remaining for the winter, others pausing for a week or two before moving south. Between 5,000 and 8,000 Canada geese begin arriving in fall; their numbers peak near Christmas. More than 10,000 waterfowl of a dozen varieties filter in to complete the wetland menagerie.

Thousands of shorebirds pass through Las Vegas in August, as they will again in April. Water levels (and resulting mudflats) partly determine whether they settle in for a while or move on. In winter, raptors are everywhere, drawing on wetland and prairie small-prey protein. Bald eagles may number more than 50 during the colder months. Golden eagles, falcons, and hawks—particularly harriers, kestrels, and red-tails—enhance the predatory presence.

By midspring, waterfowl numbers decrease at Las Vegas, though a few individuals from as many as 2 dozen species may hang around. Spring along the refuge's canyon walking trail offers good songbird possibilities. Mule deer, beaver, bobcat, and herptiles that include frogs, lizards, and 2 rattler species are also out and about.

Early summer is the driest time at Las Vegas. Nesting birds remain tucked away much of the season, though raptors, such as prairie and peregrine falcons, kestrel, and red-tailed hawk, may be spotted cruising the meadows, feeding and fledging their young. Rainfall often begins around the 4th of July, turning the straw-colored grama and buffalo grass a rich green, set off by contrasting reddish bluestem, Indian ricegrass, and others. Baby birds begin wandering the refuge by mid-summer—lines of goslings trail Canada mothers, ducklings jabber in the marshes, young kestrels and other raptors learn to hunt by observing their predator parents. Harsh thunderstorms in August precede the renewal of fall migration; then the cycle turns again.

Historic Endpoint

The western edge of the Great Plains has long been a magnet for human as well as for avian species. The town of Las Vegas straddles a line separating the Rockies from Great Plains grassland, which rolls eastward deep into the nation's midsection. In the early 1800s, the town was a terminus for weary eastern and Midwest pioneers, who came by wagon from Independence, Missouri, traveling the famed Santa Fe Trail.

Las Vegas has a rich history marked by the presence of Spanish and then Mexican soldiers, Civil War–era American troops, railroad workers, and assorted tradespeople, outlaws, farmers, and ranchers. The railroad's arrival in 1880 marked the demise of the famed westward trail, but the historic legacy of Las Vegas continues in its restored buildings and civic emphasis on the town's Old West character.

The land encompassing the refuge was for decades part of a Spanish land grant. Around the turn of the century, Storrie Reservoir was built near the town, and the improvement of irrigation soon attracted farmers and ranchers. Over the years, many farmers tried hand and plow here, but most went bust. As grain fields yielded to expanding pastureland for cattle grazing, migratory species that had long drawn upon the grain crops declined.

Las Vegas refuge was established in 1965 to restimulate the area's attractiveness to Central Flyway migratory birds. Refuge impoundments were built to complement existing ponds, and grain fields were established to support wintering geese and cranes. Habitat improvements have succeeded in dramatically increasing migratory support for numerous species.

The federal policy change toward ecosystem management hasn't changed the management focus here all that much, according to staffers. Refuge impoundments, as well as grassland, riparian canyon, and 700 acres of farm fields, have long attracted "nongame" birds along with huntable species.

Shorebirds can be abundant at Las Vegas during migration, with species such as greater yellowlegs, spotted and western sandpipers, and long-billed dowitcher crowding refuge mudflats and shallows. Passerines migrate through in fairly large numbers; Audubon's warblers occupy wooded areas along McCallister Lake by the dozens (with a few Myrtle's among them), sharing habitat with house wren, Virginia's warbler, common yellowthroat, blue grosbeak, and lesser goldfinch.

Prairie Species

Up to 2 dozen resident pronghorns are often visible near the refuge office. Their range extends over the northeast to south portions of the refuge. Mule deer, porcupine, and other mammals may also be found on the refuge, which relies on grazing but avoids prescribed burning to meet its grass management requirements. Nearby farms and limited manpower render prescribed burns inappropriate for this refuge.

freshwater wetlands

Meadowlarks are often the most noticeable birds on this prairie-rich refuge. In spring, they seem to be everywhere, boldly jutting their beaks from each available perch to issue their sweet warbling calls. Blackbirds swarm in large numbers here in spring—red-wings throughout the refuge, buzzing yellow-heads along wetland edges.

Raptors find good living at Las Vegas, especially in cold months when they feed on abundant wintering birds and resident small mammals. Some, including golden eagle, kestrel, and prairie falcon, may be found here all year. Piles of fluttering feathers in the grass often mark the site of a feeding eagle.

In winter, you'll often find bald eagles perched in the elms along the road just south of the Crane Lake Overlook. The overlook itself is a good place from which to observe soaring birds, along with waterfowl and wader species using the lake and its shoreline. A scope will help.

Sparrows, towhees, and related species are abundant at Las Vegas in every season but winter. They number more than 2 dozen varieties. Many nest on Las Vegas refuge, including spotted and canyon towhees, vesper, fox, song and Brewer's sparrows, and a few lark buntings. Clay-colored, Lincoln's, sage, and Harris's are some of the rarer sparrows; vesper, savanna, and white-crowned are often abundant. Chestnut-collared longspur and rufous-crowned sparrow may show up in fall and winter, though locating them usually requires effort.

Wetlands and Ponds

As you enter the refuge from the north, a small seasonal pond on your right may hold numerous waders and shorebirds during migration. Farther down the road, the Middle Marshes create larger habitat areas where many species may be found.

The Crane Lake Overlook, located a few miles south of HQ along the main highway, is a good place to spot the sandhill cranes who winter at Las Vegas, along with Canada geese and more than a dozen waterfowl species. Shallows and mudflats around the lake may harbor shorebirds in migration.

Along the northeastern shoreline of state-managed McCallister Lake, tree snags draw double-crested cormorants, herons, egrets, and raptors. (Note: Visitors are sometimes confused by the management status of McCallister Lake. The refuge is not involved in lake management; despite its location within

refuge borders, McCallister is solely managed by the state of New Mexico.) The area is visible both from the side of the highway and from the lake's wooded southeastern shoreline. From here you may also observe various deeper-water birds, including bufflehead, Clark's and eared grebes, canvasback and redhead, lesser scaup, and common merganser. Muskrats live near the shore all around the lake, scurrying about, rising occasionally to scrub their faces and munch on aquatic vegetation.

As you continue traveling clockwise around the lake, fences and trees lining the dirt road along the western edge of your route may offer good views of sparrows, blue grosbeaks, meadowlarks, and other perching birds.

In November, your auto-cruising options increase when the refuge opens a 4-mile tour loop that begins from the office parking lot. A slow cruise along the Sunday-only loop (from 1 to 4:30 P.M.) carries you across prairie, past several impoundments, and through cropland acres that are inaccessible at other times of the year. Here you may spot any of 20 waterfowl species, along with numerous waders and shorebirds. Pronghorns often range about this area, and mule deer, skulking coyotes, and smaller mammals may be here, too.

Gallinas Canyon Trail

On the southwestern edge of the refuge, the grasslands end abruptly as the diminutive Gallinas River carves a path through its rocky, pine-decked canyon. Visitors may hike a short trail into the canyon from a parking area surrounded by the crumbling remains of old stone ranching structures.

After a steep descent, the trail rolls along past pools rippling with algae then on to pine uplands. Here you may spot any number of larger creatures, ranging from the beaver, who in 1995–96 worked diligently to bring down the canyon's cottonwoods, to mule deer, badger, coyote, bobcat, and others. Birds may include both woods and grassland species, including Stellar's and scrub jays, canyon wren with its mournful descending trill, Lewis's woodpecker, northern flicker, and flycatchers that may include ash-throated, western and Cassin's kingbirds, cordilleran flycatcher, and Say's phoebe. Layered rock formations on canyon slopes harbor rattlesnakes, which may emerge from hibernation when daytime temperatures rise above 50 degrees F. Always be careful where you put hands and feet.

The historic stone structures near the parking area are not accessible, but several are within easy view. Visiting the canyon requires a permit from HQ, where you'll be given the combination to 2 gate locks and instructions to remain on the trail. Return your permit before leaving the refuge. Permits are available until 2 P.M. on weekdays and must be returned by 4 P.M.

Highway Touring

Wildlife observers who drive slowly or who stop along the highway should exercise caution—the road is often empty of traffic but at times it's a high-speed thoroughfare. Unless you have a spotter to warn you of oncoming vehicles, pull onto shoulders and into parking spots before absorbing yourself in the wild sights around you.

Las Vegas is a small refuge that at first may appear unremarkable. To plumb the depths of this rich habitat may require time to beat its bushes, settle in beside ponds and marshes, immerse yourself in its prairie reaches. Time and effort pay off here in any season. And even when animals are relatively few, the dramatic landscape around Las Vegas NWR is enchanting enough to make a trip here worthwhile any time of the year.

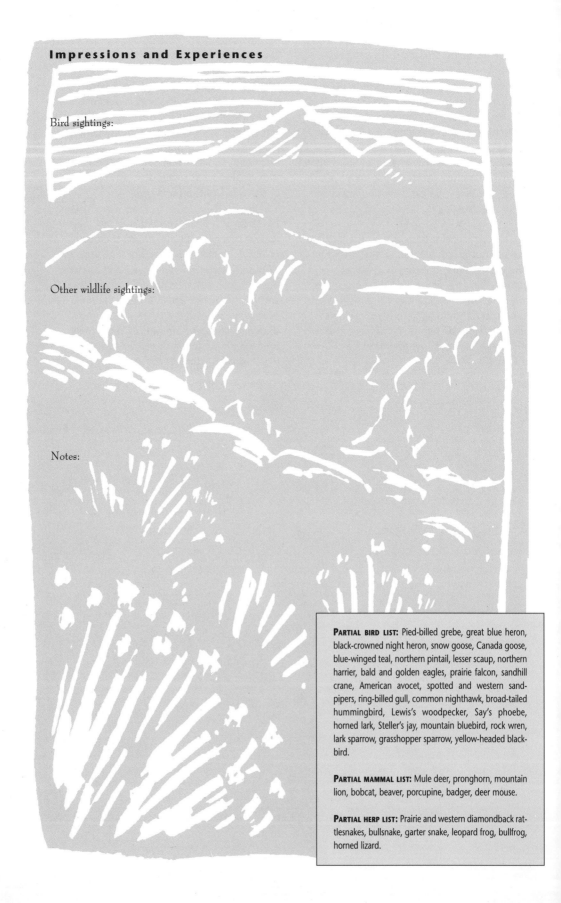

Impressions and Experiences

Bird sightings:

Other wildlife sightings:

Notes:

PARTIAL BIRD LIST: Pied-billed grebe, great blue heron, black-crowned night heron, snow goose, Canada goose, blue-winged teal, northern pintail, lesser scaup, northern harrier, bald and golden eagles, prairie falcon, sandhill crane, American avocet, spotted and western sandpipers, ring-billed gull, common nighthawk, broad-tailed hummingbird, Lewis's woodpecker, Say's phoebe, horned lark, Steller's jay, mountain bluebird, rock wren, lark sparrow, grasshopper sparrow, yellow-headed blackbird.

PARTIAL MAMMAL LIST: Mule deer, pronghorn, mountain lion, bobcat, beaver, porcupine, badger, deer mouse.

PARTIAL HERP LIST: Prairie and western diamondback rattlesnakes, bullsnake, garter snake, leopard frog, bullfrog, horned lizard.

The yellow-headed blackbird prefers marshy habitat, where it perches on the tips of emergent plants, spreads its wings and tail, and buzzes like an oversized locust.

Monte Vista NWR is part of a refuge complex that soon may include both Alamosa refuge and a new unit that provides good shorebird habitat.

Mule deer in velvet.

The Illinois River cuts a meandering path through Arapaho NWR's damp meadowland.

American badger.

Islands, sandbars, and cottonwood forests provide for numerous species at Browns Park.

(Opposite) A Great Plains gopher snake emerges from a globemallow bush.

The Green River cuts through Browns Park NWR in northwestern Colorado.

Porcupine is a common tree dweller at Rocky Mountain Arsenal. The big-toothed rodent feeds on bark and can strip the protective skin off a tree in short order.

Shortgrass prairie makes up much of the Denver-area Rocky Mountain Arsenal NWR.

Cactus wren is an uncommon inhabitant
of Bitter Lake's desert reaches.

The 700-acre Lake St. Francis Research Natural Area at Bitter Lake NWR includes a deep
sinkhole lake inhabited by native fish. The lake is not accessible to visitors.

Chihuahuan pronghorns range over parts of Bitter Lake and the vast prairie acres to the north.

Bobcat.

Kit fox.

Sandhill cranes.

Marshes and impoundments at Bosque del Apache
NWR support dozens of water-loving species;
riparian and desert reaches support many more.

Tens of thousands of snow geese winter at Bosque del Apache. To supply them with
food and keep them from ravaging nearby farm fields, grain crops are grown on the refuge
and parceled out to the geese at a measured rate.

Golden eagle.

Coyotes range throughout Las Vegas refuge, feeding on rodents and birds.

(Opposite) A microhabitat along Las Vegas NWR's Gallinas Canyon hiking trail.

Great horned owl is a common year-round resident of Maxwell refuge.

Northern shoveler

One of several irrigation district lakes on Maxwell NWR, Lake 13 and its shoreline provide waterfowl and other wildlife habitat; human fishing and camping opportunities; and a spectacular view that includes volcanic mountains to the east.

MAXWELL NWR

	R	C		W			F	

ADDRESS, PHONE: PO Box 276, Maxwell, NM 87728, (505) 375-2331.

DIRECTIONS, HOURS: From Las Vegas, NM, go N on I-25 to Maxwell exit; from town of Maxwell, refuge is 3 miles N off Hwy 445 three-quarters of a mile, then W on Hwy 505 2.5 miles to refuge entrance. Refuge open sunrise to sunset 7 days a week. HQ open 7:30 a.m. to 4 p.m. weekdays.

OVERVIEW, ACTIVITIES: Some 3,800 acres of prairie with several *playa* impoundments harboring abundant water-fowl in migration; wildlife observation, photography, hiking along roadways, fishing, camping, boating.

ELEVATION: Around 6,050 feet.

WEATHER: Cold to freezing in winter; mild spring and fall; moderately hot in summer. Strong winds often come in spring; late summer may bring torrential rains. Fall and winter best seasons to visit.

SPECIAL NEEDS: Camping and fishing gear if needed; water.

LODGING, CAMPING: Numerous motels in Raton; RV facilities in Raton and Cimarron; primitive camping on refuge; national forest camping to the W, including Cimarron Canyon State Park.

NEARBY POINTS OF INTEREST: Capulin Volcano National Monument (2 miles N of town of Capulin on Hwy 325); Sugarite Canyon State Park (10 miles NE of Raton); Cimarron, St. James Hotel, Cimarron Canyon State Park (just W of town of Cimarron); Taos; Las Vegas NWR and the historic town of Las Vegas; several national grasslands nearby in New Mexico, Texas, Oklahoma, and Colorado.

DISABILITY ACCESS: Rest rooms at HQ accessible; rest room at Lake 13 accessible; concrete pad at parking lot overlooking Lake 12; fishing from dike at Lake 13 from vehicle.

Once part of a vast Spanish land grant owned by a contemporary of mountain man Kit Carson, Maxwell NWR in northern New Mexico has come full circle—from wilderness prairie to developed farm and ranchland to (managed) wilderness once again. Throughout this squared-off 3,800-acre refuge, tall grasses wave alongside *playa* lakes often brimming with migratory waterfowl. Coyote and bobcat roam the uplands while smaller mammals, including long-tailed weasel and various rodents, evade them. Porcupines gnaw on cottonwood bark near scattered homesites now abandoned; meadowlarks and mountain bluebirds perch on the splintered ruins. Squadrons of raptors cruise the airways, alert for meals.

In fall, coyote willow lining the watercourses turns crimson and cottonwood leaves burn gold, sparking the landscape with color. Three major impoundments on the refuge reflect the clear New Mexico sky and the peaks of surrounding mountains: the Raton Range to the north, the Sangre de Cristos to the west. To the east, lower hills of volcanic origin rise from the prairie with dark distinction.

prairie

Maxwell is the smallest of New Mexico's federal refuges, but in terms of waterfowl numbers it can hold its own among any of the others. Irrigated *playa* lakes on the refuge provide habitat for tens of thousands of waterfowl, as well as for a lesser, more erratic population of waders and shorebirds.

The water on the refuge is owned by the local Vermejo Irrigation District; thus, management on and around the ponds here is limited to law enforcement and wildlife support. Whatever the district is doing as it shifts water about for utilitarian purposes, wildlife responds with enthusiasm. More than 100,000 ducks pass through in fall, including as many as 40,000 gadwalls, an equal number of wigeons, 100,000 coots, and lesser numbers representing more than a dozen species. Up

to 15,000 Canada geese arrive in late autumn. If conditions are good, many Canadas will stay for the winter.

Common loon is an occasional resident (I spotted one in April of 1996, wailing its mournful mating call in loonless surroundings); other oddball accidentals, such as surf scoter and oldsquaw, make appearances some years, along with Barrow's goldeneye, scaled quail, lesser golden plover, and yellow-billed cuckoo.

Water fluctuations are unpredictable on Maxwell, varying the breadth of mudflats from year to year. When snowmelt is meager and the ponds are low, mudflats expand. Then thousands of shorebirds and waders may spend several migration days here, including long-billed curlew, Baird's and stilt sandpipers, American avocet, marbled godwit, and sanderling. Sometimes the shorelines appear to be crawling as thousands of "peeps" dart about in synchronized bursts. In 1995, 1,500 Wilson's phalaropes wandered the shallows on a single day, twirling and feeding in a frenzy of motion.

Historic Crossroads

The region where Maxwell lies has hosted a parade of notable characters and events. Nomadic Indians used the area for some 12,000 years. In 1696, Spanish conquistador Don Diego de Vargas passed through after claiming New Mexico as Spanish territory. (He came here to quell a riot by displeased natives.) Several more Spanish incursions are recorded in the area, most involving disputes with indigenous people.

In the early 1800s, Spain decided it needed a buffer in this undeveloped area to protect its territorial claims, at a time when American explorers such as Zebulon Pike were admiring the countryside; the short-lived Republic of Texas to the south was also showing expansionist tendencies. When Mexico claimed the land as its own in the 1830s, that newest landlord took its turn worrying about land-lusting interlopers.

Its position near the end of the Santa Fe Trail brought the area more and more notice by Americans. (Maxwell lies 2 miles from one branch of the trail.) In 1841, Mexico granted Charles Beaubien virtually all the land visible from the refuge in every direction. When Beaubien's son was killed in an uprising by Taos Indians, trapper Lucien Maxwell, Charles's son-in-law by then, took over administrative duties for the 1.7-million-acre grant, a size vastly greater than any average land grant.

"Administering" the land in time came to mean "owning" it (though Maxwell did eventually pay Beaubien's business partner $40,000). Over the years, the former trapper and cohort of Gen. John C. Frémont developed a sizable empire in the region.

By the 1880s, a new wave of settlers, many of them European immigrants, had entered the area as miners or contract farmers. Maxwell had since sold out and moved south. Newcomers resented the concentration of now British-held land ownership that prevented them from pursuing their own dreams of land-based independence. Their resentment bubbled over, resulting in the Colfax County War, in which several people were shot or lynched.

Maxwell's son had meanwhile settled on a farm in Lincoln County, where—in yet another bout of history-making activity—he was hosting Billy the Kid the night Sheriff Pat Garrett gunned down the little antihero.

The range wars were finally settled with the help of New Mexico Gov. Lew Wallace, himself a legend as the author of the 1880 novel *Ben Hur*. Ownership of the land was gradually divided among a number of businesses and individuals. Later farmers would occupy much of the area, scratching out a difficult existence from this arid, poor-soiled, and often freezing environment.

Roaming the Refuge

The refuge was created in 1965 (puchased from 26 separate owners) to mitigate waterfowl depredation on surrounding grain fields, as well as to protect migratory and resident wildlife habitat. Shortly after Maxwell NWR was born, area farmers gave up their failing efforts to grow grain and switched to alfalfa, which has done well in this harsh environment.

Migratory geese continue to raid area fields, but alfalfa is a resilient plant. The geese merely clip its tops, doing little or no damage and probably enhancing fertility by leaving behind nitrogen-rich droppings. Today, most of the grain that visiting ducks and geese eat is grown by staffers and co-op farmers on 440 acres of refuge ground.

Thousands of Canada geese arrive at Maxwell each year in late October. They immediately begin gorging themselves frantically, with hourly forays from fields to ponds. If the winter is mild, the geese may stay at Maxwell. If snow and ice cut off their foraging too early, they'll head south to Las Vegas NWR, 80 miles away, or to Bitter Lake NWR near the southern end of the state.

freshwater wetlands

In either case, grain crops are mowed down a few acres at a time to support the geese at a measured rate. The mowing is necessary because bulky Canadas won't enter tall grainfields. They're slow on the takeoff and prefer to maintain 10 or 15 feet of open ground around them as a safeguard against predator attacks.

Getting Around

A network of refuge and county roads carries you through this square-shaped refuge and around its 3 major ponds. Lake 12 is never accessible to visitors (though you can see it from the roadway, along with the wildlife that often hangs out on the shoreline nearest to the road). The birds respond to the lake's sanctuary status by doing much of their breeding there. Sandhill cranes that pass through in spring and fall often roost here, moving to grainfields by day. If the winter is mild, some cranes will remain; in colder winters, they'll move on to the Las Vegas or Bitter Lake refuges.

The small size of the refuge is one reason hunting is not allowed here; a single shotgun blast might otherwise chase half of Maxwell's winged residents into the next county. Numerous nearby farmhouses around the grounds are another reason.

Lake 14 is a treeless impoundment that in early summer may support more than a hundred floating grebe nests. It's also a productive area for waterfowl birders in every season but summer. Fishing is allowed here, but relatively few anglers seem to take advantage.

Lake 13 is the largest of Maxwell's three lakes. A roadway lines the southern shoreline. Here anglers may fish from the riprap or directly from their vehicles (deep water lies immediately behind the roaded dike). Some 100,000 rainbow trout are stocked at Maxwell by the state each year; they often reach impressive sizes. Primitive camping also is allowed along this stretch of the dike, which catches the wind and so discourages insects in summer and fall. Small boats at wake speed are allowed on the lake between March 1 and October 30.

Birders can find more than a dozen waterfowl species on and around Lake 13. A marshy area near the entry road harbors killdeer and possibly sora and Virginia rails. Yellow-headed blackbird and marsh wren are some of the species attracted to the cattails along this stretch. Muskrats rise in the lake shallows, standing on their haunches to wash themselves before slipping into the pondweed and gliding off like furry submarines.

In winter, eagles perch in the cottonwoods on the north side of the lake; a few man-made perches offer them additional support in this perch-poor area. Often you'll spot them in winter standing on the ice. The eagles are joined in aerial hunt by dozens of harriers, as well as by sharp-shinned hawk, merlin, prairie

falcon, and kestrel. Osprey come in spring and fall, but that majestic fish hunter moves on during summer and winter. Golden eagle may be spotted occasionally throughout the year.

During a late April visit in 1996, I tallied 26 bird species within an hour, most of them in and around Lake 13. Eastern and Say's phoebes, as well as numerous meadowlarks, yellow-headed blackbirds, and horned larks, inhabited the grassy area near the entrance to the pond.

On the water, small numbers of waterfowl representing more than a dozen species dabbled in the shallows or bobbed on the deeper midlake area—stragglers from the spring migration or breeding birds preparing to nest. Among them were blue-winged and cinnamon teal, bufflehead, ruddy, shoveler, gadwall, Clark's grebe, common loon, eared grebe, and others.

Prairie Prowlers

The refuge is largely prairie upland, with blue grama regaining a foothold against less desirable native interlopers, such as galleta, sand dropseed, and threeawn. All of those out-of-place species rose behind a century's worth of farm plows.

Maxwell's grasslands support a few white-tailed and mule deer, as well as a small menagerie of mammals, such as coyote, bobcat, badger, curious long-tailed weasels, and numerous rodents.

Raptors take advantage of smaller furred prey as well as abundant water birds, which they help keep in good genetic shape by culling out weaker members. Ferruginous, Swainson's, and red-tailed hawks are often plentiful, along with prairie falcon and kestrel. Bald eagles come by the dozens in winter; they perch on ice or in the 2 dozen stands of cottonwood, elm, and locusts on the refuge, nearly all of which were planted by settlers. Great horned owls are plentiful throughout the refuge. Many nest here, producing 1 or 2 fluffy white young by April. As you travel the area, you'll note that there are nests in nearly every tree in the area. Some are magpie or passerine structures, but many belong to raptors of several species.

The lack of forested habitat at Maxwell means relatively few passerines stay here for long during migration. Throughout the year, the refuge manager may grant permits for birders to cross fences and enter small patches of woods in search of passerine species.

Waves of warblers, mountain bluebirds, and others show up briefly in early spring. Generally, they stay just long enough to refill their tanks before heading south. Catching sight of them is a chance occurrence. (My wife, Susan, and I caught the mountain bluebird influx during a March visit; spots of blue seemed to light the top of nearly every fence post and mullein stalk.)

Meadowlarks are plentiful, along with Say's phoebe, horned lark, and the grasshopper sparrow, which arrive in midspring. A study in 1995 revealed that Maxwell is home to more of these declining grassland sparrows than any other spot in New Mexico.

One secretive upland resident is the prairie rattler. The snake is not common on the refuge, but it's here. Any time you delve into grassy or brushy areas, keep your eyes open.

Vesper sparrows flock from brush to grasses, mainly near canals, where they often flutter down in lively groups for communal sips. The ungrazed grasses provide the sort of wild habitat that has supported birds in grand style for millennia. Grazing is not allowed on the refuge, which largely accounts for the pristine condition of the grasses.

Mammals are here, too, but few species occupy Maxwell in great numbers. Black bear have shown up on occasion, generally spending just a week or two before moving on to surrounding mountains. Pronghorn can be found in profusion north and south of the refuge, though numerous fences on Maxwell discourage these native ungulates from entering. Elk move through on occasion, though they prefer higher country to the north and west.

Long-tailed weasel is fairly common at Maxwell; staffers have seen them perched like birds on fence posts, scanning for prey. Occasionally, a staffer has glanced out an HQ window only to meet the eye of a curious weasel peering back.

Summer is Maxwell's least interesting season, but with patience and a good eye, you'll still find numerous species in the ponds and pale grass. A prairie dog town lies roughly a mile southeast of the office, a sight that children often find enjoyable—though adults like myself may also spend an hour or more watching the sociable rodents as they prance about, whistling, nudging one another, and dodging in and out of sight in their subterranean condos. Sparrows and meadowlarks, as well as a variety of raptors, spend the summer here, along with numerous nesting ducks, a few geese, ring-necked pheasant, several flycatchers and kingbirds, doves, owls, and herons.

Autumn is Maxwell's prime time for visitors—a season when the sky is crowded with wings and calls, when the lakes ripple with life, and when warm fields glow against the backdrop of distant mountains. However, any time of year can make for a worthwhile visit to this small refuge, a protected prairie land rich in history, wildlife, and scenic beauty.

Impressions and Experiences

Bird sightings:

Other wildlife sightings:

Notes:

PARTIAL BIRD LIST (OF 200 LISTED SPECIES): Pied-billed grebe, great blue heron, green-winged teal, northern pintail, gadwall, wigeon, common merganser, northern harrier, bald and golden eagles, sandhill crane, killdeer, spotted sandpiper, ring-billed gull, barn owl, great horned owl, northern flicker, eastern kingbird, sedge wren, yellow-rumped warbler, grasshopper sparrow, yellow-headed blackbird.

PARTIAL MAMMAL LIST: Mule and white-tailed deer, bobcat, coyote, long-tailed weasel, porcupine, badger, muskrat, beaver, deer mouse.

PARTIAL HERP LIST: Prairie rattler, bullsnake, garter snake, tiger salamander.

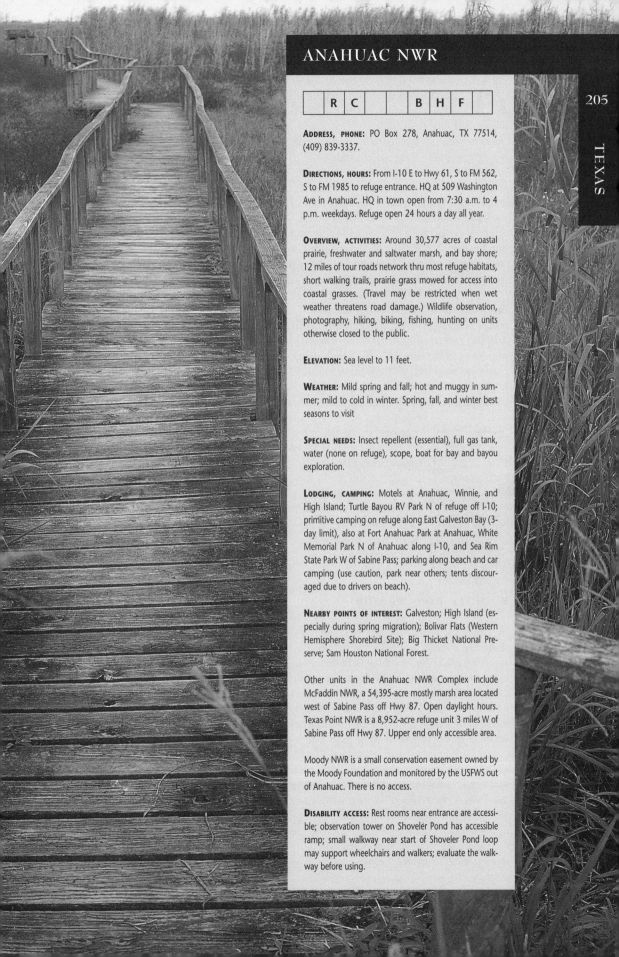

ANAHUAC NWR

	R	C		B	H	F	

ADDRESS, PHONE: PO Box 278, Anahuac, TX 77514, (409) 839-3337.

DIRECTIONS, HOURS: From I-10 E to Hwy 61, S to FM 562, S to FM 1985 to refuge entrance. HQ at 509 Washington Ave in Anahuac. HQ in town open from 7:30 a.m. to 4 p.m. weekdays. Refuge open 24 hours a day all year.

OVERVIEW, ACTIVITIES: Around 30,577 acres of coastal prairie, freshwater and saltwater marsh, and bay shore; 12 miles of tour roads network thru most refuge habitats, short walking trails, prairie grass mowed for access into coastal grasses. (Travel may be restricted when wet weather threatens road damage.) Wildlife observation, photography, hiking, biking, fishing, hunting on units otherwise closed to the public.

ELEVATION: Sea level to 11 feet.

WEATHER: Mild spring and fall; hot and muggy in summer; mild to cold in winter. Spring, fall, and winter best seasons to visit

SPECIAL NEEDS: Insect repellent (essential), full gas tank, water (none on refuge), scope, boat for bay and bayou exploration.

LODGING, CAMPING: Motels at Anahuac, Winnie, and High Island; Turtle Bayou RV Park N of refuge off I-10; primitive camping on refuge along East Galveston Bay (3-day limit), also at Fort Anahuac Park at Anahuac, White Memorial Park N of Anahuac along I-10, and Sea Rim State Park W of Sabine Pass; parking along beach and car camping (use caution, park near others; tents discouraged due to drivers on beach).

NEARBY POINTS OF INTEREST: Galveston; High Island (especially during spring migration); Bolivar Flats (Western Hemisphere Shorebird Site); Big Thicket National Preserve; Sam Houston National Forest.

Other units in the Anahuac NWR Complex include McFaddin NWR, a 54,395-acre mostly marsh area located west of Sabine Pass off Hwy 87. Open daylight hours. Texas Point NWR is a 8,952-acre refuge unit 3 miles W of Sabine Pass off Hwy 87. Upper end only accessible area.

Moody NWR is a small conservation easement owned by the Moody Foundation and monitored by the USFWS out of Anahuac. There is no access.

DISABILITY ACCESS: Rest rooms near entrance are accessible; observation tower on Shoveler Pond has accessible ramp; small walkway near start of Shoveler Pond loop may support wheelchairs and walkers; evaluate the walkway before using.

Anahuac NWR may be one of the Gulf Coast's more important migratory bird resting areas, but to me it will always be Gator Country. The primitive, predatory reptiles inhabit every watery nook and cranny of this flat coastal prairie and marsh environment south of Beaumont, Texas. Lazy gators, endearing microgators, massive gators with gaping jaws and too-confident expressions on their leathery faces— scores of evolutionary hangers-on live through-out Anahuac. There's virtually no wet place on the refuge where you won't find them, except maybe in the rest rooms. Check anyway.

Even without the gators, which are most visible in spring and fall, wildlife viewing on Anahuac can be spectacular. During avian migration, birders crowd in for a look and the roads and trails can get fairly busy; summer and early fall offer a quieter environment, though it does get hot and muggy then and

coastal

mosquitoes can be a serious nuisance. In late fall, the refuge roars as up to 80,000 snow geese, as many as 200,000 ducks (1993 survey figures) representing 2 dozen species, and a prolific cast of waders and other marsh birds move in for their winter stay.

Wildlife-Rich Region

Nature-viewing opportunities in the region around Anahuac begin well before you reach the 30,577-acre refuge (additional acres were being sought in 1996), part of a complex that includes three other units. Good birding extends throughout the area, including east and south on the county roads from Anahuac to the coastal town of High Island.

High Island is itself a famed birding hot spot. A discrete coastal rise amid monotonous plains, the town is blanketed in live oak, willow, and other trees and vegetation that are beacons to migrating birds crossing the gulf. During their final approach to land, neotropical species head to High Island by the thousands.

Especially during fallouts, the town resembles a cageless pet shop, jammed to its highest limbs with colorful species.

A few miles east of the refuge turnoff on FM 1985, a private hunting club maintains road-side grainfields that attract ducks, snow and white-fronted geese, white-faced and white ibis, and other species. In spring, the refuge maintains a shorebird management area east of East Bay Bayou; from the entrance, the field is 7 miles east. Stay in your vehicle and most of the birds will tolerate your presence. The exceptions are skittish white ibises, who fly off to distant field edges when you get too close.

Along the dirt road into the refuge you'll usually spot an assortment of critters, including armadillo, various flycatchers, loggerhead shrike, any of several hawk species, and possibly a merlin or prairie falcon. Caracara, the falcon-family bird on which the Mexican flag's icon is based, many be here, too.

In spring, any of 3 dozen warbler or other passerine species may be perching in trees along the road. One common mammal you probably won't see is white-tailed deer; surprisingly, Anahuac rarely hosts this ubiquitous Texas mammal. You may see coyotes, though, some bearing the black or reddish fur of the red wolf, whose hybridized genes they still hold, though the wolf in pure form has been extirpated from the region.

On Refuge Ground

After you register in the kiosk visitor book and enter the refuge, you immediately face a choice of three travel routes. Continue straight on Salt Cedar Road and your journey passes upland reaches and then skirts a lengthy slough that sometimes harbors gators and often pied-billed grebe, common moorhen, and other rails. Gators are here in great numbers, including big lazy ones that lay low in the water, looking like gnarled black driftwood. Keep pets leashed and children close.

About a mile down the road, check the cluster of salt cedars on your left for passerines.

Along the slough you'll likely spot killdeer, long-billed curlew, willet, various sandpipers, and many other species. Watch the willows and Chinese tallow trees for songbirds and raptors. Water hyacinth chokes many of the canals and shallow pools along the road; both their shovel-shaped leaf structure and exotic blooms are works of art, though they do create management problems and must be cleared occasionally by staffers.

Salt Cedar Road takes you on a roundabout journey along the edge of Deep Marsh; then the road's name changes to Windmill Road, which winds along Teal Slough, where many species may be found. Near Teal Slough along Barker Road are two Goose Grit Stations. Since coastal soil lacks good bird grit, refuge staffers supply geese with this essential gizzard-grinding material. You may see hundreds of geese at either spot.

The road continues to the shallows of East Galveston Bay. Along the shore lies plenty of low brush, good structure for an assortment of perchers. The bayfront is a likely place to find hermit crabs. With scant emergent vegetation there, you won't find many water birds along this stretch other than willets and pelicans. Seaside sparrows hang out around this area, too, along with clapper rails and a few terns (6 species are here, including gull-billed) cruising for fish. Several seagull species—ever the opportunists—hover over local anglers who set up camp here. Shrikes and others may also occupy the uplands and shoreline brush.

If you camp, bring water; no facilities exist in the camping area. Fires are discouraged and may be prohibited during your visit, depending on conditions. On bright nights, watch for short-eared owls hunting along the bay.

From the entrance again (where barn owls may sometimes be seen at night), a road to the left takes you to a boat ramp from which you may cruise to Oyster Bayou. The channel is often thick with wildlife, particularly waders such as roseate spoonbill, a species common here from spring through fall. In late summer, the bayou and nearby flood ponds may also harbor wood storks.

Continue along the watercourse and you'll gradually enter East Galveston Bay. Wade fishing on the bayou draws the lion's share of Anahuac's 60,000-plus visitors each year. Redfish, sea trout, and flounder are the main game fish pursued in the bay, one of Texas's most productive fisheries.

Shoveler Pond Route

A third road option just past the refuge entrance veers to the right. This is the route to Anahuac's most active wildlife area. A 3-mile loop runs past numerous habitats, including recently planted winter rye grass acres on some of Anahuac's prairie upland reaches.

The first quarter mile of the road passes a canal where you may see gators and moorhens, along with any of several grebe species. Great blue and little blue herons, killdeer, great egret, and other waders and shorebirds also use the canal and surrounding habitat.

Behind the visitor contact station, along the road to the north, is a newly planted coastal wood lot; oaks and other native species offer abundant perching habitat. A short distance down the road, on the right, lies a tiny wetland. A walkway made of recycled plastic has been laid out to provide access to a small willow-shaded pond.

The pond and surroundings create a serene setting. Willows here may harbor warblers and many others. In migration, check the trees for such neotropical migrants as yellow warbler, northern parula, indigo bunting, palm warbler (an Anahuac specialty), and others, including both black- and yellow-billed cuckoos. Northern water thrush may be here, too, slightly east of its acknowledged range. Louisiana water thrush—slightly west of its normal range—come occasionally as well.

Beyond a short, usually mowed strip of grass lies a fenced private woodland area of Chinese tallow and other trees, where numerous passerines are often found.

Continuing west on the tour road, you'll soon reach a 1-way loop that begins a cruise around extensive wetlands. A scope will serve you well as you make your way around sprawling Shoveler Pond. Narrow watercourses along the way, some draped in duckweed and water hyacinth, support gators and grebes, various waterfowl species, and often numerous egrets and herons.

Watch for river otters in the drainage area just before you get to Shoveler Pond. The playful otter also lives along Oyster Bayou and in the nonaccessible East Bay Bayou.

You may encounter a cottonmouth (also known as "water moccasin") anywhere along the tour road—and throughout Anahuac. The nearly black venomous species is abundant throughout the refuge. Nonpoisonous snakes live here, too, including mimic water snakes, which resemble the cottonmouth in their general shape and dark tones. When agitated, water snakes often swell their heads to impersonate their bad-boy cousin, though they lack the snowy inner mouth lining that gives the cottonmouth its name. Since water snake temperament is similarly aggressive, they often pull off convincing impersonations. An important distinction is the cottonmouth's tendency to hold its ground when threatened, whereas the water snake will usually slink off at the first opportunity.

Herp enthusiasts come here to catch sight of a relatively rare water serpent, Graham's crayfish snake. This slender freshwater dweller is brown with a single yellowish line along its side. It feeds on freshly molted crayfish as well as on frogs and other aquatic morsels. The gulf salt marsh snake also lives at Galveston Bay and presumably at Anahuac. Its double-lined brown body is otherwise similar to the crayfish snake's, though the former can grow to 5 feet in length—a foot longer than its crawdaddy-snacking cousin.

The Shoveler Pond loop bears a lookout platform offering good overviews of the marsh and its many inhabitants, which may include wood storks in late summer. A little farther south, a wooden walkway provides access deep into the shallow, vegetation-choked marsh (an upgrade of this ailing structure may come soon). Settle in along the walkway; your presence at first will discourage animal activity, but once they get used to you, many critters will continue about their business. Here you'll probably see a variety of waterfowl, along with egrets, herons, a ratlike nutria or two, muskrat, and, in the sky above, raptors that may include northern harrier in most seasons and osprey in spring and fall. Masked duck has nested here, one of the first records of nesting by this Mexican species in the state of Texas.

The loop continues around both vegetated and open wetlands, some deep, some shallow, with plentiful mudflats that provide habitat for waders and peeps. A leisurely trip around the Shoveler Pond loop in November of 1995 yielded sightings of shoveler, moorhen, coot, green-winged teal, marsh hawk, kestrel, red-tailed hawk, white-fronted goose, glossy and white ibises, little blue, great blue, and black-crowned night herons, great and snowy egrets, several nutrias, red-eared turtles, dozens of gators, and one of the most spectacular sunsets I've ever witnessed.

The sunset was awesome; the mosquitoes that accompanied it were, in their own way, equally spectacular. Legions of incessant stingers made even the simplest act nearly impossible to accomplish without dancing, gyrations, and the uttering of words that most moms don't allow. The moral: Bring bug repellent and keep your doors and windows closed.

Prairie Grasslands

Close to 9,000 acres of Anahuac are coastal prairie. This is a wet grassland, much of it former rice farm acres from which levees have been removed and grass restoration accomplished by refuge staffers. Prescribed burns and controlled grazing are two main tools used to keep the prairie in good shape. Most of the grassland here is made up of wetland plant species, but prairie upland species are mixed in as well.

Among the most intriguing prairie wildlife residents are rails, including a birder's magnet species, the yellow rail. All 6 North American rail species are represented on Anahuac—king, clapper, black, yellow, and Virginia, as well as sora, regarded by specialists as a near relative of true rails. Refuge staffers mow down short pathways off Windmill Road into the grasses, where you may walk in search of rails and other wildlife. Often when several people move along a mowed strip in tandem, the secretive "marsh chickens" will rise into view.

A fire in the spring of 1996 wiped out much of the grass here, but the habitat should be back in shape—possibly in improved condition—by the spring of 1997. Numerous cottonmouths inhabit prairie grasses as well as marshes. Keep your eyes open during prairie forays, as you should anywhere on the refuge.

Another birder's favorite here in winter and early spring is Le Conte's sparrow. To locate this unusual sparrow, listen for a sharp, insect-like buzz. The sharp-tailed sparrow is also here, its song a raspy trill that ends in a single low note. The sharp-tail looks much like the Le Conte's except that it has a gray stripe across the crown, which the Le Conte's lacks; dark bars across its head are also thicker than the Le Conte's crown bars. Seaside sparrow is another common resident of Anahuac throughout the year.

Resisting the Tide

Since the Gulf Intracoastal Waterway was dredged through coastal freshwater wetlands in the early 1900s, the marshes of Anahuac and other areas on the coast have suffered from saltwater intrusion, which has turned wide areas of formerly freshwater habitat into salt marsh; unfortunately, boat traffic along the GIWW has encouraged widespread erosion that is gradually widening the bay.

On the refuge, staffers work to combat both problems. One-way water-control devices (flap gates) on freshwater impoundments allow excess rainwater to be drained from the marshes while preventing saltwater from getting in. Riprap has been placed along vulnerable refuge bayfront; cordgrass planted behind the rocks helps stabilize bay shores. Budgets and manpower are the biggest obstacles in the effort to protect the bay shore—nothing new in the national wildlife refuge system.

Prescribed burns around wetland areas help control marsh vegetation; managed grazing is another tool that helps create plant diversity in the marshes, as it helps open and improve habitat for various wetland species.

Other salt-related problems have arisen from straight-line channeling and drainage projects along the coastal shoreline. Often such channels allow salty tides to move much farther inland than they once did. Salt is sometimes injected into ditches to discourage unwanted plants, but the technique is rarely used in the marshes.

Visiting Anahuac can be invigorating for the spirit. Good, varied habitat, abundant bird life from fall through spring, and all those gators make this a fascinating destination for any nature lover blessed with access to the wildlife-rich Texas coast.

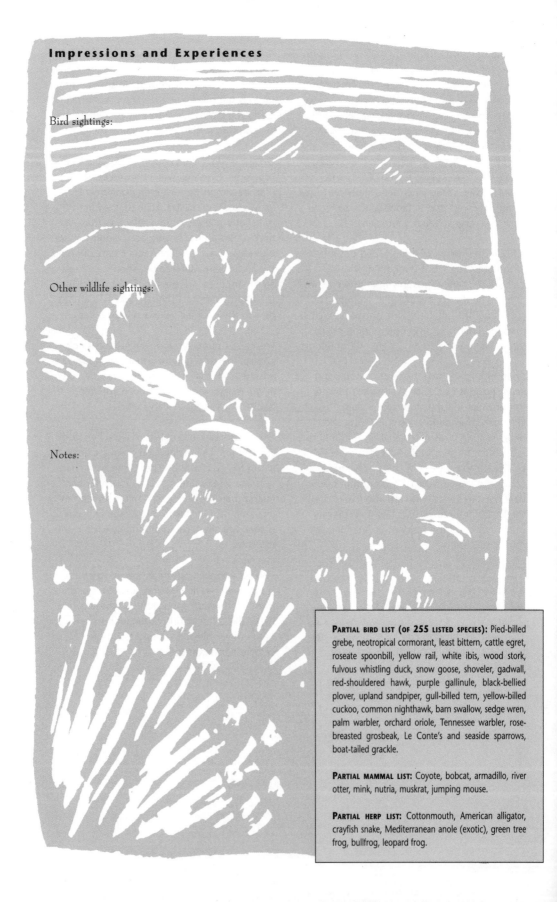

Impressions and Experiences

Bird sightings:

Other wildlife sightings:

Notes:

PARTIAL BIRD LIST (OF 255 LISTED SPECIES): Pied-billed grebe, neotropical cormorant, least bittern, cattle egret, roseate spoonbill, yellow rail, white ibis, wood stork, fulvous whistling duck, snow goose, shoveler, gadwall, red-shouldered hawk, purple gallinule, black-bellied plover, upland sandpiper, gull-billed tern, yellow-billed cuckoo, common nighthawk, barn swallow, sedge wren, palm warbler, orchard oriole, Tennessee warbler, rose-breasted grosbeak, Le Conte's and seaside sparrows, boat-tailed grackle.

PARTIAL MAMMAL LIST: Coyote, bobcat, armadillo, river otter, mink, nutria, muskrat, jumping mouse.

PARTIAL HERP LIST: Cottonmouth, American alligator, crayfish snake, Mediterranean anole (exotic), green tree frog, bullfrog, leopard frog.

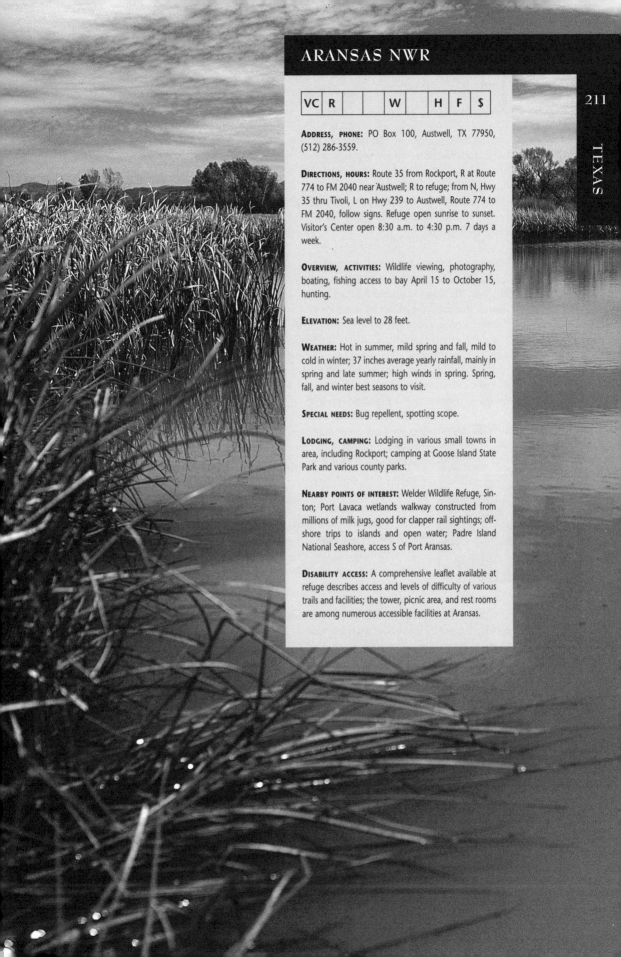

ARANSAS NWR

VC	R			W		H	F	$

ADDRESS, PHONE: PO Box 100, Austwell, TX 77950, (512) 286-3559.

DIRECTIONS, HOURS: Route 35 from Rockport, R at Route 774 to FM 2040 near Austwell; R to refuge; from N, Hwy 35 thru Tivoli, L on Hwy 239 to Austwell, Route 774 to FM 2040, follow signs. Refuge open sunrise to sunset. Visitor's Center open 8:30 a.m. to 4:30 p.m. 7 days a week.

OVERVIEW, ACTIVITIES: Wildlife viewing, photography, boating, fishing access to bay April 15 to October 15, hunting.

ELEVATION: Sea level to 28 feet.

WEATHER: Hot in summer, mild spring and fall, mild to cold in winter; 37 inches average yearly rainfall, mainly in spring and late summer; high winds in spring. Spring, fall, and winter best seasons to visit.

SPECIAL NEEDS: Bug repellent, spotting scope.

LODGING, CAMPING: Lodging in various small towns in area, including Rockport; camping at Goose Island State Park and various county parks.

NEARBY POINTS OF INTEREST: Welder Wildlife Refuge, Sinton; Port Lavaca wetlands walkway constructed from millions of milk jugs, good for clapper rail sightings; offshore trips to islands and open water; Padre Island National Seashore, access S of Port Aransas.

DISABILITY ACCESS: A comprehensive leaflet available at refuge describes access and levels of difficulty of various trails and facilities; the tower, picnic area, and rest rooms are among numerous accessible facilities at Aransas.

Each fall, an ageless ritual begins in the cold reaches of Wood Buffalo National Park in Saskatchewan, Canada. Responding to some obscure genetic travel advisory, close to 150 whooping cranes begin to look south, where warm weather and good coastal marsh habitat await. The cranes rise and circle their summer home, filling the autumn sky with their raucous calls. Alone, in pairs, or in family groups of three, they head south.

Those cranes who complete the grueling 2,600-mile journey eventually alight at Aransas NWR on the Texas coast. At Aransas and in nearby marshes, they'll spend the next 6 months alone or in small family groups, loafing and feeding on clams, crabs, and other aquatic invertebrates. (Whoopers may also eat rodents, berries, and sometimes small birds.) If they survive the season at Aransas, most will return to their northern breeding grounds by late March, fulfilling a biogeographical cycle that has survived, if precariously, the obstacle course that is modern-day North America.

coastal

An equally predictable autumn ritual coincides with that of the cranes. Eager birders from around the world descend upon Aransas from late October through mid-April. For some, the trip offers a first glimpse of the perilously endangered whooper; others, tugged by irresistible enchantment, come to renew their communion with this winged spirit of the South Coast.

The whooping crane is Aransas's chief claim to fame, as it is an emblem of all the world's at-risk species. Down to just 16 individuals in 1941—despite protection afforded by the 1918 Migratory Bird Treaty Act—by 1995 there were just over 250 whoopers left on planet earth. Half inhabited the Aransas–Canada Flyway, some were in an introduced flock in Florida, 2 or 3 faltered in a dwindling New Mexico test group (see Bosque del Apache, NM), and the rest were in captivity.

Observing a whooper in the wild is a breathtaking experience, a sad and wonderful vision of recent human and natural history, a cautionary glimpse of the price we pay for progress.

There is irony in the whoopers' choice of Aransas as their wintering spot. Irony because like the cranes themselves, this coastal stretch north of Corpus Christi is one of the most threatened habitats on the gulf. Aransas lies directly along the Gulf Intracoastal Waterway (GIWW), which provides passage each year for millions of tons of highly toxic chemicals—around $23 billion worth, if measured in money—ferried through the shallows in a parade of barges and tankers. One toxic spill while the whoopers are in residence could signal the end of this majestic species.

That's a big reason why USFWS biologists and others have struggled to create new flocks and new flyways, to create ecological buffers should the unthinkable happen. Neither the Florida nor the New Mexico flock is doing well, however; Aransas remains the whoopers' most critical ground.

Given our record as a species, an Aransas calamity will likely come. It's just a matter of when and how bad the spill will be. What will we tell ourselves if the whooper vanishes in the space of a newsflash? Could we blandly accept its absense from our world, and would that be enough to make us change?

More Than Whoopers

The spotlight at Aransas is on cranes, but the refuge is much more than a whooper sanctuary. The 70,504-acre refuge complex, midway along the Texas coast 75 miles north of Corpus Christi, was originally established in 1937 for support of migratory waterfowl and other birds. Attention on the cranes came shortly after.

Aransas NWR is composed of Blackjack Peninsula and three satellite units, including a portion of nearby Matagorda Island. Together, the refuge units represent a great variety of habitat and support a corresponding bounty of avian and other species. Gators, deer, bobcats, a large number of herptiles, and at least 392 species of birds—second only to the Laguna Atascosa refuge's 401 bird list—inhabit Aransas at least part of the year.

The satellite unit on Matagorda Island provides significant wildlife support for migratory birds in fall and spring; thousands of passerines use the island in migration, including hundreds of loggerhead shrikes that reside there in winter. Around a quarter of the whooper flock winters at Matagorda. A varied cast of sea mammals and imperiled turtles also lives and plays along island shores.

The drive down Hwy 2040 from Austwell toward the refuge makes clear one reason Aransas is such an important place for wild creatures. Farm fields stretch to the horizon in all directions, offering virtually no habitat for any of the area's wildlife except for a few clouds of blackbirds, squawking grackles and cowbirds, meadowlarks, a handful of sparrows, and sometimes caracaras and vultures, often seen hunched over road kills.

Before Euro-Americans came to crop farm the ecosystem, the area was inhabited by Native Americans known as Karankawas, whom some say were cannibalistic. Long before their presence, other peoples may have come here—surveys of the mesquite forest country to the west, for instance, have yielded 10,000-year-old Clovis points.

Even before the most ancient people trod the coastline, mammoths, wild horses, giant armadillos, and other prehistoric critters made the region their home, including a lion that resembled the present African species so closely that only an expert paleontologist can differentiate their bones.

Grassland on the refuge may not look like much to untrained eyes, but to those who know grass, Aransas's bluestem prairie is a well-balanced piece of natural art. Numerous creatures depend on the prairie for sustenance. Soon their numbers will include the

endangered Attwater's prairie chicken, whose dedicated refuge near Houston has had major problems bolstering the bird's fast-declining numbers. Reintroduction of prairie chickens on Aransas's Tatten Unit may begin before the turn of the century.

Aransas's oak motte brush country makes a good home for numerous species. Javelinas, white-tailed deer, bobcats and raccoons, and an extensive roster of grassland birds, including thousands of sparrows, visit or live in the knee-high grasses.

In 1996, Laguna's 401 count of bird species had moved well ahead of Aransas's 392 bird list, but a single exceptional year at Aransas—perhaps after a couple of hearty storms blow errant migrants onto the refuge—could shift the balance in their longtime, good-spirited contest. It's possible; since 1988, several oddball species have shown up on Aransas, including surf scoter, little gull, acorn woodpecker, clay-colored robin, greater black-backed gull, glaucous gull, and rock wren.

Many of Aransas's waterfowl species come each fall to luxuriate in the tidal marshes, formed when strong prevailing winds push water onto low-lying shoreline, creating shallow feeding areas and protected roosting spots. The warm, highly saline waters of Aransas Bay provide rich stores of marine food plants, as well as a cornucopia of invertebrates and finned morsels.

freshwater wetlands

Nineteen state or federal threatened or endangered species reside at Aransas and Matagorda, including the piping plover, state-listed reddish egret and roseate spoonbill, several federally endangered sea turtles, and the recently list-downgraded American alligator.

An in-depth book covering all aspects of Aransas ecology, as well as basic biological principles governing the region, was written by local naturalists Wayne and Martha McAlister. The book is available at the Visitor's Center.

Getting Around

A visit to the refuge begins at the Aransas Visitor's Center, where you're required to register and pay a small entry fee. Here you'll find good exhibits on coastal ecology, as well as a display on the whooper's lifeways and perils. A collection of stuffed coastal birds offers up-close inspections. Outside, watch for a pair of great horned owls that has lived around the center for years; they're affectionately known to staffers as "Steve and Edie." Passerines often inhabit trees in the parking lot.

Across the tour road lies a gated stretch of forested wetland where you'll nearly always find a gator or two sunning on the lawn or peering from the waterline. Keep your pets leashed and remind the kids, if they need reminding, that this is no zoo. Here you may also spot various waterfowl, including pied-billed grebe and an assortment of ducks. In spring and fall, Gator Pond is also a good place to begin your search for songbirds.

Along the 16-mile tour road you'll pass five main trails that wind through most Aransas habitats. The Rail Trail carries you into a thick forest of live oak and other species and then flanks an emergent-blanketed wetland. Gators, ducks, wild boars and javelinas, flycatchers, snakes, and tree frogs are among the residents here. Numerous reddish and great egrets, as well as several heron species, are often wading in nearby marshes.

Heron Flats Trail may be the most wildlife-rich walking route on the refuge. This 1.5-mile trail takes you into the heart of Aransas's canopied forest and freshwater wetlands and provides views of the bay and estuarine reaches from a raised platform. The trail offers so much, in fact, that the Southwest Natural and Cultural Heritage Association publishes a small book covering its ecology. (This book is also available at the Visitor's Center.)

Red-breasted merganser may be found among many species on the large pond here, and groove-billed ani sometimes cruise nearby woodlands; 4 of the parrotlike anis have wintered at Aransas in recent years. A red-shouldered hawk has recently claimed Heron Flats as its territory; the bird isn't too people-shy and can be easily observed. Numerous spring passerine migrants may also be found among the forest areas here. Look for purple gallinule at the intersection of Heron Flats Trail and Rail Trail.

Notes on Nippers, Pokers, and Chompers

Gators generally stay well away from the walking trail, but don't count on it. Cottonmouths live here and elsewhere on the refuge, too. In November of 1995, a 5-footer with a radiant smile crossed the trail nearly beneath my feet and then turned to gloat from a nearby yucca. As well-ordered as this refuge may appear, never forget that it's a wild place, as it has been for centuries. There are things here that can hurt you if you're careless.

Such hazards include fire ants, ticks that may carry Rocky Mountain spotted fever, and chiggers, which burrow into unprotected skin and leave nasty welts. The simple solution is to use bug repellent when you're out and about, especially on feet, ankles, and legs or pants. For nastier biters, such as snakes and Africanized bees, alertness and common sense will keep you safe. In fact, you may enjoy the thrill of sharing space with a dangerous wild critter. Leave them alone and they'll return the favor.

Don't be afraid of Aransas; 72,000 people visit each year with few incidents. Just be prepared. One insect that appears frightening but isn't is the tussock moth that sometimes arises in the millions. The tiny moth has three long, hairy protuberances on its head, none of which will harm you. The moth's eruptions in late April and early May often coincide with influxes of migratory birds, who surely appreciate the free meals after their long, exhausting flights from the south.

Back on the Trails

Other short paths off the tour loop bring you to overlooks of Aransas Bay, where in fall and winter you'll see thousands of ducks, snow geese, white pelicans, and a great blue heron virtually every 50 yards. Spoonbill, reddish egret, and tricolored and little blue herons are among many species that may reside on and near the bay. Trailside brush and trees may bear numerous songbirds in spring and fall. The oaks along the coastline are works of art, some sculpted by the wind into incredible shapes.

Jones Lake Overlook is particularly rich in wildlife. Part of it is open water, part congested with emergent vegetation. The pond itself may appear unproductive at first glance. On my second Aransas visit in November, I grew discouraged after an initial scan of the area. All I noticed at first were 5 or 6 coots bobbing at the pond's western end.

I settled in and began to glass the shoreline and marsh. Over the next several minutes I noted 2 common moorhens, a juvenile black-crowned night heron, several young gators (and one gigantic one, possibly 40 or 50 years old), a leopard frog, a few massive bullfrogs—one of which startled a moorhen, who bolted wildly—2 buffleheads in that crowd of coots, a harrier, several marsh wrens, and a common yellowthroat. A noisy flock of cranes and a vee of ducks winged overhead, topping off the experience. That unpromising stroll turned out to be one of the most enjoyable parts of my visit.

During an April trip (wind blew briskly both days), the trailside at Hog Lake was one of the better spots my wife, Susan, and I found for songbirds. Indigo and painted bunting, black-throated green warbler, and many others showed up in trees near the trailhead. Springtime songbirds may be found throughout the refuge, particularly by walking the

trails but also by driving slowly and scanning the trees along the road. Two additional birding trails may increase your passerine tally even more: one lies between the Visitor's Center and the picnic area; the other is just beyond Dagger Point. They're marked on the refuge brochure with the letter B.

Upland Wildlife

The tour loop passes on through bluestem meadows punctuated by live oak and red bay mottes (or "hammocks"), where deer, javelina, various bird species, and other wildlife may be found. Short trails through the meadow also access the bay. Flowers here in spring and summer, and after a rainfall, can be spectacular at times, with Indian blanket, Mexican hat, gayfeather (an unusual flower that is common here), scarlet pea, Turk's cap, meadow pink, Texas prickly pear, clover, and goldenrod among the hundreds of species inhabiting Aransas meadows and marshes. Scores of butterfly species, including the pipe vine swallowtail, respond to this colorful feast, further adding to Aransas's beauty and diversity.

A developed picnic area located just before the open prairie begins is notable for the javelina that sometimes gather there. Please don't feed them; that's the reason they're hanging around, but you're not helping their cause by providing them with human food. Besides, they can tusk you if you get too close. Passerines, including cuckoos and hummingbirds, may be found in the trees here as well.

Raptors that hunt the grassland and forests may include black-shouldered kite, red-shouldered hawk, both Krider's and Harlan's red-tailed hawk, caracara, prairie and peregrine falcons (both somewhat rare), sharp-shinned hawk, and carrion-eating black and turkey vultures.

Crane Watching

At the end of the 2-way route lies Aransas's prime viewing spot for whooping cranes. After that, the road continues on a twisty 1-

way loop (something of a squeeze for large RVs). The 40-foot observation tower bears two telescopes often in demand during heavy visiting periods—bring your own scope if possible.

White spots far out on the marshes may or may not be whoopers. Look for the characteristic black-and-red head patches, which similar great egrets lack. In flight, look for neck and legs that extend and black on the back outer wing margins. (Similar white pelicans and egrets both tuck their necks in during flight; the black on pelicans extends the full length of the wing on the trailing edge.) If you spot a flock of half a dozen or more birds, you're not looking at whoopers. They don't flock that way.

At least 1 pair of whoopers has resided in the marshes just west of the tower for many seasons. From the tower you may also spot numerous passerines in the nearby treetops and possibly a clapper rail, Virginia rail, or soar on the Mustang Lake mudflats.

To see whoopers close up, consider a boat trip from nearby harbors at Rockport and Fulton. Most captains guarantee a sighting, and whoopers allow boats a much closer approach than they do with people on foot or in vehicles. (The Rockport/Fulton Chamber of Commerce maintains toll-free information numbers: if out of state call [800] 826-6441; in Texas call [800] 242-0071.)

Five feet tall with 7-foot wingspans, whoopers would be impressive even if they weren't seriously endangered. Their flight is a graceful ballet of slow wing beats and bugling calls; their mating and territory-defense behavior is a delicate, comical display of high leaps and flailing wings. The species has probably never been too prolific. Some biologists estimate only about 1,400 existed in 1870, before shooting and widespread farming and grazing destroyed them and much of their habitat. Such pressures eventually forced them into 2 remnant flocks in Aransas and southwestern Louisiana.

The nonmigratory Louisiana flock failed decades ago after a hurricane ravaged the population. Until 1957, when a pilot spotted the summer nesting grounds of Aransas whoopers at Wood Buffalo National Park, no one knew for sure where they went in spring. Our understanding of their migratory pathway has helped protect them, though hunting, power lines, avian diseases, pollution, and predation continue to keep their small population at risk.

Serious recovery efforts began in 1967, drawing on a captive population to supply juvenile releasees. In 1975, a New Mexico–Idaho flock was created to boost their numbers and provide a safety valve for the species. That flock of several dozen has declined dramatically in recent years for a number of reasons.

A nonmigratory flock of 14 birds was released at the Kissimmee Prairie in Florida in 1993, and dozens more birds have been added to that flock. By 1996, that population wasn't doing too well, either. A third release site is now under consideration in Canada. Meanwhile, the Aransas–Wood Buffalo flock has slowly increased. Barring disaster, their population seems relatively stable.

Matagorda Island NWR

A bombing range until 1978 and a century-old cattle grazing spot, Matagorda Island is now owned by both the state and federal government in a unique management-sharing arrangement that has offered protection for this barrier island.

Through a complex process of legal maneuvering, easement exchange, and purchase and management agreements, 11,502 acres of Matagorda now comprise a refuge unit managed from Aransas. Nearly 44,000 acres are managed by the state of Texas in the form of the Matagorda Island State Park and Wildlife Management Area.

The Matagorda Island Unit is critical to the well-being of numerous land, air, and ocean species. Neotropical migrants and shorebirds come to the island each spring in vast numbers. Nineteen wild inhabitants there are listed by the federal government or by the state of Texas as endangered or threatened. Numerous sea creatures use island shoreline and marshes.

During a refuge compatibility review that began in the late 1980s, livestock grazing was determined to be incompatible with the wildlife-support purposes of the island refuge unit. Following extensive public review and more than a little controversy, cattle were removed from Matagorda Island in 1991 for the first time in a century.

Refuge manager Brent Giezentanner received a habitat-protector award from the Sierra Club for his island management efforts, as well as praise from virtually all concerned environmental groups. The removal of cattle ran counter to a long-held local tradition and provoked anger in some quarters—this crucial change didn't come without struggle— but the removal of cattle from Matagorda has already brought dramatic improvement to the island's wildlife habitat.

Close to a dozen gas wells have been sunk in the sands of Matagorda, most of which have since been capped. Despite oil company operations, however, the island remains largely pristine, with limited access and only foot or bike travel allowed on its 59,000-acre reach.

Controlled burning, which mimics natural prairie fires crucial to grassland health, is one management technique used on Matagorda. Burning has yielded rich wildlife habitat, and new shoots of tender grass and forbs that rise soon after a burn provide food for a variety of life-forms.

Sea turtles often visit Matagorda's shoreline, though not always in a way concerned turtle lovers would prefer: As many as 70% of the turtles who wash up dead here each year appear within 30 days of the start of the summer shrimping season. That's despite a law requiring turtle excluder devices (TEDs) in shrimpers' nets. A few uncooperative renegades among Texas Gulf fishermen continue

to slaughter scores of endangered Kemp's ridleys and other turtle species each season.

Enforcement of TED laws is difficult and relies largely on the integrity of commerical fisherman. Sadly, a few careless individuals are having a grave impact on legally protected sea turtles. Ninety-one turtles fell victim to shrimping nets here over a recent 3-year period.

On a happier note, the Enron Environmental Education and Research Center operates on the portion of the island managed by USFWS. The center was once an oil company resort; Enron endowed the Nature Conservancy with $2 million to refurbish it for use as an ecological education facility. A boat operated by the Conservancy regularly ferries students and workshop participants to the site.

Matagorda State Park also operates a ferry that crosses to the northern end of the island, providing visitors with beachcombing, camping, fishing, and swimming opportunities.

Critical Responsibilities

At Aransas, protection is being sought or enacted to stem coastal erosion that has eaten away countless acres of shoreline, largely the result of barge traffic through the GIWW. The refuge does what it can about the problem with limited funding. Recently, the Corps of Engineers has accepted responsibility to protect the refuge shoreline and provide some resources needed in case of a chemical spill in the area.

Two private energy companies have also done their bit for the area's ecology and seem to merit congratulations. Conoco has instituted the use of double-hulled tankers, the first large oil company to do so, and has taken pains to protect the environment while drilling and operating more than 80 wells on Aransas. They drill only during the 6 months when whooping cranes are not in residence; they restrict drilling sites to upland areas; and they've committed to avoiding whooper marshes when drilling and exploring. Conoco has also accepted 32 additional restrictions set by the refuge manager, including such minutiae as detouring seismic-test access routes to avoid harming individual plants of concern to biologists. For their stewardship, Conoco has received several environmental stewardship awards, both from the USFWS and from the Office of the President of the United States.

Another private energy company, Mitchell Energy, has provided funding and materials to build artificial barrier islands in the bay, creating marsh habitat with dredging material. Both Mitchell and Conoco are taking responsibility as concerned citizens—the deep-pocketed, high-impact types whose environmental ethics can make all the difference.

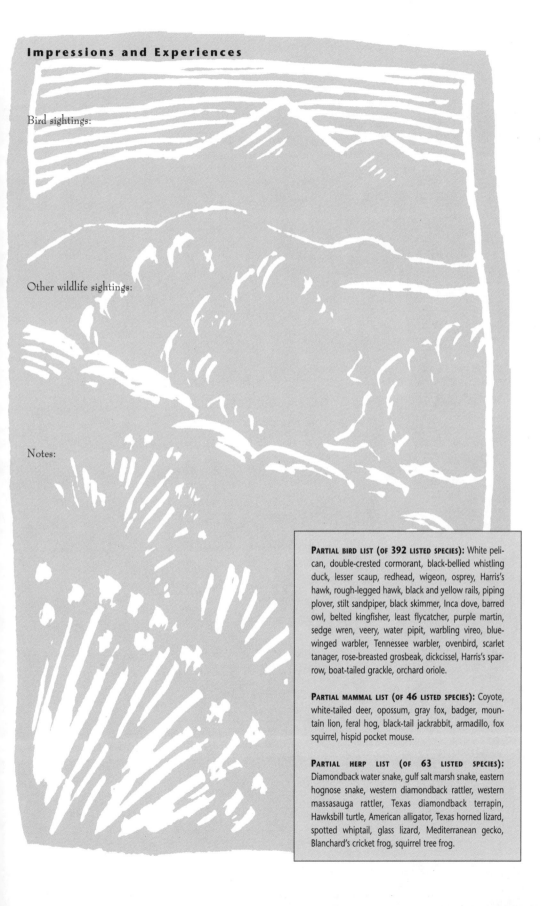

Bird sightings:

Other wildlife sightings:

Notes:

PARTIAL BIRD LIST (OF 392 LISTED SPECIES): White pelican, double-crested cormorant, black-bellied whistling duck, lesser scaup, redhead, wigeon, osprey, Harris's hawk, rough-legged hawk, black and yellow rails, piping plover, stilt sandpiper, black skimmer, Inca dove, barred owl, belted kingfisher, least flycatcher, purple martin, sedge wren, veery, water pipit, warbling vireo, blue-winged warbler, Tennessee warbler, ovenbird, scarlet tanager, rose-breasted grosbeak, dickcissel, Harris's sparrow, boat-tailed grackle, orchard oriole.

PARTIAL MAMMAL LIST (OF 46 LISTED SPECIES): Coyote, white-tailed deer, opossum, gray fox, badger, mountain lion, feral hog, black-tail jackrabbit, armadillo, fox squirrel, hispid pocket mouse.

PARTIAL HERP LIST (OF 63 LISTED SPECIES): Diamondback water snake, gulf salt marsh snake, eastern hognose snake, western diamondback rattler, western massasauga rattler, Texas diamondback terrapin, Hawksbill turtle, American alligator, Texas horned lizard, spotted whiptail, glass lizard, Mediterranean gecko, Blanchard's cricket frog, squirrel tree frog.

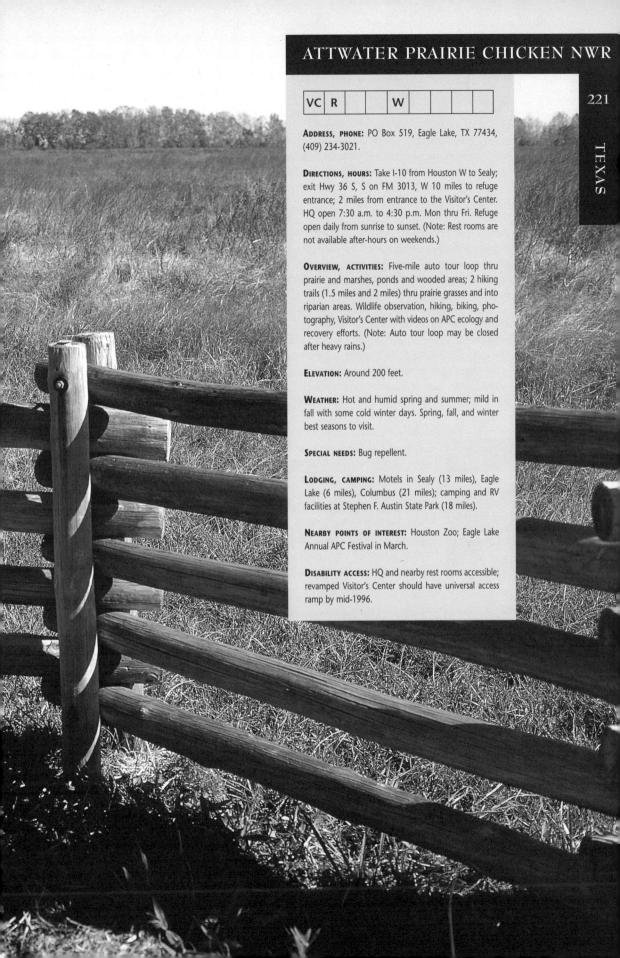

VC	R		W				

ADDRESS, PHONE: PO Box 519, Eagle Lake, TX 77434, (409) 234-3021.

DIRECTIONS, HOURS: Take I-10 from Houston W to Sealy; exit Hwy 36 S, S on FM 3013, W 10 miles to refuge entrance; 2 miles from entrance to the Visitor's Center. HQ open 7:30 a.m. to 4:30 p.m. Mon thru Fri. Refuge open daily from sunrise to sunset. (Note: Rest rooms are not available after-hours on weekends.)

OVERVIEW, ACTIVITIES: Five-mile auto tour loop thru prairie and marshes, ponds and wooded areas; 2 hiking trails (1.5 miles and 2 miles) thru prairie grasses and into riparian areas. Wildlife observation, hiking, biking, photography, Visitor's Center with videos on APC ecology and recovery efforts. (Note: Auto tour loop may be closed after heavy rains.)

ELEVATION: Around 200 feet.

WEATHER: Hot and humid spring and summer; mild in fall with some cold winter days. Spring, fall, and winter best seasons to visit.

SPECIAL NEEDS: Bug repellent.

LODGING, CAMPING: Motels in Sealy (13 miles), Eagle Lake (6 miles), Columbus (21 miles); camping and RV facilities at Stephen F. Austin State Park (18 miles).

NEARBY POINTS OF INTEREST: Houston Zoo; Eagle Lake Annual APC Festival in March.

DISABILITY ACCESS: HQ and nearby rest rooms accessible; revamped Visitor's Center should have universal access ramp by mid-1996.

On a drizzly November morning in 1995 I entered one of several avian enclosures at Texas A&M University's breeding center for native birds, where 4 endangered Attwater's prairie chicken (APC) males strutted about in their dignified/comical way. I was immediately touched by the grace and fragility of this native Texan fowl, one of America's most endangered creatures.

Each of the 4 prairie chickens in the pen showed a distinct personality: One dashed about nervously in a smooth stride, keeping its distance. As he hurried about, his twin pinnate neck feathers remained stiffly extended, his tail fanning out like an undersized turkey's. Another male stood by the door, gazing at me without a hint of fear, holding his ground. The other 2 maintained an attitude somewhere in between: One showed little nervousness but led its slightly less confident partner about, strutting in short bursts to keep a comfortable distance between us.

prairie

The sight of a prairie chicken can evoke both admiration and melancholy. Less than 50 of these native prairie dwellers still existed in the wild by mid-1996. At one time they were among the most abundant bird species in the tallgrass coastal prairies of Texas and Louisiana.

The large, brown "pinnaceous" fowl (the term refers to those long, dark neck feathers), elegantly patterned with dark barred feathers from neck to belly, is best known for the male's colorful breeding display. Each spring a congregation of hormone-driven males moves onto the lek, or "booming ground," where they commence a dramatic routine to attract females.

The show is an ostentatious one, characterized by the males' strutting and posing and by their "booming" to attract females. They make the sound by expanding the gullar sac—a loose yellow pouch of skin beneath the beak that swells to hardball size—to serve as a resonating chamber. (Such vocalizations

are similar to the sound made by blowing across the mouth of a glass bottle.)

Dominant older males do nearly all the mating with females who respond to their displays; younger males hover on the outskirts of the lek, looking on with envy and frustration. They spend much of their lives trying to breach that inner circle.

Historians theorize that some Plains Indian dances may have originated from observations of the chicken's springtime antics. A finer model of unrestrained celebratory behavior would indeed be hard to find.

Struggle for Survival

Before visiting the prairie chickens at Texas A&M, I'd explored the federal refuge in southeastern Texas that bears their name. The Attwater Prairie Chicken NWR (sans the apostrophe "s" in the species name) is primarily a region of tallgrass prairie, spotted with wetland ponds and marshes and lined with a few patches of riparian and upland woods. Later on as I stood in those breeding pens with the refuge namesake, Attwater reentered my thoughts in a new light. That patch of grassy ground, I realized, might be the last stronghold for a truly magnificent fellow creature.

Even with the great gift of protected habitat, the Attwater's prairie chicken remains in desperate trouble. The fowl's range, which once spanned 6 million acres and 2 states, has dwindled to the point that it may no longer support viable wild populations. With so few APCs left, computers and geneticists are required to track the genes of captive birds— a scientific dating service critical to discouraging recessive traits, which would lower their survival chances even more.

Just Us Chickens

Until the Euro-American influx into its range in the 1800s, the APC (*Tympanuchus cupido attwateri*) was abundant. The expansion of agriculture has been a major culprit in the chicken's decline, though unrestrained hunting in the early years, overgrazing, and the sprawl of Houston and other cities over the prairie landscape can also take their share of the blame.

As they often do when wildlife is in peril, the Nature Conservancy responded early to the realization that these birds were approaching extinction. In the mid-1960s, the conservation group purchased 3,500 acres of land near Houston for the APC habitat. That initial plot was transferred to the USFWS, which added 4,500 more acres to what became Attwater Prairie Chicken NWR in 1972. Presently, wild prairie chickens live only on the refuge and at two other sites in Texas's Refugio and Galveston counties.

Fortunately, captive breeding of APCs has been successful, and reintroduction efforts continue to offer some hope for APC survival. Thirteen males were released onto the refuge in 1995; by the following spring, 2 of those birds were still living alongside a dozen of their wild brethren, a good survival ratio by captive-release standards.

More than a hundred recently hatched young were scheduled for release in the fall of 1996 (at around 12 to 15 weeks of age). That single event may already have tripled the refuge APC population—at least until natural predation from raccoons, skunks, raptors, and other species brings the number down again. Future release sites at Brazoria NWR and Aransas NWR, both in Texas, will expand the APC's range into additional protected areas, helping ease the impact of losses within local populations.

Wildlife Abundance

Don't expect to encounter a prairie chicken during your APC refuge visit. You may get lucky, but with just a small number of APCs living on the 8,000-acre refuge (in early 1996), and with public access limited to a third of the refuge, your chance of seeing one is very slim. Leks on the refuge were once fitted with blinds for visitor observations, but

population declines caused by a late 1980s drought, followed by too much rain in the early 1990s—along with unacceptable disturbances by visitors—spurred refuge overseers to remove the blinds in 1992.

Aside from prairie chickens, Attwater refuge offers abundant reasons for a visit. Tallgrass prairie comprises most of the refuge, supporting numerous bird species, including northern bobwhite, meadowlark, and several interesting sparrows, as well as mammals, herptiles, plants, and flowers. Marshes, ponds, woodland, and riparian stretches add richness and diversity to the visitor portion of the refuge. During migration, Attwater's varied habitats attract a variety of neotropical migrants and shorebirds. A total of 266 bird species has used the refuge in recent years.

Summer is Attwater's least productive season for birders, though many species do reside during the hot season, including long-billed dowitcher, pectoral and least sandpipers, king rail, purple gallinule, numerous flycatchers, and at least 3 warbler species.

Among dozens of spring and summer nesters are white-faced ibis, American and least bittern, black-bellied whistling duck, mottled duck, white-tailed hawk, northern bobwhite, black-necked stilt, 3 species of doves, barn, barred, and great horned owls, red-bellied woodpecker, scissor-tailed flycatcher, Carolina wren, and painted bunting.

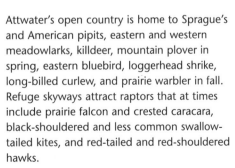

freshwater wetlands

Attwater's open country is home to Sprague's and American pipits, eastern and western meadowlarks, killdeer, mountain plover in spring, eastern bluebird, loggerhead shrike, long-billed curlew, and prairie warbler in fall. Refuge skyways attract raptors that at times include prairie falcon and crested caracara, black-shouldered and less common swallow-tailed kites, and red-tailed and red-shouldered hawks.

Sparrow lovers will enjoy a literal field day here. Common among Attwater's more than 20 sparrow species (most leave for the summer) are grasshopper, Lincoln's, lark, white-throated, and Harris's. Lark bunting and Cassin's sparrow show up occasionally. Dickcissels are abundant from spring to early fall.

Among the more colorful perching birds found in Attwater's woodlands and riparian stretches are indigo and painted buntings, blue- and rose-breasted grosbeaks, northern cardinal, and sometimes vermilion flycatcher and the chunky-beaked cardinal lookalike, pyrrhuloxia.

The prairie supports an abundance of wildflowers, most of which bloom in late March and into April if rain clouds cooperate. Texas bluebonnets often steal the show, their rich blue petals set off by Indian paintbrush, coreopsis, phlox, and many others. Many visitors come in spring as much to see the flower show as anything else; the nearby town of Eagle Lake holds an APC festival in March, which may coincide with the floral magic.

Cooling Down

Attwater's marshes ripple with life in fall and throughout winter, with 21 species of ducks and 4 geese (snow, Ross's, Canada, and white-fronted) occupying the wetlands—most of which are visible from the tour loop. Nearly all the Central Flyway's duck varieties visit or nest on Attwater. Shorebirds and waders may occupy mudflats and shallows here by the thousands, including least, pectoral, and stilt sandpiper, dunlin, common snipe, Wilson's phalarope, yellowlegs, and Hudsonian godwit. A regular visiting wader in summer and fall is the dignified wood stork, which may be found perched on snags or wading in marshes and shallow ponds.

Emergent-lined shores harbor birds that include black- and yellow-crowned night herons, little blue heron, white and white-faced ibises, roseate spoonbill, and king and sora rails (yellow rails may be here during migration). Snags and trees over water sup-

port cormorants and sometimes bald eagles. Belted kingfishers—some as large as robins—perch over the water, alert for careless fingerlings.

Snakes are abundant on the refuge from spring through fall, propped on snags, sunning themselves on rocks, or hunting in the grasses. Cottonmouths and rat snakes live throughout the refuge. Be attentive and don't wander into heavy grass. If you encounter a cottonmouth, you're the one who'll have to back off; the snake tends to hold its ground.

Other marsh dwellers here include the nutria, which may sometimes be seen lounging on the banks. Its smaller cousin, the muskrat, is here, too.

One interesting feature along the tour loop is a stretch on the south end that runs low past a portion of the marsh. The roadway here allows you to observe the marsh from your car window at a duck's-eye view.

Riparian habitat lies in and around the marsh areas and lines Coushatta Creek on the Sycamore hiking trail. Settle in and scan for any of the refuge's 28 visiting or resident warbler species, many of them present only in spring or autumn. Among the most common are black-and-white, Wilson's, bay-breasted, yellow-rumped, orange-crowned, and Nashville, along with American redstart and northern parula. But with luck and a good eye, you may also pick up a worm-eating, blue-winged, prothonotary, hooded, or Blackburnian.

Take a Hike

For those with adequate time, conditioning, and drinking water, the 5-mile auto tour loop doubles as a hiking trail. Two footpaths also pass through prairie acres and go on to riparian stretches along the San Bernard River and Coushatta Creek. Both areas can be extremely productive for birders in the spring and again, but to a lesser extent, in the fall.

Of North America's 3 accipiters, Cooper's and sharp-shinned hawks are found among

Attwater forested areas. Both use their short, rounded wings and long tails to maneuver with lightning agility in pursuit of woodland birds and other small prey.

Pounding the Prairie

Your grassland wanderings may yield sightings of some of Attwater's newest arrivals. Six American bison—5 cows and a bull—were released here in the spring of 1996. Their presence adds one more piece of historic prairie biota to Attwater.

The test release, if successful, may help encourage greater species diversification at other refuges. For the time being, staffers hope that the huge beasts will prove to be manageable and sound additions to the refuge. These are not tame animals, and staffers request that visitors stay out of buffalo pastures. It's always a good idea to keep some distance between yourself and a 6-foot, 1-ton mass of muscle and horns.

The bison probably won't have much impact on one prairie invader, McCartney's rose, an exotic that steals large amounts of grassland soil and space. The showy bush was introduced to the area from India in the early 1900s; it spread, and now claims large areas for itself. Besides intruding on prairie grasses, larger rose plants may also serve as predator perches. They offer effective hideouts for prairie chicken nest predators, including rac-

coons and skunks, the two biggest offenders. Control of the rose is difficult and ongoing.

A prairie chicken's preferred habitat is grass that is somewhat clumped—not too sparse, not too overgrown, but somewhere in between. At one time bison roamed the area in the thousands. Their tromping and feeding behaviors helped support the ongoing health of our presettlement prairies; running buffalo on the refuge adds that missing component to the system. It also allows biologists to compare the creatures' grassland habits to that of cows, which can serve as a sort of buffalo substitute in prairie ecosystems. By understanding the way bison impact grassland, biologists can better manage cattle in a way that enhances the prairies on which they graze.

Meanwhile, the tenacious Attwater's prairie chicken hangs on, the last remnant of a once-abundant species. The bird is relying totally on human effort to save it from the fate of the passenger pigeon and the Carolina parakeet—two widespread 19th-century birds that now exist only in the pages of books.

With 20th-century science on its side, coupled with a new realization of the importance of diversity to our world, the Attwater's prairie chicken may still have a chance. Saving this noble bird is a goal that doesn't occupy the highest levels of our federal priority list—but it should.

Impressions and Experiences

Bird sightings:

Other wildlife sightings:

Notes:

PARTIAL BIRD LIST (OF 266 LISTED SPECIES): Pied-billed grebe, white pelican, snowy egret, little blue heron, white and white-faced ibises, Canada goose, black-bellied and fulvous whistling ducks, black vulture, white-tailed hawk, crested caracara, king rail, long-billed dowitcher, black tern, yellow-billed cuckoo, short-eared owl, red-bellied woodpecker, great-crested flycatcher, Sprague's pipit, black-and-white warbler, northern cardinal, dickcissel, Le Conte's sparrow, Harris's sparrow.

PARTIAL MAMMAL LIST: White-tailed deer, American bison, bobcat, coyote, raccoon, opossum, armadillo, nutria, striped skunk, red fox, Louisiana pocket gopher, least shrew.

PARTIAL HERP LIST: Alligator, cottonmouth, coral snake, Texas rat snake, Baird's rat snake, diamondback water snake, Graham's crayfish snake, western slender glass lizard, Texas horned lizard, three-toed box turtle, Houston toad.

					B	H	F	

ADDRESS, PHONE: PO Drawer 1088, 1212 N Velasco, Angleton, TX 77516, (409) 849-6062.

DIRECTIONS, HOURS: Refuge office is at 1212 N Velasco in Angleton. To Brazoria refuge from Houston, S on Hwy 288 to Lake Jackson, E on FM 2004 to FM 523, R to refuge (5.5 miles). To San Bernard from Lake Jackson, W on FM 2004, 11 miles to refuge. Brazoria is open on the first and third weekends each month from 8 a.m. to 5 p.m. San Bernard is open sunrise to sunset thruout the year. Big Boggy is only accessible to waterfowl hunters in the fall and winter.

OVERVIEW, ACTIVITIES: Tour roads thru coastal marshes, impoundments, riparian, and grassy uplands. Wildlife viewing; photography, hiking; fishing on Alligator, Nicks, Salt, and Lost lakes; boating in Chocolate and Bastrop bays and Bastrop Bayou; hunting at all three units.

ELEVATION: Sea level to 11 feet.

WEATHER: Hot in summer, mild spring and fall, mild to cold in winter. Good visiting all year.

SPECIAL NEEDS: Insect repellent (a must), spotting scope.

LODGING, CAMPING: Motels in Angleton, Lake Jackson, and other nearby towns; camping on county beaches, Brazos Bend State Park N of Angleton on FM 1462; other county parks in area.

NEARBY POINTS OF INTEREST: Varner-Hogg State Plantation Historical Park (W of Angleton on Hwy 35); Galveston Island; Houston Zoo (whooping cranes and other endangered species are maintained there); Anahuac NWR near High Island (both great songbird migratory rest stops).

In mid-1996, the 170,000-acre area known as Columbia Bottomlands was the subject of much discussion and political debate to determine a protection strategy for this unique forest floodplain of the Brazos, San Bernard, and Colorado rivers. Columbia Bottomlands represents an important breeding and landfall area for neotropical migrants (30 species nest here). The area also supports a variety of resident species. Its thick stands of water oak, live oak, green ash, cedar elm, hackberry, and willow are all that remain of a 700,000-acre forest that once existed here and represent some of the only remaining forest on the Texas Gulf Coast. That forest is presently visible along Hwy 35 from Angleton to Bay City and along FM 1301. When management plans are enacted, access will likely be increased into this onetime plantation land.

DISABILITY ACCESS: Newly developed disability-accessible areas at the fishing pier and Teal Pond at Brazoria; Bobcat Woods Trail at San Bernard is accessible.

The Gulf Coast of Texas is one of America's great birding meccas. A boundless variety of avian species lives or visits the thousand-mile-plus shoreline, inhabiting the skies, fresh and salt marshes, mudflats, and coastal prairie. Some 50 species of migrating passerines, including 30 warblers, stop here on their circuit to and from Mexico's Yucatán Peninsula and surrounding jungles. In spring, they swarm the coast in great numbers, resting before they move farther south. Many more perching species reside here all year round. Unusual birds, such as groove-billed ani, black-billed cuckoo, caracara, and worm-eating warbler, can sometimes be found flitting about coastal forests, prairies, and riparian reaches.

Winter bird numbers on the third coast are often overwhelming, with more than a hundred wading, waterfowl, and shorebird species gathering from across the north country to sit out the cold months in comfort.

coastal

Birders come in large numbers, too, and revel in this concentrated avian display at Brazoria NWR Complex, comprising the 43,000-acre Brazoria refuge, the 27,414-acre San Bernard refuge, and the 4,400-acre Big Boggy NWR. Together they host a huge share of winged creatures, including more than 100,000 migratory shorebirds and an equal number of waterfowl in fall and winter.

The refuges are made up primarily of three habitats: extensive saltwater marshes and mudflats, which support tens of thousands of shorebirds and waterfowl species; freshwater canals, lakes, and more mudflats, where birds and others also find good habitat and where shorebirds are so prolific that the world biological community has named the complex a Western Hemisphere Shorebird Reserve Network site; and coastal uplands, including prairie grassland, where many bird and other species nest, loaf, and feed.

Less prolific than the 300-plus bird species inhabiting Brazoria are mammals that also take advantage of this hospitable habitat. Predators, which once included the red wolf, relish the store of easy meals here. In drawing from the slow, sick, or weak portion of the bird population, they help minimize avian diseases in their ancient cleansing way. In doing so, they contribute to the ecological balance in a largely unbalanced region, long supplanted by agriculture and ranching.

Red wolves no longer exist here, though some of their genes remain extant in local wolf-hybridized coyotes, who retain some of the larger dog's build, gait, and coloration. Bobcats are common, too; they can be effective bird snatchers. (A bobcat reputedly scored a whooping crane at Aransas NWR in the mid-1990s.) Numerous avian predators, including hawks and falcons, find a protein-rich life at Brazoria and its sister refuges.

Despite the absence of the noble wolf, who long ago preyed on the region's bison population, the Brazoria complex offers a wealth of animal encounters. One gauge of the avian riches at Brazoria is the wealth of species tallied here during the annual Freeport Christmas Bird Count. That event draws participants from around the world and often yields more than 200 identified species in a single day's count. Smaller San Bernard has its own Christmas Bird Count, which always ends with a tally of at least 150 species.

Reptiles, especially snakes, are abundant at Brazoria and San Bernard. Cottonmouths frequent the roads, as well as refuge brush, grasslands, and marshes. The diamondback rattler—a species whose eastern and western forms are responsible for more fatalities than all other US snakes combined—is also a common upland resident here. Along with ticks, fire ants, and other nippers, snakes are a good reason not to wander into areas where grass and brush obscure your path. The cottonmouth can be a particularly aggressive species, often standing its ground in situations where rattlers choose to flee.

Part-Time Visitor Access

Open the first and third full weekends of each month, as well as for prearranged group tours, Brazoria visits require advance planning. Nearby San Bernard refuge is open every day from sunrise to sundown. San Bernard is smaller with less varied habitat, but wildlife excursions along its 3-mile Moccasin Pond loop and several hiking trails can yield bountiful wildlife sightings. Big Boggy NWR is closed to all but waterfowl hunters during the winter bird-shooting season.

The refuge complex is a major stopover for migrating songbirds. Fallouts (the settling of thousands of exhausted passerines after fighting winds as they cross the gulf) are especially notable, but amid birders' jubilation over the wealth of species that a fallout can bring, some respectful reflection is in order. For every indigo bunting or bay-breasted warbler perched on a Brazoria shrub, dozens or hundreds more lay floating in the gulf, having failed to make sufficient headway against the wind's lethal breath.

In fall, the raptor population skyrockets at Brazoria and San Bernard, with merlin, black-shouldered kite, harrier, redtail and broad-wing, kestrel, and an occasional peregrine falcon occupying trees, stumps, snags, and fence posts. Mississippi kite also come through in spring and summer, and the refuge supports the orange-faced caracara and stunning white-tailed hawk. The latter, a 2-foot hawk with a snowy tail banded in black, has rusty shoulders that resemble those of the mature Harris's hawk. The Harris's tail, however, is more black than white, and its undersides are dark. The white-tail's breast and belly are white or lightly barred.

In fall and winter, geese and ducks swarm onto the refuge, along with a population of sandhill cranes that may number 1,500. Once in a long while, a whooper may stray here from Aransas, as 2 did in the late 1980s. A lookout platform near Teal Pond on the tour loop offers good views of sandhills, snow and Canada geese, and a variety of shorebirds and waders. The platform stands a hundred yards from the pond, partly hidden by huisache and salt cedar; a spotting scope can be valuable here for close-ups. In the grassy upland below the lookout, disk plowing sometimes encourages the growth of wild millet, which may attract numerous waterfowl and wader species.

An interesting symbiosis occurs between the 50,000 snow, white-fronted, and Canada geese that use the refuge in winter, as well as the shorebirds who visit in the spring and fall. All those webbed goose feet roil and tear at the soil in some freshwater shallows. By the time they leave in late winter, they've created a fertile mudflat that in turn supports an influx of waders and shorebirds. By the time the shorebirds depart, new food plants have begun to arise from the muddy earth, providing food for the next crop of wintering geese.

That cycle doesn't go so smoothly in salty tidal shallows. When geese tear up a patch of earth in the salt marshes (such as those occurring south and east of the Brazoria tour loop), plants can't regenerate so easily in this more restrictive environment. Instead, tidal action tears at the mud wallow, opening a scar that may take years to heal. To mitigate such damage, refuge managers provide attractive freshwater habitats that help attract geese and keep them out of the salt marsh.

freshwater wetlands

Seaside Wonders

An incredible number of shorebirds and waders use Brazoria and San Bernard, especially in spring migration (and to a lesser extent in the late summer and fall return trip). Some, like the roseate spoonbill and white ibis, make the refuges their home all year. Migratory shorebirds here include the snowy and endangered piping plover, marbled godwit, ruddy turnstone, sanderling, snipe, least and white-rumped sandpiper, and American oystercatcher. (Catching oysters is so easy your grandma could do it; it's the ability to pry them open that sets this black, orange-beaked bird apart.) Wood storks visit the refuge most summers, remaining into early fall.

Summer is Brazoria's least spectacular wild-life season, but it does offer the benefit of a diminished mosquito population. Mosquitoes in the fall and spring can be awesome here, creating dense clouds that generally encourage tightly closed car windows.

Seabirds of all types make their home at Brazoria and San Bernard. Black skimmers nest at Brazoria, sometimes on the raised-earth oil drilling platforms on the refuge. Staffers have supplied such nesting sites with crushed oyster shell and gravel, which sits well with skimmers as well as with terns.

Eight tern species, including the gull-billed variety, inhabit the refuges. As many as 15 pairs of brown pelicans nest at Dressing Point Island off Big Boggy refuge. Their south coast numbers have rebounded after egg thinning and toxicity from DDT and other pesticides nearly extirpated them. The California race of brown pelican hasn't snapped back as well and remains endangered.

Extensive colonial rookeries exist in the salt marshes, accessible only by boat. That's just as well because disturbances can be lethal to the colonies. If a mother tern, spoonbill, cormorant, egret, heron, or white ibis leaves its nest for just a few minutes in the summer sun, hard-boiled eggs may result. Warning signs have been placed around some rookeries, and boaters can be hit with harsh fines for lingering too long or too close to these sensitive nesting communities.

Raccoons wreak a more natural, though equally destructive, impact on colonial eggs and young. One colonial nesting spot, Cedar Lakes at the San Bernard refuge, was recently fitted with an antipredator fence to discourage them. (Brasosport Birders, Friends of Brazoria Refuge, and other supporters render valuable volunteer hours for such tasks.)

On Dressing Point Island, up to 2,000 white ibises, 400 tricolored herons, and thousands of other herons, reddish and great egrets, cormorants, and terns maintain one of the gulf's largest colonial nests.

One of the most beautiful—and oddly constructed—birds of all North American species, the roseate spoonbill is a colonial nester and year-round resident. The "Texas flamingo" is easy to spot on mudflats and marshes, its large, pinkish color and flattened bill distinguishing it from other tall waders. The spoonbill uses its pancake proboscis to sweep the shallow water column for insects and aquatic invertebrates.

Spoonbills often feed in freshwater and salt marshes throughout the refuge. White ibis is another impressive permanent resident. The small ibis, with its long, red, down-curved bill, is as skittish as the spoonbill. Both are often the first waders to flee when humans or other perceived threats approach.

Upland Brooders and Loafers

A 30,000-acre inland tract that includes the elevated Hoskins Mound has recently come under refuge management (not yet visitor accessible but part of the new tract is visible from County Road 227). Much of the Duck Stamp–funded acquisition comprises uplands, including rice fields that provide nesting and feeding habitat for some 600 mottled ducks, Brazoria's only resident duck species. The new tract also includes wetlands.

Major management challenges accompany the acquisition, including the scores of Chinese tallow trees that have taken over huge areas. Like many exotics, the tallows were brought to this country as ornamentals. Their attractive whitish bark and large delicate berries make them desirable landscaping plants; but like other ornamental exotics, they escaped their domestic settings and now compete heavily with indigenous plants.

As a food source, tallow seeds are favored by grackles and nest-parasitic cowbirds. Few

Cottonmouth (aka, water moccasin).

Gators inhabit the wetlands of Anahuac and thrive in freshwater marshes along much of the Texas coast.

Yellow-rumped warbler.

A small, emergent-filled wetland on Anahuac NWR offers good birding
and a spot for peaceful contemplation.

The long-billed thrasher is a south Texas resident. It often perches at treetop level, singing a melodious song.

The westward view from Aransas NWR's viewing tower reveals sprawling bay and marsh habitats that support many of its yearly wintering whooping cranes.

Great blue heron.

Close to 150 endangered whooping cranes visit Aransas and its surrounding marshes each October and remain until late winter or early spring.

White-tailed deer range about Attwater refuge.

(Opposite) The Attwater's prairie chicken fights for survival on the refuge and in a few other Texas prairie habitats.

Attwater Prairie Chicken NWR's limited wetlands draw dozens of species. Here a non-native nutria dozes on the shore as egrets, herons, and half a dozen waterfowl species browse and rest along a spit of land.

(Opposite) Sunset colors the marsh at San Bernard NWR.

(Opposite, below) Freshwater marshes throughout Brazoria NWR support dozens of waterfowl and wader species.

Ospreys hunt along coastal shores and freshwater marshes throughout Texas and much of the West.

The nine-banded armadillo is nearly blind. It relies on thick armor plating to protect it from predators as it roots for insects and grubs, usually at night.

Mixed-grass prairie, rugged canyon walls, and a small
wetland area make up Buffalo Lake NWR.

The Texas horned lizard is an odd yet gentle creature that ranges from western Kansas southwest to southern Arizona.

Canada goose.

Snow, Canada, and white-fronted geese browse Hagerman NWR's green
wheat fields, which overlook the Big Mineral Arm of Lake Texoma.

(Opposite) Western meadowlarks occupy much of the
grassland and farm field acres of Hagerman NWR.

White-crowned sparrow.

Great egret.

Laguna Atascosa NWR's upland desert makes up a significant part of this bayside refuge, which boasts the longest bird list in the entire national wildlife refuge system.

(Top) Green jay is one of Laguna Atascosa's many regional avian "specialty" species.

Redheads visit Laguna Atascosa during the fall in the hundreds of thousands.

Raised edges around prairie dog burrows keep floodwater out and provide a raised platform for "guard dogs."

Prairie dogs inhabit townsites that dot much of Muleshoe refuge.

Red-tailed hawk is a common predator at Muleshoe
and at refuges throughout the West.

Prairie overlooks a series of *playa* lakes at Muleshoe NWR. Lower Pauls Lake
playa is often dry, but in winter it may support thousands of sandhill cranes, who
get their water from a spring in nearby Upper Pauls Lake.

Green kingfisher is one of many species on Santa Ana's exhaustive list of rare birds.

Brush-enshrouded ponds and marshes at Santa Ana NWR
harbor hundreds of birds and other species.

The groove-billed ani, a favorite of birders, inhabits Santa Ana's thick brush.

A few highly endangered jaguarundis may still roam throughout the brush at Santa Ana refuge.

An extensive trail system carries visitors into the magic reaches of Santa Ana NWR.

refuge staffers wish to encourage either species. They also crowd out desirable trees, such as willow. The refuge will serve as a release site (probably by the summer of 1996) for the endangered Attwater's prairie chickens—yet another reason the trees are a problem, as they offer good perches for avian predators.

Baccharis is another overbearing species on the refuge. It's a native but has captured more than its share of territory due to past overgrazing. On the marshes, California bulrush and common reed have also moved in to capture otherwise good habitat acres.

Controlled burning is one of the best ways to control such species, but burning is difficult here. In spring and summer, southerly winds carry smoke directly toward Houston and nearby major roadways. Winter burns are less disruptive, since the common northerly winds carry smoke out to sea and fewer people are affected. Herbicides, such as a biodegradable product known as Rodeo®, are coming into favor as control tools for marsh invaders. Used carefully in spot treatments, the chemical may help expand critically needed bird habitat on this and other refuges while causing what the EPA regards as minimal contamination. Controlled grazing is another management tool used to keep Brazoria grasslands healthy and productive as feeding, nesting, and loafing grounds for geese, waterfowl, and other species.

The refuge's proximity to saltwater provides a more natural way to control marsh plant succession, which otherwise would result in vegetation-choked wetland habitat. By occasionally channeling saltwater into freshwater impoundments, and by maintaining brackish conditions in some wetland areas, refuge managers can control the succession of most emergents.

Wolves and Coyotes: Connubial Confusion

The red wolf once ranged throughout the coastal prairies here, its range formerly extending across the south coastal states to Florida and the Carolinas. The last confirmed sightings of wild red wolves were in the area; the last pure red wolf was captured nearby in a USFWS effort to save the shrinking, genetically diluted population from extinction.

Now only a handful of captive wolves remains in a few scattered facilities. Their keepers have begun to release their progeny into the wild again, but such releases won't take place here—ranching and development in this crowded region make it a sure loser as a wolf recovery site. Alligator River NWR in North Carolina has become one red wolf sanctuary, its secure island habitat helping ensure that coyotes will corrupt its genes no further.

Though its status as a red wolf habitat has faded, Brazoria/San Bernard NWR Complex can still claim great significance as one of relatively few remaining protected gulf reaches. It's also one of the most spectacular destinations for birders and wildlife lovers anywhere along the Texas coast.

Impressions and Experiences

Bird sightings:

Other wildlife sightings:

Notes:

PARTIAL BIRD LIST (OF 301 LISTED SPECIES): American white pelican, fulvous whistling duck, blue-winged teal, least bittern, green heron, wood stork, crested caracara, black and clapper rails, purple gallinule, black-necked stilt, willet, western sandpiper, Sandwich tern, groove-billed ani, ruby-throated hummingbird, pileated woodpecker, wood thrush, white-eyed vireo, palm and black-and-white warblers, northern cardinal, seaside sparrow, American goldfinch.

PARTIAL MAMMAL LIST: Coyote, white-tailed deer, raccoon, river otter, armadillo, cotton rat.

PARTIAL HERP LIST: Cottonmouth, diamondback rattler, coral snake, fox snake, American alligator, Texas toad.

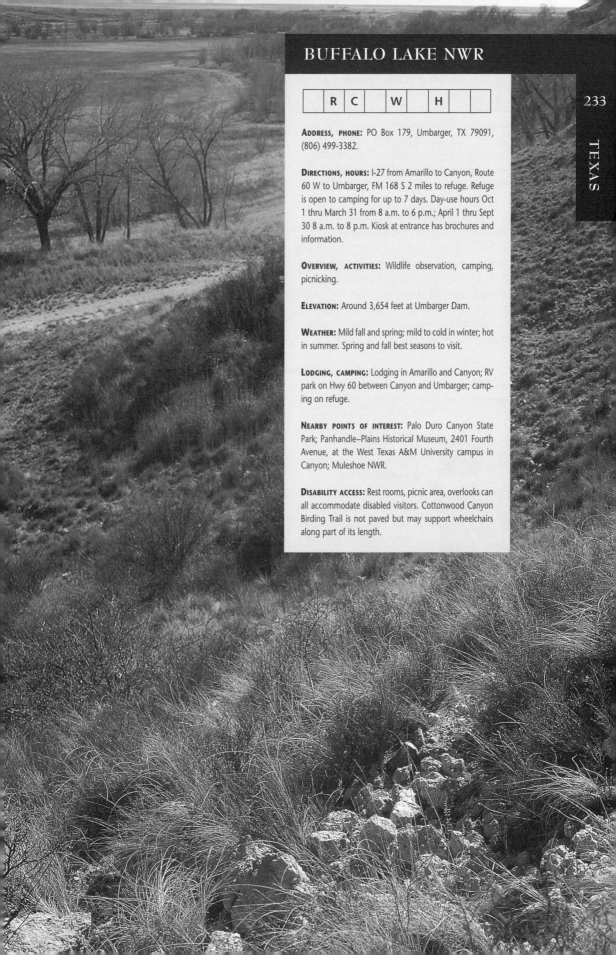

BUFFALO LAKE NWR

	R	C		W		H		

ADDRESS, PHONE: PO Box 179, Umbarger, TX 79091, (806) 499-3382.

DIRECTIONS, HOURS: I-27 from Amarillo to Canyon, Route 60 W to Umbarger, FM 168 S 2 miles to refuge. Refuge is open to camping for up to 7 days. Day-use hours Oct 1 thru March 31 from 8 a.m. to 6 p.m.; April 1 thru Sept 30 8 a.m. to 8 p.m. Kiosk at entrance has brochures and information.

OVERVIEW, ACTIVITIES: Wildlife observation, camping, picnicking.

ELEVATION: Around 3,654 feet at Umbarger Dam.

WEATHER: Mild fall and spring; mild to cold in winter; hot in summer. Spring and fall best seasons to visit.

LODGING, CAMPING: Lodging in Amarillo and Canyon; RV park on Hwy 60 between Canyon and Umbarger; camping on refuge.

NEARBY POINTS OF INTEREST: Palo Duro Canyon State Park; Panhandle–Plains Historical Museum, 2401 Fourth Avenue, at the West Texas A&M University campus in Canyon; Muleshoe NWR.

DISABILITY ACCESS: Rest rooms, picnic area, overlooks can all accommodate disabled visitors. Cottonwood Canyon Birding Trail is not paved but may support wheelchairs along part of its length.

Look out over the 7,764-acre Buffalo Lake NWR and, with a touch of imagination, you might conjure up images of bison herds roaming across the prairie, rutting and fighting, kicking up dust, and browsing the endless blue grama that blankets the refuge and much of the Texas Panhandle.

Waves of grass blaze in golden strands beneath an aquamarine sky untouched by industry. Rock ledges and outcroppings line the northward canyon, where a dam once held back rainfall and agricultural runoff. Canyon woodlands stand thick with cotton-woods and Chinese elm, enticing migratory passerines to some of the only good perching habitat for miles.

In farm fields carved in the former lake bottom, pheasants call from secret places, bolting occasionally to reveal their thick, fluttering forms.

prairie

Blackbirds perch sideways on reeds, shouting multinote songs, part passion, part grinding machine. Western meadowlarks flash their yellow formal wear from yucca fronds and mesquite snags. In the thickets, mule deer crouch beneath red-tailed hawk, merlin and kestrel, and golden and bald eagles in winter.

In Chinese elms planted throughout the refuge in the 1940s and 1950s, porcupines gnaw tender bark; they're notable as dark patches in the higher limbs. Move slowly and talk softly and they'll likely continue their bark stripping, untroubled by your thin-skinned presence. Badger is here, too, along with coyote, bobcat, and numerous other mammals.

Prairie dogs cavort in a colony on the east side of Hwy 168, 2 miles south of the Hwy 1714 intersection. From a nearby viewing area you can spend hours watching the slapstick critters. Children seem especially entranced by the little rodents and their frenetic behavior.

Death of a Lake

Placed under USFWS control in 1958, Buffalo Lake refuge was once the site of a 2,000-acre reservoir. The namesake lake is gone now, partly due to the draining of our nation's largest aquifer—the Ogallala—by more than 80 feet in 20 years. Once a higher water table helped fill numerous *playas* and streams throughout Ogallala's thousand-mile reach. Were all agriculture to cease right now from Minnesota to Texas, it would still take decades to replenish the ancient aquifer. Reduced rainfall and runoff have also changed the refuge's character; whether the change is due to global warming or to a long-term cyclic event, no one knows for sure.

In place of the lake, a 300-acre wetland has been developed near the south end of the tour road, providing some habitat for migratory birds. Masses of waterfowl, such as the 800,000 ducks and 40,000 Canada geese who came in the fall of 1960, will never again find the extensive wetland habitat that once drew them in, but a lesser number still come to Stewart Marsh, including green-winged teal, mallard, pintail, and more than a dozen other species. Sandhills used to come, but never in large numbers. Now they rarely show up at all.

Other animals besides birds are drawn to the marsh. Coyote and bobcat are 2 year-round residents often found nearby; you'll most likely spot them near dawn and dusk. Badger visits, too, along with some of the 5 dozen or so mule deer and 2 dozen white-tailed deer on the refuge. A large wooden blind at the end of a short trail from the parking area is fitted with viewing slats, from which you can observe and photograph wildlife.

Moist-soil units totaling 40 acres were being developed in 1995–96 just south of Stewart Dike. These native-plant growth plots, managed to simulate normal flood-and-dry cycles, will provide for the foraging needs of numerous species. The units are visible from the observation deck. The dike itself is off-limits to humans, whose presence would disrupt the peace in the marsh.

In times of heavy rain, Buffalo Lake does manage to hold some water (its dam is designated as a "flood-control structure"). When the water rises, birds respond by the thousands, but the reality of the lake's demise is made stark by the presence of a permanent farm field on its bed. Here co-op farmers maintain about 600 acres of milo and winter wheat for Buffalo Lake's waterfowl visitors, a third of which is reserved for the birds.

The lakebed is almost too rich for agriculture, largely the result of decades of creek drainage through the stockyard capital of the world, Hereford, Texas, which has delivered nitrate-saturated water to Buffalo Lake. To help reduce that chemical overload, which can actually burn plants, farmers at harvest remove crop roots along with grains and stalks. The practice steadily decreases the concentration of plant-scorching chemicals in the soil.

Despite the near lack of water, Buffalo Lake still manages to attract a large number of bird species. At least 333 species have used the refuge at one time or another, with closer to 274 listed as common or semiregular visitors or residents. The old bird list contains many species seen when the lake was full; many no longer visit the area. A new list will soon offer a better representation of birds that continue to reside or visit.

More common waterfowl include green-winged teal, mallard, gadwall, wigeon, and shoveler. Common shorebirds and open-water species include lesser yellowlegs, killdeer, and spotted and least sandpipers.

Accidentals who may still visit Buffalo Lake include waterfowl, such as American black duck, fulvous whistling duck, and red-breasted merganser. Shorebird and open-water species that only rarely show up include Sabine's gull and Caspian and least tern. Black tern may show up in small numbers but not every year.

A walking trail on the northern part of the refuge just past the entrance takes you a mile into a canyon of cottonwood and Chinese elm. This is the best place on the refuge for passerine sightings. The Cottonwood Canyon Birding Trail is a good dirt hiking path, flanked by the canyon wall on the west and thick prairie grasses to the east.

The passerine presence at Buffalo Lake can be notable, especially during migration. Some resident and migratory perching birds here include yellow-billed cuckoo, mourning dove, scissortail and willow flycatchers, eastern and western kingbirds, ruby-crowned kinglet, loggerhead shrike, blue grosbeak, clay-colored and song sparrows, and American goldfinch.

A handful of warbler species passes through in spring and fall, but most of the 3 dozen warblers on the list are accidentals, including rarities such as Cape May and palm warblers. Regular visitors include yellow-rumped, black-and-white, and Wilson's warblers. Worm-eating and Nashville are 2 warbler species who may come occasionally.

One of Buffalo Lake's chief claims to fame is its abundant raptor population. Numerous aerial predators take advantage of the refuge's grassland and marsh prey. Raptors here include red-tailed, Swainson's, and ferruginous hawks, golden and bald eagles, peregrine falcon, kestrel, merlin, prairie falcon, Cooper's hawk, Mississippi kite, great horned and short-eared owls, and burrowing owl, who inhabit the prairie dog town. Each spring a buzzard roost forms in old, dead trees between the picnic and camping areas. As many as 144 vultures have been spotted in the sky around the roost.

Habitat for Wild and Human Animals

Buffalo Lake's habitat changes have resulted in its transformation to one of the more visitor-oriented refuges in the system. Excellent shaded campgrounds and picnic areas are now in place, with grills, good parking, and rest rooms. Disabled access is first-rate—concrete pads are in place at several viewing areas and overlooks, making for easy wheelchair on- and off-loading. Rest rooms and trailheads are similarly equipped.

Despite the first-rate conveniences, it's a little sad that the refuge has become such a human-oriented place; it's a measure of what's been lost to wildlife. Supporting its wild residents remains the prime goal at Buffalo Lake, but with the decline of bird visitors by the hundreds of thousand, the refuge has placed greater emphasis on its human visitors. At the same time, many species do continue to use the refuge, including numerous mammals and upland birds. Waterfowl and other migrants still benefit from Buffalo Lake's marsh, riparian, and grassland habitats.

A trip here in early March yielded sightings of northern cardinal, loggerhead shrike, northern harrier, red-tailed hawk, American kestrel, northern flicker, golden-fronted woodpecker, and several flycatchers; deer, coyote, and porcupine were also spotted.

Managing on the Prairie

Prairie grasses require periodic thinning and cropping to keep them healthy and robust. Such natural tending was once accomplished by nature, through the browsing of buffalo and through wildfires sparked either by nature or human hands. These days frequent high winds and short staffing make prescribed burning a risky endeavor. Instead, controlled grazing is used during years of normal rainfall to help keep grasses from growing bunched and decrepit. Drought in 1994 and 1995 resulted in a grazing ban in 1995 and may mean that 1996 is a nongrazing year as well.

Buffalo Lake is a rewarding place to visit in every season but summer, when the heat can be uncomfortable. Whether wildlife is abundant or scarce during your time here, there's always good camping, picnicking, and hiking, as well as prairie views that any visitor, whether buffalo, bird, or human, will appreciate.

Impressions and Experiences

Bird sightings:

Other wildlife sightings:

Notes:

PARTIAL BIRD LIST (OF 274 LISTED SPECIES AND 59 ACCI-DENTALS; LIST IS BEING UPDATED TO REFLECT CHANGED HABITAT CONDITIONS): Pied-billed grebe, great blue heron, black-crowned night heron, Canada goose, mallard, blue-winged teal, northern harrier, Swainson's and red-tailed hawks, golden and bald eagles, sandhill crane, killdeer, greater and lesser yellowlegs, western sandpiper, ring-billed gull, black tern, yellowbilled cuckoo, ladder-backed woodpecker, western kingbird, tree swallow, rock wren, Townsend's solitaire, cedar waxwing, northern cardinal, yellow warbler, blue grosbeak, savanna sparrow, lark bunting, northern oriole.

PARTIAL MAMMAL LIST: Mule deer, coyote, bobcat, badger, jackrabbit, cottontail, porcupine, short-tailed mouse, wood rat.

PARTIAL HERP LIST: Prairie rattler, bullsnake, hognose snake, Texas horned lizard, several toad species, leopard frog.

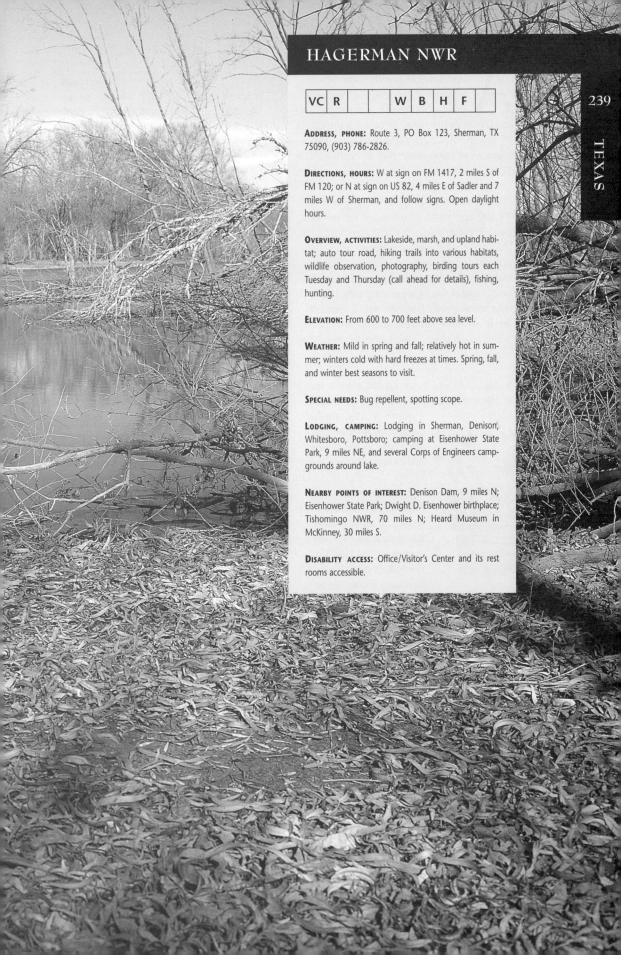

VC	R			W	B	H	F	

ADDRESS, PHONE: Route 3, PO Box 123, Sherman, TX 75090, (903) 786-2826.

DIRECTIONS, HOURS: W at sign on FM 1417, 2 miles S of FM 120; or N at sign on US 82, 4 miles E of Sadler and 7 miles W of Sherman, and follow signs. Open daylight hours.

OVERVIEW, ACTIVITIES: Lakeside, marsh, and upland habitat; auto tour road, hiking trails into various habitats, wildlife observation, photography, birding tours each Tuesday and Thursday (call ahead for details), fishing, hunting.

ELEVATION: From 600 to 700 feet above sea level.

WEATHER: Mild in spring and fall; relatively hot in summer; winters cold with hard freezes at times. Spring, fall, and winter best seasons to visit.

SPECIAL NEEDS: Bug repellent, spotting scope.

LODGING, CAMPING: Lodging in Sherman, Denison, Whitesboro, Pottsboro; camping at Eisenhower State Park, 9 miles NE, and several Corps of Engineers campgrounds around lake.

NEARBY POINTS OF INTEREST: Denison Dam, 9 miles N; Eisenhower State Park; Dwight D. Eisenhower birthplace; Tishomingo NWR, 70 miles N; Heard Museum in McKinney, 30 miles S.

DISABILITY ACCESS: Office/Visitor's Center and its rest rooms accessible.

Approachable geese, huge rafts of waterfowl and seagulls, remnant prairie, and marshes harboring pelicans, cormorants, and, at times, a multitude of shorebirds—these are just a few of the surprises at Hagerman NWR in north-central Texas.

Despite obvious oil-drilling activity on this 11,320-acre patch of managed north Texas habitat, Hagerman is first and foremost a wildlife refuge, one that supports an impressive array of species, both resident and migratory. Habitats here that include wetlands, woodlands, and remnant tallgrass prairie draw migratory species from the Arctic Circle to South America. Resident species are numerous, too, promising good wildlife viewing all year round.

A total of 316 bird species has been identified at Hagerman, a figure that includes nearly

4 dozen accidentals that have been seen at least once here in the refuge's half-century history. Such rarities have included brant, whimbrel, wood thrush, MacGillivray's warbler, mountain plover, curve-billed thrasher, northern goshawk, and black rail. Black duck and red knot have also shown up at

freshwater wetlands

Hagerman at least once—the sort of uncommon yet possible sightings that create pleasant anticipation for those who revel in wildlife surprises.

Much of Hagerman's fundamental magic consists of species you're more likely to encounter. They number into the dozens and also include some uncommon, and uncommonly beautiful, creatures. Winter geese are both plentiful and relatively undisturbed by human presence, creating excellent opportunities for up-close observation.

Oil activity on the refuge leads some people to question Hagerman's sanctity as a wildlife refuge. Indeed, nearly a 150 oil rigs dot the

rolling hardwood and grass-covered landscape of this 11,320-acre lakeside refuge. The rigs churn day and night, their soft, rhythmic thumping muted by distance. Oil company vehicles sometimes move along the main dirt road artery, which is also a major local route to Gordonsville and the state of Oklahoma.

Still, Hagerman remains a peaceful and rewarding place for wildlife, as it is for nature lovers, especially those who leave the main road and their vehicles to hike refuge trails. Even on the main tour road, drilling noise recedes from consciousness in time, the landscape is beautiful, and except for brief periods when workers head to and from work during the week, tranquility can be found here, too.

Three-quarters of Hagerman's 175,000 yearly visitors are anglers who concentrate at a few spots along the lakefront. A small number are hunters who visit in the fall and winter. The rest come to observe and appreciate the wildlife. Visitors come largely from the Dallas metroplex, but Hagerman has been a destination for wildlife lovers from around the country; even international visitors may cruise through after landing at Dallas–Fort Worth International Airport.

Located along the southern edge of Lake Texoma, much of the refuge is heavily influenced by water levels of this constantly fluctuating reservoir. When the lake recedes, shallows, mudflats, and nearby impoundments may attract thousands of shorebirds—most heavily in spring and again in late summer and fall.

Anytime from October through late March, the Big Mineral arm of the lake along the refuge may be covered in huge rafts of redheads, canvasbacks, and "puddle ducks" such as pintail, mallard, and green-winged teal. Thousands of gulls create feathered white islands, bobbing and feeding, rising in thunderous clouds. The majority are often ring-billed gulls, with Franklin's and a few Bonaparte's scattered among them. In the fall of 1995, some 6,500 gulls were counted in 1 day by Hagerman's vigilant volunteer observers.

Four hundred acres of farm fields, most located along the tour road, are planted with crops such as green wheat, milo maize, and mung beans. They attract hundreds of geese in the fall and winter, including snow and Ross's, white-fronted, and members of the Tall Grass Prairie flock of Canada geese. Deer also browse the fields, their heads and necks rarely rising when food is plentiful.

In recent years, Hagerman's attractiveness to Canada geese has diminished, probably due to a dramatic regional increase in precipitation. From around 30 inches of yearly precipitation, rainfall now approaches 40 inches per year. Canadas that once numbered as high as 7,500 in past years have shown a recent preference for areas of western Oklahoma, including the Washita NWR.

In place of the Canadas, snow geese who once winged along a more easterly corridor have begun arriving at Hagerman in increasing numbers. A small proportion of blue-phase snow geese make up those visitors. Blues tend to increase in proportion to whites as you travel eastward across their range.

A Well-Defined History

Hagerman NWR was created in 1946, mainly to provide waterfowl habitat for migratory birds. At the time it was established, the Corps of Engineers, which originally purchased the land, declined to purchase mineral rights. Within a decade, the Discovery Well was sunk on the refuge and yielded black gold. A stampede ensued; dozens of wells were drilled over the following years until some 200 were in place. A significant part of Hagerman's character was set for the long term.

That character will likely begin changing soon. Some wells here no longer produce— a sign the field is drying up. When wells are decommissioned, they're usually filled and abandoned. However, the refuge may benefit as supportive oil companies agree to reconfigure some as water wells to support refuge

wetlands. One company recently agreed to do so, and Ducks Unlimited has offered to fund the purchase of a pump to complete that new water-delivery system. Despite Hagerman's proximity to Lake Texoma, water is still a valued resource here, limited by water rights. Additional water means more valuable wetlands habitat; more habitat means more numerous and diverse wildlife.

Dikes that support well access roads have already proven valuable as habitat-making dams. Drilling companies maintain the dikes; when they leave, the task will go to the underfunded refuge, leaving the future of the habitats created by these levees in some doubt. As it stands, some diked impoundments lack adequate water-control structures, rendering them vulnerable to siltation and making them less valuable as habitat. Money is once again the culprit and the solution. But with the USFWS receiving per-acre funding that seems to decrease every year, managers make do with what they have. President Bill Clinton recently injected the refuge system with a moderate funding increase, promising a revolution in the system, but in the face of a budget-cutting Congress, the reality of his expressed good intentions remains to be seen.

prairie

Touring Hagerman

As you enter the refuge near headquarters and pass the information kiosk (where you'll find brochures and displays), you cruise past fields of low, succulent green wheat maintained by refuge staffers for wintering geese. A broad expanse of lake stretches to the north and west, often covered in rafts of birds that may include ring-billed gull, teal, redhead, and others. Western grebe have shown up here, far from its normal western range, and even white-winged scoter, commonly regarded as a seabird.

In fall and winter, the road also takes you within a few yards of browsing snow, Ross's, white-fronted, and Canada geese, who seem to adjust to vehicle traffic within weeks of their initial fall arrival. Snow, Ross's, and Canadas are generally at ease with your presence; white-fronts appear somewhat less confident and maintain a wider safety zone.

Remain inside your vehicle and the birds pay you little mind; get out and you may startle them into flight. The ability to approach Hagerman's geese closely without frightening them is a rare privilege, allowing intimate observation and easy photography. A window tripod, reasonably fast film, and a moderately long telephoto lens will allow you to get good, sharp close-ups. Meadowlarks, horned larks, and killdeer are also common in the same areas.

Several ponds formed from wellhead access roads are located just a few miles from the entrance along the main road, along with smaller wetlands all along the lakeshore stretch. Mineral Marsh, one of the diked impoundments, creates good resting and feeding areas for a variety of water birds, including white pelicans who may occupy the refuge throughout the year. White-faced ibises arrive some spring and summer seasons. Steadman Marsh, conversely, lacks adequate water control and stays flooded for long periods. There you may find such deep-water birds as cormorants and redheads.

Great blue herons, white pelicans, and neo-tropical cormorants are among many birds that occupy the impoundments and nearby wetlands. Trotline regulations have been altered mainly for their benefit; fixed trot-lines have snagged fish-loving birds. Legal trotlines are limited to the free-floating types that rise and fall with changing water levels. (While freeing snagged pelicans, one refuge staffer noted that their massive, vein-rich mouths harbor oversized lice, which look something like deformed crabs.)

When water conditions are right, shorebirds flock to the edges of these impoundments. Gradations in their depth, depending on the fluctuation of Lake Texoma during wet and dry periods, create temporary biomes that may support thousands of mudflat and shallows dwellers.

Waders and shorebirds on Hagerman include yellowlegs, a dozen sandpiper species, dunlin, and marbled godwit, among others. More than 20 duck species reside here from fall through spring, and tundra swans may appear in colder months. Sandhill cranes pass through occasionally on their way to and from coastal wintering grounds.

Upland Wildlife

Despite the extensive lake water you see along the first stretch of the tour road, nearly three-quarters of Hagerman is upland, including broad reaches of hardwood forest and tallgrass prairie. The Crow Hill Trail is a good route for seeing both. That walking path begins from a parking area less than a mile south of the main tour road (a sign leads you there). The trail first passes through a forest of cedar elm where numerous passerines are often found, including a rich variety of sparrows. Song, Lincoln's, Harris's, white-throated, and white-crowned sparrows and other LBJs (little brown jobs) reside here. Clay-colored sparrow is a less common resident of the area's trees and brush in spring and fall. Particularly abundant are scissor-tailed fly-catchers, who seem to inhabit every available power line or other high perch during warmer months.

A variety of other forest birds are here, too, including chickadee, pine siskin, yellow-billed cuckoo, ladder-backed woodpecker, cardinal, summer tanager, and several flycatchers. Indigo and painted bunting and blue gros-beak are often found in the area from spring through fall.

Warblers are not well-represented at Hagerman, though a few species pass through in migration, including such species as prothonotary, bay-breasted (rare), Blackburnian, and black-throated green. Yellow warbler is one of a few warbler species found here most months of the year. Orange-crowned warbler is common in winter, and Kentucky warbler has nested here.

A short distance beyond the forest, the trail enters open big bluestem prairie. (In warm weather, watch for venomous snakes, as you should throughout the refuge.) Here you may spot numerous perching birds, including sometimes hundreds of meadowlarks and red-winged and yellow-headed blackbirds.
Le Conte's sparrow, a prairie-obligate and one of Hagerman's specialties, can be found here without difficulty. Grasshopper sparrow may be found in the grasses, along with vesper and field sparrows, several thrushes, and an occasional bobolink in the spring. When conditions are right, all 4 longspur species that inhabit the United States may appear at Hagerman. Look for them on lawns, road-sides, and farm fields. McCown's is the rarest of the 4; Smith's is the most likely of these rare northerners to show up at Hagerman.

Raptors can be numerous in prairie skyways and surrounding perches. Red-tailed and red-shouldered hawk, eastern screech owl, northern harrier, Mississippi kite, and bald eagle are some of the nearly 20 raptors residing at or visiting Hagerman.

A Walk Through Woods and Wetlands

A 2½-mile vehicle-restricted road delivers hikers into what is at times some of Hagerman's best woodland and marsh habitat. Beginning at a gate on the right, located along the road about 2½ miles from headquarters, foot-traffic-only Meadow Pond Trail serves as hunter access during various periods in the fall and winter; but it can provide a good binocular hunt area, too.

As you hike down the westward-running road, you're flanked on the right by a low-land forest of oak, walnut, and lotus trees. Along Meadow Pond Trail, you may encounter deer, raccoon, opposum, fox squirrel, and other forest species. Copperheads wander the leaf-covered forest floor, so watch your step

if you leave the road. Likewise, marsh areas of Hagerman support cottonmouths, so be alert for this thick, black venomous species, too.

On your left are a couple of ponds that, when full, can be great waterfowl, wader, and shore-bird habitats. Dever Pond is the first impoundment along the way. In 1995, erosion problems resulted in its being drained, and bulldozers were attempting to make low-budget bank and channel repairs. When Dever is full, it often supports abundant ducks, as well as shorebirds, who begin arriving in late August and early September and are largely gone by mid-November. Rarely, the water-loving crowd here may include such rarities as roseate spoonbill, white ibis, and black rail.

Forest habitat along the southern edge of the impoundment may, if water levels can be stabilized, provide good wood duck breeding habitat in the future. The impoundment is also configured nicely for colonial nesters, such as great blue and black-crowned night herons, with raised areas, "bodark" (bois d'arc) snags, and other good structure helping to serve their familial needs. Black rail have been spotted here, though king and Virginia rails, and sora, are more common. As always, the coot, a rail family member, finds living space wherever there's water. A scope will aid your viewing efforts at Dever Pond, which can reach a hundred yards south of the road when full.

Smaller wetlands lie along the road farther to the west, where eventually you'll reach a bridge that crosses the black water of Big Mineral Creek. The steep-banked watercourse may attract various wildlife species and can be a good viewing "tunnel" into the woods. The refuge boundary lies at the railroad bridge farther down the road. Look for belted kingfishers in limbs that overhang the creek and wetlands; some of Hagerman's kingfishers are surprisingly robust.

Overlook, Overview

The Sandy Point day-use area lies on the far western side of the refuge. The picnic and lounging spot overlooks a broad reach of the lake; with a scope you can get a good view from here, sometimes of thousands of ducks who raft over the water in the fall. Erosion along the exposed shoreline here is serious, approaching possibly 5 feet of lost bank each year. In the face of an estimated half-million-dollar repair cost, though, refuge managers are resigned to watching the lake enlarge itself a little more each year.

Grazing has been reduced at Hagerman over past decades, but cows can be a good management tool to keep prairie grasses healthy and vibrant. Control is the key, and here such control is careful and thoughtful.

Managing an oil-bearing preserve creates challenges for refuge officials, but the situation seems more or less in balance, given the realities of commercial activity here. Spillage around rigs has been minimal, with oil spills into watery areas almost unknown. The largest companies, particularly Shell Oil, seem to be the most responsible while the record of smaller independents has been more spotty. One good sign: Like casual visitors, oil field workers often pause beside rafts of white pelicans or flocks of geese to sit and watch them. They see the value of wildlife here, and most probably strive to accommodate their wild charges.

The proprietary feeling of workers toward the refuge and its residents at times has aided in management efforts; poachers have been reported by oil field workers, and an ethic of respect toward wildlife seems to be the norm. Shell Oil, which originally drilled most of the wells on Hagerman, has reportedly been a careful steward, reflecting a respect for wildlife that seems to extend from the top of the corporation down through the ranks—the kind of wildlife/land ethic our national family depends upon.

Impressions and Experiences

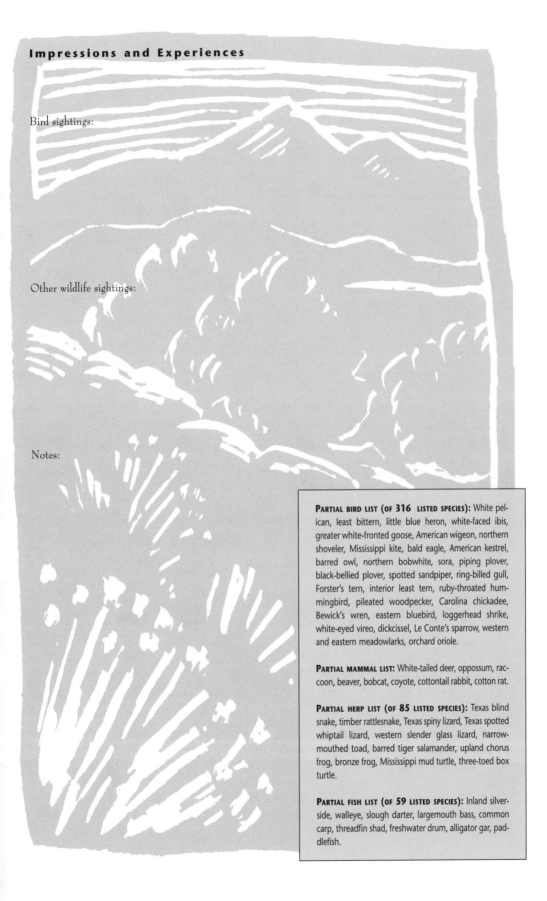

Bird sightings:

Other wildlife sightings:

Notes:

PARTIAL BIRD LIST (OF 316 LISTED SPECIES): White pelican, least bittern, little blue heron, white-faced ibis, greater white-fronted goose, American wigeon, northern shoveler, Mississippi kite, bald eagle, American kestrel, barred owl, northern bobwhite, sora, piping plover, black-bellied plover, spotted sandpiper, ring-billed gull, Forster's tern, interior least tern, ruby-throated hummingbird, pileated woodpecker, Carolina chickadee, Bewick's wren, eastern bluebird, loggerhead shrike, white-eyed vireo, dickcissel, Le Conte's sparrow, western and eastern meadowlarks, orchard oriole.

PARTIAL MAMMAL LIST: White-tailed deer, oppossum, raccoon, beaver, bobcat, coyote, cottontail rabbit, cotton rat.

PARTIAL HERP LIST (OF 85 LISTED SPECIES): Texas blind snake, timber rattlesnake, Texas spiny lizard, Texas spotted whiptail lizard, western slender glass lizard, narrow-mouthed toad, barred tiger salamander, upland chorus frog, bronze frog, Mississippi mud turtle, three-toed box turtle.

PARTIAL FISH LIST (OF 59 LISTED SPECIES): Inland silverside, walleye, slough darter, largemouth bass, common carp, threadfin shad, freshwater drum, alligator gar, paddlefish.

VC	R			W		H	F	$

ADDRESS, PHONE: PO Box 450, Rio Hondo, TX 78583, (210) 748-3607.

DIRECTIONS, HOURS: From Harlingen on Hwy 106; 14 miles past Rio Hondo, take a L; 3 miles to Visitor's Center. From South Padre Island, take Hwy 100 from Port Isabel, R onto Farm Road 510 at Laguna Vista; 5.4 miles to Cameron County Airport road; take a R, 7 miles to Visitor's Center. From Brownsville, N on Paredes Line Road (1847) thru Los Fresnos to Hwy 106; turn R, 10 miles to T; take L, 3 miles to Visitor's Center. Tour roads open sunrise to sunset every day; Visitor's Center open 10 a.m. to 4 p.m. daily Oct thru April; 10 a.m. to 4 p.m. weekends in May; closed June–Sept. Small entry fee.

OVERVIEW, ACTIVITIES: Around 45,000 acres of coastal plains, fresh and salt marshes, open bay and other habitats, foot trails thru riparian habitat; wildlife viewing, hiking, photography, fishing and camping at Adolph Thomae County Park on N end, Harlingen Ship Channel, and Cayo Atascoso; hunting; fishing.

ELEVATION: Sea level to 34 feet.

WEATHER: Mild in spring and late fall; hot in summer and early fall; mild to very cold in winter. Spring, fall, and winter best seasons to visit.

SPECIAL NEEDS: Insect repellent.

LODGING, CAMPING: Lodging in Port Isabel, South Padre Island, and other towns in the area; camping at Thomae County Park (including RV sites); beaches N of the town of South Padre Island; Bentsen–Rio Grande State Park.

NEARBY POINTS OF INTEREST: South Padre Island, Bentsen–Rio Grande State Park, Santa Ana NWR, Brownsville dump (for Mexican crows and white-necked ravens).

DISABILITY ACCESS: Visitor's Center and Osprey Overlook are accessible.

As you enter Laguna Atascosa NWR along Hwy 106 from the town of Rio Hondo, this far-south Texas refuge at first appears unremarkable, little more than an extension of surrounding coastal prairie and farmland. In spring and summer, you might wonder: If this is such a world-renowned refuge, where's the wildlife?

That impression falls away as you enter Laguna Atascosa's varied habitats and begin to encounter the vitality of this environment. Laguna harbors more types of birds than any other US refuge, as well as a wide range of other creatures. A little exploration will confirm that you've entered one of the nation's truly spectacular refuges.

In fall and winter, you may find yourself in the midst of hundreds of thousands of rising, squawking waterfowl—a scene that will surely take your breath away. In spring, countless passerines inhabit Laguna's mesquite forest and sub-tropical uplands. Year-round, a fascinating array of wild creatures live, breed, and loaf on the refuge, in some of the last natural habitat of its kind left in the entire region.

coastal

The 45,000-acre Laguna Atascosa, established in 1946, is a mostly flat tract made up of 6 ecological zones, including coastal prairie, upland coastal scrub, savanna, marsh, and open fresh- and saltwater. Each harbors a unique cast of life.

The great numbers of birds and other creatures on the refuge result from its proximity to several distinct climatic zones, as well as at least 2 migratory pathways. Chihuahuan Desert, subtropical, temperate, and gulf climates all meet here, resulting in a hodge-podge biota mix found in few other places. Migratory species from the Central and Mississippi Flyways both pass through Laguna,

along with wildlife visitors from all along the southern coast.

In one small area of Laguna you might find cactus wrens mingling within calling distance of wading reddish egrets while painted buntings and Harris's hawks perch in nearby trees that also shelter groove-billed anis. A few yards away, willets and piping plovers may be exploring a *playa* pond.

Laguna is a de facto part of the lower Rio Grande wildlife corridor, if not directly connected. One of the largest remaining plots of undeveloped land in the entire south Texas region, the refuge is a significant part of that system. All the wild country in south Texas, of which relatively few acres remain, represents an ecologically connected system—discrete patches of land bordered by wide swathes of farmland but a system nevertheless. The connectedness of those separated acres represents a true corridor, especially for highly mobile birds but also for land mammals, bats, and possibly some of the more mobile herptiles. In the case of even the smallest herps, as well as for many plants, the more an area is buffered from development, the healthier it will be.

Scores of rare critters prowl the uplands here, including 2 endangered cats: the ocelot, a shy nocturnal feline with a beautiful spotted coat; and the gray or reddish-haired jaguarundi, an even more furtive cat whose US population may number less than 10 individuals. The Aplomado falcon, an endangered species extirpated from the region by habitat loss and DDT-induced egg thinning, is now making a comeback at Laguna with the help of the non-profit Peregrine Fund, the federal government, and cooperative Mexican interests.

Laguna's coastal and inland lake habitats provide for many thousands of waterfowl and also support innumerable shorebirds. Its canals and backwaters support alligator, various heron species, egrets, and dozens of other species.

Getting Around

Auto, foot, and bike trails vein the refuge, providing access to each of its habitat types. In spring and especially in summer (which can be extremely hot and humid), locating wildlife sometimes requires settling in at a promising spot and taking time to scan and study the area. Brisk spring winds can be a problem (these are the same winds that birds ride north from the Yucatán) but shouldn't discourage a visit. In fall and winter, productive wildlife observation is a simple matter of showing up, as this is a time when countless waterfowl and shorebirds crowd the waterways and shorelines.

Plants on Laguna number more than 450 species. Some 40 mammals live here, including several wildcats, raccoons, gray fox, bottlenosed dolphin along the Harlingen Ship Channel, and long-tailed weasel, a brown-and-white, open-field dweller who feeds on birds, insects, and mammals as large as rabbits. The weasel will climb trees in search of prey, moving in a deadly fluid motion. Occasionally, an individual seems to fall under a blood-induced murder spell, killing and eating whatever is around, including its own wounded siblings. Like its distant cousin the skunk, the weasel possesses anal glands that can issue a nasty scent, but that doesn't always stop predators such as eagles, hawks, and cats from making meals of the creature.

Forty reptile and 20 amphibian species, including rattlesnake, American alligator, and Texas horned lizard and a variety of frogs, toads, and salamanders, are found in Laguna's uplands and wet areas.

In the scrub and savanna country, a colorful assortment of birds either lives or visits, including an occasional northern wheatear, a rock-hopping, ground-nesting bird whose confirmed presence in November of 1994—far from its normal range in the Frozen North—elevated Laguna's bird count to an incredible 399 species, highest in the national wildlife refuge system. (The list has more recently swelled to 401 species.) Audubon Christmas counts on the refuge always turn up more than 150 species.

Canals, Coypus, and Creeping Carnivores

Wildlife-viewing opportunities at Laguna begin within a short distance of the Hwy 106 entrance 14 miles east of the town of Rio Hondo. Soon after passing the refuge sign you come to a narrow canal. Park well off the road on either side of the bridge and approach the waterway stealthily. Here you may find a variety of egrets, herons, ducks, terns, and shorebird species. Nesting under the bridge is a colony of swallows that swoops below you with little concern for your presence. A gator or two may be spotted in the slow-moving canal.

A small number of nonnative nutrias, also known as coypus, inhabit the canals and *resacas* (ponds created from old river oxbows). This hyper-glandular rat resembles a large beaver, though its tail is thin rather than paddle-shaped. The South American transplant damages banks, devours crops, and is considered a pest on this and all refuges.

freshwater wetlands

Fortunately, its geographic expansion is limited here by water salinity, so the nutria isn't a serious nuisance.

As elsewhere in the region, nonnative feral hogs are a different story. The destructive porkers are hunted both by refuge staffers and by Texan bow and gun hunters during the short winter hunting season. An exotic-control policy also allows the removal of these animals from the refuge to protect habitat. Deer are also hunted on the refuge, subject to the manager's determination of appropriate numbers that may be "harvested."

Across the road to the northeast, a service road takes you less than a mile by foot or bike to the southern edge of Laguna Atascosa Lake. The trail's terminus is a good place to find geese, cranes, and a variety of shorebirds in season. In 1994–95, a flamingo of mysterious origin resided on the lake. If it's still around, the graceful pink wader may be visible from this spot.

A few miles down the road on Hwy 106, Resaca de los Cuates, the shallow remains of an old river oxbow, curves off from both sides of the road. The western side of this narrow pond is home to numerous waders and waterbirds, gators, and other species. Black-bellied whistling ducks browse and loaf here; the long-legged birds may sometimes be observed at sunset perched atop cottonwood snags on the hill north of the *resaca*—an amusing, incongruous sight.

Several gators ply the waterway, stalking little blue, green, and great blue herons, as well as ducks and egrets who inhabit the shore. Often 2 or more gators will glide toward a bankside wader so slowly they appear to be driftwood. They pause 10 or 20 yards offshore, sometimes for an hour or more, before creeping in for the kill. This patient stalking ability has likely contributed to the gator's largely unaltered physiology through millions of years of evolution. If something works, why change it?

Laguna Atascosa Lake

Osprey Overlook, north of the Visitor's Center, offers a broad view of the mostly freshwater Laguna Atascosa Lake, where an array of water-loving species may be found. In the spring of 1995, that lone, out-of-place flamingo was one of the lake's many large waders, visible a mile to the northwest through one of the overlook's two telescopes. Roseate spoonbills, various egrets and herons, avocets and stilts, and a variety of terns, skimmers, plovers, sandpipers, and other water lovers also make the lake their home for all or part of the year. They often play in the shallows off the lake's broad, curving shore.

A trail running east along the shoreline from Osprey Overlook passes through thick sub-

tropical desert scrub. A hike there may turn up a dozen or more species of warblers, raptors, and others, including the olive sparrow, a favorite of list-conscious birders. Biologists sometimes erect mist nets on the trail to catch and survey birds during spring migration. Some of the efforts support MAPS, a nationwide program that monitors migratory passerines—and tracks their present decline—throughout North America.

The importance of avian research is clear despite the unfortunate disturbance that net trapping causes the birds. At Laguna Atascosa, researchers (who may be trained Americorp workers supervised by staff biologists) check their nets every 20 minutes and promptly remove them at the end of each session. Such research will help us develop ways to support declining migrant populations.

A gated service road off the main route to Osprey Overlook takes you on foot or bike a quarter mile to Alligator Pond, which often contains a few gators.

This is no petting zoo; gators can eat kids and pets if given the chance, and they've given adults some nasty bites. Alligators grow to more than 19 feet and live up to 50 years, though Laguna's population runs no higher than the 14-foot range. On land they can move surprisingly fast, and they're even more agile in water. For that reason, wading in any gator-inhabited watercourse is a truly lousy idea.

Keep your pets leashed and your kids close by when you're around gators. If an individual shows agitation, back off. (Interpreting such a loud, ferocious message is not difficult. One staffer jokes that anyone who ignores the creature's awesome intimidation display may deserve to be selected out of the evolutionary stream.) None of this is meant to discourage hiking or gator-watching. Few people ever experience problems with these majestic reptiles, and observing them can be an exciting and rewarding experience. They simply require a measure of respect.

Here as throughout the refuge, grass and brush also hide rattlesnakes, mites, ticks, and other creatures that can damage body and spirit. Stay on the trails, be observant, use insect repellent, and you should have no problems.

Bayside Tour Loop

On the gulf side of the refuge, a 15-mile, 1-way tour road takes you across the slough that runs to Pelican Lake, where vast rafts of wintering ducks (particularly redheads) congregate, then on to the shore of Laguna Madre. The first mile or two of the road is a brushy stretch where Botteri's and Cassin's sparrows can be found in every season except winter. Clay dunes below a large pullout overlooking the bay support numerous Texas horned lizards (we always called them horny toads), whose cryptic coloration helps hide them from predators. Willets, sandpipers, and other shorebirds and waders browse the small pools lying all along the roadway.

Laguna Madre is one of only three hypersaline lagoons in the world (another lies off the coast of Mexico a short distance to the south). Its high salinity is the result of limited inflow and outflow to the Gulf of Mexico. Water trapped in this barrier bay constantly evaporates, keeping the salt concentration high and creating a fertile growth zone for seagrass and algal mats. Those plant communities in turn provide food, directly and indirectly, to many avian and marine species. Tidal flats along the shoreline are constantly inundated, and fish trapped in small pools make for easy pickings, too.

This natural feast hardly goes unnoticed. Eighty percent of the planet's redheads winter at Laguna (400,000 to 600,000 winter in the general area). Waterfowl hunting was halted here several years back after managers accepted the fact that with overflying redheads virtually blotting out the sun, a shotgunner couldn't hope to limit his bag to the legal take.

Many other creatures feed on the riches at Laguna. The endangered piping plover is one species that relies on Laguna's algal mats and mudflats. Watching the plovers in spring can make for good entertainment. The male plover's mating ritual includes a spectacular figure-eight flight, along with a ground display that includes whistling, crouching, wing spreading, and other behavior meant to impress a potential mate.

Pelican Lake, a shallow, brackish extension of Laguna Madre that lies inside the loop, is at times so packed with wintertime ducks that they appear as solid islands. Canvasback is another species that sometimes finds the area attractive, though the majority of canvasbacks prefer Laguna Atascosa Lake. Wintering canvasbacks now number in the 20,000 range at Laguna and may be increasing.

Along the shore of Laguna Madre you might see any number of species, including desert dwellers such as cactus wren and roadrunner on the arid upland reaches. There, desert plants such as yucca and prickly pear thrive just a few feet above cordgrass and other marine flora and fauna.

Ospreys hunt over Laguna Madre and Pelican Lake, often bringing freshly caught fish to the shore. The ospreys here exhibit a curious habit: They sometimes allow shorebirds such as ruddy turnstones and others to snack on their catch. Occasionally, a frustrated osprey will escape with its meal to a nearby field, presumably to avoid those overbearing neighbors.

Reddish egret, white and brown pelicans, and dozens of other seabirds, shorebirds, and waders use Laguna's water and offshore strip islands. If you're lucky, a magnificent frigate bird may soar overhead. The name of this bird, which inflates a huge red pouch beneath its beak, says it all.

At Redhead Ridge Overlook you can climb high enough to see a good portion of Laguna Madre, as well as two ponds lying on either side of you. With good glass you can spot numerous species from here. Just below the overlook, the 3-mile Moranco Blanco Trail takes you past a couple of tidal ponds and into yucca country—very nice in spring due to the profusion of snowy yucca blooms.

Desert birds flit among the vegetation that lines the bay shore, another of Laguna's pleasing incongruities.

Songbirds, including gray-cheeked thrush, long-billed thrasher (whose song is melodic and complex), and dozens of warbler species, live in the brush along the southern reach of the auto loop. Warbler watchers should give this area some extra time and attention.

Migratory "fallouts" can be spectacular, when exhausted passerines just in from the Yucatán swarm every tree and shrub. In late April and early May, when migration is most intense, human visitors also swarm the refuge. Visitation at Laguna runs to 200,000 people per year. Additional visitors come to fish at Thomae Park on the northern side of the refuge.

Passerines can also be found near headquarters, along two walking trails that take you into dense canopies of mesquite and other plants, and in the brush along the entrance. Avoid beehives along the trails and elsewhere on the refuge; Africanized bees inhabit the entire south Texas area and can be dangerous. Generally, staffers remove bees from visitor-accessible areas, but don't take a chance by lingering near any hive you encounter.

Aplomado Falcon

The endangered Aplomado falcon is often seen hunting over the last third of the tour road. One of 8 falcon-family birds traditionally inhabiting the United States, the Aplomado was at one time common in southern Texas and southern Arizona. Habitat destruction by the middle part of this century—coupled with DDT poisoning that also ravaged peregrines and other predators of crop-dwelling insects and small mammals—conspired to eradicate the beautiful brown-and-gray falcon from the region.

Since 1985, efforts by the Peregrine Fund, a private nonprofit group of dedicated falcon savers, the World Center for Birds of Prey in Boise, Idaho, and refuge staffers have brought the Aplomado back to some of its former Texas range.

Laguna Atascosa's open prairies offer good, protected habitat for the 16-inch bird, whose strikingly marked face, gray crown, and barred brownish tail set it apart from the similar young Mississippi kite, also found here. Between 7 and 30 young Aplomados have been transplanted to Laguna each year since the early 1990s. Future releases may number as many as 50 young birds per year.

Careful study has revealed that the survival rate of "hacked" (human-raised) Aplomados is enhanced by releasing them away from the haunts of predatory great horned owls and coyotes, who feed on young, inexperienced falcons. Unlike peregrines, hacked Aplomados tend to roost on the ground, a practice that would likely be discouraged by overseeing parents. Since these birds lack parental tutelage, their critical trial-and-error youth is a time of great danger that human overseers are struggling to understand and help them overcome.

Efforts by the Peregrine Fund and refuge biologists have been impressive so far, with survival rates hovering between 58% to 85%, far higher than expected. Upgrading of the peregrine falcon from the endangered to the threatened list in mid-1995—though some believe the move was premature and politically based—is testimony to the good work of the Peregrine Fund. That organization deserves praise and donations, not necessarily in that order. We can only hope their efforts with the Aplomado are equally fruitful.

Ocelot Ecology

The 30 or so endangered ocelots who inhabit Laguna Atascosa are another species of prime concern, as are the handful of jaguarundis who may live here. For years, radio collars have helped biologists track the lifeways of Laguna's ocelots, who range in the thick brush hunting rabbits, rodents, and other small prey. Experts believe the relatively small amount of habitat at Laguna harbors an optimal number of ocelots, to perhaps 40 individuals. That can be a problem for upcoming young cats, who are regularly forced out of the territory by older adults. With most of the region's brush habitat gone to development, far-ranging 1- and 2-year-olds invariably end up at the edge of highways. Shy, nervous ocelots sometimes dart across roads impulsively, which often results in their deaths. In some areas, culverts installed beneath roadways now provide them with safe passage.

Refuge biologists try to keep about 10 cats radio-collared at a time in order to track them and better understand their behavior. Thus far, they've found that some ocelots swim back and forth across the arroyo at Thomae Park on the northern boundary; that they sometimes use sugarcane fields as habitat; and that they cross farm fields on their way to isolated patches of cover. Once ensconced in those brush patches, ocelots may starve to death for lack of prey. It isn't easy being an ocelot in south Texas.

Laguna's connection to the King Ranch and other huge private holdings north of the refuge represents the best hope for many of these critters, offering them crucial expansion area into wild country when older males force young ones from their territory. Close to 3 million wild acres comprise that big-time Texas ranch country, and many ranchers in the area have agreed that wildlife in the area needs protection and nurturing. Good habitat is good habitat, whether it's on refuge property or not.

South Texas ranchers in general support the presence of ocelots. They express admiration for the cats, are thrilled to see them enter their headlights at night, and treasure the idea of having this wild creature on their land—another example of the common ground between cowpokes and environmentalists. However, it isn't fear of livestock depradation that makes ranchers nervous about ocelots; it's the thought of having an endangered species on their property, which they fear may lead to government control of their land.

Nervous landowners in south Texas have sometimes bulldozed or otherwise altered land containing endangered species, believing they've eliminated a threat to their economic sovereignty. More enlightened individuals work with private, federal, and state officials to enhance the survival of ocelots and other rare species. Most often, cooperation arises from conversation—the informal kind, one-to-one over a cup of coffee. More often than not, such encounters are the key to recognizing common interests, which often results in greater habitat protection.

Impressions and Experiences

Bird sightings:

Other wildlife sightings:

Notes:

PARTIAL BIRD LIST (OF 401 LISTED SPECIES): Redhead, ring-necked and canvasback ducks, reddish egret, roseate spoonbill, sandhill crane, Aplomado falcon, peregrine falcon, Harris's hawk, groove-billed ani, cactus wren, curve-billed thrasher, northern bobwhite, northern wheatear, MacGillivray's warbler, olive sparrow.

PARTIAL MAMMAL LIST (OF 40 LISTED SPECIES): Mountain lion, jaguarundi, ocelot, coyote, collared peccary, armadillo, Brazilian free-tailed bat, raccoon, long-tailed weasel, bottle-nosed dolphin, wood rat.

PARTIAL HERP LIST: Western diamondback rattler, desert king snake, Texas indigo snake, Texas coral snake, whiptail lizard, skink, Texas spiny lizard, Texas tortoise, Rio Grande siren, giant toad, Couch's spadefoot toad.

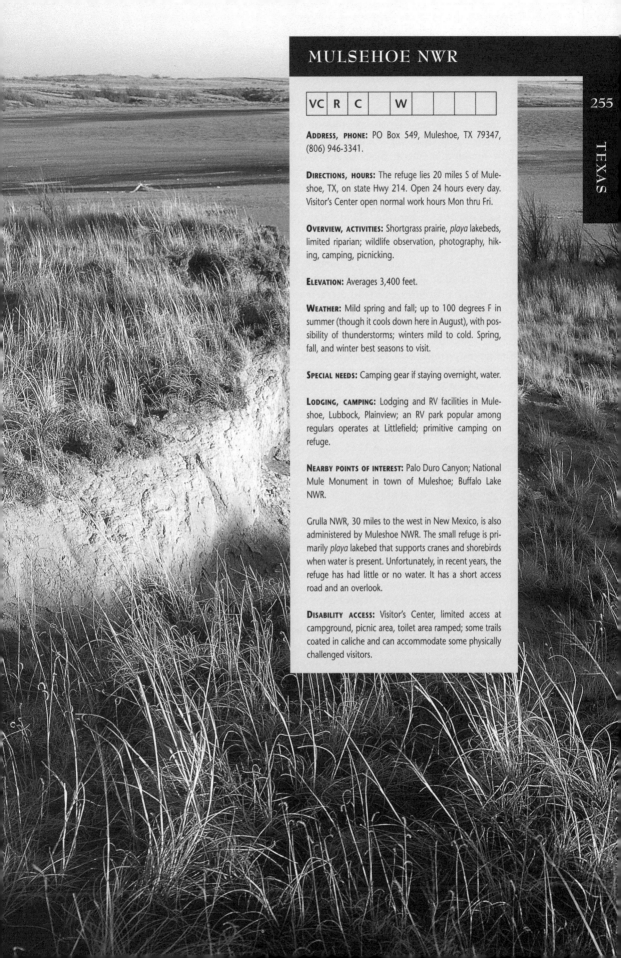

MULSEHOE NWR

VC	R	C		W				

ADDRESS, PHONE: PO Box 549, Muleshoe, TX 79347, (806) 946-3341.

DIRECTIONS, HOURS: The refuge lies 20 miles S of Muleshoe, TX, on state Hwy 214. Open 24 hours every day. Visitor's Center open normal work hours Mon thru Fri.

OVERVIEW, ACTIVITIES: Shortgrass prairie, *playa* lakebeds, limited riparian; wildlife observation, photography, hiking, camping, picnicking.

ELEVATION: Averages 3,400 feet.

WEATHER: Mild spring and fall; up to 100 degrees F in summer (though it cools down here in August), with possibility of thunderstorms; winters mild to cold. Spring, fall, and winter best seasons to visit.

SPECIAL NEEDS: Camping gear if staying overnight, water.

LODGING, CAMPING: Lodging and RV facilities in Muleshoe, Lubbock, Plainview; an RV park popular among regulars operates at Littlefield; primitive camping on refuge.

NEARBY POINTS OF INTEREST: Palo Duro Canyon; National Mule Monument in town of Muleshoe; Buffalo Lake NWR.

Grulla NWR, 30 miles to the west in New Mexico, is also administered by Muleshoe NWR. The small refuge is primarily *playa* lakebed that supports cranes and shorebirds when water is present. Unfortunately, in recent years, the refuge has had little or no water. It has a short access road and an overlook.

DISABILITY ACCESS: Visitor's Center, limited access at campground, picnic area, toilet area ramped; some trails coated in caliche and can accommodate some physically challenged visitors.

The oldest national wildlife refuge in Texas may be primarily dry, rolling shortgrass prairie, but water—or lack of it—determines Muleshoe's biological character. That character changes constantly from month to month and year to year and affects virtually all plant and animal life that inhabits these 5,809 acres.

In February 1981, when water (and thus food) was plentiful, the number of wintering sandhills at Muleshoe reached 250,000. In the winter of 1987–88, around 58,000 sandhill cranes resided at this northwest Texas refuge. Over the past decade, rainfall has decreased; consequently, sandhill numbers on Muleshoe have hovered in the 7,000 to 10,000 range.

During the wettest years, tens of thousands of ducks, geese, and shorebirds may visit three *playa* lakes on the refuge, when those undrained natural concavities might provide nearly 1,000 wetland acres. When the refuge was founded in 1935, the aquifer beneath this prairie region had not yet been sucked dry by extensive farming from Texas to the Canadian border. Waterfowl numbers often approached 300,000 in those days.

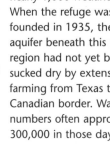

prairie

In drier years that have become the rule, water bird activity is minimal. Then the refuge is more important for resident species, such as coyote, prairie rattler, a handful of lesser prairie chickens, and roadrunners, which have lately increased in number after a period of scarcity. A minimum of a few thousand sandhill cranes normally show up here unless water is completely lacking.

Muleshoe lies on the northern reach of a region of west Texas known as the Llano Estacado, a Spanish-derived term that translates to "staked plain." Theories on the origin of the area's name abound. One legend has it that early Spanish explorers drove wooden stakes into the featureless plains for navigation purposes. Another ascribes the name to the

yucca stalks that jut from the grassland. A third credits prairie dog guards perched (stakelike?) on their raised front porches, alert for danger. The theories range from utilitarian to fanciful; your choice probably says something about the degree of romance or playfulness in your nature.

Four-fifths of the refuge is swathed in shortgrasses that include blue, side oats, and black grama. Dustings of "cottontop," a grass species nicknamed for its feather-duster topknot, lend the prairie a lustrous, snow-flecked quality in the fall and winter. Like the beast of burden for which it's named, Muleshoe's dominant colors are brown and buff, with patches of brighter hues that arise with spring and summer blooms of verbena, mallow, prickly pear, and many others. After good rains, the tawny grasses turn green almost overnight, retaining their growth hues as long as the moisture holds out.

Three saline lakes comprise nearly a fifth of the refuge—*playas* with no drainage that fill mainly from runoff and rain, along with whatever artesian springwater erupts from the depleted aquifer. *Playa* water evaporates over time, leaving an ever-thickening white coat of salt on the surfaces.

As with the origin of the region's name, various theories exist to explain the creation of *playa* lakes in prairie country. Some believe huge buffalo herds that once roamed the region wallowed en masse, stamping out the lakebeds. Another theory attributes the depressions to meteor strikes. Still others suggest they developed from differential soil compaction or wind scouring. Take your pick.

Moisture and Missions

At one time the vast Ogallala aquifer, underlying the nation's midsection for more than a thousand miles north to south, fed these lakes and kept them full; life swelled their surfaces and banks. Back then, 60-year-old Muleshoe served as a migratory waterfowl resting area.

Unfortunately, half a century of farming has drawn the aquifer down to the point that artesian pressure is lacking except in times of heavy precipitation. (Ogallala has dropped by as much as 2 feet per year in recent decades.) The lack of water has changed Muleshoe's major role from waterfowl to sandhill crane resting support, though it still provides a haven for local wildlife.

A single remnant perennial spring in Upper Pauls Lake continues to feed the diked *playa*. Its trickling flow has become critical to migratory species and locals alike; there you can often find water-loving birds when they're absent elsewhere on the refuge.

After heavy rain, the spring may increase its flow, spilling water over the dike into the much larger Lower Pauls Lake, where an overlook offers good viewing. When Lower Pauls is wet, it may support extensive waterfowl and shorebird habitat (a scope is usually necessary to observe its far shoreline). During those rare seasons of heavy rainfall (generally rain falls hardest in late summer), other springs may erupt briefly at the two *playas* near the refuge headquarters, and the precipitation can fill those large natural impoundments, too. In recent years, however, water has been minimal, and the *playas* have served more as crane resting habitat than as waterfowl dabbling and diving spots.

Even with its dramatic moisture fluctuations, Muleshoe represents one important site in a meager link of protected Central Flyway habitats that supports long-distance winged travelers. One problem that has arisen from the flyway's shrunken habitat has been sporadic outbreaks of avian cholera, a soil-based waterfowl killer that is aggravated by crowding. Several epidemics have occurred since the mid-1950s, killing millions of migratory birds.

Little can be done about the disease other than reducing waterfowl concentrations when the bacteria grows virulent. But relatively little habitat is left in our nation's midsection. If you chase birds from places such as Muleshoe, where do they have left to go? One manager

regards the national wildlife refuge system as "a network of Band-Aids on a very sick system." These days, such first aid can make all the difference for wildlife.

From Subtle to Spectacular

The variety of birds that use the refuge can be extensive when conditions are right. Muleshoe's bird list includes 282 species, 45 of which are rare accidentals that show up only in odd years.

Crane-watching is the main reason people visit Muleshoe; some years the tall, graceful birds, who begin arriving by the first of October, seem to occupy every foot of wetland and associated uplands, flying into *playa* edges around sunset, leaving again at sunrise to glean food from agricultural fields as far as 30 miles away. Their soaring, screaming flights are always a joy to behold. The lesser sandhills that come usually remain until February, when they rise in circling flocks and then head north, stopping along the way to forage from the leavings of cornfields and other croplands along their way.

For a wondrous view of the sandhill migratory cycle, visit the Panhandle area here from mid-February to early March. At that time, you'll likely see thousands of lesser sandhills winging north over far-reaching farm fields as they return to their summer nesting grounds. Fall migration can also be spectacular.

When water and mudflats appear on Muleshoe, waders and shorebirds may arrive in huge numbers. Greater and lesser yellow-legs, great blue heron, snowy plover (a nester here), western and Baird's sandpipers, and long-billed dowitcher are often in residence. Enochs Pond, a few miles south of the campground on a walking-only road, can sometimes be productive for a variety of water birds, as well as for passerines in its surrounding trees and brush.

Various duck species make up a significant portion of wintering birds on Muleshoe, and many stay to nest. Lesser scaup, redhead, American wigeon, ruddy duck, and northern pintail are a few nesting species. They arrive beginning in late August and reach their peak around year's end—if conditions are good. In all, some 2 dozen types of waterfowl may show up. Rare accidentals, including old-squaw, brant, white-winged scoter, and an occasional common loon, have come in odd years.

Raptor species who visit or reside at Muleshoe are fairly diverse, drawn by a good prairie rodent and small mammal population. Northern harrier is here in every month. Swainson's hawk stays from spring through fall and is replaced by ferruginous hawk in winter; generally, the handful of ferruginous hawks here is gone by spring, often after fledging their 2 to 4 young from nests they construct of sticks, bones, cow dung, and garbage. Their courtship ritual can be impressive; during the ritual the couple "parachutes" downward on spread wings then the male swoops down on the female to lock talons with her in a twisting aerial display.

Scattered mesquite, willow, and salt cedar groves—most in the draws leading to *playas* and low spots—lure migratory passerines and support resident birds, both in small numbers. Probably the best area for passerine observation is the draw next to the refuge campground. Planted in ash, locust, and willow, that stretch (accessible via a short hiking trail) is the thickest grove on the refuge.

Another small grove of good perching trees lies 2 miles north of the campground on a refuge-boundary road that you may hike but not drive. Likewise, much of the area off the main road and *playa* access roads is walkable, but you must leave vehicles behind.

Orange-crowned, Nashville, MacGillivray's, and yellow warbler, blue grosbeak, and northern oriole are some of Muleshoe's more common migrants. Resident passerines include rock and Bewick's wren, northern mockingbird, loggerhead shrike, and rufous-crowned sparrow, among others.

On Muleshoe's prairie hills and flats, ground-dwelling birds include northern bobwhite, scaled quail, roadrunner, and an occasional ring-necked pheasant. Killdeer and mourning dove are common, and brown towhee, savanna sparrow, and lark sparrow aren't too hard to find. Both eastern and western meadowlarks sing from low shrubs and other perches throughout the refuge.

Low Society

Hundreds of acres on and below the refuge, including an extensive area along the entrance road and around the Visitor's Center (also along the road to Pauls Lake), are occupied by one of the most socially-organized of small mammals, the black-tailed prairie dog. You can't miss their townsites, which cover more than 300 refuge acres; many are skirted by raised earthen ramparts, which protect their homes from flooding and provide a raised platform for the guards who watch for predators. When an owl, hawk, coyote, or badger approaches, the guard dog may utter any of a number of whistles, chucking sounds, wheezes, or other vocalizations.

Research reveals that the prairie dog has a language of its own: One sound if by air; another if the threat is a ground-skulker; and still others to call fellow towndogs to meetings or matings. Their calls distinguish a coyote from a badger or a hawk from a person. Talking rodents, you say? All the evidence affirms it.

The endearing critter, attacked mercilessly in many regions because its burrows threaten cow ankles and its major-league teeth strip away crop roots, is protected on Muleshoe, where it thrives.

The last evidence of black-footed ferrets here was reported in 1964. The highly endangered weasel eats almost nothing but prairie dogs and probably enjoyed a good livelihood on this grocery-rich hunting ground. Other, more recent ferret sightings in the Canadian River area indicate that the ferret likely inhabited the Muleshoe region until development and other forces extirpated it from all but a tiny patch of north-country acreage.

Numerous nonendangered mammals live on the refuge or sometimes visit. A very occasional cougar, whose range can span several hundred miles, has passed through, possibly from a home range in nearby Palo Duro Canyon. Coyotes are here, along with blacktail jackrabbit, least shrew, a few raccoons and bobcats, a small number of gray foxes, and pallid bat. Herptiles here include the prairie rattler, which can be out and about during any season. Western hognose snake, coachwhip, lesser earless and collared lizards, Great Plains toad, and western spadefoot are some of the cold-blooded creatures you may encounter on the refuge.

Money and Management

Hunting is nonexistent at Muleshoe. That hasn't been an issue, probably due to the low population nearby and subsequent lack of pressure for a refuge hunt. That's fortunate for the cranes who visit since they're legally hunted in Texas, as they are in Utah, New Mexico, and other southwestern states.

Likewise, people management has been relatively uneventful, according to refuge staffers. Muleshoe's 13,000 yearly visitors seem to appreciate wildlife and respect wild lands; they treat the place accordingly. Many locals from the town of Muleshoe, say refuge staffers, seem to regard the refuge as "theirs," with all the pride of ownership such a relationship suggests.

The refuge rewards that good stewardship with a basic but serviceable campground near the Visitor's Center. It's large enough for a dozen or more parties and is stocked with tables, grills (bring your own wood or charcoal), and a rest room.

Water represents the most demanding management issue here. With sporadic natural precipitation, a more reliable water-delivery system would greatly benefit local and migratory residents, even the human ones who now depend upon a single 6-gallons-per-minute well and cistern above headquarters. That water serves not only refuge housing but also the campground, the Visitor's Center, and the controlled grazing program maintained here in summer.

Grazing on the refuge helps regulate the condition of grasslands. For the past decade, tighter grazing controls have been instituted to lessen the impact on the native gramas that make up much of the prairie biota. Grazing here has come to be a management tool rather than simply a convenience for nearby ranchers. Seven areas have been fenced off to enable managers to control the intensity of cattle impacts. Local area stock is run on varying units in summer on a rest-rotation basis—at a competitive price that is much higher than BLM or Forest Service land grazing fees. The fenced partitions never allow too intensive cropping of a single area, and each unit is rested seasonally from year to year, which prevents selective encouragement/suppression of certain grass species.

Controlled burning represents the other half of the refuge grass management program, but staffers here often prefer the grazing alternative. The reason: Gramas require a bedding of litter to get them through drought times. Burning destroys that litter, whereas grazing allows it to remain. Less desirable (from a wildlife standpoint) alkali sacaton seems to respond vigorously to grazing, too, say Muleshoe staffers. Whereas burning seems to encourage merely more vigorous alkali sacaton growth, grazing helps bring it down while allowing nearby gramas the opportunity to move in on its edges.

Muleshoe's wildlife numbers vary, but the refuge is always a good place to visit for the spaciousness of the land, the broad northwest Texas sky, and all those playful prairie dogs. The well-maintained camping/picnicking area makes this a convenient getaway alternative to state and federal parks. Besides, Muleshoe's long views are always good for the spirit.

Impressions and Experiences

Bird sightings:

Other wildlife sightings:

Notes:

PARTIAL BIRD LIST (OF 282 LISTED SPECIES): Eared grebe, great blue heron, sandhill crane, mallard, blue-winged teal, bufflehead, northern harrier, golden eagle, Swainson's hawk, ferruginous hawk, northern bobwhite, roadrunner, snowy plover, yellowlegs, Baird's sandpiper, mourning dove, burrowing owl, northern flicker, scissor-tailed flycatcher, barn swallow, loggerhead shrike, Wilson's warbler, lark bunting, western meadowlark, McCown's longspur.

PARTIAL MAMMAL LIST: Coyote, black-tail jackrabbit, black-tailed prairie dog, bobcat, least shrew, long-tailed weasel, Plains pocket gopher.

PARTIAL HERP LIST: Prairie rattlesnake, bullsnake, western hognose snake, prairie racerunner, Texas horned lizard, spotted chorus frog, ornate box turtle.

SANTA ANA NWR

VC	R		NP	W				

ADDRESS, PHONE: Route 2, PO Box 202A, Alamo, TX 78516, (210) 787-3079.

DIRECTIONS, HOURS: Take Hwy 83 to Alamo, turn S onto FM 907. At Hwy 281 turn L and continue a quarter mile to refuge. Daylight hours. Visitor's Center open weekdays during normal work hours.

OVERVIEW, ACTIVITIES: Some 2,000 acres of thorn forest woodlands, marsh, and riparian; hiking, photography, wildlife observation, and nature study.

ELEVATION: Sea level to 50 feet.

WEATHER: Very hot in summer, mostly mild other seasons. Spring, fall, and winter best seasons to visit.

SPECIAL NEEDS: Water for long excursions on refuge trails; binoculars; insect repellent.

LODGING, CAMPING: McAllen and Brownsville have hundreds of motel and hotel rooms; camping at Bentsen–Rio Grande State Park; primitive camping on South Padre Island beach N of town. Numerous RV parks are found thruout the area, including several large ones near the entrance to Bentsen–Rio Grande State Park.

NEARBY POINTS OF INTEREST: Sabal Palm Grove Sanctuary; Laguna Atascosa NWR; Bentsen–Rio Grande State Park (good birding); South Padre Island.

DISABILITY ACCESS: Visitor's Center, rest rooms, Trail A, and tram are all accessible to mobility-impaired visitors.

Pause for half an hour along any path at Santa Ana NWR—perhaps alongside one of its many canopied wetlands—and you'll likely spot a dozen or more species of birds, 4 or 5 mammals, several reptiles, an amphibian or two, and scores of butterflies and other insects, all creeping and winging their way through a small biome consisting of hundreds of plant species.

No field guide is adequate for this species-rich refuge at the southern tip of Texas; if you go, resign yourself to an experience that includes blissful ignorance, constant delight, and a desire to return again and again.

Diminutive Santa Ana NWR is a nature lover's paradise. In some ways, this 2,088-acre plot of native "midvalley riparian woodland" and wetlands, perched amid endless farm fields in a busy agricultural region, resembles an unbarred zoo, densely crowded with a dazzling array of life-forms.

Close to 2,000 plants make up the habitat base, many of them Mexican species found nowhere else in the United States. Nearly 400 bird species, along with scores of other creatures, live here or visit seasonally.

freshwater wetlands

If not for Santa Ana and a few other scattered patches of natural habitat, it would be hard to imagine what the surrounding region looked like before agricultural overkill stripped virtually every tillable acre in the Rio Grande Valley down to the roots. Fields of cotton, sorghum, various fruits, and other crops create a flattened, barren look to the region, which isn't really a valley but a fertile delta. Santa Ana represents much of the surviving semitropical thorn forest habitat that once dominated here, before improved land-clearing technology developed early in this century. That technological revolution launched a virtual clear-cutting of the native landscape, threatening a large-scale catastrophe: the destruction of an entire ecosystem.

Santa Ana serves as home to an amazing number of species. The reasons are many: The refuge stands at a funnel-like confluence of major migratory flyways; its sphere of influence includes tropical, subtropical, coastal plain, Gulf Coast, and temperate zones (with a growing season that averages 11 months per year); and, sadly, it's part of less than 5% of native habitat in the area that has survived city and plow. Migratory species can't help but pause here during their journeys. In an ocean of agriculture, Santa Ana is one tiny isle of good habitat along their way.

Fortunately, a nearby satellite refuge, Lower Rio Grande NWR (not accessible to the public as of early 1996), takes up some of the habitat slack for Santa Ana. The 64,149-acre preserve, established in 1979, is, in turn, part of a network of more than a hundred separate tracts of land—an even larger assemblage of habitats that together make up the expanding "Lower Rio Grande Valley Wildlife Corridor." The goal of this regional habitat conservation program is reestablishment and preservation of wild south Texas lands that will—with luck, funding, and political cooperation—eventually total a quarter of a million acres.

Congregation of Exotica

Santa Ana's staggering array of plant species attracts an abundance of animal life. Unusual botanical species are commonplace here, supported by the region's 18 to 22 inches of yearly rainfall, which facilitates a junglelike environment.

The refuge is populated largely by huisache, a tree similar to mesquite, along with spiny and sugar hackberry, honey mesquite, towering cedar elm, Texas persimmon, and willows in the wetlands. Less common species include *retama,* a small, thorny tree whose seedpods were once ground by Native Americans to make flour; great leadtree, which grows to 60 feet in height; Texas ebony, an evergreen with wood much denser than oak; the drought-resistant *anaqua,* or sandpaper tree, whose rough leaves are the source of its name; and the brasil, or bluewood, a shrub with spoon-shaped leaves and wood that produces a blue dye. Its sweet blackberries provide sustenance for numerous wildlife species.

Because Santa Ana lies within a subtropical latitude, seasonal changes here are less pronounced than at most refuges—it's warm all year round, though it can get downright toasty in summer. Many migratory birds follow the same rituals as elsewhere, passing through on their way north and south. For some, Santa Ana is the terminus of southerly or northerly flights.

Most serious birders are eventually drawn to Santa Ana. Avian lovers need only consider a few of the unique accidentals that have been spotted here before yielding to the inevitable: hook-billed kite, crane hawk, tropical parula, military macaw, clay-colored and rufous-backed robins, golden-crowned warbler, Mexican crow, gray-crowned yellowthroat, blue bunting, white-collared seedeater, and crimson-collared grosbeak.

More commonly seen Santa Ana species are nearly as exciting as the accidentals. They include green jay, chacalaca, buff-bellied hummingbird, Altamira oriole, black-shouldered kite, and gray hawk. Groove-billed ani is often seen here, and northern jacana show up some years.

Three dozen warblers pass through during migration and a few species remain year-round. More than 2 dozen varieties of ducks, geese, and swans are found on the refuge in season. Shorebird and wading species crowd the shorelines of Santa Ana's 4 lakes, and 25 flycatchers—including the bright-yellow, raucous great kiskadee, largest of US flycatchers—hunt throughout the refuge.

Superexotics, such as the jabiru stork, endangered Aplomado falcon, clapper rail, and even the elegant trogon, have been encountered at Santa Ana in some years, along with the more common but equally stunning roseate spoonbill, white and white-faced ibises, sandhill crane, reddish egret, and other large waders.

Birds are Santa Ana's most obvious inhabitants, but a wealth of other species occupy the dense refuge vegetation. At least 42 mammals make Santa Ana their home, including bats (9 species), armadillo, pygmy mouse, gray fox, long-tailed weasel, and the endangered ocelot. The nocturnal jaguarundi, also endangered, may skulk about in the brush, though years have passed since the last confirmed sighting. Jaguars were seen in the area until the 1950s but sadly come no longer.

Reptiles and amphibians are also well represented, including 11 lizards, 18 snakes, 4 turtles, 10 frogs and toads, and at least 1 state-threatened salamander, the Rio Grande lesser siren. Ten species of mollusk occupy refuge microhabitats, along with more butterfly species than on any other refuge—265 species have been found here, enough to spur the creation of a separate refuge brochure that covers strictly butterflies (most common in summer and fall). Common species include gold rim and Ornythion swallowtails, leaf wing, white peacock, and silver-blue hairstreak. Butterfly poaching is an increasing problem here, and refuge staffers are pretty sure that reptile thieves also ply their felonious trade on Santa Ana's back trails.

riparian

Several introduced species, including the Mediterranean gecko, fox squirrel, nutria, and feral hog, cause minor disruption to plant and animal communities. Nearby Lower Rio Grande NWR, on the other hand, suffers more intensely from intruder-species damage, especially by the feral hog, long-wild relative of swine brought in by settlers. The hogs tear up plants, foul water sources, and compete for food with local species. Contract trapping by locals, who are allowed to butcher and eat the hogs they capture, keeps numbers down to somewhat manageable levels.

Happy Trails

The foundation of Santa Ana's visitor program is the Visitor's Center itself, a large, modern structure harboring good exhibits on brush country ecology, wildlife poaching, and

Africanized bees that have moved into the area. A wildlife list in the center details recent sightings, giving newcomers a good idea of what to look for. Local hawk-watchers regularly update the list of raptor flybys.

Along with such information, Santa Ana's staff maintains a retail outlet that features a good selection of nature-oriented books, Wildlife Corridor T-shirts, and other items that help raise needed revenue.

The broad, shaded mall outside the Visitor's Center is a good place to see a variety of species, including buff-bellied hummers, who frequent the lush flower gardens, especially favoring the Turk's cap bushes near the entrance; yellow-billed cuckoos, often heard, and occasionally seen, at the trailhead; and chacalacas, who favor the parking lot vegetation but are found throughout the refuge. Virtually any of Santa Ana's other nonwater bird species may be spotted here.

Be sure to drink a healthy amount of water before hitting the trails and take drinking water with you; the hot, humid environment here can quickly sap your fluid content and leave you cross-eyed and stumbling. After you note the density of mosquitoes, chiggers, and biting flies, you'll also be glad you applied insect repellent before heading out (lower legs and ankles are prime targets). The refuge staff knows the true value of repellent: about five bucks a bottle. They sell it at the Visitor's Center.

Just down the central concrete pathway you'll encounter a trail hub from which you may embark on meandering foot journeys through the refuge. Each trail intersects with at least one other trail, allowing for a nonstop tour of the entire refuge. The visitor map simplifies navigation, though you still might get "displaced" within the thick vegetation, distracted by the many natural wonders. If that happens, periodic trail signs and the refuge brochure map eventually reorient you.

Trail A takes you in a short circle past Willow Lake, a broad, open pond surrounded by a thick forest of huisache, willow, and other native species that shade a near-impenetrable understory. The woodlands along the way are home to a wide variety of species, including the great kiskadee, northern beardless tyrannulet, groove-billed ani, and rose-throated becard. At the water your view opens up to reveal a scattered assortment of waterfowl. In the fall and winter, densely packed congregations of species, such as shoveler, gadwall, wigeon, pintail, and others, are found here.

A narrow spit of land bisects the lake, supporting least, royal, and Forster's terns, yellowlegs, black-necked stilts, American avocets, Wilson's phalaropes, a variety of gulls, and numerous other waders and shorebirds. The surrounding forest is a haven for innumerable species, including common yellowthroat, various warblers, and the loudmouthed kiskadee, which shouts its name repeatedly for all to hear.

Around the shore you may spot a green kingfisher, often perched atop a cattail or snag in search of prey (its call resembles the rapid clacking of steel ball bearings), or the ringed kingfisher—largest of North America's 3 kingfisher subspecies—which favors both shoreline trees and open-water snags. The belted kingfisher also lives here, making Santa Ana the only US refuge supporting all 3 species. Water clarity is key to kingfisher sightings; clear water encourages them, while the roiled muck that sometimes develops in summer due to the play of "rough fish," such as carp and suckers, can keep them in hiding.

Small islands and peninsulas on the lake's east end support black-bellied and fulvous whistling ducks year-round, along with other ducks, white-faced ibises, and several varieties of egret and heron. Expect to see at least a dozen water-oriented species here at any time of the year. Whistling ducks often perch on the nest boxes propped on stilts over open water.

Trail B takes you back into some of Santa Ana's more interesting wetlands. The area is densely vegetated, often rendering the trail tunnel-like. Along its reach you'll pass through moss-draped forests and thick stands of brush that shelter numerous bird, mammal, and reptile species. A bridge along the way signals your approach to a canopied marsh where ibises and green and little blue herons cavort alongside common moorhens and other species.

Here you might also encounter the giant toad, a lumbering amphibian as broad as a small dinner plate, with oversized parotid glands on its side from which toxic defensive secretions can flow if the creature is molested, or the sheep frog, a smooth, pointy-snouted critter that bleats much like its namesake.

Veer to your right just past the footbridge and you'll soon arrive at Resaca Lake (not named on the map), a pond that supports some of the more skittish waterbirds. We were fortunate to encounter a female masked duck here in the spring of 1995; the species reportedly visits Santa Ana every 2 to 5 years on average.

Our April visit to Resaca Lake also revealed a pair of yellow-crowned night herons, northern shoveler, little blue heron, ringed kingfisher, great kiskadee, black-bellied whistling duck, snowy egret, ruddy duck, lesser scaup, and others. Your tally will be different, but you'll likely see at least a score of species on and around Resaca.

Trail C winds around and through Pintail Lake, the largest body of water on the refuge, then goes on to the Rio Grande. Extensive cattail marsh lines the segmented lake, providing excellent habitat for a variety of species. Five or 6 types of rail can be found in this area, including yellow, Virginia, king, and sora.

In spring and fall, king rails tend to favor the cattails to your left as you approach Pintail Lake along the auto tour road. The 15-inch, chickenlike bird, which calls with a *kek-kek-kek* similar to that of clapper rails, is secretive but might be seen with sufficient patience and immobility. You may spot, or at least hear, rails anywhere in the cattail marshes throughout Santa Ana. Get a tape and learn a few rail calls before making the trip; such knowledge will allow you to zero in on the usually secretive but often noisy birds.

The lake supports a variety of waterfowl during migration. A few species, such as the gangly black-bellied whistling duck (one of a few tree-perching ducks), Forster's tern, and mottled duck, as well as individuals from other species, remain throughout the year.

Several other trails offer good wildlife viewing and enhanced solitude since these are longer and attract only people willing to do serious shoe-leather touring (probably less than 10% of the visiting population). During times of lesser visitation, some of the trail network is open as part of a 7-mile auto tour loop that allows access deep into Santa Ana's forest and lowlands.

The Vireo Trail, which branches off the auto loop at its southeast corner, takes you all the way to the Rio Grande River and is a good place to find songbirds. The Owl and Resaca trails, running off the roadway just north of the Vireo Trail, are two of the better routes for spotting tropical parulas, as well as other passerines, especially during migration.

In the case of a springtime "fallout," when generally favorable south winds abruptly turn against northward-winging species, the refuge may take on the look of a fully decorated Christmas tree farm, with colorful species crowding onto every available roost. Watch the weather report; if a northerly cold front moves into the area, a fallout is likely. Fallouts aren't all-or-nothing events, by the way. Sometimes a weak front will create a minor fallout, with migrating species increasing noticeably for a day or so. The best fronts come at night, causing birds that frequently leave the Yucatán in the evening to struggle all night against the wind. By morning, survivors are sometimes so exhausted you can walk over to them and pick them up. But don't.

The Owl Trail connects with the Mesquite Trail to the west, which takes you to Cattail Lake. This wetland was dry in 1995 due to lack of a good water-delivery system. The problem has been corrected, however, and Cattail Lake is now being fed via an underground pipeline. It may be an attractive alternative to more accessible lakes, especially if your aim is solitude. The lake lies along the auto tour loop, but the loop is closed to vehicles during the busy season, putting Cattail Lake out of reach for the majority of visitors.

Among numerous other species, the northern jacana, a brightly colored "lily trotter," arrives in spring and spends much of the summer and fall perched on or strolling across water-borne plants. Purple gallinule, pied-billed, and least grebe can also be found at Cattail.

To spot the numerous hawks, falcons, and kites (including the uncommon swallow-tailed kite) that overfly the refuge, good vantage points are found atop dikes lining the north and west sides of the refuge. The trails around Pintail Lake also offer the kind of open viewing that enhances raptor-watching. During migration, you'll likely tire of counting broad-winged hawks—tens of thousands sometimes pass overhead within a few weeks.

Managing the Mob

Though Santa Ana is compact and well over 100,000 people visit each year, the density of its vegetation creates a buffer; you can often find privacy here even when others are strolling just a few yards away. Still, heavy visitation represents one of the thornier problems for Santa Ana's management. The refuge is a wildlife sanctuary first, an educational/recreational site second. Public education is critical to the political survival of public refuge lands, but keeping wildlife stress levels down to a minimum is a primary refuge goal.

To lessen the impact, auto tour roads are closed and an open tram is employed along the loop during busy seasons, generally from late November through the end of April. A small fee is charged for tram rides; some morning time slots are reserved for school tours, but general visitors can ride with the kids when space allows.

The guided tour provides good information about the ecology of the refuge. Whether or not you take the ride, try to explore Santa Ana on foot if possible. Some of your most memorable experiences will come from solitary moments along the trails. When you walk, please stay on the paths, no matter what incredible species pops up in the nearby

brush. This precious acreage is vulnerable to ground compaction, plant damage, and wildlife disruption; it needs your protection.

Habitat Expansion

Saving wild habitat in the valley has been accomplished through the dedication and foresight of many people, including concerned farmers and ranchers. Farmers whose fields abut the refuges have worked cooperatively with managers regarding the best timing for and types of chemical applications; some have gone further, leaving portions of their land in a wild state for the benefit of wildlife.

Santa Ana is the most visible habitat among a vast number of protected areas in the region. Its sister refuge, Lower Rio Grande Valley NWR, is the largest parcel of indigenous valley land outside of Laguna Atascosa NWR. But these are only pieces in a discretely connected system that dots the south Texas landscape. Their effectiveness is limited by their size, funding, and water rights (as well as by the money to pay for water from the local conservation district); additional habitat is critically needed to support the valley's potentially rich wildlife.

A variety of methods have been employed to secure wild habitat or return farmland to its natural state. Ten diverse biomes have been identified in the region, stretching from Falcon Dam to the Gulf of Mexico. Some of them are *clay loma wind tidal flats,* coastal stretches with clay dunes that jut above the landscape except when tides and winds combine to inundate them; *ramaderos,* green strips of land along dry arroyo where numerous species live or visit; and *pothole and basin* biomes, which now make up around 12,000 acres in the valley.

The federal government's Acquisition Plan is designed to preserve and increase such habitats, mainly for the support of migratory species but also to support indigenous non-migratory animals, as well as plants, including more than 115 unique vertebrate species that are endangered, threatened, or reside here on the edge of their natural range.

The federal program is supplemented by the efforts of state, local, and private entities, such as the National Audubon Society, which operates nearby Sabal Palm Grove Sanctuary (protecting 172 acres and one of the last US communities of the indigenous *Sabal texana* palm), and the Nature Conservancy. The latter has also purchased land and turned it over to the refuge.

Habitat acquisition and protection are accomplished through a range of creative approaches, each providing a different level of protection. They include outright land purchases by the USFWS (from willing sellers); land donations; management agreements, where, for example, entities such as conservation districts agree to clear brush from only one side of a canal, leaving the other side wild; and limited protection arrangements, whereby refuge staffers place signs and fencing, and provide law enforcement, in areas such as the port authority acreage along the Harlingen Ship Channel.

The refuge maintains a vibrant nursery and replanting program, supported by the efforts of more than a dozen area farmers on 10,000 acres of land. The refuge nursery, seed collection, and seedling production efforts generate some 50 species of plants, including huisache, *retama,* mesquite, and many other regional specialties. Nursery vegetation is used to return farmlands to their ancient state. In some cases "co-op farmers" plant a portion of a refuge plot for profit, repaying the refuge with labor rather than cash by prepping land and replanting wild species, such as Montezuma bald cypress, ash, cedar elm, and Rio Grande ash, on the remaining acres.

Private lands are sometimes protected through establishment of short- or long-term "conservation easements," which leave the land in a

private owner's hands but allow the USFWS to manage and preserve its wild habitat. These methods together provide a critical lifeline for local and migrating species.

Across the Rio Grande, some Mexican environmentalists are taking steps to preserve and protect wild brush country. Recognizing the old ecosystem as a valuable part of their cultural heritage, Mexican environmentalists are setting up private refuges, including one just across from Santa Ana on an *ejido,* one of many communal land tracts set up after the Mexican Revolution. The refuge supplies biological expertise to support Mexican scientists in species surveys and habitat protection methods.

All of this is good for the animals, who recognize no borders or federal preserves. Ocelots on Santa Ana, for instance, are known to swim across the border in search of prey and other animal pleasures.

In the case of Santa Ana NWR, small is definitely beautiful. Here you can observe abundant species within a very limited area, which, through excellent management, remains wild and largely untrammeled.

For birders, I recommend the National Geographic's field guide (see Suggested Reading), which includes numerous Mexican species not found in other general guides. Peterson's *Birds of Texas,* devoted to the avian species of this oversized state, is another option but covers fewer species than does the National Geographic guide.

If you haven't yet visited Santa Ana, expect to swell your bird list by at least 10 to 30 species, possibly more. You'll find it difficult to top this refuge in terms of variety. A menagerie of exotic creatures is always in residence at Santa Ana, making this a conveniently magnificent place to visit any time of the year.

Impressions and Experiences

Bird sightings:

Other wildlife sightings:

Notes:

PARTIAL BIRD LIST (OF 388 LISTED SPECIES PLUS 11 HYPOTHETICALS): Groove-billed ani, great kiskadee, rose-breasted becard, reddish egret, northern jacana, tropical parula, green kingfisher, ringed kingfisher.

PARTIAL MAMMAL LIST (OF 42 LISTED SPECIES): Ocelot, Virginia opossum, Mexican ground squirrel, Mexican free-tailed bat, coyote, long-tailed weasel, badger, feral hog, javelina.

PARTIAL HERP LIST (OF 46 LISTED SPECIES): Rio Grande lesser siren, Mexican tree frog, Texas tortoise, red-eared slider, Texas horned lizard, Laredo striped whiptail, Texas indigo snake, speckled racer, Mexican hooknosed snake, diamondback water snake, Texas coral snake.

In our relationship with the natural world, some of us act out of dirt-ignorance, a condition we are all born with and some get over. The common perception that animals are somehow "lesser" beings due to their apparently low intelligence has yet to fall away. Still, attitudes toward wildlife are changing. When I was a kid, my friends and I shot sparrows off power lines with BB guns, a senseless pastime but hardly deviant given the times. In the early 1960s animals were regarded as little more than objects for our amusement. Gradually, most people who spend time with nonhuman animals come to understand that they possess a profound intelligence, an awareness we have yet to grasp. Proximity to animals—whether dogs, cats, parakeets, or wildlife at federal refuges—can help us understand their uniqueness, their intelligence and awareness, and their communal or solitary natures. If we observe carefully with our hearts as well as our minds, we may find the path to wisdom.

Take the avian world, for example. To paraphrase F. Scott Fitzgerald, birds are different than you and me. Their brains are unique; many are highly intelligent, yet they don't seem to think like dogs or cats or people. Stubborn, curious, intelligent, impetuous, emotional—such description can only hint at the complex mental and emotional side of our winged neighbors.

So it is with other species. Lizards gaze at you with a look that resembles contemplation.

Prairie dogs address friends and neighbors in a dialect that differentiates the presence of hawks, coyotes, or humans. Bees dance on their hives, explaining to other bees the distance and direction of pollen sources. Some egrets blow bubbles and cast bait to attract fish. Elephants possess a highly developed language; they comfort their young with soothing vocalizations.

To dominate nature is still regarded by many people as our God-given role in the food chain. Vice President Al Gore insists the biblical term is actually "dominion," a distinctly different concept. Domination implies that the earth is ours to stripmine, to plow and plant and cover in plastic. Dominion, on the other hand, implies respectful stewardship.

Jerry Falwell, I believe, spoke eloquently for ecological menaces everywhere when he said we can treat the world any way we like, because it'll all be destroyed on Judgment Day anyway. Saner voices offer a more fundamentally spiritual view: We are part and parcel of nature, no better and no worse. Because we're blessed with high intelligence and opposable digits, we're charged with dominion over our planet and all its creatures. Wildlife is, in the strictest sense, part of the family.

Though they're called refuges, most lands in the national wildlife refuge system are managed under conditions falling short of true sanctuary status, a fact that surprises most people. Within the boundaries of many refuges, animals are legally shot and trapped for sport, the earth is drilled, mined, or logged, and powerboats and other recreational diversions disrupt the equilibrium. Rarely do these uses represent legitimate management practices.

Hunting is allowed on two-thirds of our national wildlife refuges. A legacy of the Duck Stamp land-funding bargain we made with the hunting community in 1934, and of the continuing political aggressiveness of hunters, this custom dies hard. Support for this use comes from the ranks of the USFWS as well, though the situation is changing as younger, nonhunting employees enter the Service.

The issue is complex. For years, hunters supplied needed funding for refuge land acquisition. (These days, less than ten percent of refuge funding comes from duck stamps, and nonhunters buy them, too.) In a sense, hunters and nonconsumptive nature lovers alike are allies in the common cause of preserving wildlife habitat. Some environmental organizations have recognized that alliance and tacitly accept—and occasionally encourage—refuge hunting.

Does tradition justify the use of wildlife refuges as public hunting clubs for the four percent of visitors who come to kill the wildlife? Amateur herpetologists and lepidopterists also support the system with their tax dollars. Should they be allowed to remove snakes or butterflies for their personal collections? Is one form of "harvesting" more legitimate than another? Of course not. Neither is appropriate on land deemed a "refuge."

When Teddy Roosevelt founded the system, he envisioned it as a network of inviolate sanctuaries for wild creatures. Teddy was a passionate hunter, but he thought it only fair that wildlife should have a few places where they might live unmolested. Teddy was right. Wildlife refuges are hopeful places, cathedrals in a sense, where living, breathing nature should be honored and valued above all else, where each action should be designed strictly to preserve and protect wild creatures and wild systems.

The issue of refuge hunting elicits strong emotion on both sides. Please share your views respectfully with refuge employees. I believe most would like to know where you, the refuge owners, come down on this subject.

One refuge manager expressed his fear that TV nature programs create the illusion that wildlife is secure and abundant. In reality, he points out, wildlife refuges are little more than "Band-aids" on a disturbed ecological system. Numerous species have declined dramatically throughout North America; even species not considered "at risk" are rarely encountered in the wild without diligent effort.

Supporting the maintenance and acquisition of protected public land should be one of our nation's top priorities. Budgets and tax laws, and even the poisons of terrorism and militant paranoia, will eventually yield to some level of equilibrium, but extinct animals and sterile landscapes generally stay that way.

In 1995, the national refuge system received less than one-sixth of the per-acre funding the National Park Service received, and less than a third of the US Forest Service's yearly per-acre funding. The result of inadequate USFWS funding is that on most refuges, necessary habitat enhancement is regularly deferred—wetlands go unbuilt, water rights are not exercised, public-use facilities are allowed to deteriorate. To do its job effectively, the refuge system needs more money.

Recent surveys reveal that most Americans strongly support wildlife programs and nature-related expenditures. At the same time, many people are unfamiliar with wildlife behavior and needs. (First and foremost, they need habitat.) Urban dwellers tend to be frightened by nondomesticated creatures, having lived all their lives among humans, by far the most dangerous species ever evolved. Refuges are a great place to begin the educational process so critical to renewing the ancient bond between human and nonhuman animals.

Such awareness grows ever more important. Antinature forces are pervasive in our society, relentlessly striving to grasp, to use up, to destroy. Due in part to their efforts—though the over-riding problem is overpopulation, along with our convenience-driven lifestyle—animals are going extinct in our world faster than at any time in history, and probably as fast as they have in a million years. As our society continues its relentless march towards technological Utopia, some experts say we've eliminated half of all species that existed just a century ago.

Legions of greedy people are at work—politicians, mill owners, timber slashers, cow farmers, unprincipled developers, industrial polluters—doing all they can to destroy what's left of our natural birthright. Such people care nothing for nature because they don't believe they're a part of nature. In their acquisitory minds, they've risen above the natural world. They're only in it for the money.

The antidote is action.

Write to someone in power. Join a nature organization. Groups such as the Nature Conservancy, the Audubon Society, Defenders of Wildlife, the Sierra Club, the Natural Resources Defense Council, and Forest Guardians are critical in resisting antinature forces. If you haven't joined an environmental organization, now is the time. If you're not a joiner, at least give them support.

Don't stop there. Make your voice heard in public meetings, in churches and grocery lines and restaurants and office cubicles, wherever people talk about land, wildlife, heritage, choices. Your voice counts, it has influence.

When another addled senator insists we sell our national parks and refuges to some green-eyed friend with a fat wallet, voice your disgust. When the next congressman tries to trash the Endangered Species Act so his campaign contributors can make a few extra bucks, let him know you'll do your best to send him packing. We simply can't afford to have these people in leadership positions. Vote them back into the private sector where they'll do less damage. Remember that our natural land is finite; once we sell it off or lay asphalt over it, it's irretrievably gone.

Despite the assaults on our priceless natural heritage, there are plenty of reasons for hope. Many people acknowledge the problems and strive for solutions. Recent bills that would weaken basic environmental protections are still being beaten down. In 1995, a federal judge in Arizona ordered a halt to all logging in the Southwest, in order to safeguard Mexican spotted owl habitat. The order didn't last, but what a bright beacon of hope! Send that judge some flowers.

As the refuge system is a noble enterprise, its employees are heroic individuals. I greatly admire them and their work. For me, the lands they oversee represent a national, and personal, treasure. As a measure of that feeling, my wife, Susan, and I were married in October 1995 at Bosque del Apache National Wildlife Refuge, beneath the evening spectacle of soaring geese and sandhill cranes. Phil Norton, Bosque's superb manager, honored us with his presence. We couldn't think of a better place to begin our married life together. Our children will know Bosque well.

See you at the refuges!

Occasionally visitors leave a national wildlife refuge feeling that the nature there has been assaulted. To some it appears that refuge managers, in an arrogant abuse of power, have chosen to play god with the lands under their control. However, rarely is that true. In most cases, tampering with nature on refuge land is crucial to supporting the wildlife species that rely upon it.

That may sound like twisted logic, but it's actually plain common sense. If you comprehend the history and character of our wildlands, you can more easily understand the reasons for such tampering.

A hundred years ago, natural land was abundant. Wildlife had the option of moving from one area to another when natural succession or sudden traumatic events, such as floods or storms, rendered a habitat unsupportive. Today, most species have few habitat options. With more than 50% of our wetlands destroyed, for instance, migratory waterfowl must make do with the relatively few remaining marshes along their flyways. Pronghorns who require vast acres for feeding and mating confront uncrossable barbed wire over much of their range. Prairie chickens who once roamed millions of acres in Texas and Louisiana now find natural tall- or mixed-grass prairie in just a few isolated spots.

Managing wildlife means managing habitats. If left alone, refuge habitats would indeed revert to their natural state. Over a period of several years, grasslands would grow too thick and decrepit to support bobwhite quail; marshes would become choked with cattails and bulrushes, too congested to allow for nesting redheads; salt cedar would literally swarm over wetland edges, overwhelming their banks.

True, if such habitats were left alone, fire would eventually come to burn the grasses, and, afterward, nourishing new shoots would emerge from the blackened soil. Floods would drown the cattails, and open water would gradually reappear. Tamarisks might burn, though they would soon return, probably thicker than ever.

If nature were allowed to rule unfettered, refuges would support abundant wildlife for one year, maybe less the next, perhaps none at all for the next few years. Then a natural event or a gradual cycle would return the area to a wildlife-friendly state.

Unfortunately, with so little good wildlife habitat remaining in the United States, we no longer enjoy the luxury of allowing nature to work its slow evolution on refuge acres. Managers must keep these tiny patches of habitat at a maximum carrying capacity—year after year after year. That means altering natural succession and expanding supportive habitat when possible. Such management might involve the burning of plants, the cutting of marsh vegetation, the plowing of new dikes and the eradication of old ones, or the channeling of water from here to there.

While such activities may create "unsightly" conditions on refuges, once visitors understand the reasons behind such tampering, they may come to appreciate it. You may, as I am, be grateful that resident wildlife experts, using the best ecological science available, are maximizing the value of these tiny life rafts of habitat bobbing on a sea of development, agriculture, and overgrazed land.

Biodiversity: The full range of associated and interactive life-forms existing within an *ecosystem*. Ecological experts have determined that the greater the diversity in a particular system, the healthier and more stable that system will be.

Biome: A geographic area characterized by a particular *habitat* that supports a specific group of plants and animals, for example, sage upland or riverine marsh.

Carrying capacity: The number and variety of species a particular *habitat* can support based on space, available nourishment, and territorial needs.

Ecosystem: The dynamic system arising from interactions between an area's life-forms and their environment. Generally, the system is more or less balanced until outside forces alter one or more aspects of the system.

Ecosystem management: A concept injected into the *NWR* management agenda in the early 1990s. Basically, the concept mandates that diversified habitats be encouraged in order to support the maximum number of species. This landmark policy change is largely credited to the late USFWS director Mollie Beattie

Ecotone: An area where two distinct ecosystems grade into one another. Often an ecotone harbors species representing both ecosystems.

Edge: A more restrictive term than *ecotone*, describing the abrupt line where, for instance, a farm field meets uncut brush or a seashore meets desert upland. Edges generally harbor life from both adjoining habitats and are productive places for wildlife observation.

Emergent: A plant, such as cattail, that grows in wet or submerged soil and "emerges" above the surface.

Exotic: A biological term for animals and plants that have encroached into nonnative areas. Exotics often create *ecosystem* imbalances that create problems for native species, though sometimes—as in the case of pheasants—they appear to integrate well into their new environment.

Feral: Refers to animals or their progeny from domesticated stock, such as burros or dogs, that have gone wild. They often cause problems on refuges. And other wildlife-oriented programs.

Habitat: An area's specific physical structure and plants as they relate to various species' needs for nutrition, shelter, breeding, and nesting space.

Herptiles: A jury-rigged term encompassing both reptiles and amphibians.

Moist soil management: An artificial, seasonally timed water management system that encourages indigenous food plants and associated invertebrates to grow. Generally mimicking predevelopment flood conditions along rivers, moist soil management is often used to raise food for waterfowl.

Neotropical migrants: Birds that migrate back and forth each year from North America to Central or South America. Often used to refer to migratory *passerines*. Migratory *shorebirds* are usually referred to separately, for example, "neotropical migrants and shore-birds." For various reasons, many of our neotropical migrants have declined over the last few decades.

NWR: National Wildlife Refuge.

Passerine: A large, diverse class of birds characterized by their practice of perching.

Riparian: *Ecosystems* along watercourses, often characterized in the West by cotton-wood-willow associations, along with under-story shrubs and water-oriented plants.

Shorebird: Any in a large class of birds that forage along shallows and shorelines.

Upland: An area of land not directly supplied with water from a lake or watercourse. In the West, uplands are often blanketed in sage, grasses, saltbush, or greasewood.

USFWS: Shorthand for the US Fish and Wildlife Service, the federal division of the US Department of the Interior responsible for managing our national wildlife refuges and other wildlife-oriented programs.

Wader: Any in a class of birds characterized by long legs and shallow water foraging behavior.

Wilderness: In the federal land system, a legal term that mandates an area shall not be roaded or developed and that only nonmotor-ized travel be allowed within its boundaries.

F or more information on desert ecology, good sources include Peggy Larson's The *Deserts of the Southwest* (1977, Sierra Club Books), James MacMahon's *Deserts* (1985, National Audubon Society Nature Guides/Knopf), George Olin's *House In the Sun: A Natural History of the Sonoran Desert* (1985, Southwest Parks and Monuments Assoc., Tucson, AZ), and the late Edward Abbey's whole inspiring body of work. Basic wetlands ecology is well described in Milton Weller's *Freshwater Marshes* (2nd edition, 1987, University of Minnesota Press).

My preferred pair of birding books are F*ield Guide to the Birds of North America* (1983, 2nd edition, National Geographic Society) along with an excellent source of avian information, *The Birder's Handbook*, by Erhich, Dobkin, and Wheye (1988, Simon and Schuster). For additional information on the specialty birds of Texas and where to find them, a good source is Edward Kutac's *Birder's Guide to Texas* (1982, Gulf Publishing Co.)

Sage uplands ecological information, as well as an excellent guide to wildflowers of the Great Basin desert, mountains, and steppe, can be found in Ronald Taylor's *Sagebrush Country: A Wildflower Sanctuary* (1992, Mountain Press). Good information on plant and human ecology in the high deserts and mountains of New Mexico and surroundings is available in Dunmire and Tierney's *Wild Plants of the Pueblo Province* (1995, Museum of New Mexico Press). The Southwest Parks and Monuments Association's four-book series on southwestern plants (available at most national park, refuge, and monument book-stores) provides good identification keys and information on a number of species that western travelers are likely to encounter.

Laura and William Rileys' *Guide to the National Wildlife Refuges* (rev. 1993, Collier) offers a comprehensive overview of most US refuges. An out-of-print book on the federal refuge system that I found well-written and inspiring is Robert Murphy's *Wild Sanctuaries* (1968, E. P. Dutton and Co.).